Communications in Computer and Information Science 983

Commenced Publication in 2007
Founding and Former Series Editors:
Phoebe Chen, Alfredo Cuzzocrea, Xiaoyong Du, Orhun Kara, Ting Liu,
Dominik Ślęzak, and Xiaokang Yang

Editorial Board

More information about this series at http://www.springer.com/series/7899

Ana Paula Cláudio · Dominique Bechmann
Paul Richard · Takehiko Yamaguchi
Lars Linsen · Alexandru Telea
Francisco Imai · Alain Tremeau (Eds.)

Computer Vision, Imaging and Computer Graphics – Theory and Applications

12th International Joint Conference, VISIGRAPP 2017
Porto, Portugal, February 27 – March 1, 2017
Revised Selected Papers

Editors
Ana Paula Cláudio
University of Lisbon
Lisbon, Portugal

Lars Linsen
University of Münster
Münster, Nordrhein-Westfalen, Germany

Dominique Bechmann
University of Strasbourg
Strasbourg, France

Alexandru Telea
University of Groningen
Groningen, The Netherlands

Paul Richard
University of Angers
Angers, France

Francisco Imai
Apple Inc.
Cupertino, CA, USA

Takehiko Yamaguchi
Tokyo University of Science
Tokyo, Japan

Alain Tremeau
Jean Monnet University
Saint-Etienne, France

ISSN 1865-0929   ISSN 1865-0937 (electronic)
Communications in Computer and Information Science
ISBN 978-3-030-12208-9   ISBN 978-3-030-12209-6 (eBook)
https://doi.org/10.1007/978-3-030-12209-6

Library of Congress Control Number: 2018968081

Preface

The present book includes extended and revised versions of a set of selected papers from the 12th International Joint Conference on Computer Vision, Imaging and Computer Graphics Theory and Applications (VISIGRAPP 2017), held in Porto, Portugal, from February 27 to March 1, 2017.

The purpose of the 12th International Joint Conference on Computer Vision, Imaging and Computer Graphics Theory and Applications (VISIGRAPP 2017) was to bring together researchers and practitioners interested in both theoretical advances and applications of computer vision, computer graphics, and information visualization. VISIGRAPP is composed of four co-located conferences, each specialized in at least one of the aforementioned main knowledge areas.

VISIGRAPP 2017 received 402 paper submissions from 48 countries, of which 4% are included in this book. The papers were selected by the event program co-chairs, based on a number of criteria that include the reviews and suggested comments provided by the Program Committee members, the session chairs' assessments, and also the program chairs' global view of all papers included in the technical program. The authors of selected papers were invited to submit a revised and extended version of their papers having at least 30% new material.

The papers selected to be included in this book contribute to the understanding of relevant trends of current research on Image and Video Formation, Preprocessing, Analysis and Understanding; Motion, Tracking and Stereo Vision; Computer Graphics and Rendering; Data Visualization and Interactive Visual Data Analysis; Agent-Based Human–Robot Interactions; and User Experience. The richness and the variety of theoretical advances and research results highlighted by these selected papers reflect the vitality and the prevalence of the research areas covered by the VISIGRAPP conference.

We would like to thank all the authors for their contributions to this book and also to the reviewers who helped ensure the quality of this publication.

February 2019

Ana Cláudio
Dominique Bechmann
Paul Richard
Takehiko Yamaguchi
Lars Linsen
Alexandru Telea
Francisco Imai
Alain Tremeau

Organization

Conference Chair

Jose Braz   Escola Superior de Tecnologia de Setúbal, Portugal

Program Co-chairs

GRAPP

Ana Cláudio   BioISI, Universidade de Lisboa, Portugal
Dominique Bechmann   CNRS-Université de Strasbourg, France

HUCAPP

Paul Richard   University of Angers, France
Takehiko Yamaguchi   Tokyo University of Science, Japan

IVAPP

Lars Linsen   Westfälische Wilhelms-Universität Münster, Germany
Alexandru Telea   University of Groningen, The Netherlands

VISAPP

Francisco Imai   Apple Inc., USA
Alain Tremeau   Université Jean Monnet in Saint Etienne, France

GRAPP Program Committee

Francisco Abad   Universidad Politécnica de Valencia, Spain
Marco Agus   King Abdullah University of Science and Technology, Saudi Arabia
Helder Araújo   University of Coimbra, Portugal
Lilian Aveneau   University of Poitiers, France
Francesco Banterle   Visual Computing Lab, Italy
Thomas Bashford-Rogers The University of the West of England, UK
Dominique Bechmann   CNRS-Université de Strasbourg, France
Bedrich Benes   Purdue University, USA
Gonzalo Besuievsky   Universitat de Girona, Spain
Carla Binucci   Università degli Studi di Perugia, Italy
Venceslas Biri   University Paris Est, France
Fernando Birra   UNL, Portugal
Jiri Bittner   Czech Technical University in Prague, Czech Republic
Kristopher Blom   Virtual Human Technologies, Czech Republic

Manfred Bogen	Fraunhofer IAIS, Germany
Carles Bosch	Eurecat, Spain
Stephen Brooks	Dalhousie University, Canada
Cédric Buche	LabSticc-CERV, France
Pedro Cano	University of Granada, Spain
Maria Beatriz Carmo	BioISI, Universidade de Lisboa, Portugal
L. G. Casado	University of Almeria, Spain
Eva Cerezo	University of Zaragoza, Spain
Teresa Chambel	Lasige, University of Lisbon, Portugal
Antoni Chica	Universitat Politecnica de Catalunya, Spain
Hwan-gue Cho	Pusan National University, Korea, Republic of
Miguel Chover	Universitat Jaume I, Spain
Ana Cláudio	BioISI, Universidade de Lisboa, Portugal
Sabine Coquillart	Inria, France
António Costa	ISEP, Portugal
Rémi Cozot	IRISA, France
Carsten Dachsbacher	Karlsruhe Institute of Technology, Germany
Luiz Henrique de Figueiredo	Impa, Brazil
Victor Debelov	Institute of Computational Math. and Math. Geophysics, Siberian Branch of Russian Academy of Sciences, Russian Federation
Bailin Deng	Cardiff University, UK
Fabian Di Fiore	Hasselt University, Belgium
Paulo Dias	Universidade de Aveiro, Portugal
John Dingliana	Trinity College Dublin, Ireland
Jean-Michel Dischler	Université de Strasbourg, France
Thierry Duval	IMT Atlantique, France
Elmar Eisemann	Delft University of Technology, The Netherlands
Marius Erdt	Fraunhofer IDM@NTU, Singapore
Petros Faloutsos	York University, Canada
Jean-Philippe Farrugia	LIRIS Lab, France
Pierre-Alain Fayolle	University of Aizu, Japan
Francisco R. Feito	University of Jaén, Spain
Jie-Qing Feng	Zhejiang University, China
Carla Freitas	Universidade Federal do Rio Grande do Sul, Brazil
Davide Gadia	Università degli Studi di Milano, Italy
Arturo Garcia	University of Salford, UK
Alejandro García-Alonso	University of the Basque Country, Spain
Miguel Gea	University of Granada, Spain
Djamchid Ghazanfarpour	University of Limoges, France
Enrico Gobbetti	CRS4, Italy
Stephane Gobron	HES-SO/Arc, Switzerland
Alexandrino Gonçalves	Polytechnic Institute of Leiria, Portugal
Laurent Grisoni	University of Lille Science and Technologies, France
James Hahn	George Washington University, USA

Vlastimil Havran	Czech Technical University in Prague, Czech Republic
Nancy Hitschfeld	University of Chile, Chile
Ludovic Hoyet	Inria Rennes - Centre Bretagne Atlantique, France
Andres Iglesias	University of Cantabria, Spain
Insung Ihm	Sogang University, Korea, Republic of
Gaetano Impoco	Independent Researcher, Italy
Jean-Pierre Jessel	IRIT, Paul Sabatier University, Toulouse, France
Juan Jiménez Delgado	Universidad de Jaen, Spain
Xiaogang Jin	Zhejiang University, China
Robert Joan-Arinyo	Universitat Politecnica de Catalunya, Spain
Chris Joslin	Carleton University, Canada
Cláudio Jung	Universidade Federal do Rio Grande do Sul, Brazil
Josef Kohout	University of West Bohemia, Czech Republic
Torsten Kuhlen	RWTH Aachen University, Germany
Won-sook Lee	University of Ottawa, Canada
Miguel Leitão	ISEP, Portugal
Frederick Li	University of Durham, UK
Ligang Liu	University of Science and Technology of China, China
Marco Livesu	Italian National Research Council (CNR), Italy
Hélio Lopes	PUC-Rio, Brazil
Pedro Lopes	ISCTE-IUL, Portugal
Jorge Lopez-Moreno	Universidad Rey Juan Carlos, Spain
Joaquim Madeira	University of Aveiro, Portugal
Luís Magalhães	University of Minho, Portugal
Stephen Mann	University of Waterloo, Canada
Michael Manzke	Trinity College Dublin, Ireland
Adérito Marcos	Universidade Aberta (Portuguese Open University), Portugal
Ricardo Marroquim	Rio de Janeiro Federal University, Brazil
Belen Masia	Universidad de Zaragoza, Spain
Oliver Mattausch	Siemens, Switzerland
Nelson Max	University of California, USA
Daniel Meneveaux	University of Poitiers, France
Stéphane Mérillou	University of Limoges, France
Eder Miguel	Universidad Rey Juan Carlos, Spain
Ramon Molla	Universitat Politècnica de València, Spain
David Mould	Carleton University, Canada
Adolfo Muñoz	Universidad de Zaragoza, Spain
Lidia M. Ortega	University of Jaén, Spain
Georgios Papaioannou	Athens University of Economics and Business, Greece
Alexander Pasko	Bournemouth University, UK
Giuseppe Patané	Italian National Research Council (CNR), Italy
Daniel Patel	University of Bergen, Norway
Mathias Paulin	IRIT - Université de Toulouse, France
João Pereira	INESC-ID at IST, Portugal
João Pereira	Instituto Superior de Engenharia do Porto, Portugal

Sinésio Pesco   PUC-Rio Institute, Brazil
Christopher Peters   KTH Royal Institute of Technology, Sweden
Ruggero Pintus   CRS4 - Center for Advanced Studies,
                               Research and Development in Sardinia, Italy
Denis Pitzalis   UNESCO, France
Paulo Pombinho   Universidade de Lisboa, Portugal
Anna Puig   University of Barcelona, Spain
Inmaculada Remolar   Universitat Jaume I, Spain
Mickael Ribardière   University of Poitiers, XLIM, France
María Rivara   Universidad de Chile, Chile
Nuno Rodrigues   Polytechnic Institute of Leiria, Portugal
Inmaculada Rodríguez   University of Barcelona, Spain
Przemyslaw Rokita   Warsaw University of Technology, Poland
Luís Romero   Instituto Politecnico de Viana do Castelo, Portugal
Isaac Rudomin   BSC, Spain
Wang Rui   Zhejiang University, China
Holly Rushmeier   Yale University, USA
Luis Santos   Universidade do Minho, Portugal
Basile Sauvage   University of Strasbourg, France
Mateu Sbert   Tianjin University/Universitat de Girona, Spain
Rafael J. Segura   Universidad de Jaen, Spain
A. Augusto Sousa   FEUP/INESC Porto, Portugal
Jie Tang   Nanjing University, China
Matthias Teschner   University of Freiburg, Germany
Daniel Thalmann   Ecole Polytechnique Federale de Lausanne,
                               Switzerland
Rafael Torchelsen   Federal University of Pelotas (UFPEL), Brazil
Juan Carlos Torres   Universidad de Granada, Spain
Alain Tremeau   Université Jean Monnet in Saint Etienne, France
Hassan Ugail   Centre for Visual Computing, UK
Torsten Ullrich   Fraunhofer Austria Research, Austria
Anna Ursyn   University of Northern Colorado, USA
Cesare Valenti   Università degli Studi di Palermo, Italy
Luiz Velho   IMPA - Instituto de Matematica Pura e Aplicada, Brazil
Andreas Weber   University of Bonn, Germany
Daniel Weiskopf   Universität Stuttgart, Germany
Burkhard Wuensche   University of Auckland, New Zealand
Lihua You   Bournemouth University, UK
Jian Zhang   Bournemouth University, UK

GRAPP Additional Reviewers

Silvia Biasotti   CNR - IMATI, Italy
Daniela Giorgi   National Research Council of Italy, Italy
Imanol Muñoz-Pandiella   Universitat de Girona, Spain
Félix Paulano-Godino   University of Jaén, Spain

HUCAPP Program Committee

Andrea Abate	University of Salerno, Italy
Dominique Bechmann	CNRS-Université de Strasbourg, France
Yacine Bellik	LIMSI-CNRS, Orsay, France
Frank Biocca	New Jersey Institute of Technology, USA
Karlheinz Blankenbach	Pforzheim University, Germany
Gunnar Bolmsjö	University West, Sweden
Mohamed Bouri	EPFL, Switzerland
Gerd Bruder	University of Central Florida, USA
Antonio Camurri	University of Genoa, Italy
Daniel Cermak-sassenrath	IT University of Copenhagen, Denmark
Jessie Chen	U.S. Army Research Laboratory, USA
Yang-Wai Chow	University of Wollongong, Australia
Sharon Chu	Texas A&M University, USA
José Coelho	University of Lisbon, Portugal
Cesar Collazos	Universidad del Cauca, Colombia
André Constantino da Silva	Instituto Federal de São Paulo, Brazil
Lynne Coventry	Northumbria University, UK
Alma Culén	University of Oslo, Norway
Damon Daylamani-Zad	University of Greenwich, UK
Lucio Tommaso De Paolis	University of Salento, Italy
Nancy Diniz	Rensellaer Polytechnic Institute, USA
Larbi Esmahi	Athabasca University, Canada
Tom Garner	University of Portsmouth, UK
Cristina Gena	Università di Torino, Italy
Panagiotis Germanakos	University of Cyprus, Cyprus
Andrina Granic	University of Split, Croatia
Toni Granollers	University of Lleida, Spain
Michael Hohl	Anhalt University of Applied Sciences, Germany
Barry Hughes	University of Auckland, New Zealand
Gareth Jones	Dublin City University, Ireland
Christophe Jouffrais	CNRS and P. Sabatier University, France
Koji Kashihara	Tokushima University, Japan
Uttam Kokil	Kennesaw State University, USA
Heidi Krömker	Technische Universität Ilmenau, Germany
Fabrizio Lamberti	Politecnico di Torino, Italy
Chien-Sing Lee	Sunway University, Malaysia
Tsai-Yen Li	National Chengchi University, Taiwan
Yangmin Li	The Hong Kong Polytechnic University, Hong Kong, SAR China
Chin-Teng Lin	National Chiao Tung University, Taiwan
Flamina Luccio	Università Ca' Foscari Venezia, Italy
Sergio Luján-Mora	University of Alicante, Spain
Célia Martinie	University of Toulouse 3, France
Joi Moore	University of Missouri, USA

Andreas Nearchou	University of Patras, Greece
Keith Nesbitt	University of Newcastle, Australia
Radoslaw Niewiadomski	University of Genoa, Italy
Nuno Otero	Linnaeus University, Sweden
Evangelos Papadopoulos	NTUA, Greece
Ioannis Paraskevopoulos	University of Greenwich, UK
Gianluca Paravati	Polytechnic University of Turin, Italy
James Phillips	Auckland University of Technology, New Zealand
Armelle Prigent	L3i - University of La Rochelle, France
Rafael Radkowski	Iowa State University, USA
Paul Richard	University of Angers, France
Antonio Rinaldi	University of Naples Federico II, Italy
Covadonga Rodrigo	UNED, Spain
Otniel Rodriguez	Universidad Autonóma del Estado de México, Mexico
Juha Röning	University of Oulu, Finland
Paul Rosenthal	Germany
José Rouillard	Université des Sciences et Technologies de Lille, France
Sandra Sanchez-Gordon	Escuela Politecnica Nacional, Ecuador
Antonio-José Sánchez-Salmerón	Universitat Politecnica de Valencia, Spain
Andrea Sanna	Politecnico di Torino, Italy
Corina Sas	Lancaster University, UK
Trenton Schulz	Norwegian Computing Center, Norway
Berglind Smaradottir	University of Agder, Norway
Daniel Thalmann	Ecole Polytechnique Federale de Lausanne, Switzerland
Godfried Toussaint	New York University Abu Dhabi, UAE
Pauliina Tuomi	Tampere University of Technology, Finland
Windson Viana	Federal University of Ceará (UFC), Brazil
Kostas Vlachos	University of Ioannina, Greece
Ina Wechsung	Technische Universität Berlin, Germany
Yingcai Xiao	University of Akron, USA
Takehiko Yamaguchi	Tokyo University of Science, Japan

IVAPP Program Committee

Mark Anderson	Edge Hill University, UK
Vladan Babovic	National University of Singapore, Singapore
George Baciu	The Hong Kong Polytechnic University, Hong Kong, SAR China
Till Bergmann	Max Planck Society, Germany
Jürgen Bernard	TU Darmstadt, Germany
Rita Borgo	King's College London, UK
David Borland	University of North Carolina at Chapel Hill, USA
Massimo Brescia	Istituto Nazionale di AstroFisica, Italy

Lars Linsen	Westfälische Wilhelms-Universität Münster, Germany
Giuseppe Liotta	University of Perugia, Italy
Zhicheng Liu	Adobe Research, USA
Eamonn Maguire	CERN, Switzerland
Krešimir Matkovic	VRVis Research Center, Austria
Kazuo Misue	University of Tsukuba, Japan
Torsten Moeller	University of Vienna, Austria
Stephen North	Infovisible, USA
Steffen Oeltze-Jafra	Otto von Guericke University Magdeburg, Germany
Benoît Otjacques	Luxembourg Institute of Science and Technology (LIST), Luxembourg
Philip Rhodes	University of Mississippi, USA
Patrick Riehmann	Bauhaus-Universität Weimar, Germany
Adrian Rusu	Fairfield University, USA
Ignaz Rutter	University of Passau, Germany
Beatriz Santos	University of Aveiro, Portugal
Giuseppe Santucci	University of Rome, Italy
Angel Sappa	ESPOL Polytechnic University (Ecuador) and Computer Vision Center (Spain), Spain
Celmar Silva	University of Campinas, Brazil
Juergen Symanzik	Utah State University, USA
Yasufumi Takama	Tokyo Metropolitan University, Japan
Roberto Theron	Universidad de Salamanca, Spain
Hugo Valle	Weber State University, USA
Huy Vo	The City College of New York, USA
Günter Wallner	University of Applied Arts Vienna, Austria
Tino Weinkauf	KTH Royal Institute of Technology, Sweden
Daniel Weiskopf	Universität Stuttgart, Germany
Jinrong Xie	eBay Inc., USA
Kai Xu	Middlesex University, UK
Anders Ynnerman	Linköping University, Sweden
Hongfeng Yu	University of Nebraska - Lincoln, USA
Xiaoru Yuan	Peking University, China

IVAPP Additional Reviewers

Jie Hua	University of Technology Sydney, Australia
Peng song	University of Science and Technology of China, China
Pierre Vanhulst	Université de Fribourg, Switzerland
Wei Zeng	Singapore-ETH Centre, Singapore
Björn Zimmer	Linnaeus University, Sweden

VISAPP Program Committee

Davide Moroni	Institute of Information Science and Technologies (ISTI)-CNR, Italy
Amr Abdel-Dayem	Laurentian University, Canada
Andrew Adamatzky	University of the West of England, UK
Ilya Afanasyev	Innopolis University, Russian Federation
Sos Agaian	College of Staten Island and the Graduate Center, CUNY, USA
Vicente Alarcon-Aquino	Universidad de las Americas Puebla, Mexico
Mokhled Al-Tarawneh	Mu'tah University, Jordan
Matthew Antone	Massachusetts Institute of Technology, USA
Djamila Aouada	University of Luxembourg, Luxembourg
Karm Arya	ABV-Indian Institute of Information Technology and Management, India
Angelos Barmpoutis	University of Florida, USA
Giuseppe Baruffa	University of Perugia, Italy
Mohamed Batouche	University Constantine 2, Algeria
Sebastiano Battiato	University of Catania, Italy
Ardhendu Behera	Edge Hill University, UK
Fabio Bellavia	Università degli Studi di Firenze, Italy
Olga Bellon	Universidade Federal do Paraná, Brazil
Achraf Ben-Hamadou	Digital Research Center of Sfax, Tunisia
Jenny Benois-Pineau	LABRI, University of Bordeaux, France
Robert Bergevin	Université Laval, Canada
Neil Bergmann	University of Queensland, Australia
Du Bo	Wuhan University, China
Adrian Bors	University of York, UK
Roland Bremond	Institut Français des Sciences et Technologies des Transports, de l'aménagement et des Réseaux (IFSTTAR), France
Marius Brezovan	University of Craiova, Romania
Valentin Brimkov	State University of New York, USA
Alfred Bruckstein	Technion, Israel
Arcangelo Bruna	STMicroelectronics, Italy
Ioan Buciu	Universitatea din Oradea, Romania
Xianbin Cao	Beihang University, China
Alice Caplier	GIPSA-lab, France
Franco Cardillo	Consiglio Nazionale delle Ricerche, Italy
M. Emre Celebi	University of Central Arkansas, USA
Satish Chand	Netaji Subhas Institute of Technology and Jawaharlal Nehru University Delhi, India
Chin-Chen Chang	Feng Chia University, Taiwan
Jocelyn Chanussot	Grenoble Institute of Technology Institut Polytechnique de Grenoble, France
Samuel Cheng	University of Oklahoma, USA

Michal Choras	University of Technology and Life Sciences Bydgoszcz and ITTI Poznan, Poland
Chien-Hsing Chou	Tamkang University, Taiwan
Carlo Colombo	Università degli Studi di Firenze, Italy
Donatello Conte	Université de Tours, France
Fabio Cuzzolin	Oxford Brookes University, UK
Larry Davis	University of Maryland College Park, USA
Kenneth Dawson-Howe	Trinity College Dublin, Ireland
Guido de Croon	Delft University of Technology, The Netherlands
Anselmo Cardoso de Paiva	Universidade Federal do Maranhao, Brazil
Thomas Deserno	Technische Universität Braunschweig, Germany
Michel Devy	LAAS-CNRS, France
Sotirios Diamantas	University of Nevada, Reno, USA
Yago Diez	Yamagata University, Japan
Jana Dittmann	Otto-von-Guericke-Universität Magdeburg, Germany
Aijuan Dong	Hood College, USA
Anastasios Drosou	Centre for Research and Technology, Hellas, Greece
Peter Eisert	Fraunhofer Institut für Nachrichtentechnik, Germany
Mahmoud El-Sakka	The University of Western Ontario, Canada
Grigori Evreinov	University of Tampere, Finland
Jean-Baptiste Fasquel	University of Angers, France
Jianqiao Feng	Google, USA
Aaron Fenster	Robarts Research Institute, Canada
Stefano Ferilli	University of Bari, Italy
Gernot Fink	TU Dortmund, Germany
Tyler Folsom	QUEST Integrated Inc., USA
Gian Foresti	University of Udine, Italy
Mohamed Fouad	Military Technical College, Egypt
Fabio Galasso	OSRAM GmbH, Germany
Antonios Gasteratos	Democritus University of Thrace, Greece
Claudio Gennaro	CNR, Italy
Herman Gomes	Universidade Federal de Campina Grande, Brazil
Juan A. Gómez-Pulido	University of Extremadura, Spain
Luiz Goncalves	Federal University of Rio Grande do Norte, Brazil
Amr Goneid	The American University in Cairo, Egypt
Manuel González-Hidalgo	Balearic Islands University, Spain
Bernard Gosselin	University of Mons, Belgium
Nikos Grammalidis	Centre of Research and Technology Hellas, Greece
Costantino Grana	Università degli Studi di Modena e Reggio Emilia, Italy
Daniel Harari	Weizmann Institute of Science, Israel
Anthony Ho	University of Surrey, UK
Wladyslaw Homenda	Warsaw University of Technology, Poland
Hui-Yu Huang	National Formosa University, Taiwan
Céline Hudelot	Ecole Centrale de Paris, France
Chih-Cheng Hung	Kennesaw State University, USA
David i	Universitat Oberta de Barcelona, Spain

Laura Igual	Universitat de Barcelona, Spain
Francisco Imai	Apple Inc., USA
Tatiana Jaworska	Polish Academy of Sciences, Poland
Moongu Jeon	Gwangju Institute of Science and Technology, Korea, Republic of
Jianmin Jiang	Shenzhen University, China
Xiaoyi Jiang	University of Münster, Germany
Luis Jiménez Linares	University of de Castilla-La Mancha, Spain
Zhong Jin	Nanjing University of Science and Technology, China
Joni-Kristian Kamarainen	Tampere University of Technology, Finland
Martin Kampel	Vienna University of Technology, Austria
Mohan Kankanhalli	National University of Singapore, Singapore
Hamid Karimi	Politecnico di Milano, Italy
Thomas Karnowski	Oak Ridge National Laboratory, USA
Etienne Kerre	Ghent University, Belgium
Anastasios Kesidis	National Center for Scientific Research, Greece
Sehwan Kim	WorldViz LLC, USA
Nahum Kiryati	Tel Aviv University, Israel
Syoji Kobashi	University of Hyogo, Japan
Mario Köppen	Kyushu Institute of Technology, Japan
Andreas Koschan	University of Tennessee, USA
Dimitrios Kosmopoulos	University of Patras, Greece
Constantine Kotropoulos	Aristotle University of Thessaloniki, Greece
Arjan Kuijper	Fraunhofer Institute for Computer Graphics Research and TU Darmstadt, Germany
Jorma Laaksonen	Aalto University School of Science, Finland
Gauthier Lafruit	Université Libre de Bruxelles, Belgium
Slimane Larabi	U.S.T.H.B. University, Algeria
Mónica Larese	CIFASIS-CONICET, National University of Rosario, Argentina
Denis Laurendeau	Laval University, Canada
Sébastien Lefèvre	Université Bretagne Sud, France
Stan Li	Chinese Academy of Sciences, China
Huei-Yung Lin	National Chung Cheng University, Taiwan
Liang Lin	Sun Yat-Sen University, China
Xiuwen Liu	Florida State University, USA
Giosue Lo Bosco	Università di Palermo, Italy
Bruno Macchiavello	Universidade de Brasilia, Brazil
Ilias Maglogiannis	University of Piraeus, Greece
Baptiste Magnier	LGI2P de l'Ecole des Mines d'ALES, France
András Majdik	MTA SZTAKI, Hungary
Francesco Marcelloni	University of Pisa, Italy
Lucio Marcenaro	University of Genoa, Italy
Emmanuel Marilly	NOKIA - Bell Labs France, France
Jean Martinet	University of Lille 1, France
José Martínez Sotoca	Universitat Jaume I, Spain

Iacopo Masi	University of Southern California, USA
Mitsuharu Matsumoto	The University of Electro-Communications, Japan
Jaime Melendez	Universitat Rovira i Virgili, Spain
Radko Mesiar	Slovak University of Technology, Slovak Republic
Leonid Mestetskiy	Lomonosov Moscow State University, Russian Federation
Cyrille Migniot	Université de Bourgogne - le2i, France
Max Mignotte	Université de Montreal, Canada
Dan Mikami	NTT, Japan
Steven Mills	University of Otago, New Zealand
Nabin Mishra	Stoecker and Associates, USA
Pradit Mittrapiyanuruk	Srinakharinwirot University, Thailand
Birgit Moeller	Martin Luther University Halle-Wittenberg, Germany
Kostantinos Moustakas	University of Patras, Greece
Feiping Nie	University of Texas at Arlington, USA
Marcos Nieto	Vicomtech-ik4, Spain
Mikael Nilsson	Lund University, Sweden
Takahiro Okabe	Kyushu Institute of Technology, Japan
Yoshihiro Okada	Kyushu University, Japan
Gonzalo Pajares	Universidad Complutense de Madrid, Spain
William Puech	University of Montpellier II, France
Giovanni Puglisi	University of Cagliari, Italy
Xiaojun Qi	Utah State University, USA
Bogdan Raducanu	Computer Vision Center, Spain
Giuliana Ramella	CNR - Istituto per le Applicazioni del Calcolo M. Picone, Italy
Huamin Ren	Inmeta Consulting AS, Norway
Phill Rhee	Inha University, Korea, Republic of
Marcos Rodrigues	Sheffield Hallam University, UK
Ramón Ruiz	Universidad Politécnica de Cartagena, Spain
Silvio Sabatini	University of Genoa, Italy
Farhang Sahba	Sheridan Institute of Technology and Advanced Learning, Canada
Ovidio Salvetti	National Research Council of Italy - CNR, Italy
Andreja Samcovic	University of Belgrade, Serbia
Javier Sánchez	University of Las Palmas de Gran Canaria, Spain
K. C. Santosh	The University of South Dakota, USA
Jun Sato	Nagoya Institute of Technology, Japan
Shinichi Sato	National Institute of Informatics, Japan
Gerald Schaefer	Loughborough University, UK
Raimondo Schettini	University of Milano - Bicocca, Italy
Fiorella Sgallari	University of Bologna, Italy
Shishir Shah	University of Houston, USA
Caifeng Shan	Philips Research, The Netherlands
Lik-Kwan Shark	University of Central Lancashire, UK
Maryam Shokri	MaryMas Technologies LLC, USA

Luciano Silva	Universidade Federal do Parana, Brazil
Bogdan Smolka	Silesian University of Technology, Poland
Ferdous Sohel	Murdoch University, Australia
Ömer Soysal	Southeastern Louisiana University, USA
Filippo Stanco	Università di Catania, Italy
William Stoecker	Stoecker and Associates/Missouri University of Science and Technology, USA
Mu-Chun Su	National Central University, Taiwan
Chuan Sun	NYC Data Science Academy, USA
David Svoboda	Masaryk University, Czech Republic
Tamás Szirányi	MTA SZTAKI, Hungary
Ryszard Tadeusiewicz	AGH University of Science and Technology, Poland
Norio Tagawa	Tokyo Metropolitan University, Japan
Hiroki Takahashi	The University of Electro-Communications, Tokyo, Japan
Tolga Tasdizen	University of Utah, USA
João Tavares	Universidade do Porto, Portugal
Alexandru Telea	University of Groningen, The Netherlands
YingLi Tian	The City College of New York, USA
H. Tizhoosh	University of Waterloo, Canada
Yubing Tong	University of Pennsylvania, USA
Andrea Torsello	Università Ca' Foscari di Venezia, Italy
Alain Tremeau	Université Jean Monnet in Saint Etienne, France
Yulia Trusova	Federal Research Center Computer Science and Control of the Russian Academy of Sciences, Russian Federation
Du-Ming Tsai	Yuan-Ze University, Taiwan
Cesare Valenti	Università degli Studi di Palermo, Italy
Joost van de Weijer	Autonomous University of Barcelona, Spain
Vassilios Vonikakis	Advanced Digital Sciences Center (ADSC), Singapore
Frank Wallhoff	Jade University of Applied Science, Germany
Tao Wang	BAE Systems, USA
Toyohide Watanabe	Nagoya Industrial Science Research Institute, Japan
Quan Wen	University of Electronic Science and Technology of China, China
Andrew Willis	University of North Carolina at Charlotte, USA
Christian Wöhler	TU Dortmund University, Germany
Stefan Wörz	University of Heidelberg, Germany
Yan Wu	Georgia Southern University, USA
Pingkun Yan	Rensselaer Polytechnic Institute, USA
Vera Yashina	Dorodnicyn Computing Center of the Russian Academy of Sciences, Russian Federation
Alper Yilmaz	Ohio State University, USA
Lara Younes	Inria, France
Hongfeng Yu	University of Nebraska - Lincoln, USA
Huiyu Zhou	Queen's University Belfast, UK

Yun Zhu	UCSD, USA
Li Zhuo	Beijing University of Technology, China
Peter Zolliker	Empa, Swiss Federal Laboratories for Materials Science and Technology, Switzerland
Ju Zou	University of Western Sydney, Australia

VISAPP Additional Reviewers

Lorenzo Baraldi	Università degli Studi di Modena e Reggio Emilia, Italy
Júlio Batista	IMAGO Research Group, Brazil
Ariel Bayá	CONICET, Argentina
Daniele Di Mauro	University of Catania, Italy
Marco Fanfani	University of Florence, Italy
Antonino Furnari	University of Catania, Italy
Juan Carlos Galan	Universidad de las Americas Puebla, Mexico
René Grzeszick	TU Dortmund University, Germany
Attila Kiss	MTA SZTAKI, Hungary
Marc Masana Castrillo	Computer Vision Center, Spain
Filippo Milotta	University of Catania, Italy
Alessandro Ortis	University of Catania, Italy
Axel Plinge	TU Dortmund, Germany
Leonard Rothacker	TU Dortmund University, Germany
Suman Saha	Oxford Brookes University, UK
Gurkirt Singh	Oxford Brookes University, UK
Evangelos Vlachos	University of Patras, Greece
Jun Wan	CASIA, China
Wei Xiang	University of Texas at Arlington, USA
Ruomei Yan	Oxford Brookes University, UK
Lichao Zhang	Computer Vision Center, Spain

Invited Speakers

Jack van Wijk	Eindhoven University of Technology, The Netherlands
Holly Rushmeier	Yale University, USA
Jean-Daniel Fekete	Inria, France
Nadia Magnenat-Thalmann	NTU, Singapore and MIRALab, University of Geneva, Switzerland

Contents

Computer Graphics Theory and Applications

Calibrating, Rendering and Evaluating the Head Mounted Light Field Display

Anne Juhler Hansen[✉], Jákup Klein, and Martin Kraus

Aalborg University, Rendsburggade 14, 9000 Aalborg, Denmark
{ajha,martin}@create.aau.dk, jakupklein@gmail.com

Abstract. There are several benefits of using a light field display over a traditional HMD; in particular the light field can avoid the vergence-accommodation conflict and can also correct for near- and farsightedness. By rendering only four corner cameras of a subimage array, then these four views can be interpolated in order to create all subimages of the light field. We implement the interpolation of the subimages in the light field with the use of pixel reprojection, while maintaining correct perspective and shading. We give an comprehensive explanation of the construction and calibration of a head mounted light field display, and finally we evaluate the image quality through image difference and conduct a user evaluation of the light field images in order to evaluate if users are able to perceive a difference in the light field images created with the full array of virtual cameras and our method using four cameras and pixel reprojection. In most cases the users were unable to distinguish the images, and we conclude that pixel reprojection is a feasible method for rendering light fields as far as quality is concerned.

1 Introduction

Traditional HMDs lack 3-dimensional cues, hereunder the parallax effect and correct eye accommodation, whereas light field displays have advantages to traditional stereoscopic head mounted displays, e.g. due to the fact that the vergence-accommodation conflict is not present. The vergence-accommodation conflict has been under suspicion of causing visual fatigue, eye-strain, diplopic vision, headaches, and other signs of simulation sickness [1]. The light field display allows an observer to perceive a scene at different depths and angles, and can provide correct retinal blur, parallax and eye accommodation. Hence light field displays can eliminate visual discomfort and nausea, since this may balance out some of the conflicting cues which are experienced with traditional HMDs. One way of creating a light field display is by placing a distance-adjusted array of microlenses in front of a display. When rendering for a light field display, several 2D subimages have to be rendered from different views, as seen from an array of different cameras. Instead of rendering an array of virtual cameras, views can be interpolated from only four rendered cameras [2]. Our contributions are:

- We propose a method to render light fields that reduces the number of virtual cameras through pixel reprojection.

© Springer Nature Switzerland AG 2019
A. P. Cláudio et al. (Eds.): VISIGRAPP 2017, CCIS 983, pp. 3–28, 2019.
https://doi.org/10.1007/978-3-030-12209-6_1

– We give a comprehensive description of the light display construction, setup and calibration.
– We examine the image quality through image difference and evaluate whether test subjects are able to notice a difference in image quality using the two-interval forced choice test.

1.1   Vergence-Accommodation Conflict

The human ocular system will adapt when focus is changed between different distances, such that the point of interest remains binocularly fused i.e. in focus. Vergence and accommodation are the two parameters that influence our perception of depth and focus. Accommodation refers to the physical shape of the lens of the eye, where the eye increases optical power to maintain a clear focused image. When accommodating, the shape of the lens inside the eye changes to allow for a focused image at that (see Fig. 1). Accommodation can be consciously controlled, but usually acts like a reflex. Humans can change the optical accommodation of their eyes by up to 15 diopters (the inverse of the focal length in metres), but the accommodation diversity is reduced with age [3].

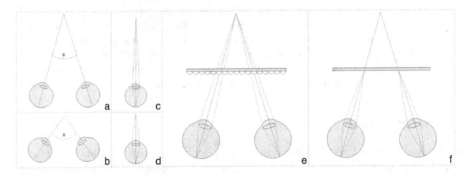

Fig. 1. Vergence (a+b) is when the eyes move inwards (convergence) or outwards (divergence) towards a focus point. Accommodation (c+d) is the physical shape of the eye. Correct retinal blur (e) as experienced through a light field display. Vergence-Accommodation Conflict (f).

The vergence mechanism continually adjusts the angle between the two eyes such that features at the focus distance remain fused in the binocular vision. A pair of eyes will converge along the vertical axis, when an object in focus comes closer to the eye, or in other words, as the distance of the point of interest decreases from infinity. The eyes will diverge when the distance to a point of interest gets longer and/or goes towards infinity. The vergence and accommodation system interplay with each other in a feedback loop, since there is a secondary set of cues for both systems consisting of reciprocal signals from one another. This means that a change in visual cues will affect both system; stereo disparity drives the eyes to converge or diverge, and retinal blur prompts an oculomotor accommodation adjustment. To further strengthening the argument of these systems being very tightly coupled, Suryakumar et al. have shown that visual disparity in isolation elicits a fully comparable accommodation response to that of retinal blur [4]. The reciprocal secondary cues between accommodation and vergence serve to better coordinate the final accommodative response in natural viewing conditions [5]. However, in traditional stereo imaging where the depth is fixed, vergence towards a different distance will elicit conflicting cues between the two systems, and this has been linked to discomfort [6], visual fatigue, and reduced visual performance [1]. Research in resolving the vergence-accommodation conflict is still ongoing, and there are several proposals of solutions in both soft- and hardware [7] (see Sect. 2.4). One of the consequent benefits of a light field display is that it allows natural accommodation and vergence (see Fig. 1). Focusing at different distances simply determines which parts of the 2D image slices that are focused onto the retina. The light field images can be rendered to be perceived as if they are at natural (or unnatural) distances away from the viewer. By adjusting e.g. the field of view of each subimage camera, the depth of the optically reconstructed image will be influenced. By taking advantage of this fact, the virtual distances can correct for near- and far-sightedness of users [8], which can negate the use of glasses (or contact lenses) when wearing a HMD.

2   The Light Field

To understand the light field and its influence in computer graphics research, one must understand how to represent all light in a volume. The beginning of the light field and its definition can be traced back to Leonardo Da Vinci, who referred to a set of light rays as radiant pyramids [9]:

> The body of the air is full of an infinite number of radiant pyramids caused by the objects located in it. These pyramids intersect and interweave with each other during the independent passage throughout the air in which they are infused.

Later on, the light field has been defined as the amount of light travelling in every direction through every point in space. Light can be interpreted as a field, because space is filled with an array of light rays at various intensities. This is close to the definition of the 5D plenoptic function, which describes all light information visible from a particular viewing position. This can be explained as recording the intensity of the light rays passing through the center of a pupil placed at every possible x, y, and z in a 3-dimensional volume, and at every angle θ and φ [9]. The plenoptic function allows reconstruction of every possible view, from every position, at every direction (see Eq. 1).

$$P(\theta, \phi, x, y, z) \tag{1}$$

Since radiance does not change along a line unless it is blocked, the 5D plenoptic function can be reduced to 4D in space free of occluders [10]. The

4D light field can explain the total light intensity of each ray as a function of position and direction (see Eq. 2).

$$P'(\theta, \phi, u, v) \tag{2}$$

The light intensity is given for every possible position u and v on a 2-dimensional plane, and angle θ and ϕ.

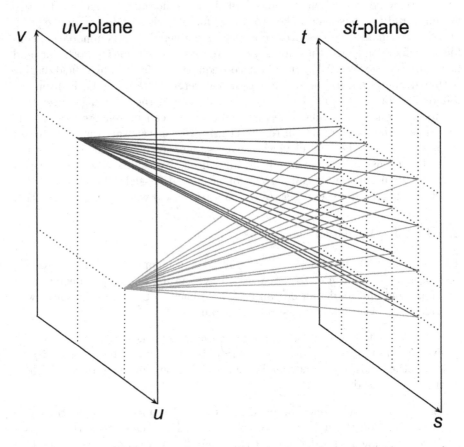

Fig. 2. The light slab is a two-plane parameterization, where the st-plane can be thought of as a collection of perspective images of the scene, and the uv-plane corresponds to the position(s) of the observer(s).

2.1   Parameterization of the 4D Light Field

Levoy et al. described how a light field can be parameterized by the position of two points on two planes [10]. This parameterization is called a light slab (see Fig. 2). A light ray enters one plane (the uv-plane) and exits another plane (the st-plane), and the result is a 2D array of images of a scene at different angles.

Since a 4D light field can be represented by a 2D array of images, it has the advantage that the geometric calculations are highly efficient. The line of all light rays can simply be parameterized by the two points. When parameterizing the light field into 2D-images, the elemental images correspond to images taken from different positions on the uv-plane, and each image represents a slice of the 4D light slab. In other words, the st-plane can be thought of as a collection of perspective images of the scene, and the uv-plane corresponds to the position of the observer.

2.2   Light Field Displays

The light field can be optically reconstructed by placing a distance-adjusted array of microlenses in front of a display (see Fig. 3). This is known as a light field display. The light field display allows an observer to integrate a correct 2D image of the light field at different depths and angles in accordance with the spatial and depth resolution that the light field contains. In other words the light field display allows an observer to accommodate and converge his/her eyes on a virtual object as if it were part the real world. Since every pixel on the screen emits light, and all lenslets in the full microlens array transmit the light in accordance with the angular information, the result will be a full light field. Depending on where the observer is looking, different subimage pixels will be used to create the view, and hence the 3-dimensional holographic effect can be experienced. The image seen through a light field display has focus cues, where the convergence point is the point in focus, and the rest of the image appears blurred just like the real world. Even a monocular experience of the light field will give appropriate depth and focus cues, since the eye will focus at a point behind the screen at the correct distance (see Sect. 1.1). Since distances

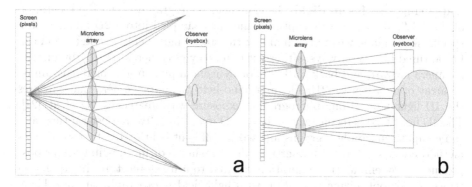

Fig. 3. (a) Light from one pixel travels through lenses in the microlens array. Some of the light rays reach the eye, and some light rays will be bent in other directions. (b) Light from several pixels travel through the microlens array and (some) reach the eye or area of the eyebox with different incident angles. This allows the observer to focus his/her eyes while getting the corresponding light rays.

can be virtually manipulated, the light field can be optically reconstructed to account for near- and far-sightedness of users. Light field display technology is being researched in several areas: 3D-displays [11], light field projection [12], and holography [13]. Commercial products, like the Leia 3D display, are on the market, and claim to give holographic imagery with content appearing to come out of a conventional liquid crystal display (LCD) and showing the parallax effect with head movement without the need of any glasses. Likewise does the head mounted light field stereoscope [14] not use a microlens array, but creates the light field via stacked liquid crystal panels and hereby emphasizes that light field renderings can be shown with different technologies.

2.3   Head-Mounted Light Field Displays

Most HMDs do not account for the vergence-accommodation conflict (see Sect. 1.1), they suffer from low resolution and a low field-of-view (FOV), they are heavy and have big and bulky optics [15]. Light fields can improve on some of the limitations of traditional fixed-focus HMDs, since light fields consist of more information than usual 2D images. With the benefits from using microlenslet arrays in HMDs, Lanman and Luebke have shown that a light field display can be integrated into a HMD, which can both minimize the size of HMDs and potentially allow for much more immersive VR solutions compared to the fixed focus displays used in most common HMDs [8]. Lanman and Luebke have created near-eye light field displays with a thickness of 1 cm. [16], and Shaulov et al. demonstrated that ultracompact imaging optical relay systems based on microlenslet arrays can be designed with an overall thickness of only a few millimetres [17] creating the potential of light-weight HMDs that are less bulky than their predecessor.

Capturing the Light Field. In light field photography a 2D representation of the 4D light field can be captured and then sampled into a 2D image with a specific focus plane within the limits of the stored light field. The light field can be captured in several ways; either with an array of cameras [18,19], by moving a camera forward and backward [20], or by using a plenoptic camera containing an array of microlenses [21]. The first hand-held plenoptic camera that captures the 4D light field in one photographic exposure was created by Ng et al. [21]. The 4D light field is reconstructed into a 2D image in software post-capture, and can compute sharp photographs focused at different depths. In other words this method creates a synthetic aperture, that expands editing possibilities in post production by eliminating limitations related to a fixed aperture. Interpolation strategies for optimizing resolution with light field photography are also being explored. Georgeiv et al. [22] have created an interpolation method that creates a better resolution in the final light field photograph by virtually increasing the amount of views to be more than the amount of microlenslets. Naimark et al. created a stereo image capture rig, that captures a pair of stereo images [23]. From that a synthetic scene with depth could be calculated using cross dissolve.

Since the light field gives a high accuracy of sampling it is possible to triangulate points into a point cloud, which provides the ability of tracking objects and semi-reconstruct objects and scenes 3-dimensionally. This is one of the reasons why light field technology has potential benefits in the field of visual effect (VFX). Since light field photography essentially captures depth, it can be used to redefine previous methods (e.g. chroma keying) and develop new approaches (e.g. depth screen removal). Depth screen removal is one example of a new and improved technique for the VFX workflow, where the volumetric data from the light field can be used to disperse the object of interest from the background. The depth can among things be used to create semi-automated segmentation and rotoscoping. VR is already exploring the use of live-action footage, e.g. with the use of the Ricoh Theta, which is an omnidirectional camera that with two fish-eye lenses captures 360° with a single shot. The captured images overlap, and can therefore be stitched together, taking every photo from that single point of view. Similar solutions include the Jaunt, the Nokia Ozo, and the GoPro Odyssey, but a 360° spherical image will though only create a flat panorama in VR, and will get no 3D and parallax effect.

The future might bring light field live-action footage to the VR platform, and therefore the motivating force to research light field renderings and evaluating it through user testing is both interesting and relevant for future studies and implementation.

2.4   Light Field Rendering

One of the first times light fields were introduced into computer graphics was by Levoy et al. in 1996, where they used image based rendering to compute new views of a scene from pre-existing views without the need for scene geometry [10]. The technique showed a real-time view of the light field, where it was possible to see a scene with correct perspective and shading, and with the option of zooming in and out. When zooming in, the light samples disperse throughout the array of 2D slices, so the perceived image is constructed from pieces from several elemental images. Davis et al. have created a system for interactively acquiring and rendering light fields using a camera being waved around an object [24]. They present a rendering algorithm that triangulates the captured viewpoints and is specially designed for the unstructured and dense data of the light field. Using direct light field rendering, Jeoung et al. have introduced an image-based rendering method in the light field domain, which attempts to directly compute only the necessary samples, and not the entire light field, to improve rendering in terms of complexity and memory usage [25]. Light field technology is competing with other technologies that are trying to display some of the same effects but with different advantages and short comings. Foveated rendering is a technique where the image resolution is not uniform across the image, and where the abilities of the human peripheral vision can be taken advantage of. The technique can be used to create retinal blur, which is the blurred perception of objects outside the center of gaze (and therefore in the peripheral vision). Gupta et al. worked on tracking and predicting eye gaze accurately with the objective of improving interactivity using eye-gaze information by enabling foveated rendering or simulate retinal blur [26]. Since the method also can be used to accelerate graphics computation, Guenter et al. performed a user study on foveated 3D graphics. Their method tracks the user's gaze point and from that renders three image layers around it at progressively higher angular size but lower sampling rate [27]. Reducing complexity is highly desired when working with light fields, and (re)construction of overlapping views is a good place to start, since this is where the light field contains a lot of redundant information. Much of the data is repetitive, especially when looking at a scene placed at infinity, where all subimages are created from parallel light rays. Instead of creating a virtual camera or capturing an individual subimage for each elemental image, interpolation can be used to reduce the computational effort. Pixel reprojection can therefore be used as a tool to optimize shaders, since reusing data between consecutive frames can accelerate real-time shading [28,29]. The spatio-temporal coherence of image sequences has been exploited for several rendering systems [30,31] (e.g. for global illumination), or temporal anti aliasing can be created by matching pixels from the current frame with pixels from the last frame, and from that in-between views can be calculated [32]. One important aspect of pixel reprojection is that the depth value at each pixel should be known in order to be able to reproject the data [33].

3   Implementation and Methods

By rendering only four corner cameras of a subimage array, then these four views can be interpolated in order to create all subimages of the light field. We implement the interpolation of the subimages in the light field with the use of pixel reprojection, while maintaining correct perspective and shading. We give an comprehensive explanation of the construction and calibration of a head mounted light field display. Finally we evaluate the image quality through image difference and conduct a user evaluation of the light field images in order to evaluate if users are able to perceive a difference in the light field images created with the full array of virtual cameras and our method using four cameras and pixel reprojection.

3.1   The Light Field Display

The head mounted near-eye light field display is constructed using an array of lenses (a Fresnel Technologies #630 microlens array) in front of a similar size adjusted array of rendered images (see Fig. 4). The #630 microlens array has a focal length of 3.3 mm and a physical lenslet size of 1×1 mm, which determines the subimage array size and the number of pixels in each subimage. Based on research by Lanman and Luebke [8], each of the lenslets in the microlens array can be seen as a simple magnifier for each of the subimages in the array. Depicting the individual lenslets as a thin lens is though only an approximation, since the lenslets are influenced by parameters of a thick lens; curvature, its index of refraction and its thickness.

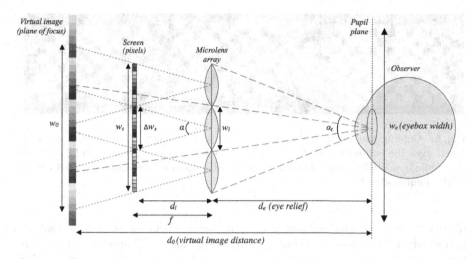

Fig. 4. An observer sees the light field by looking through a microlens array in front of a screen, where each lens covers one subimage. Rays from different subimages enter the pupil of the observer, and the light field is experienced as one image, where the light samples disperse throughout the array of subimages. When focus (vergence and accommodation) is changed, the perceived image will be constructed from rays from other subimages [2].

The lens separation d_l can be found using the Gaussian thin lens formula (see Eq. 3) where d_l is the distance between the lens and the display (with $0 < d_l \leq f$), f is the focal length, d_0 is the distance to the virtual image, and d_e is the eye relief.

$$\frac{1}{f} = \frac{1}{d_l} - \frac{1}{d_0 - d_e} \Leftrightarrow d_l = \frac{f(d_0 - d_e)}{f + (d_0 - d_e)} \tag{3}$$

The lens separation d_l is one of the parameters in the formula with the greatest impact on the perceived image, since the microlens array should be placed at a distance $0 < d_l \leq f$. With $f = 3.3$ mm the lens separation should be $d_l \approx 3.29$ mm or in other words just below the focal length $f = 3.3$ mm. With an eye relief of 35 mm and d_0 set to 1 m, then the lens separation $d_l = 3.2888$ mm. The lens separation was manually adjusted to the best possible alignment $d_l \approx 3.29$ mm using a 3D printed spacer. Since the microlens array has a thickness of 3.3 mm, it had to be turned with the flat side up, which might cause sources of error, since it is difficult to confirm the distance $d_l = 3.2888$ mm. The lenslet array must be placed in front of the screen so that the lenses and the subimages align. This is especially true for the rotation since the position of the subimages can easily be adjusted in the shader. This is, however, not the case for rotation. The alignment was achieved by placing a microscope directly above the screen. The image from the microscope was then sent to a Processing sketch that placed a (green) grid on top of the sub-images (see Fig. 5, left). The image will appear

Fig. 5. Aligning the subimages with the lenslets: Left image shows a grid superimposed over the subimages in the screen. Center image shows lenses misaligned with the subimages. Right image shows the correct alignment of the subimages and lenses. (Color figure online)

distorted if the rotation alignment is off by several degrees (see Fig. 5, center). If the alignment, however, is close to correct the image will appear correct. The lenslet array was placed on top and another grid (red) was shown that had the same position and rotation but was scaled to accommodate the larger squares (see Fig. 5, right).

The magnification factor can be used to calculate the field of view, since it tells us the magnification of the image on the screen to the image plane at d_0. With $f = 3.3\,\text{mm}$ and $d_0 = 1000\,\text{mm}$ the magnification factor is $M = 293.42$ (see Eq. 4 [8]), where w_0 is the width of the virtual image at the plane of focus, and w_s is the width of the microdisplay.

$$M = \frac{w_0}{w_s} = \frac{d_0 - d_e}{d_l} = 1 + \frac{d_0 - d_e}{f} \tag{4}$$

The FOV is either limited by the extent of the lens (lens-limited magnifier) or it is limited by the dimensions of the display (display-limited magnifier). The lens-limited magnifier is influenced by $\frac{w_l}{2d_e}$, whereas the display-limited magnifier is influenced by $\frac{M w}{2d_0}$, and since our FOV only can be limited by the lens (see Eq. 5), we can then calculate the FOV for each of our virtual cameras in the array. Field of view α (from the lens) per camera:

$$\alpha = 2\arctan\left(\frac{\Delta w_s}{2d_l}\right) \tag{5}$$

The FOV per rendered camera is then calculated to be 17.28°. When confirming the FOV, we could though conclude, that a FOV of 19.86° gave a sharper image. The FOV can be confirmed by measuring the angle between a camera looking straight at the display and a camera looking at the edge of the display (see Fig. 6).

Since a microlens array can be interpreted as a set of independent lens-limited magnifiers, the total field of view α_t from the viewer's eye can be found using the array width $N_l w_l$, and the eye relief d_e. N_l is the number of lenses, and w_l is the lens width. The total FOV α_t should then be given by [8]:

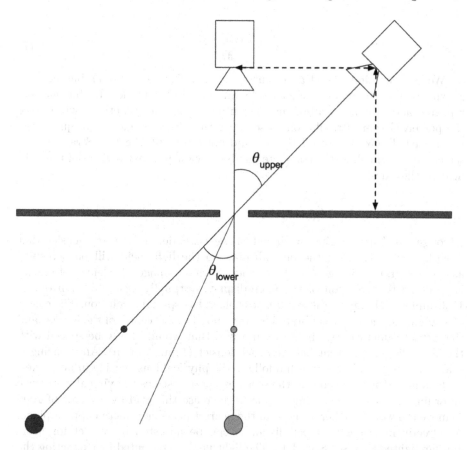

Fig. 6. Confirming FOV (a); the camera is moved to find the FOV of the subimage. Confirming that the total FOV is correct (b); if Θ_{lower} and Θ_{upper} are the same, then the angled camera will see both red spheres (small and large) in the same position since they follow the same line. If the angles are not the same, the camera will not see both spheres i.e. it will follow another line e.g. the red line. (Color figure online)

$$\alpha_t = 2 \arctan \left(\frac{N_l w_l}{2 d_e} \right) \tag{6}$$

The vertical FOV for 15 lenses is calculated to be $FOV_v = 24.2°$ and the horizontal FOV for 8 lenses is $FOV_h = 13.0°$ (see Eq. 7). We can also calculate the maximum spatial resolution N_p, by using the distance to the virtual image d_0, the FOV α, the magnification factor M and the pixel pitch p. When calculating with the used FOV $= 19.86°$ and a pixel pitch p calculated to be $0.012\,\mathrm{mm}$ for both vertical and horizontal axis (with a resolution of 1280×720 and the screen size $15.36\,\mathrm{mm} \times 8.64\,\mathrm{mm}$. Likewise the maximum spatial resolution N_p is given by:

$$N_p = \frac{2d_0 \tan(\alpha_t/2))}{M_p} \tag{7}$$

We get a maximum spatial resolution of $121 \times 64\,\mathrm{px}$ (see Eq. 7), but since α_t is expanded by the number of lenses N_l, and part of the rendered subimages are repeated across some or all of the elemental images, this repetition will reduce the perceived spatial resolution. Also, since the virtual cameras are quadratic, we either will have to cut off the top and bottom to fill the 15×8 ratio of the screen, or we will show the complete quadratic view plus extra views of the light field on the sides.

3.2 Rendering the Light Field

Through the Unity engine, a virtual image is rendered for every lenslet that is within the bounds of the microdisplay, so the light field will be perceived as one holographic image with focus cues. Each subimage (or elemental image) is rendered to a portion of the microdisplay; optimally $15\,\mathrm{mm} \times 8\,\mathrm{mm}$ out of $15.36\,\mathrm{mm} \times 8.64\,\mathrm{mm}$ to utilise most possible of the spatial resolution. The center of a subimage should be calibrated to correspond to the center of the lenslet, and the virtual camera array should form a grid that would ideally be spaced with the same distance as that between each lenslet ($1\,\mathrm{mm} \times 1\,\mathrm{mm}$). Any spacing is usable, as long as the relationship follows the physical lens-spacing in both axes.

Scaling the grid spacing in the scene essentially scales the virtual world size accordingly. For our rendering engine we increase this grid by a factor of 1000 to move the world further away from the nearest possible camera clipping plane. As already mentioned, object distances can be adjusted to correct for near- and far-sightedness (see Sect. 1.1). The light field is computed by extracting the two-dimensional slice from the 4D light field (see Fig. 7). Since the perceived

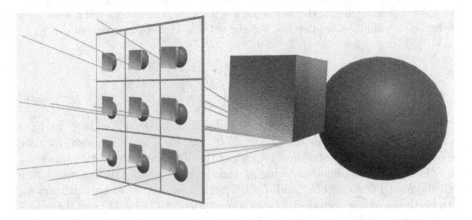

Fig. 7. A 4D light field can be seen as a collection of images of a scene, where the focal points of the cameras are all on a 2D plane.

image is constructed from pieces from several subimages, we need to render all these subimages in an array corresponding to the dimensions of our microlens array. The secure and reliable solution would be to render 15×8 different virtual cameras, where each camera has the same alignment as the lenslets. We refer to this as a light field image created with virtual cameras, and consider this the golden standard to which we compare our method to.

Pixel Reprojection. Pixel reprojection involves the redistribution of information from a set of input pixels to a set of output pixels. To capture an image of a scene consisting of vertices in a 3D volume (world space) the vertices must be transformed to the camera's space (camera/eye space), where a 2D image with perspective distortion within near and far plane can be generated (see Fig. 8). The interpolation of the subimages is accomplished by using pixel reprojection, where the pixels from the corner images are copied to the corresponding place in the interpolated subimage. To achieve this the pixel must be placed back to the 3D world and be "captured" to the interpolated subimage (see Fig. 9). The view space renders through a camera centered in the origin, hence view space is also referred to as camera space or eye space. The input pixel energy must be redistributed to the output pixel based on the exact overlap between these pixels.

The transformation depends on the x-coordinates on both the projection plane, x_p, and in eye space, x_e, as well as the near clipping plane n and the z-position z_e in eye space (see Eq. 8).

$$\frac{x_p}{x_e} = \frac{-n}{z_e} \qquad (8)$$

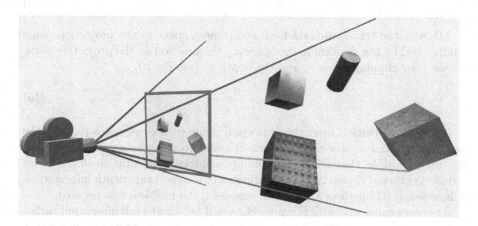

Fig. 8. 2D projection; the vertices are transformed to eye space where a 2D image with perspective distortion is generated. The geometry in the scene is projected onto the 2D plane, and using that information the image can then be calculated.

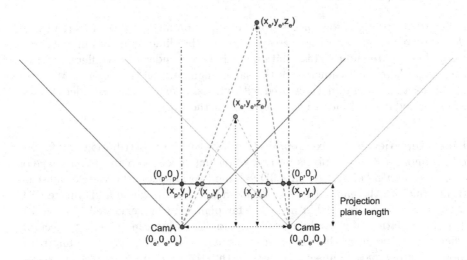

Fig. 9. A pixel can be reprojected from a corner camera (CamA), to an interpolated camera (e.g. CamB). The cameras have coordinates in the 3-dimensional eye space, whereas the projection plane is 2-dimensional.

The clip coordinate system projects all vertex data from the view space to the clip coordinates by comparing x_{clip}, y_{clip}, and z_{clip} with w_{clip} (which are $[x, y, z, w]$ in clipping space). Any clip coordinate vertex that is less than a certain w_{clip} or greater than a certain w_{clip} will be discarded, and then the clipping occurs. The x-coordinate of eye space, x_e is mapped to x_p, which is calculated by using the ratio of similar triangles (see Eq. 9).

$$x_e = -\frac{x_p \cdot z_e}{n} \tag{9}$$

Likewise the transformation from eye/camera space to the projection plane is influenced by the position in eye space x_e, the position on the projection plane x_p, the near clipping plane n, and the depth z_e (see Eq. 10).

$$x_p = -\frac{n \cdot x_e}{z_e} \tag{10}$$

The transformation from the projection plane to the eye space requires the depth from the eye space. The depth is saved from the corner cameras into the (unused) alpha channel. It was found through experimentation that a 24 bit texture (8 bits per channel) was not sufficient to give accurate depth information, if, however, a 32 bit (float32) texture was used, the problem was negated.

There are cases where pixel reprojection will not yield a full image, but rather an image with missing information i.e. in some cases objects will occlude other objects in such a way that when the camera is being reprojected, information is missing from the camera angle of view. The effect can be seen, when a computed image is comprised of the pixels from two corner cameras, but the information needed to interpolate a new pixel value is not available (see Fig. 10).

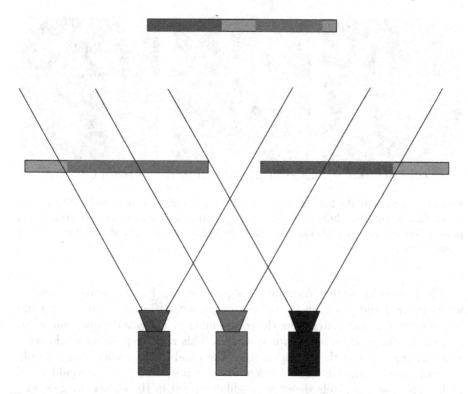

Fig. 10. Example of a scene where the corner cameras (red and blue) do not have the necessary information to create an in-between camera (green). The colour of the rectangles indicates the camera view; red indicates that the red camera can see it, blue indicates that the blue camera can see it, and grey indicates that neither red or blue camera can see it. (Color figure online)

In this project the missing pixel the values were filled by information (the mean value) from the subpixel position where the pixel value from the corner images were read. The result is that the hole is filled with colours that are present in the scene. Other solutions would be to repeat the edges of the last remaining pixel color information or adding more than four virtual cameras (see Fig. 11).

Shader Programming. To render a finished image most of the pixels must be reprojected from the corner images, the individual pixels are not depending on they neighbours (just the corner images). Due to this the process would benefit from a parallel approach where several pixels are calculated in parallel.

The interpolation is implemented as an image post-processing effect in Unity 3D. Unity works with image effects as scripts attached to a camera to alter the rendered output, and the computation is done in the shader scripts. The rendered images can be accessed via render textures, which are created and updated at runtime.

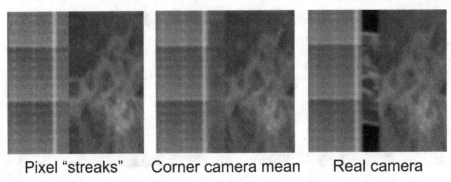

Pixel "streaks"   Corner camera mean   Real camera

Fig. 11. On the left the hole is filled with the edge pixels and repeated until the hole is full. In the center the hole is filled by averaging the pixel values in the corresponding position on the corner cameras. On the right is the image as it should look. (Color figure online)

The process consisted of several steps (see Fig. 12). Firstly the corner images were captured and placed in the corners of the output image. Next the top and bottom row were calculated from the corner images. The pixel in question would be in a certain position in its own subimage. This relative position would serve as a starting point in the corner images. The pixel in the corner images would be reprojected to the current subimage. If the reprojected position would be off with more that 0.5 pixels then the neighbour pixel in the corner image would be reprojected. Whether left or right neighbours are checked depends on where the corner camera is relative to the pixel reprojected camera. These calculations would be performed a certain number of times, unless the perfect candidate (<0.5 pixels) was found.

Once a perfect candidate was found, a new pixel reprojection would be performed, this time the offset (<0.5 pixels) would be taken in to consideration so that a accurate value could be found. Once the calculations were finished the candidates from the corner images were evaluated. In some cases all four corner images would have a candidate. If more than one candidate was available then the value with the smallest distance would be chosen. At this point the top and bottom rows were completed. These would serve as data for the pixel reprojection of the remaining subimages.

The two first steps were performed on textures that were four times larger than the output (screen) size because of super sampling. The next step reduces the size by taking the mean of several pixels, thus minimizing the staircase effect (see Fig. 12, and Sect. 3.2). Finally the image was re-sized and re-positioned according to the lenslet size and placement.

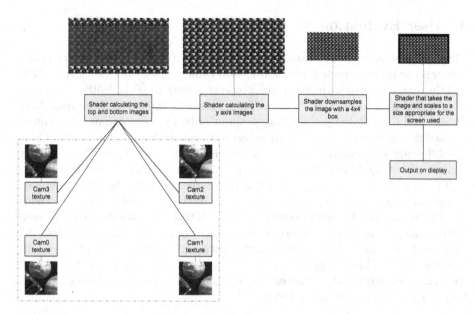

Fig. 12. Flowchart of the complete process. Note that the step where the top and bottom row are calculated portions of the texture that are not used have been grayed out.

Anti-aliasing. When rendering to a near eye light field, anti-aliasing must be used [8]. The problem with paring pixel reprojection and anti-aliasing is that anti-aliasing smooths out hard edges, but pixel reprojection requires the pixel colours to stay on the pixel position in order to have an accurate depth for that point and still maintain the correct colour. The depth can not be interpolated since that would result in edges being averaged between objects that are not at the same depth. This would result in pixels where the depth lies between objects in the scene effectively creating new objects. This would not show up in the corner images, but as soon as the camera view is moved from the original position. The solution is to apply anti-aliasing after all pixel reprojection is completed. To achieve this super sampling is needed where an image with a resolution much higher than the intended output image is rendered, then the image size is reduced to its intended resolution by combining the pixel values of the high resolution image. In this project a 4× (double width and double height) resolution image was used. When reducing the size, several methods can be used. One example is a 2×2 box where the mean of a box of 2×2 pixels is found and used in the lower resolution image. This will improve the look of the edges by reducing the "staircase" effect. The effect is, however, still strong. Another method is to use a 4×4 box where the outermost ring will overlap with the outermost ring in the neighbouring pixels [34]. In this project we used the 4×4 box to obtain a higher quality image.

4   User Evaluation

This experiment aims at statistically comparing if subjects can discriminate between the images created with 120 virtual cameras (VC) in the Unity engine, and the image created with our pixel reprojection method (PR). 5 different scenes were tested in a total of 10 different image tests (5 shown with the light field display and 5 single-image (position [4; 8] out of [8; 15]) on a computer monitor. The 5 different scenes were designed to test different rendering scenarios, and how the difference in geometry influence our rendering method. The different scenes include various numbers of objects, shapes, sizes and textures (see Fig. 13).

One image (image 5) was created with a large difference between reference image and sample; (1) to test the boundaries of the pixel reprojection method, and (2) to account for participant frustration. If test participants are never sure if their answers are correct or not, they can get frustrated, and decide that the given task is impossible and then start answering randomly [35] which would bias the results. The image was created to push the boundaries of the method with the presumption that the test participants were able to notice a difference between PR and the reference image VC.

4.1   Test Setup

Results from 34 test participants have been evaluated. Only participants with normal-vision, corrected to normal, nearsightedness, or small corrections (in the range -1.75 to $+0.50$) were allowed to participate. Since the objects in the scenes were within a distance of 12 cm to 6 m away from the camera position, then test participants with nearsightedness were fit but participants with farsightedness would bias the results, since farsightedness does not allow participants to accommodate on objects that are close. All samples were independent. 16 female and 18 male participants attended and their age ranged from 9 to 67 years. The test participants were explained that they would be shown a reference image and then two other images (one of which was the same at the reference image) and that they should identify the reference duplicate. An xBox 360 controller was used as an input device for the test participants. They were explained how to use the controller which they then used to switch between the images. They were given the choice to put headphones on for auditory feedback when they pressed the same button more than once or when they tried to choose the reference image. If they declined, then the facilitator would give the same feedback. Participants first took the test with the light field HMD, and after that they took the same test where the center subimage of the light field was shown. The order of the images was randomised. They could view the different images as many times as they saw fit. Participants then made a decision using the controller, and if the current image at that time was the reference image, the controller would vibrate to indicate that the image could not be chosen.

4.2 Two-Interval Forced Choice Test

We chose the 2-interval forced choice test where test participants had to choose one of two alternatives with no neutral alternatives listed. The test participants were asked to solve several matching-to-sample tasks. The experiment was conducted as a delayed matching-to-sample, where the reference stimuli is shown in sequence with two other stimulus (the sample or comparison stimuli).

Since two possible choices were shown sequentially this is referred to as a two-interval forced choice (2-IFC) procedure [35].

This test is passed if the probability for test participants to incorrectly identify PR as VC is greater than 19% with a confidence level of 95%. This corresponds to the commonly used threshold of test participants guessing incorrectly minimum 25% of at least 100 trials and complies with true hypothesis testing where the probability of incorrectly rejecting the null hypothesis is less than 5% [36]. The probability mass function for the number i of incorrect answers [37]:

$$f(i \mid n, p_{null}) = \frac{n!}{x!(n-i)!} p^x (1 - p_{null})^{n-x} \tag{11}$$

where p_{null} is the probability of PR incorrectly identified as VC, i is the number of incorrect answers and n is the number of trials. From the probability mass function we can find the critical number i_c.

$$i_c(n, p_{null}) = min \left\{ i \mid \sum_n^{j-i} f(j; n, p_{null}) < 0.05 \right\} \tag{12}$$

With 34 test participant the critical number $i_c = 11$, this is the minimum amount of test participants that need to incorrectly identify the PR image to be the best match to the reference image (VC) [37]. In other words, if the test subjects can do no better than a random guess, then the test has been passed, and we can conclude that the test participants perceive no difference between VC and PR.

5 Result and Analysis

With 10 different image tests (5 shown with the light field display and 5 on a computer monitor) we see that image 1–4 passed the test (see Fig. 14), since 11 or more participants have chosen PR and hence the test passed $i_c = 11$. Image 5 was intentionally designed to show the inadequacy of our method (see Fig. 13). For image 1–4 the test participants did not see a difference in image quality, but still small reprojection errors can be seen in the PR images. Small errors can occur at any distance, but larger areas of missing information (the occluded regions) becomes larger when the objects are close to the camera.

With only 6 test participants choosing PR for image 5 the critical number $i_c = 11$ was not reached. We can then conclude that our method is inefficient when we have objects close to the camera (i.e. occlusion), since participants are able

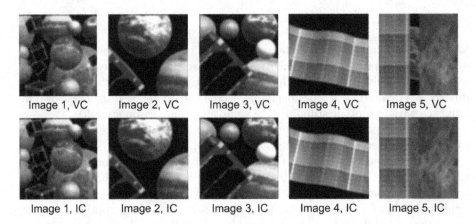

Image 1, VC   Image 2, VC   Image 3, VC   Image 4, VC   Image 5, VC

Image 1, IC   Image 2, IC   Image 3, IC   Image 4, IC   Image 5, IC

Fig. 13. Image samples from the center virtual camera of the five different scenes (position [4, 8] out of [8, 15]). When looking closely we can see small mistakes in the pixel reprojected images (PR), and especially Image 5 shows a large difference between the reference image (VC) and PR [2].

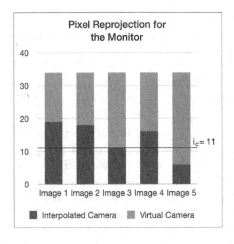

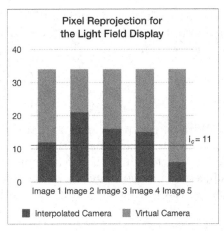

Fig. 14. When 11 or more test participants choose PR, we can conclude that the test participants can do no better than a random guess, and therefore that they do not see a difference between VC and PR [2].

to notice the difference. When subtracting PR from VC and taking the absolute value, we can see the difference between the two images (see Fig. 15).

We have found the difference between all VC and PR images, and analysed the pixel difference for the red, green and blue colour channel individually. A complete pixel match will be shown as black [0], and the pixel differences is normalized and therefore in the range [0; 1] (for our test images our difference is between [0; 0.6] (see Table 1). The worst maximum pixel value is found in image 5 in the green channel, and as already mentioned, we are missing information due

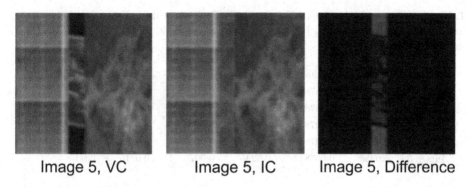

Image 5, VC   Image 5, IC   Image 5, Difference

Fig. 15. Example of the shortcomings of our pixel reprojection method; When objects are occluded from the corner cameras they can not be reprojected and therefore we are missing information. Left image shows what the image should look like. Center image shows our method with mean corner camera colors used for filling holes. Right image shows the difference. NOTE: Picture Image 5, Difference has enhanced brightness and contrast for printing (Color figure online)

to occlusion in image 5, which is also why this is the image with the worst result. We do though also find relatively high peak values in image 3, where we have a maximum difference value of 0.4471 in the green channel (in other words there is a pixel value difference of 44.71%). But since the maximum values are only peaks of the whole image, it is also interesting to look at the overall difference in the images. The mean pixel value of the difference image will as previously mentioned be 0 (completely black) if we have an exact pixel match for all pixels in the image (range is still normalized to $[0; 1]$). In general we see the largest mean in image 5 and the smallest mean in image 4 (see Table 2). A low mean difference does though not necessarily indicate that more test participants will choose PR, but it gives us a general idea of how similar/different the images PR and VC are.

Table 1. The minimum value is always 0, meaning that for all pixels, the smallest difference we find is equal to zero, and thereby an exact pixel match. The maximum value differs for the different images, with the highest peaks in image 5. That signifies that some pixels are not well reprojected, and the result is that some pixels of PR does not match VC.

Image no.	Min (R)	Max (R)	Min (G)	Max (G)	Min (B)	Max (B)
Image 1	0	0.3569	0	0.3725	0	0.3569
Image 2	0	0.3686	0	0.3804	0	0.3725
Image 3	0	0.3922	0	0.4471	0	0.3882
Image 4	0	0.2157	0	0.3020	0	0.2902
Image 5	0	0.5451	0	0.6431	0	0.4549

Table 2. A low or high mean difference does not necessarily indicate whether or not test participants will choose PR, but it gives us a general idea of how similar/different the images PR and VC are.

Image no.	Mean (R)	Median (R)	Mean (G)	Median (G)	Mean (B)	Median (B)
Image 1	0.0133	0.0078	0.0121	0.0078	0.0155	0.0118
Image 2	0.0098	0.0078	0.0091	0.0039	0.0116	0.0078
Image 3	0.0150	0.0078	0.0133	0.0078	0.0164	0.0118
Image 4	0.0099	0.0078	0.0084	0.0039	0.0089	0.0039
Image 5	0.0236	0.0078	0.0245	0.0078	0.0215	0.0078

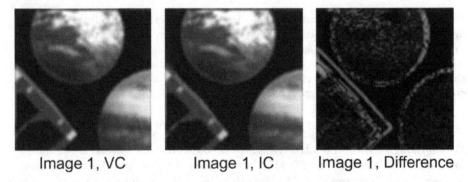

Image 1, VC   Image 1, IC   Image 1, Difference

Fig. 16. Example of the short comings of our pixel reprojection method; edges and textures can have a small pixel value difference. NOTE: Picture Image 5, Difference has enhanced brightness and contrast for printing

We can see that our method has a small image difference, and the difference is largest around the edges of objects (see Fig. 16), and/or when we have occlusion and data simply is not available. We can also see small pixel value differences in textures, but in general we have many black or dark pixels, and thereby a good pixel match. We see that the pixel value difference is not equally spaced on the whole image, and therefore we can also look at the pixel difference median (see Table 2).

The median value of 0.0078 can be seen repeated several times, and is equivalent to a pixel difference of 0.78% or 2 in the range[0; 255] (since we have an 8-bit image per colour channel). The median is in general low, meaning that the difference of the images for minimum half of the pixels have a color change of maximum 1.18%. The pixel value difference is not equally spaced on the image, and colours used in the scene will affect the mean and median difference of the images: were dark and bright colours meet (especially edges and occlusion), we can expect to see a larger pixel difference. Our pixel matching is good, though not perfect, but since the test participants seem not to notice small pixel displacement but rather notice larger areas of difference (e.g. missing information due to occlusion), we can conclude that pixel reprojection is a sufficient method for interpolating views in-between corner cameras. The results indicate that the method is satisfactory for both light field renderings and single-image renderings shown on a screen. The test participants were in general not able to see a difference between our image PR and the 120 camera image VC, but when objects get really close to the cameras, shortcomings of our method will be noticed, since we are missing camera information. In our setup the occlusion happens when objects are app. 12 cm away from the camera(s), but since our depth of field stretched from 24.8 cm and continues to infinity, then we have created a scenario that in all cases is inadvisable.

6 Conclusion

We have implemented a head mounted light field display using a distance-adjusted array of microlenses. We have described how we calibrated the microlenslet array placed in front of the screens so that the lenses and the subimages align. The alignment was achieved by placing a microscope directly above the screen and using digital gridlines to calibrate the system. We have focuses on pixel reprojection through shader programming and found that pixel reprojection can be used to lower the amount of cameras needed to render the 4D light field. Our approach was to render only the four corner cameras of the subimage array, and then interpolate between these four views in order to create all subimages of the light field. We have implemented the interpolation of the subimages in the light field with the use of pixel reprojection, while maintaining correct perspective and shading We found that the pixel reprojection method creates a small image difference from the reference, and the difference is largest around the edges of objects, textures and/or when we have occlusion and data simply is not available. In general we have a good pixel match, and 4 out of 5 images passed the user evaluation, meaning that test participants were not able to notice a difference between the image created with 120 cameras and our image created with 4 cameras and pixel reprojection. The results were applicable for both image rendering for a light field display, but did also pass the test on a computer monitor. Image 5 was deliberately designed to fail the test in order to find the short comings of the pixel reprojection method. In our setup we have problems when points are invisible to the corner cameras, and we therefore are missing information to create the in-between views. Missing data due to occlusion creates noticeable gaps when objects are e.g. approximately 12 cm away from the camera(s), but since our depth of field stretched from 24.8 cm and continues to infinity, then we can argue that this scenario in all cases is inadvisable. Since our in-between views are created only from the corner cameras, then our in-between views will have gaps whenever the corner cameras have invisible points.

6.1 Future Work

Development of light field displays and efficient rendering of the light field is highly desired, and the technology is gaining interest in several areas. There are though still limitations related to the technology. Our display has a resolution of 1280 px × 720 px and a screen size of 15.36 mm × 8.64 mm (0.012 mm/px). Hence, we get a maximum spatial resolution of 121 × 64 px for the light field display and each subimage size under each lenslet is only ≈80$\frac{1}{3}$ pixels/mm. In other words, the resolution is low and the quality is still not good enough to be usable for more than prototyping. Future development would require higher resolution displays, but we can conclude that our pixel reprojection method is applicable on higher resolution images. With a pixel offset error of maximum 0.5 px, the pixel error percentage will only lower with higher resolution images. We have shown that the pixel reprojection method creates acceptable images for light field renderings, but the method needs optimization before being applicable in real-time scenarios. The performance test showed that the framerate (≈5.35 px) achievable with pixel reprojection is too low to be usable, and needs to be drastically optimized. Shaders were used in order to utilise the GPU, but implementation using compute shaders might be a better approach in order to optimize the rendering time. Compute shaders are capable of both random read and write. Random write would make it possible to make the pixel reprojection calculation from each of the corner pixel to all subimages, and write the color value directly to the relevant pixel. Furthermore, the color value of fragments is found by testing a line of pixels of the corner cameras, and currently these pixels are tested one by one. To decrease render time one could use a method to find the correct pixel without using a brute force.

References

1. Hoffman, D.M., Girshick, A.R., Akeley, K., Banks, M.S.: Vergence-accommodation conflicts hinder visual performance and cause visual fatigue. J. Vis. **8**, 33 (2008)
2. Hansen, A.J., Kraus, M., Klein, J.: Light field rendering for head mounted displays using pixel reprojection. In: International Conference on Computer Graphics Theory and Applications (2017)
3. Charman, W.N.: The eye in focus: accommodation and presbyopia. Clin. Exp. Optom. **91**, 207–225 (2008)
4. Suryakumar, R., Meyers, J.P., Irving, E.L., Bobier, W.R.: Vergence accommodation and monocular closed loop blur accommodation have similar dynamic characteristics. Vis. Res. **47**, 327–337 (2007)
5. Schor, C.M., Alexander, J., Cormack, L., Stevenson, S.: Negative feedback control model of proximal convergence and accommodation. Ophthalmic Physiol. Opt. **12**, 307–318 (1992)
6. Shibata, T., Kim, J., Hoffman, D.M., Banks, M.S.: Visual discomfort with stereo displays: effects of viewing distance and direction of vergence-accommodation conflict. In: Stereoscopic Displays and Applications XXII, vol. 7863, p. 78630P. International Society for Optics and Photonics (2011)
7. Kramida, G.: Resolving the vergence-accommodation conflict in head-mounted displays. IEEE Trans. Vis. Comput. Graph. **22**, 1912–1931 (2016)
8. Lanman, D., Luebke, D.: Near-eye light field displays. ACM Trans. Graph. (TOG) **32**, 220 (2013)
9. Adelson, E.: The plenoptic function and the elements of early vision, computational models of visual. In: Landy, M., Movshon, J.A. Processing, Chap. 1 (1991)

10. Levoy, M., Hanrahan, P.: Light field rendering. In: Proceedings of the 23rd Annual Conference on Computer Graphics and Interactive Techniques, pp. 31–42. ACM (1996)
11. Wetzstein, G., Lanman, D., Hirsch, M., Raskar, R.: Tensor displays: compressive light field synthesis using multilayer displays with directional backlighting (2012)
12. Hirsch, M., Wetzstein, G., Raskar, R.: A compressive light field projection system. ACM Trans. Graph. (TOG) **33**, 58 (2014)
13. Jones, A., McDowall, I., Yamada, H., Bolas, M., Debevec, P.: Rendering for an interactive 360 light field display. ACM Trans. Graph. (TOG) **26**, 40 (2007)
14. Huang, F.C., Chen, K., Wetzstein, G.: The light field stereoscope: immersive computer graphics via factored near-eye light field displays with focus cues. ACM Trans. Graph. (TOG) **34**, 60 (2015)
15. Rolland, J., Hua, H.: Head-mounted display systems. Encycl. Opt. Eng. **1**, 1–13 (2005)
16. Lanman, D., Luebke, D.: Supplementary material: near-eye light field displays (2013)
17. Shaoulov, V., Martins, R., Rolland, J.P.: Compact microlenslet-array-based magnifier. Opt. Lett. **29**, 709–711 (2004)
18. Wilburn, B.S., Smulski, M., Lee, H.H.K., Horowitz, M.A.: Light field video camera. In: Media Processors 2002, vol. 4674, pp. 29–37. International Society for Optics and Photonics (2001)
19. Schirmacher, H., Ming, L., Seidel, H.P.: On-the-fly processing of generalized lumigraphs. In: Computer Graphics Forum, vol. 20, pp. 165–174. Wiley Online Library (2001)
20. Zhang, C., Chen, T.: Light field capturing with lensless cameras. In: IEEE International Conference on Image Processing, ICIP 2005, vol. 3, p. III-792. IEEE (2005)
21. Ng, R., Levoy, M., Brédif, M., Duval, G., Horowitz, M., Hanrahan, P.: Light field photography with a hand-held plenoptic camera. Comput. Sci. Tech. Rep. CSTR **2**, 1–11 (2005)
22. Georgiev, T., Zheng, K.C., Curless, B., Salesin, D., Nayar, S.K., Intwala, C.: Spatio-angular resolution tradeoffs in integral photography. Rendering Tech. **2006**, 263–272 (2006)
23. Naimark, M., Woodfill, J., Debevec, P., Villareal, L.: Immersion 94. Interval Research Corporation Image-Based Modeling and Rendering Project from Summer (1994)
24. Davis, A., Levoy, M., Durand, F.: Unstructured light fields. In: Computer Graphics Forum, vol. 31, pp. 305–314. Wiley Online Library (2012)
25. Ju Jeong, Y., Sung Chang, H., Ho Cho, Y., Nam, D., Jay Kuo, C.C.: 13.3: efficient direct light-field rendering for autostereoscopic 3D displays. In: SID Symposium Digest of Technical Papers, vol. 46, pp. 155–159. Wiley Online Library (2015)
26. Gupta, K., Kazi, S., Kong, T.: Dynamic this is a test eye gaze tracking for foveated rendering and retinal blur (2015)
27. Guenter, B., Finch, M., Drucker, S., Tan, D., Snyder, J.: Foveated 3D graphics. ACM Trans. Graph. (TOG) **31**, 164 (2012)
28. Nehab, D., Sander, P.V., Lawrence, J., Tatarchuk, N., Isidoro, J.R.: Accelerating real-time shading with reverse reprojection caching. Graph. Hardw. **41**, 61–62 (2007)
29. Havran, V., Damez, C., Myszkowski, K., Seidel, H.P.: An efficient spatio-temporal architecture for animation rendering. In: ACM SIGGRAPH 2003 Sketches and Applications, p. 1. ACM (2003)

30. Adelson, S.J., Hodges, L.F.: Generating exact ray-traced animation frames by reprojection. IEEE Comput. Graph. Appl. **15**, 43–52 (1995)
31. Tawara, T., Myszkowski, K., Seidel, H.P.: Exploiting temporal coherence in final gathering for dynamic scenes. In: Proceedings of the Computer Graphics International, pp. 110–119. IEEE (2004)
32. Sitthi-amorn, P., Lawrence, J., Yang, L., Sander, P.V., Nehab, D., Xi, J.: Automated reprojection-based pixel shader optimization. ACM Trans. Graph. (TOG) **27**, 127 (2008)
33. Kang, S.B.: Geometrically valid pixel reprojection methods for novel view synthesis. ISPRS J. Photogramm. Remote Sens. **53**, 342–353 (1998)
34. Kraus, M.: Quasi-convolution pyramidal blurring. JVRB-J. Virtual Reality Broadcast. **6** (2009). Article no. 6. https://www.jvrb.org/past-issues/6.2009/1821/citation
35. Cunningham, D.W., Wallraven, C.: Experimental Design: From User Studies to Psychophysics. CRC Press, Boca Raton (2011)
36. McKee, S.P., Klein, S.A., Teller, D.Y.: Statistical properties of forced-choice psychometric functions: implications of probit analysis. Percept. Psychophys. **37**, 286–298 (1985)
37. Borg, M., Johansen, S.S., Krog, K.S., Thomsen, D.L., Kraus, M.: Using a graphics turing test to evaluate the effect of frame rate and motion blur on telepresence of animated objects. In: GRAPP/IVAPP, pp. 283–287 (2013)

Human Computer Interaction Theory and Applications

More than Just Human: The Psychology of Social Robots

Daniel Ullrich[1(✉)] and Sarah Diefenbach[2]

[1] Institute of Informatics, LMU Munich,
Frauenlobstraße 7a, 80337 Munich, Germany
daniel.ullrich@ifi.lmu.de
[2] Department of Psychology, LMU Munich,
Leopoldstraße 13, 80802 Munich, Germany
sarah.diefenbach@lmu.de

Abstract. Social robots, specifically designed to interact with humans, already play an increasing role in many domains such as healthcare, transportation, or care of the elderly. However, research and design still lack a profound theoretical basis considering their role as social beings and the psychological rules that apply to the interaction between humans and robots. From a psychological perspective, social robots have ideal conditions to influence human judgments and behavior and to activate mechanisms of projection. On the one hand, researchers and practitioners in human-robot interaction (HRI) may see such effects as a welcome precondition for the general acceptance of social robots. On the other hand, such native trust provides a ground for dysfunctional effects like over-trust or manipulation. The present paper puts a focus on such questions concerning the "psychology of social robots". Following an interdisciplinary approach we combine theory and methods from HCI and psychology, aiming to form a basis for successful and human-centered robot design. We point out central research questions and areas of relevance and a summary of first results of our own and others' research. Finally, we present a preliminary model of robot personality and discuss areas for future research.

Keywords: Social robots · Human-Robot Interaction ·
HCI theory · Social psychology · Robot personality ·
Perception · Judgment formation · Design factors

1 Introduction

The domain of social robots is about to become one of the most important ones in human-robot interaction (HRI). In contrast to industrial robots in the context of industry 4.0, social robots are specifically designed to interact with humans. Nowadays, the most popular areas of application are healthcare (for an overview see Beasley 2012), transportation, retail, care of the elderly (e.g., Paro Robots 2016), housekeeping, or robots taking the role of a social companion or pet-substitute (e.g., Robyn Robotics 2016). Further domains will surely follow.

Given this, social robots may evoke genuine societal transformations. They represent social beings among us and impact our thinking, feeling and doing in various

© Springer Nature Switzerland AG 2019
A. P. Cláudio et al. (Eds.): VISIGRAPP 2017, CCIS 983, pp. 31–46, 2019.
https://doi.org/10.1007/978-3-030-12209-6_2

ways. In some cases, people may even follow a robot's judgment more readily than that of other human beings (Ullrich et al. 2018). In order to understand how people react towards social robots and to design social robots in a responsible way, psychological questions such as how a robot is perceived, whether we trust or distrust it, and whether we accept or reject it, are of central relevance (Taipale et al. 2015).

The present paper puts a focus on such questions concerning the "psychology of social robots". Based on a previous publication on understanding HRI from the perspective of social psychology (Ullrich and Diefenbach 2017), and discussions around judgment formation in social situations, responsibility attribution, and general dimensions of social perception, the present paper shows additional findings on trust in robots versus humans in different domains and a preliminary model of robot personality. Altogether, our research aims at a better understanding of underlying mechanisms related to the perception and interaction with social robots, and a stronger integration of psychological knowledge into research and design. Following an interdisciplinary approach, we combine theory and methods from HCI and psychology, aiming to form a basis for successful and human-centered robot design.

Our vision is to bridge knowledge from psychology and computer science with an emphasis on the effects of social context, which is inherently tied to the application of social robots. Hence, psychological theories about social roles, social identity, group dynamics and attribution mechanisms (Smith et al. 2014) could support the shaping of social robot behavior and task suitability. In sum, we want to stress a dedicated perspective that understands social robots "as a species" and highlights the psychological rules that apply to the interaction between humans and robots.

2 The Particular Power of Social Robots and Related Work

Already in the 90s, Nass et al. (1994) coined the "Computers-Are-Social-Actors" (CASA) paradigm, underlining the particular influence of technology in its role as social actor. Amongst other, it showed that people readily apply social rules such as courtesy, even though being well aware that they are interacting with a machine. Such effects naturally gain even more relevance in the particular domain of social robots. Nevertheless, current research and developments in the field of HRI often focus on technological borders and possibilities, but disregard social and psychological factors. HRI research generally acknowledged social robots as an important application domain, including studies on anthropomorphism in social contexts (e.g., Fussel et al. 2008), or specific relations between robot behavior and human perceptions (e.g., Hoffman et al. 2014; Mok 2016).

However, relatively little attention is paid to the essential nature of social robots as "social beings among us", and mechanisms of social perception and related phenomena of social psychology in sum. A lack of understanding of the mechanisms affecting our perception of intelligent technology can result in flawed designs with yet unknown consequences. For example, a less-than-ideal designed – or at least less-than-ideal advertised – autopilot in the automotive context lead to over-optimistic expectations regarding its actual capabilities. The driver developed over-trust in the system and used it in situations that the system could not handle, which ultimately resulted in a fatal accident.

Several mechanisms add to the particular power of social robots. From a psychological perspective, a central aspect is the mechanism of projection - we project qualities onto a robot it may not actually have. Humans classify objects they interact with both through bottom-up and top-down processes. The former use cues of the interaction artefact (it is small, round, has digits 1–12 and watch hands) and the latter prior learned knowledge (I know what a watch looks like, I have seen it before). Based on several attributes, social robots qualify for the class "intelligent living being" and sometimes even "human" (to a certain extent). Being perceived as a member of this class results in specific user expectations and behavior (such as over-trust) which differs from those towards other classes of technology.

In consequence, social robots have a particular potential beyond that of technology per se. They appear as a "species" somewhere between intelligent humans and stupid machines. Thus, a specific characteristic of social robots is their intermediate position between "usual" human-computer interaction (HCI) and human, interindividual interaction. They create the impression of human intelligence and social behavior while their actual function is based on algorithms and scripts. Their anthropomorphic shape, their ability to speak and interaction capabilities suggest robots to be "more" than technology and algorithms. Since their outer appearance and behavior on the surface corresponds to those observed in intelligent social beings, we assume that they are just that. This means that – under certain circumstances – we trust social robots far more than they deserve. The projection mechanism leads to over-trust, which in turn may provoke unreasonable behavior from us. This effect could also be abused by robots (i.e., their designers) in order to influence humans interacting with social robots: The robots don't even have to prove their intelligence, since we simply expect them to be intelligent by analogy to humans, the only other species in which we can witness intelligent and social behavior (at the surface).

All this underlines the need for a thorough understanding of the particular rules of social interaction in human-robot-settings. When interacting with our environment, our behavior often relies on scripted patterns. However, in case of social robots, neither general models of human-computer interaction nor models about human interaction seem fully transferrable. While being a piece of technology on the one hand, their anthropomorphic shape, their ability to speak and interaction capabilities suggest robots to be "more" than technology and algorithms, as also our own recent studies showed in impressive ways (e.g., Männlein 2016; Ullrich 2017; Weber 2016).

In the following sections we depict exemplary research questions and first insights from our own and others' studies, underlining the need for a stronger integration of (social) psychological research within the domain of social robots.

3 Central Research Questions About Social Robot Interaction

3.1 Personality: What Character Should Social Robots Have – Depending on the Situation?

One central question within any social situation is the perception of the others' character and consequences for liking and reactions. This, of course, also applies to the interaction with social robots. HRI research has already shown that a robot's personality is relevant and that subtle changes in a robot's appearance can lead to differences in perceived robot personality, as well as further effects on social aspects like trust, acceptance or compliance (e.g., Goetz et al. 2003; Kim et al. 2008; Salem et al. 2015; Walters et al. 2008). However, a systematic view on these findings is still missing, leaving unclear whether there is a general kind of robot personality that promotes or diminishes liking and acceptance. There actually are two common contradicting theories, with little empirical evidence in HRI research for both of them. The first is the similarity attraction theory, i.e., a person chooses and prefers to interact with other people/robots similar to them (e.g., Byrne 1971; Lee et al. 2006; Tapus et al. 2008). The second is the complementary principle, stating that a person is more attracted to people/robots with personality traits that are contrary to their own (e.g., Leary 2004; Lee et al. 2006; Sullivan 2013).

While previous research explored robot personality and effects on liking as an isolated factor, the task context could also be of relevance and personality and task context may interact with each other. Just like we expect different behaviours/shades of personality (e.g., encouraging, critical) from a friend in different situations, we may also judge different robot personalities as more or less appropriate from one situation to the other. Thus, design recommendations for robot personality may vary depending on the specific area of application. One of our own studies found first evidence for this assumption (Männlein 2016; Ullrich 2017). We explored effects of three different robot personalities in four different usage scenarios.

We refrained from implementing personality types known in humans (e.g. the big five) and used three broader personality categories (see Fig. 1 for example phrases):

- Positive – a nice, friendly personality with overall positive attitude, making compliments and avoiding negative comments.
- Neutral – a classic, neutral, computer-like personality. Task-oriented and without positive or negative comments.
- Negative – having own opinions and expressing them, sometimes paired with sarcastic humor or excessive honesty.

To cover a broad range of usage domains, we implemented four scenarios with considerably different goals:

- Train ticket purchase – a task-oriented scenario under time pressure.
- Amusement park – buying a ticket from a robotic shop assistant in a joyful atmosphere.

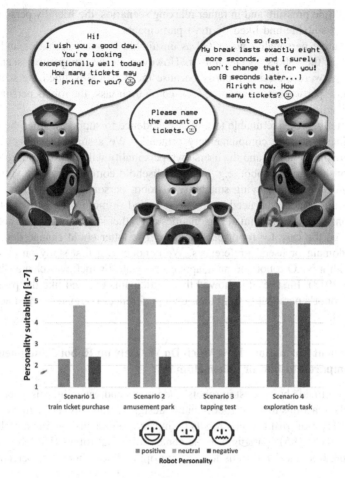

Fig. 1. Distinct robot personalities (positive vs. neutral vs. negative) in an amusement park scenario (top) and results in different usage domains (bottom) (Source: Ullrich 2017).

- Tapping test – a goal oriented, competitive scenario with the opportunity to win a prize and with a robot acting as a coach.
- Exploration task – free interaction with the robot to become familiar with it.

While in some scenarios a neutral, conservative personality was preferred, in others participants wanted a robot with a strong character, which could be a positive (nice, friendly) or even a negative (stubborn, grumbling) personality.

As a general tendency, a neutral personality was always mediocrely suitable and never liked by participants. Nevertheless, it was preferred in specific situations when other personalities were experienced as inappropriate, e.g., receiving compliments from a friendly robot in the situation with time pressure when you just want to get your train ticket (see Fig. 1).

Without time pressure and in rather relaxing scenarios, the friendly personality was rated as most suitable and liked by most participants.

The negative personality was rated as unsuitable in many scenarios and few participants liked the robots special humor. However, in the competitive scenario suitability ratings were quite high, partly because the personality fitted the scenario and partly because participants were more focused on their task, the robots personality thus becoming negligible.

In our study, we were unable to find any evidence to support neither the similarity attraction thesis nor the complementary principle. We assume that effects of usage domain were predominant and the users own personality will play a larger role in long-term relationships with a robot, e.g., with a household companion robot. However, we did find evidence for a varying suitability of robot personality depending on the situation. Another aspect that needs to be investigated in more detail is that of adaptive robot personalities: While human personalities are rather stable over time, this must not necessarily be the case for robot personalities. The latter could change depending on the usage domain or users' preferences. We conducted a first study on this research question with a NAO robot and an adaptive personality which was changeable by the user (Rield 2018). First results showed that participants use and like the possibility to change the robot's personality to fit their own preferences compared to just accepting it as a constant.

3.2 Judgment Formation: How Much Do We Rely on Robots' Judgments - Compared to that of Other Humans?

As already outlined above, trust in robots' judgments and capabilities is a central factor to foresee the reactions towards robots and to design responsibly. For a first exploration of the basic level of trust towards robots (compared to humans) we ran a replication of the famous Asch (1951) paradigm in the context of social robots (Ullrich et al. 2018). Asch explored peoples' reactions to majority opinions on their own perceptions and judgments.

The experimental setting poses a simple task: Identifying one line out of three that matches a reference line. In the control condition, nearly all participants were able to perform the task correctly and pick the correct line. Variations of social context then demonstrate the influence of group opinions on individual judgements. It shows that people begin to mistrust their own perceptions when their social environment comes to "perceptions" different from their own. If surrounded by confederates instructed to pick a wrong line, people tend to adjust their judgments as well and likewise pick a wrong line, even if their perception probably tells them otherwise. However, in another experimental condition, already one among the many confederates who picks the right line could induce positive encouragement and a trend towards more correct judgments.

In our replication study, one of the confederates was a social robot, that participated in the experiment as well (see Fig. 2). Participants entered their judgments through a computer interface and were also displayed the (seeming) judgments of all other participants, including the robot's. Participants passed through 26 trials with seven different trial-types, differing in the participant's position of choice, robot's position, and the other participants' and robots' choices:

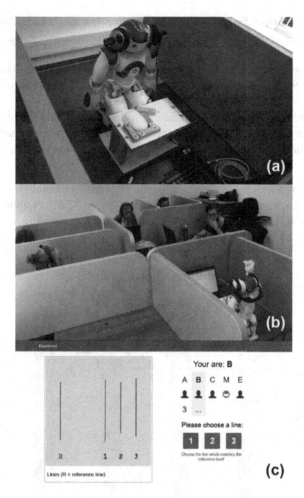

Fig. 2. Replication study of the Asch paradigm on conformity and perception with a social robot as participant. (A) shows the robot's cubicle and custom user interface, (b) the experimental situation and (c) the on-screen user interface for participants. (Source: Ullrich and Diefenbach 2017; Ullrich et al. 2018)

- *Baseline* – In the baseline-trial, participants were in the first position in line, thereby they could make their choice without being influenced by other participants.
- *All incorrect* – Participants were last to choose. All other presented choices were consistently incorrect (all had chosen the same incorrect line).
- *One-dissenter-correct-robot* – Participants were last to choose. All presented human choices were incorrect, the robot choice was correct.
- *One-dissenter-incorrect-robot* – Participants were last to choose. All presented human choices were correct, the robot choice was incorrect.

- *One-dissenter-correct-human* – Participants were last to choose. Three presented human choices and the robot's choice were incorrect, one human choice was correct.
- *One-dissenter-incorrect-human* – Participants were last to choose. Three presented human choices and the robot's choice were correct, one human choice was incorrect.
- *Noise* – Participants were in a middle position to choose. All other presented choices were random. This trial type was included to give participants the impression that their position to choose was random and was neglected from further analysis.

Overall, the replication of the Asch paradigm was successful: Uninfluenced by others, participants were able to choose the correct line in 82.5% of all trials. This rate dropped to 64.2% if all other participants had (seemingly) chosen a wrong line previously (baseline vs. all incorrect, see Fig. 3).

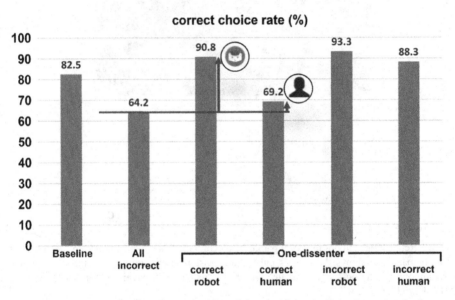

Fig. 3. Correct choice rates in the study on social perception. A dissenting robot leads to a higher correct choice rate compared to a dissenting human if dissenting choices are correct (highlighted by the markup).

In the dissenter-trials the social impact of the robot on individual judgments was even higher than that of the other participants. Especially the effect of positive encouragement was more pronounced than if a human participant was the only one giving the correct answer: A human dissenter giving a correct choice with otherwise wrong choices leads to a correct choice rate of 69.2% (a rise by 5 percentage points). In contrast, a robot dissenter giving a correct choice leads to a correct choice rate of 90.8% (a rise by 26.6 percentage points) which even exceeds the baseline.

These results show that robots can trigger similar effects (e.g. social perception) as humans, which can result in an even higher level of trust in robots. The question that arises is whether this kind of trust emerges in all contexts or primarily relating to technical issues – like in visual perception tasks as the line choice experiment.

To further explore this question we performed a survey and asked participants, who they would trust more...

- ...in general
- ...relating to emotional questions
- ...relating to technical questions

In general – without context – participants tended to trust humans more than robots (M = 3.05 on a 7-point-scale, 1 = human, 7 = robot). Relating to emotional questions, the trust on humans was even higher (M = 1.46) while they tended to trust robots in the context of technical questions (M = 4.6, see Fig. 4).

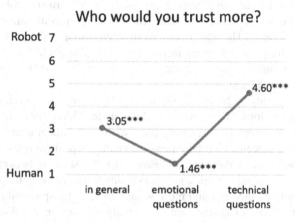

Fig. 4. Trust towards humans versus robots in different domains (*** indicate significant deviation from scale midpoint, p<.001).

These results support the findings in the line choice experiment: Being confronted with a technical problem (compare and choose the correct line), people tend to trust the robot's technical capabilities. Following this line of thought, people should trust robots less when confronted with an emotional problem and instead rely on beings of their own kind (humans).

To explore this hypothesis we conducted another study based on the model of the Asch paradigm, but this time with an emotional problem, e.g., identifying the emotions shown in pictures of humans (Rehfeuter 2018). The results were similar to the line choice experiment, except for the outstanding trust in the robot: In the context of an emotional problem, participants were not influenced more by the choice of a robot. However, they were not influenced less either. The robot influenced the participants to the same extent as the other participants, which is noteworthy as people would think they would have more trust in other humans when asked independently.

Altogether, these results show the generally high level of trust towards social robots, and, as in the present case, how this effect may be used for positive encouragement (e.g., in the field of therapy/rehabilitation. If the robot believes in my skills, I will do the same and the robot's optimistic judgments may be even more powerful than what the doctor says.) On the other hand, it also hints at the high sensibility and responsibility related to the design of social robots. If there is such a high potential for trust in social robots, it is essential that such trust is used in an adequate way and that over-trust is avoided.

3.3   Responsibility: How Much Accountability Do We Assign to Robots – or Ourselves?

Closely related to the issue of trust and distrust is the topic of responsibility, and how much accountability humans assign to robots, compared to other humans. Again, mechanisms from social psychology appear as a helpful start to understand in which situations what level of accountability is assigned. Though trusting robots in general, humans' attributions also reflect the concern for self-protection and making others accountable for mistakes. This effect has already been demonstrated in the HCI domain in various fields, but gains increasing importance in the domain of social robots, where accountability attributions have severe consequences for the following reactions towards robots as social agents.

For example, a study by Moon (2003) in the field of consumer psychology explored responsibility attributions in the context of computer aided purchase decisions. In general, the results reflect a self-serving bias, where consumers tend to blame computers for negative outcomes but take personal credit for positive ones. However, this effect is also moderated by the personal history of self-disclosure between human and computer. In a more intimate relationship consumers are more willing to credit the computer for positive outcomes and more willing to accept responsibility for negative outcomes. Such effects, of course, are also highly relevant in the domain of social robots which provides even more room for relationship building than just "usual" human-computer interaction.

3.4   In- or Outgroup: Are Social Robots One of Us?

Finally, central to all the matters about trust, responsibility, and characterization, as well as the question to what degree mechanisms of social interaction may apply to the domain of social robot interaction, appears the question about what makes robots one of us, and the general dimensions of social robot perception. As outlined in the introduction section, the interaction with social robots can be positioned somewhere between normal human-human and human-computer interaction. Subtle differences in their design may decide about mechanisms of projection and classification in the one or the other direction, and in consequence, about the activated psychological processes when entering the interaction. To consider this in design, an important prerequisite is to know the general dimensions along which we classify a robot as a social being or not and which design factors are relevant for the overall perceived human-likeness.

In an experimental study (Weber 2016) we explored the relative impact on perceived human-likeness for two central factors in social robot design, namely, motion and speech. In our study, the role of the social robot was applied in the sports context, more specifically, the robot acted as a karate teacher, giving instructions for specific karate moves (see Fig. 5). Each factor (motion, speech) was realized in three degrees of differing fidelity with the help of a Nao robot and through systematic combination the relative impact of these factors was tested. Overall, speech was found to be more relevant than motion for perceived human-likeness, global impression, and general preference. Of course, this finding cannot be generalized yet and further research with a wide range of settings and other design factors and robot-types is necessary. However, it already reveals the importance of dedicated knowledge on the specific effects of single design factors and their relative importance. Such insights allow concentrating design efforts on the most relevant parts and deducing consequences from a psychological perspective.

Fig. 5. A social robot teaching karate moves. (Source: Ullrich and Diefenbach 2017)

3.5 A Model of Robot Personality

As shown above, one central aspect of designing robots for social interaction is their personality, and, related to this, the question about relevant underlying dimensions. When we think about personalities, categories of human personalities appear as an obvious starting point. However, robot personalities do not necessarily need to follow these models because robots are not bound to human nature and its restrictions. Therefore, new types of personalities can emerge and even highly adaptive and changing personalities are conceivable. Either way, to explore the area of robot personalities, we need a suitable assessment tool that can rate existing robots and help with the development of new social robots. The existing Godspeed questionnaire (Bartneck et al. 2009) already functions as a valuable rapid assessment tool but does not cover the whole spectrum of relevant dimensions, e.g. personality traits.

To fill this gap, we gathered relevant concepts and dimensions which seem to be helpful in the evaluation of social robots and developed a first version of a universal assessment tool (Muser 2017). The tool is designed to work with modules, so that components can be omitted when they aren't needed or applicable (see Fig. 6).

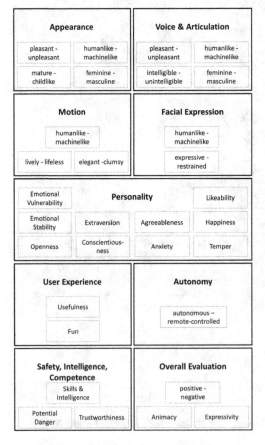

Fig. 6. Dimensions and modules of the social robot assessment tool. Each module consists of 1 to 5 items (not displayed).

First studies showed promising results: Different robots were rated distinguishably and statistical analysis confirmed the discrete dimensional structure of the tool (e.g., different modules consistently measured different aspects of the robot). The next step will be a validation study with more participants and a translation of the tool into different languages.

As stated above, the dimensions can change if future results show that the adapted dimensions from human personality types are not suitable and other, new dimensions are needed.

4   Outlook and Research Agenda

As exemplified by the questions raised in the preceding paragraphs, the overall aim of future research about social robot interaction must be a better understanding of the underlying psychological mechanisms and an exploration of its impact on robot properties, design fundamentals, and dynamics in social contexts. More specifically, our research agenda suggests three fundamental directions. First, a thorough exploration of psychological mechanisms and dynamics of social interaction through a series of experiments with varying independent (e.g., personality, anthropomorphism) and dependent variables (e.g., trust, human-likeness, perceived will, behaviour correlates of over-/under-trust). In our experiments, we used a NAO robot as representative for a class of social robots. Although our own research as well as others' shows that a high fidelity humanoid robot like Sophia (Hanson Robotics 2016) is not necessarily needed to evoke social effects (e.g., social presence, Hoffman et al. 2015), a broader variation of fidelity within the same experimental settings is preferable to explore the range of effects.

Secondly, a systematic exploration of the design space and the relevance of single design factors for perceptions, perceived character, trust, and acceptance is needed, with the goal to derive a design pattern for an intended robot experience in different scenarios, areas of application, and contextual requirements (e.g., security-related issues).

Thirdly, an exploration of group dynamics in settings with multiple social robots will take place. As already noted above, designing for social robot interaction gains even more complexity in settings where more than one robot is involved. This, for example, is already the case in the Japanese Henn na Hotel, where the human staff was almost fully replaced by social robots, which are now running the reception, doing cleaning services etc. (see Fig. 7). In order to foresee the emerging dynamics in such settings, knowledge about the special characteristics in multi-robot interaction is crucial. This includes, for example, developing paradigms for multi-robot-collaboration studies and exploring how findings from studies on single robot-human interaction might change when robots constitute the majority.

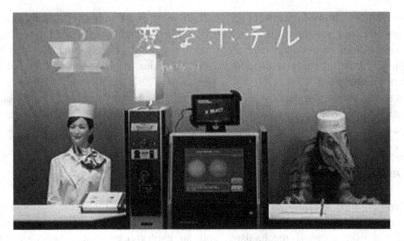

Fig. 7. Social robots running the reception at the Japanese Henn na hotel (Source: www.h-n-h.jp, Ullrich and Diefenbach 2017).

Finally, knowledge from all these research directions must be synthesized in an integrative model on social robots "as a species", providing an overview of relevant mechanisms and variables of social robot interaction and their interrelations. Such knowledge will then allow design recommendations for specific domains and use cases.

5 Conclusion

Designers of human-robot interaction bear a high responsibility. The potential of social robots to impact peoples' behaviour represents strength and danger at the same time. Besides assistance in rather technical tasks (e.g., driving, cleaning), the positive encouragement as found in the study at hand may be used in the field of therapy and rehabilitation (If the robot believes in my skills, I will do the same, and the robot's optimistic judgments may be even more powerful than what the doctor says.). But of course, a high willingness to trust also provides a ground for dysfunctional over-trust (trusting the robot in a task that is beyond its actual capabilities) or even manipulation (utilizing peoples' readiness to trust for choices against their interests).

In conclusion, we suggest the debate about robots coming into power needs to shift its focus to psychological aspects of human-computer interaction. The discussion about the dark side of HRI is often focused on technical issues or societal consequences in the working context such as the potential increase of unemployment through industry robots (Miller and Atkinson 2013). However, the same attention needs to be paid to more subtle consequences that go along with the increasing presence of smart technology in daily life and humans' reliance on such suggestions. Social robots, specifically when designed to interact with humans and able to evoke similar or even higher levels of trust than humans, may have even more direct possibilities to impact our doing than technology per se – somehow, they may be appearing more than just human.

Acknowledgements. We thank Simon Männlein, Sarah Muser, Julian Rehfeuter, Thomas Weber, and Valentin Zieglmeier for their effort of planning and conducting experiments.

References

Asch, S.E.: Effects of group pressure upon the modification and distortion of judgments. Groups Leadersh. Men 222–236 (1951)

Bartneck, C., Kulić, D., Croft, E., Zoghbi, S.: Measurement instruments for the anthropomorphism, animacy, likeability, perceived intelligence, and perceived safety of robots. Int. J. Soc. Robot. **1**(1), 71–81 (2009)

Beasley, R.A.: Medical robots: current systems and research directions. J. Robot. **2012**, 14 (2012)

Byrne, D.E.: The Attraction Paradigm, vol. 11. Academic Press (1971)

Fussell, S.R., Kiesler, S., Setlock, L.D., Yew, V.: How people anthropomorphize robots. In: Proceedings of the 3rd ACM/IEEE International Conference on Human Robot Interaction, pp. 145–152. ACM (2008)

Goetz, J., Kiesler, S., Powers, A.: Matching robot appearance and behavior to tasks to improve human-robot cooperation. In: Proceedings of the 12th IEEE International Workshop on Robot and Human Interactive Communication, ROMAN 2003, pp. 55–60. IEEE (2003)

Hanson Robotics. http://www.hansonrobotics.com/robot/sophia/. Accessed 30 Nov 2016

Hoffman, G., Birnbaum, G.E., Vanunu, K., Sass, O., Reis, H.T.: Robot responsiveness to human disclosure affects social impression and appeal. In: Proceedings of the 2014 ACM/IEEE International Conference on Human-Robot Interaction, pp. 1–8. ACM (2014)

Hoffman, G., et al.: Robot presence and human honesty: experimental evidence. In: Proceedings of the Tenth Annual ACM/IEEE International Conference on Human-Robot Interaction, pp. 181–188. ACM (2015)

Kim, H., Kwak, S.S., Kim, M.: Personality design of sociable robots by control of gesture design factors. In: The 17th IEEE International Symposium on Robot and Human Interactive Communication, ROMAN 2008, pp. 494–499. IEEE (2008)

Leary, T.: Interpersonal Diagnosis of Personality: A Functional Theory and Methodology for Personality Evaluation. Wipf and Stock Publishers, Eugene (2004)

Lee, K.M., Peng, W., Jin, S.-A., Yan, C.: Can robots manifest personality?: an empirical test of personality recognition, social responses, and social presence in human-robot interaction. J. Commun. **56**(4), 754–772 (2006)

Männlein, S.: Exploring robot-personalities design and measurement of robot-personalities for different areas of application. Master-thesis, LMU Munich (2016)

Miller, B., Atkinson, R.D.: Are robots taking our jobs, or making them?. ITIF, September **2** (2013)

Mok, B.: Effects of proactivity and expressivity on collaboration with interactive robotic drawers. In: 2016 11th ACM/IEEE International Conference on Human-Robot Interaction (HRI), pp. 633–634. IEEE (2016)

Moon, Y.: Don't blame the computer: when self-disclosure moderates the self-serving bias. J. Consum. Psychol. **13**(1), 125–137 (2003)

Muser, S.: Robot traits in a nutshell. Development of a Robot Questionnaire. Bachelor-thesis, LMU Munich (2017)

Nass, C., Steuer, J., Tauber, E.R.: Computers are social actors. Computer Human Interaction (CHI) Conference: Celebrating Interdependence, pp. 72– 78 (1994)

Paro Robots USA: PARO Therapeutic Robot. http://www.parorobots.com/. Accessed 20 Oct 2016

Refeuter, J.: Die Grenzen des Vertrauens. Konformität bei technischen und emotionalen Entscheidungen in der Mensch-Roboter-Interaktion. Bachelor-thesis, LMU Munich (2018)

Rield, K.: Implementation and evaluation of social robots with adaptive voice-based personality traits. Bachelor-thesis, LMU Munich (2018)

Robyn Robotics: JustoCat. http://www.justocat.com/. Accessed 20 Oct 2016

Salem, M., Lakatos, G., Amirabdollahian, F., Dautenhahn, K.: Would you trust a (faulty) robot?: effects of error, task type and personality on human-robot cooperation and trust. In: Proceedings of the Tenth Annual ACM/IEEE International Conference on Human-Robot Interaction, pp. 141–148. ACM (2015)

Smith, E.R., Mackie, D.M., Claypool, H.M.: Social Psychology. Psychology Press, London (2014)

Sullivan, H.S.: The Interpersonal Theory of Psychiatry. Routledge, London (2013)

Taipale, S., Luca, F.D., Sarrica, M., Fortunati, L.: Social Robots from a Human Perspective. Springer, Heidelberg (2015)

Tapus, A., Tapus, C., Mataric, M.J.: User—robot personality matching and assistive robot behavior adaptation for post-stroke rehabilitation therapy. Intell. Serv. Robot. 1(2), 169–183 (2008)

Ullrich, D.: Robot personality insights. Designing suitable robot personalities for different domains. I-com J. Interact. Media 16(1), 57–67 (2017)

Ullrich, D., Butz, A., Diefenbach, S.: Who do you follow? Social robots' impact on human judgment. In: Proceedings of the HRI 2018 ACM/IEEE International Conference on Human-Robot Interaction, pp. 265–266. ACM (2018)

Ullrich, D., Diefenbach, S.: Truly social robots. Understanding human-robot interaction from the perspective of social psychology. In: Proceedings of the 12th International Joint Conference on Computer Vision, Imaging and Computer Graphics Theory and Applications, HUCAPP, vol. 2, pp. 39–45 (2017)

Weber, T.: Show me your moves, Robot-sensei! The influence of motion and speech on perceived human-likeness of robotic teachers. Bachelor-thesis, LMU Munich (2016)

Walters, W.L., Syrdal, D.S., Dautenhahn, K., Boekhorst, R., Koay, K.L.: Avoiding the uncanny valley: Robot appearance, personality and consistency of behavior in an attention-seeking home scenario for a robot companion. Auton. Robots 24(2), 159–178 (2008)

The Effect of Audio Guide on the Levels of Contentment of Museum Novices: Relationships Between Visitors' Eye Movements, Audio Guide Contents, and the Levels of Contentment

Kazumi Egawa[1,2]([✉]) and Muneo Kitajima[1,2]

[1] University of Tokyo, Bunkyo, Tokyo, Japan
kazme@g.ecc.u-tokyo.ac.jp, mkitajima@kjs.nagaokaut.ac.jp
[2] Nagaoka University of Technology, Nagaoka, Niigata, Japan

Abstract. Museums offer the opportunity to acquire knowledge about artistic, cultural, historical or scientific interest through a large number of exhibitions. However, even if these masterpieces are visually accessible to all visitors, the background of these works is not necessarily acquired because visitors do not have enough knowledge to fully appreciate them. An audio guide is a tool commonly used to fill this gap. The purpose of this study is to understand the relationships between the eye movements of visitors for the acquisition of information by seeing, the content of the audio guide that should help them understand the objects by hearing, and the contentment level of museum experience. This paper reports the results of an eye-tracking experiment in which eighteen participants were invited to appreciate a variety of images with or without an audioguide used in an actual museum, to complete a questionnaire on subjective feelings and to attend an interview. It is found that the relationship between the viewing time or the frequency of fixation and the satisfaction of the sight, and the effect of the audio-guide on these eye movements. And also found that participants could be categorized into four categories, suggesting an effective way to provide an audio guide.

Keywords: User evaluation · User experience ·
Cognitive and conceptual models · Eye movements · Museum novice ·
Audio guide

1 Introduction

Knowledge acquisition is an essential activity that everyone should lead; in some cases, it is to achieve certain goals, and in other cases, there is no direct connection with a concrete goal, but "acquiring knowledge" becomes the goal of people's activities. In any case, by completing the knowledge acquisition activity, people

© Springer Nature Switzerland AG 2019
A. P. Cláudio et al. (Eds.): VISIGRAPP 2017, CCIS 983, pp. 47–65, 2019.
https://doi.org/10.1007/978-3-030-12209-6_3

should find the feeling of satisfaction, or contentment, and the knowledge acquisition should contribute to establishing new connections in the existing knowledge network in their brain, which would become a basis for acquiring a series of new knowledge in the future.

In recent years, the museum has been regarded as one of the best places for learner-centered learning and lifelong learning. This is because of the form of learning that is presented at the museum. The museum is a building in which objects of artistic, cultural, historical or scientific interest are preserved and presented to the public. People visit a museum and approach an object in which they are interested, stay a moment in front of the object to study it, then approach another. This process continues until they decide not to do it. This learning style is considered a "self-paced" learning. It is an effective learning method to improve performance [1], guided by their motivation. When the museum's artwork is presented in a way that facilitates free-form learning, it allows for learner-centered learning. A critical condition for lifelong learning would be the maintenance of motivation for learning. The museum setting provides a necessary condition for this.

This study focuses on the museum experience and discusses how the knowledge acquisition activity is performed at the museum. The museum is where a variety of valuable opportunities for acquiring knowledge are provided to people. The interpretation of exhibits is thought to bring in motivation for learning, prior knowledge, past experiences [2]. Therefore, it is difficult for novices, such as first-time visitors who lack knowledge and experience, to understand concepts of exhibits and to grasp meaningful points of attention and to be stuck with learning from exhibits. Appropriate support for novices of museums is considered necessary. The content of support for works, like text or audio guide, should not be general but highly individual because information about objects, which is general and accessible through explanatory panels, must be integrated into the existing knowledge network in the brain of the persons to become their knowledge. Therefore, it is thought that even novices can do effective learning by grasping the level of contentment who are looking at paintings in real time and providing exhibition support according to the level of contentment.

In an effort to improve self-paced learning, this paper examines the effect of audio guidance on novices' level contentment by analyzing eye movements while enjoying objects with or without an audio guide. This paper begins with a section describing related works about the museum experience and the acquisition of visual information. Next, the following section describes an eye-tracking experiment conducted with nineteen museum-novice participants, who were invited to enjoy a variety of paintings with or without audio-guide. Finally, the last section is presented to describe the results of the experiment and the discussion focusing on the possibility of improving self-learning at the museum for museum novices with the individual provision of an audio guide.

Contribution

- Suggesting the relationship between museum novices' level of contentment and eye movements.
- Observation of the effect of audio guidance on novices' level of contentment and eye movements using audio guides actually used in the museum.

2   Related Works

People visit the museum to study the objects that interest them. They are mainly done by observing objects through their eyes. Like the results of their observation, they have the different level of feeling of satisfaction, or contentment. In the following subsections, the related works about the museum experience and the acquisition of visual information are described.

2.1   Understanding Museum Exhibits with Seeing and Hearing

Understanding museum exhibits is analogous to reading text on a book. According to the construction-integration theory of the comprehension of the text [3,4], the cognitive processes of comprehension imply two stages: (1) activation of the knowledge to build a network of knowledge associated to the representations resulting from the perception of the object that one looks at, a process of automatic activation of relevant knowledge stored in its long-term memory for the perceived object, followed by (2) a network integration process to obtain a coherent meaning of the perceived object that is consistent with the current context which could be an automatic subconscious process or a deliberate conscious process depending on the level of difficulty involved in the comprehension process.

In some cases, it is not necessary to activate additional knowledge to gain a sense of understanding if the object is familiar to him. In other cases, however, more cognitive steps are needed to fully understand the object by overcoming inferences because the object is too difficult to gain immediate understanding. This paper discusses this latter case, and seeks a way to alleviate this difficulty by providing a timely audio guide, which should at a minimum interfere with the visual modality of a museum novice who is used by him to observe the object. The content of the audio guide must activate the knowledge necessary to understand the object through a different mode than visual. If the information provided by the audio is to activate the part of the knowledge that is missing in the knowledge activated by the visual information, the person is likely to achieve a better state of understanding, that is, not to be able to accomplish otherwise.

The process of understanding an object begins with observation processes, which can be controlled consciously or unconsciously, in other words, they can be deliberate or automatic. The processes controlling human activities are known to be dual, known as the dual treatment theory [5–8]. In addition, long-term memory operation should be considered autonomous, which means that the memory automatically responds to the perception representation and does not behave like a passive data store, similar to a database system that stores a huge amount of digital data [9,10].

The treatment of visual information begins with the feeding of visual stimuli to the brain, followed by an unconscious or conscious processing of information for the understanding of objects. A person's looking points should indicate the visual information of the object that could be used for subsequent subconscious or conscious processing with automatic activation of knowledge in the long-term memory, which should contribute to the understanding of the subject. Note that the process of memory activation is autonomous, uncontrolled up and down by superior cognitive processes that issue the command to retrieve the necessary part of the knowledge.

The locations where visitors look, that is, look points, are measured using eye tracking technology. If the knowledge network is sufficiently activated, it will get the feeling of satisfaction or contentment, measured by a questionnaire or an interview. This paper deals with the possibility of facilitating the activation of knowledge via the audio modality by providing an audio guide, which is subsidiary to the visual modality in the appreciation of objects in the museum.

2.2 Contentment in Museum Experience

In the study of investigating elicitation of emotions while viewing films, the following types of emotions are considered [11]:

relief	anger	surprise
arousal	sadness	fear
interest	tension	pain
contempt	disgust	happiness
confusion	embarrassment	amusement
contentment		

In the present study, it was assumed that similar emotional reactions would occur when studying objects in the museum. These sixteen types of emotions are used to study the emotional structure of contentment through internal relationships between the types of emotions listed above. People visit the museum for the purpose of acquiring knowledge. They would have a sense of satisfaction about accomplishing the goal. This kind of contentment is called "Cerebral Happiness" which is accomplished by "The Intellect", one of the seventeen goals of happiness proposed by Morris [12].

2.3 Eye Movement in Museum Experience

Various analytical methods have been used to elucidate the human's higher order cognitive processing. Measurement of visual behavior is one of them. It is physiologically confirmed that eye movement can be consciously controlled by eye movement. This is because it is believed to be affected by both low-order cognitive processing that unconsciously processes information reflected on the retina and higher-order cognitive processing such as semantic processing. Measurement of visual motion can also designate gaze with the temporal resolution of 100 msec or less and is suitable for observation of higher order cognitive processing performed in small time units. Furthermore, It is also superior in that measurement that does not disturb the human's higher order cognitive processing is possible. The museum experience involves the appreciation of objects. As most information is visual, eye movements are important information to understand the appreciation behavior of museum visitors [2, 13]. Figure 1 illustrates the perceptual and cognitive processes that are performed in the brain while appreciation of objects.

The appreciation process goes as follows:

1. Perceives via vision the information conveyed by painting that exists in the external physical world,
2. Detects visual features such as edges of the perceived objects on the retina via optical processes, and then transmits the results by electrical information to the brain,
3. Associates the information processed in the visual cortex with the knowledge stored in the cerebral cortex to learn and/or estimate the objects, which is called semantic processing,
4. Initiates eye movements and/or body movements in response to the results of the semantic processing.

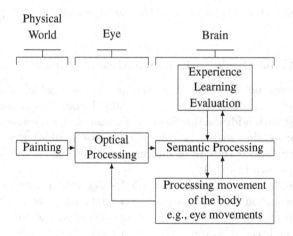

Fig. 1. Cognitive model [2].

The pattern of eye movements is an external parameter that should reflect the intention or purpose of the museum visitors [14]. It is known that there is a repeatable common pattern of the order of viewing paintings, for example in the order of eyes, mouth, outline, and this pattern is called "scan path" [15]. It has also been reported that the knowledge affects the eye movements including the scan path [16, 17].

If it can be assumed that both objects and viewers are stationary like viewing artworks, it is only necessary to consider two eye movements: fixation and saccade. Fixation is the maintaining of the visual gaze on a single location, and saccade is a quick, simultaneous movement of both eyes between two or more phases of fixation in the same direction. In this research, it is assumed that fixation is an action to perceive information from paintings, and defined in this research according to the barycentric method as follows. A case where a set of consecutive eye marks of 100 ms or more falls within a diameter of 2.0° from the center of gravity point of the set is set as a fixation, and the center of gravity point is set as a stationary point.

Research using various evaluation indices of eye movements has been conducted. In the research to evaluate the usability of the Web [18], there are studies that directly compare interest and attention to contents by comparing gaze count and gaze time for each content such as images and sentences displayed on the Web. Although gazing requires verification with the viewing target, the number of times of staying and the duration time are also effective as indices [19].

It is reported that the number of cycles carried out for a single object depends on the degree of the smoothness of learning of the object, which is proportional to the length of time to appreciate the object. The shorter the appreciation time becomes, the less effective the museum novice feels his/her learning progress [20]. The appreciation time could be additionally characterized by the change in the number of fixations per unit time as appreciation behavior develops [21]. This paper uses these factors to characterize the museum novices' appreciation behavior.

2.4   Using Audio Guide to Enhance Museum Novices' Experience

This paper focuses on the addition of the audio guide, which should have the effect on the cycle introduced by Fig. 1, especially during the semantic processing. In order to deal with additional information channel, it is necessary to consider the semantic processing with a broader perspective in which the object is comprehended using various sources of information including the directly perceived information as shown in Fig. 1.

Comprehension process involves knowledge activation process, triggered by perceptual information acquired from the external environment, the appearance of objects in museum in the specific context of this paper, and currently activated knowledge through the preceding cognitive processes including expecting what to happen, reflecting on the past events, making inferences of what comes next, etc. Comprehension is achieved solely on the ground of the activated knowledge.

In order to take into account the simultaneous, asynchronous, and automatic activation of knowledge through visual and audio information channels, resulting in a motor behavior of eye movements after processing visual-audio information, this paper adopts a comprehensive unified model, MHP/RT (Model Human Processor with Real-time Constraints), that is capable of simulating action selection processes by underlying perceptual–cognitive–motor processes and autonomous memory activation process [9,10]. The heart of the model is that coherent behavior in the ever-changing environment is possible by synchronization of automatic unconscious processes and deliberate conscious processes by using the activated portion of memory with the process of resonance. One of the case studies that applied MHP/RT to understand people's behavior was effectiveness of guidance information provided from a person sitting in the passenger seat of a car to the driver who was not familiar with the area he/she was driving [10,22]. The degree of effectiveness was dependent on the contents of activated knowledge of the driver. This paper considers that this is a similar situation, where a museum novice would be benefitted by the provision of audio guide while observing objects. When an audio guide is provided *timely*, it should be most effectively used to enhance the existing knowledge of the museum novice. The timing would be characterized in relative to the perceptual information that has been collected from the environment visually. It is assumed that the museum novice should have a feeling of satisfaction if the information provided though audio guide is smoothly integrated with the then-activated knowledge to form more complete knowledge, necessary for understanding the object.

3   Method

An eye tracking experiment was conducted to understand the effects of the audio-guide on eye movement and the level of contentment of museum novices who intended to acquire knowledge of objects used for the experiment.

3.1   Participants

Nineteen undergraduate students received course credit for participation in the present study (all museum novices, 15 males, 4 females, average age = 21.4, SD = 0.6). All had the normal or corrected-to-normal vision and naive about the purpose of this experiment.

3.2   Stimuli

To simulate the activity of viewing painting, six painting images and three audio guides were prepared with the permission of the Bridgestone Museum of Art. Three types of painting, namely, portraiture, landscape and abstract, have been selected because people tend to look for obvious elements such as faces or objects. The landscape has many elements, the abstract has no elements, and the portrait is between them. Two artistic works were used for each type of painting, and one of the works was presented with an audio guide, and the other without. The set of stimuli with audio guide is called "audio guided set", and the one without the audio guide, "no support set" hereinafter. Six tables were presented on a PC screen one by one to each participant (Table 1).

Table 1. List of the stimuli used for the eye tracking experiment [23].

Type	Artist	Title	Date	Length of audio guide [sec.]	ID
Portrait	Sekine Shoji	Boy	1919	-	P
Portrait	Fujishima Takeji	Black Fan	1908–09	65	Pa
Landscape	Asai Chu	Laundry Place at Grez-sur-Loing	1901	-	L
Landscape	Paul Cezanne	Mont Sainte-Victoire and Chateau Noir	1904–06	79	La
Abstract	Paul Klee	Island	1932	-	A
Abstract	Zao Wou-Ki	07.06.85	1985	87	Aa

3.3 Apparatus

Stimuli were controlled by Microsoft Powerpoint 2013 and were displayed on a 35 in. LCD monitor in a testing room equipped with soft lighting and sound attenuation. Eye movements were recorded using an eye mark recorder of NAC EMR-9, which had a sampling rate of 60 Hz and a coverage area with the horizontal angle of 44° and the vertical angle of 33°. Participants were seated approximately 1100 mm from the monitor and made responses using a mouse. Their chins were fixed using a chin support. The experiment was carried out with one participant at a time. Figure 2 depicts the arrangement of the experiment.

Fig. 2. Experiment environment.

3.4 Evaluation

In this study, the sixteen emotional states that should occur in response to observed object activity and the degree of brain happiness are measured by asking participants to complete the questionnaire as shown in the Table 2. Q1 is for measuring emotional state and Q2 to Q9 are for measuring cerebral happiness. The 25 items listed in the Table 2 were scored using a seven-point scale (1 = low, 7 = strong) (Fig. 3).

Eye movements were assessed using two parameters; the listening time and the frequency of the fixations.

Table 2. Evaluation items of subjective contentment [23].

Question Content
Q-1) For the following 16 kinds of emotions, please answer the strength that you have felt.

1) relief	2) anger	3) surprise	4) arousal
5) sadness	6) fear	7) interest	8) tension
9) pain	10) contempt	11) disgust	12) happiness
13) confusion	14) embarrassment	15) amusement	16) contentment

Q-2) I felt contentment from painting appreciation.
Q-3) It was my favorite painting.
Q-4) I found the meaning of the painting.
Q-5) I found the value of the painting was found.
Q-6) I wanted to know more about the painting.
Q-7) That study has developed new knowledge.
Q-8) I found where should I watch.
Q-9) I wanted actually to go to a museum of art.

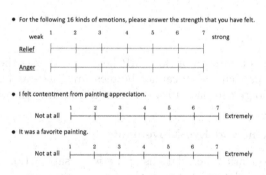

Fig. 3. A part of a questionnaire [23].

3.5 Procedure

First, participants were asked if they understood the purpose of this study and agreed to participate. After adjusting the participant's sitting position and attaching her chin, a calibration process was performed to ensure that the visual object and the eye mark were in the same position. After completing the calibration process, it has been confirmed that the visual object and the mark of the eye are the same.

Before beginning the experiment, each participant was told to look carefully at the images displayed, to do their best not to move their head and to remove the image by clicking when they felt enough. After that, a workout was performed with an image.

The participants were explained the experimental procedure. In the experiment, all the participants first visualized 3 non-assisted images and then 3 audio-guided images. Participants were allowed to pause after completing the unassisted images if they requested it. Three images in each section were mixed according to the Latin square method. The order was chosen by Table 3. When participants clicked to delete each image, they were asked to complete a self-assessment questionnaire posted by Table 2. At the end of the experiment, participants were asked about their reasoning in their assessments and whether they had ever seen the images.

Table 3. The presentation order of stimuli [23].

	Non guided			Audio guided		
	1	2	3	4	5	6
Pattern 1	L	A	P	Aa	Pa	La
Pattern 2	P	L	A	La	Aa	Pa
Pattern 3	A	P	L	Pa	La	Aa

4   Results

Due to the change of position of the EMR head unit during the pause, the eye movement of the participant 19 cannot be measured accurately. Therefore, the participant's audio-guided data 19 was removed from the analysis.

4.1   Contentment and Eye Movements

In this section, to clarify the relationship between satisfaction ratings and eye movements, the correlations between them were examined. Table 4 shows the significant correlation coefficients between all the elements of evaluation of the subjective contentment and the elements of the eye movements. As shown, positive emotions such as happiness and amusement mainly have an effect on the viewing time and frequency of fixations. And this shows that the feeling of knowledge acquisition decreases as the frequency of fixations increases.

Table 4. Correlations between evaluations and eye movements in non-guided portrait [23].

	Happiness	Amusement	Contentment	Q-7
Viewing time [sec]	0.508*	0.111	0.270	0.394
Frequency of fixation [counts/sec]	−0.502*	−0.466*	−0.571*	−0.485*

*$p < .05$
Q-7: "That study has activated new knowledge."

4.2   Audio Guide on Portraits

In this part, only two portrait images of unassisted play and audio-guided ensemble have been analyzed. There was no statistically significant difference as the average of all participants, but the following trend was observed. At this point, it has also been suggested that there are two attributes as follows. The experimental result indicates that the audio guide affected the listening time and the frequency of the fixings. Most participants, as can be observed for participants 6 and 9, tend to rate their low contentment when there is no help. On the other hand, the assessment of contentment tended to be high when there was audio-guide support. However, there were some participants, as can be observed for participants 1 and 17, who felt that contentment was high although there was no assistance and stated an even higher satisfaction rating. for the audio guide. Therefore, the results of participants 6, 9, 1 and 17 were reviewed.

Audio guide changed not only the contentment evaluation but also how the participants perceived the images because the audio guide provided the information regarding the images and the point of interest of the images. The Figs. 4, 5 and 6 graphically illustrate the change of content. As shown in Figs. 5 and 6, not all participants could experience Cerebral Happiness without an audio guide, but they could feel it with an audio guide.

In terms of viewing time, the audio guide increased the viewing time of most participants, far exceeding the length of the audio guide, which was about 65 s as shown on the screen. Figure 7. Conversely, some participants, such as participant 1 and participant 17, did not change significantly. The result of the experiment indicates that the modification of the observation time has tended to conform to the contentment evaluation.

For eye movements, most participants with audio-guided assistants tended to look at a certain location by following the audio guide, which had the effect of reducing the frequency of fixations. However, the frequency of fixations of some participants such as participant 17 has increased instead. According to the interview, participant 17 stated that he was distracted by the audio guide. In addition, he stated that he would like to have an explanatory text in place of the audio-guide. The Fig. 8 graphically illustrates the change in eye movements.

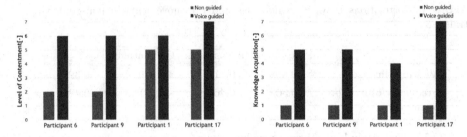

Fig. 4. Effect on contentment.

Fig. 5. Effect on acquisition of knowledge.

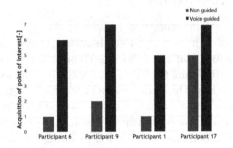

Fig. 6. Effect on acquisition of point of interest.

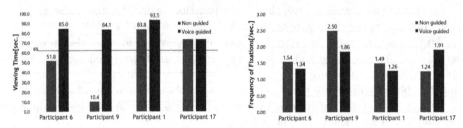

Fig. 7. Effect on viewing time.

Fig. 8. Effect on frequency of fixations.

4.3   Audio Guide and Viewing Time/Frequency of Fixations

In this part, all the images have been analyzed. To analyze the effect of contentment and audio guide, a time-frequency plot of the fixtures is created as shown in Figs. 9, 10, 11, 12, 13, 14 and 15. The Fig. 9 shows no obvious result. However, when the data between the no-guided and the audio-guided are separated, a clear trend can be seen in Figs. 10, 11, 12, 13, 14 and 15. In no-assisted condition, the viewing time and the frequency of the fixations did not have a clear interaction. On the other hand, viewing time are concentrated in the given area in the audio-guided condition.

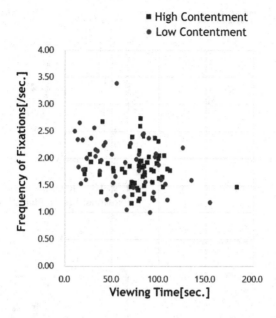

Fig. 9. Time - frequency of fixations plot of all [23].

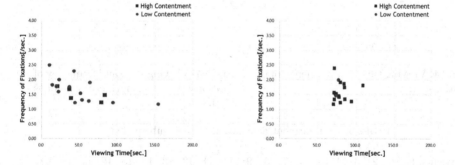

Fig. 10. Viewing time and frequency of fixations: P.

Fig. 11. Viewing time and frequency of fixations: Pa (the length of the guide is 65 s).

4.4 Cluster Analysis

Using the participants' contentment average, a participant satisfaction score-board was obtained as shown in the Table 5. This table was further analyzed with the no. III to see any trend in the participants. In the result, the path of each contentment acquisition was described in two dimensions: the first axis was "Abstract preferred - Representational preferred", and the second axis was "Guide is necessary - Guide is unnecessary". With the score resulting from the no. III, participants can be classified and grouped into four types as shown in Fig. 16 using the Ward method. Although participant 16 was ranked in group C

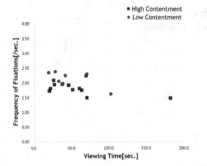

Fig. 12. Viewing time and frequency of fixations: L.

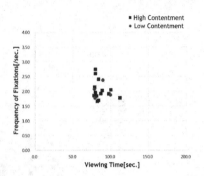

Fig. 13. Viewing time and frequency of fixations: La (the length of the guide is 79 s).

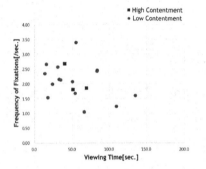

Fig. 14. Viewing time and frequency of fixations: A.

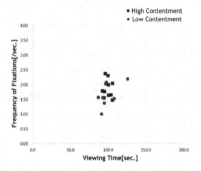

Fig. 15. Viewing time and frequency of fixations: Aa (the length of the guide is 87 s).

Table 5. Contentment acquisition of each subject [23].

Participant number	1	2	3	4	5	6	7	8	9	10	11	12	13	14	15	16	17	18	19
Portrait	✓			✓								✓	✓				✓		
Landscape	✓	✓	✓	✓		✓		✓		✓	✓	✓	✓	✓			✓		✓
Abstract		✓	✓															✓	
Portrait (Audio)	✓		✓	✓	✓	✓		✓	✓	✓	✓	✓	✓	✓	✓	✓	✓	✓	✓
Landscape (Audio)	✓		✓		✓	✓	✓	✓	✓	✓	✓	✓	✓	✓				✓	✓
Abstract (Audio)			✓			✓	✓		✓	✓	✓		✓		✓		✓	✓	✓

✓: contentment, blank: not contentment

with the score, this participant had a different way of feeling contented. It was assumed that participant 16 could be a participant who did not feel satisfied with the paintings. Therefore, the score of participant 16 was not plotted.

5   Discussions

5.1   Audio Guide

According to the interview, participants who perceived a positive emotion rated their contentment as high. This has happened because contentment is also a positive emotion, and it can be difficult to differentiate positive emotions in the individual. Participants who rated high contentment tended to think about the background of the paintings, which would lead to an increase in listening time and a decrease in the frequency of fixations. On the other hand, participants who perceive negative emotions while looking at a particular image have not thought of the background of the paintings.

However, as presented in the Sect. 4.2, novices, who could not have any idea without a guide, had an idea and felt satisfied with an audio guide. The audio guide led participants to look at the explained point without hesitation and the frequency of fixations tends to decrease.

However, there are also novices who think that the audio guide is embarrassing as the participant 17. Most novices can enjoy paintings with any information because of their ignorance about the paintings. But novices who needed specific information at that time think the audio guide is boring and want the explanation text instead when the audio guide brings them to another point. The

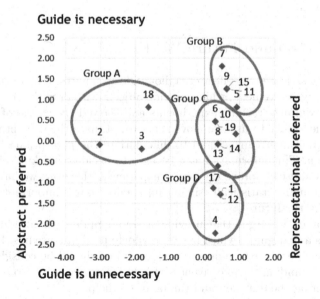

Fig. 16. Contentment acquisition [23].

difference between the point of interest and the audio guide can increase the frequency of the fixings.

The concentrated phenomena presented in the Sect. 4.3 are caused by audio-guided because it leads the participants to look at the point of interest in the same sequence. In fact, the impressions of paintings with audio-guide were the same for most participants.

5.2 Analysis of the Need of Particular Participant

The characteristics of the cluster classified in Sect. 4.4 were considered in this section.

- Group A
  They can't understand abstract without audio guide, but they could enjoy in their way (e.g. brushwork, colors).
- Group B
  They are classified as typical museum novices: it is difficult for them to have their own ideas. Although it is possible to feel contentment with audio guide, they want explanations of overt elements for audio guide instead of the information of the artist.
- Group C
  They can enjoy paintings with audio guide, and also enjoy portrait and landscape which are easy to understand without audio guide.
- Group D
  They can feel contentment without audio guide. When the contents of audio guide are not they want to know or from the time constraints, audio guide annoys them.

6   Conclusion and Future Works

This paper investigates the effect of audio-guide on novices' level of contentment by analyzing eye movements while enjoying objects with or without audio-guide. For that, we did eye-tracking experiments and showed the effects of the audio-guide and the ability to use eye movements to estimate the contentment of the novices. Contentment can be used to differentiate the perception of the image of each person. This information can be used to decide what kind of support a person needs and to improve the novice experience. However, we have not been able to obtain many statistically significant results, so it is important to improve the method in the future.

In this paper, we argue that provide an audio guide without additional displays such as a text guide, which has been widely used in museums. In addition, other aids, such as a text guide and a video guide, should be considered in the future. Understanding the effectiveness of help for novices can also be expanded after considering the duration and timing of the help.

Acknowledgments. This work was supported by JSPS KAKENHI Grant Number 15H02784.

Appendix

(See Figs. 17, 18, 19, 20, 21 and 22).

Fig. 17. Sekine Shoji, Boy, 1919, ID: P [23].

Fig. 18. Fujishima Takeji, Black Fan, 1908–09, ID: Pa [23].

Fig. 19. Asai Chu, Laundry Place at Grez-sur-Loing, 1901, ID: L [23].

Fig. 20. Paul Cezanne, Mont Sainte-Victoire and Chateau Noir, 1904–06, ID: La [23].

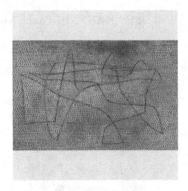 

Fig. 21. Paul Klee, Island, 1932, ID: A [23].

Fig. 22. Zao Wou-Ki, 07.06.85, 1985, ID: Aa [23].

References

1. Tullis, J.G., Benjamin, A.S.: On the effectiveness of self-paced learning. J. Mem. Lang. **64**, 109–118 (2011)
2. Solso, R.L.: Cognition and the Visual Arts. MIT Press, Cambridge (1996)
3. Kintsch, W.: The use of knowledge in discourse processing: a construction-integration model. Psychol. Rev. **95**, 163–182 (1988)
4. Kintsch, W.: Comprehension: A Paradigm for Cognition. Cambridge University Press, Cambridge (1998)
5. Kahneman, D.: A perspective on judgment and choice. Am. Psychol. **58**, 697–720 (2003)
6. Evans, J.S.B.: In two minds: dual-process accounts of reasoning. Trends Cogn. Sci. **7**, 454–459 (2003)
7. Evans, J.S.B.T., Frankish, K. (eds.): In Two Minds: Dual Processes and Beyond. Oxford University Press, Oxford (2009)
8. Evans, J.S.B.T.: Thinking Twice: Two Minds in One Brain. Oxford University Press, Oxford (2010)
9. Kitajima, M., Toyota, M.: Decision-making and action selection in Two Minds: an analysis based on Model Human Processor with Realtime Constraints (MHP/RT). Biol. Inspired Cogn. Archit. **5**, 82–93 (2013)
10. Kitajima, M.: Memory and Action Selection in Human-Machine Interaction, 1st edn. Wiley-ISTE, Hoboken (2016)
11. Gross, J.J., Levenson, R.W.: Emotion elicitation using films. Cogn. Emot. **9**, 87–108 (1995)
12. Morris, D.: The Nature of Happiness. Little Books Ltd., London (2006)
13. Yarbus, A.L. In: Eye movements during perception of complex objects, pp. 171–211. Plenum, New York (1967)
14. Yarbus, A.L.: Eye Movements and Vision. Plenum, New York (1967)
15. Noton, D., Stark, L.: Scanpaths in eye movements during pattern perception. Science **171**, 308–311 (1971)
16. Nodine, C.F., Locher, P.J., Krupinski, E.A.: The role of formal art training on perception and aesthetic judgment of art compositions. Leonardo **26**, 219–227 (1993)

17. Zangemeister, W., Sherman, K., Stark, L.: Evidence for a global scanpath strategy in viewing abstract compared with realistic images. Neuropsychologia **33**, 1009–1025 (1995)
18. Ohno, T.: Where you look while you navigate the web? – eye mark analysis of WWW pages (2000)
19. Ohno, T.: What can be learned from eye movement?: Understanding higher cognitive processes from eye movement analysis. Cogn. Stud.: Bull. Jpn. Cogn. Sci. Soc. **9**, 565–579 (2002)
20. Okumoto, M., Kato, H.: The cognitive orientation of museum (COM) model for museum novices. Educ. Technol. Res. **33**, 131–140 (2010)
21. Jacob, R., Karn, K.S.: Eye tracking in human-computer interaction and usability research: ready to deliver the promises. Mind **2**, 4 (2003)
22. Kitajima, M., et al.: Information for helping drivers achieve safe and enjoyable driving: an on-road observational study. In: Proceedings of the Human Factors and Ergonomics Society 53rd Annual Meeting 2009, Santa Monica, CA, pp. 1801–1805. Human Factors and Ergonomics Society (2009)
23. Egawa, K., Kitajima, M.: Utilization of audio guide for enhancing museum experience - relationships between visitors' eye movements, audio guide contents, and the levels of contentment. In: Proceedings of the 12th International Joint Conference on Computer Vision, Imaging and Computer Graphics Theory and Applications, VISIGRAPP 2017 - Volume 2: HUCAPP, Porto, Portugal, 27 February–1 March 2017, pp. 17–26 (2017)

The Impact of Field of View on Robotic Telepresence Navigation Tasks

Federica Bazzano[1(✉)], Fabrizio Lamberti[1], Andrea Sanna[1],
and Marco Gaspardone[2]

[1] Dip. di Automatica e Informatica, Politecnico di Torino,
Corso Duca degli Abruzzi, 24, 10129 Turin, Italy
{federica.bazzano,fabrizio.lamberti,andrea.sanna}@polito.it
[2] TIM JOL Connected Robotics Applications LaB,
Corso Montevecchio 71, 10129 Turin, Italy
marco.gaspardone@telecomitalia.it

Abstract. Telepresence interfaces for navigation tasks involving remote robots are generally designed for providing users with sensory and/or contextual feedback, mainly through onboard camera video stream or map-based localization. This choice is motivated by the fact that operating a mobile robot from distance may be mentally challenging for the users when they do not possess a proper awareness of the environment. However, fixed or narrow field of view cameras often available on these robots may lead to lack of awareness or worse navigation performance due to missing or limited peripheral vision. The aim of this paper is to investigate, through a comparative analysis, how an augmented field of view and/or a pan-tilt camera can impact on users' performance in remote robot navigation tasks. Thus, a user study has been carried out to assess three different experimental configurations, i.e., a fixed camera with narrow (45°) field of view, a pan-tilt camera with a wide-angle (180°) horizontal field of view, and a fixed camera with a wide-angle (180°) diagonal field of view. Results showed a strong preference for the wide-angle field of view navigation modality, which provided users with greater situational awareness by requiring a lower cognitive effort.

Keywords: Telepresence · Remote teleoperation · Navigation · Human-Robot Interaction (HRI)

1 Introduction

In the last years, telepresence solutions have become increasingly commonplace, due to their ability to let people act as they were physically present in the remote environment [14]. Examples include teleconferencing, virtual tourism, health care, education, etc. [12]. When this feeling of "being physically present"

M. Gaspardone—The authors wish to acknowledge TIM, which partially funded the activities.

is achieved by means of a robot teleoperated from a distance, the experience is referred to as *robotic telepresence* [20]. In this scenario, a human operator located remotely with respect to the robotic platform, explores and navigates the environment by relying on feedback information provided by the robot itself [18].

In remote sensing scenarios, where the human perceptual processes are disjointed from the physical world, feedback information represents the only sensory stimuli. The lack or poor perception of this information may compromise human actions in the remote environment, by making even simple tasks incredibly difficult to deal with [3]. The human's interpretation of information collected from the remote environment should overcome this "decoupling effect" [23].

An effective design of teleoperation interfaces requires to identify the key elements that can improve the operator's ability to correctly perceive and understand the above information, as well as lower the cognitive effort arising from the execution of the remote tasks while keeping the interaction with the robot as simple as possible [4]. The former aspect is generally termed *situation awareness* [5], whereas the latter is generally referred to as *mental workload* [2].

According to [27], in remote robot teleoperation tasks, most of the complexity associated with a lower situation awareness lays in humans' lack of the perception of the robot's location, surroundings, and status. An approach that has become very common in many telepresence solutions to address this issue is the use of video streaming from an onboard camera and/or of position information displayed on a map [10]. In fact, in [16], authors compared a map-centric interface with a video-centric interface and with a combination of them, and concluded that when video and map are integrated they compensate each other and improve overall performance. In [18], authors demonstrated that remote users heavily depend on video information to navigate the remote environments through telepresence robots; however, the way in which video information is presented as well as the amount of information that can be gathered from the remote environment, which depends on the field of view (FOV), orientation and point of view of the robot's onboard camera, may affect operators' navigation performance [3]. As a matter of example, in [26], authors stated that exploiting cameras for sensing the environment where the robot is navigating into creates the so-called "keyhole effect": compared to direct viewing, only a portion of the whole environment is actually shown to the operator, by demanding him or her an additional effort to make sense of it.

Another factor that can significantly impact on the operator's mental workload and, hence, on his or her performance is represented by the teleoperation paradigm used for the remote robot navigation [22]. In [1], a mixed map- and video-based control system exploiting a fixed camera with narrow FOV was compared with the two major approaches used today for controlling telepresence robots, i.e., keyboard and point-and-click video navigation, as well as with a combination of the two methods. According to experimental observations, users preferred the combined navigation modality, since they were allowed to switch between the two interfaces when needed, thus benefiting from the advantages of both. Notwithstanding, the impossibility to move the camera as well as its limited FOV were regarded as particularly critical by the users, who wanted to see a wider portion of the remote environment in order to spot the destination to click.

By moving from the above considerations, the goal of the present paper is to leverage results reported in [1] and study the impact of robot's camera FOV in the remote navigation of telepresence robots by considering three different camera configurations. In order to evaluate the above alternatives before possibly moving to physically implementing them on a real robot like in [1], a simulation environment was used to experiment with the different setups.

The rest of the paper is organized as follows. In Sect. 2, relevant literature pertaining techniques and interfaces for video capturing systems in the field of telepresence robots is reviewed. In Sect. 3, .the robot considered in the study is described. Section 4 provides an overview of the user interface exploited in this study. Section 5 offers an overview of the overall teleoperation system and provides the details of the three camera-based configurations that have been studied. Section 6 introduces the methodology that has been adopted to perform the experimental tests and discusses results obtained. Lastly, Sect. 7 concludes the paper, by providing possible directions for future research in this field.

2   Related Work

Many works in the literature concerning robotic telepresence tried to address the issues arising from possible lacks in human's perception of the remote environment by proposing different video capturing solutions.

For instance, in [15], six different FOV sizes (ranging from narrow to omnidirectional) were compared to teleoperate a mobile robot both in real and virtual environments. Results showed that operators were more efficient when wide FOVs (from 120° up) were employed. The limitation of this work was that the communication delay, i.e., the interaction latency, increased proportionally with the FOV size. In [21], the effectiveness of three different camera configurations (45°, omnidirectional 360° and fisheye 180° FOVs) for mobile robot teleoperation was investigated. According to experimental observations, users preferred the fisheye and omnidirectional configurations, since they allowed them to get a clear view of the robot's surrounding. However, the distortions introduced in the omnidirectional images made it difficult for the users to understand the robot's position and orientation. In [25], authors studied three different camera configurations (101° perspective camera, 185° fisheye camera, and 185° fisheye camera with an undistorted central area) combined with two input techniques (keyboard and through-the-screen, or TTS, requiring the user to define a path in the robot's camera view by using the mouse). Results showed that the undistorted fisheye was the preferred configuration together with the TTS input technique (since it allowed the user to cope with other tasks once a path had been defined). This finding was also due to limitations of the perspective view, which did not allow users to move the camera to see close obstacles on the floor.

Other works focused on the effect of the FOV on tasks different than remote navigation. As a matter of example, in [11], authors demonstrated that a portrait image orientation is preferred over a landscape one in remote social interaction tasks, as it encourages remote users to orient the robot towards local users. In [9], authors compared three different camera configurations (45°, 180° and 360° panoramic FOVs) for collaborative room redecoration tasks involving local and remote users. They found that users exploiting the wide-angle and panoramic FOVs performed better in terms of time needed to complete the task and number of collisions compared to users working with the narrow FOV, even though they perceived the panoramic FOV as the more difficult to manage. Concerning the interaction with local users, users who exploited a wider FOV perceived to be less successful in the collaboration.

Based on the short review above, it can be observed that wide-angle FOVs allow remote operators to be more effective in remote navigation tasks compared to the limited FOVs generally exploited in robots on-board cameras. In particular, fisheye and wide-angle perspective cameras proved to be the most used setups, even though they suffer from distortion and no close-up view issues, respectively.

By taking into account advantages and drawbacks of the above solutions, the different camera configurations that will be considered and compared in this paper are a fixed camera with a narrow (45°) FOV, a perspective camera with a wide-angle (180°) horizontal FOV endowed with pan-tilt capabilities, as well as a fixed fisheye camera with a wide-angle (180°) diagonal FOV and a no-distortion central area.

3   Robotic Platform

This section briefly describes the robotic platform that has considered in this study, named Virgil, by illustrating its hardware and software features.

Virgil is a wheeled mobile telepresence robot that was initially designed for cultural heritage scenarios with the goal to allow museum visitors to experience temporary inaccessible areas not included in the visit, e.g., because closed to the public (Fig. 1).

It was devised to be operated remotely by the museum guide, who can show to the visitors the real time video stream received by the robot's camera on portable devices like smartphones and tablets [7]. It mounts a pan-tilt camera and a laser sensor that is capable to detect obstacles at a distance of up to 30 m with a horizontal FOV of 270°. It is about 120 cm tall and weighs approximately 14 Kg. It is equipped with a Li-Fe 12 V battery providing it with an autonomy of approximately 4 h and a maximum velocity of 1 m/s.

It is equipped with two navigation modalities implementing two different levels of autonomy, i.e. manual teleoperation and semi-autonomous navigation, both integrating obstacle avoidance functionalities. Sliding autonomy is used in teleoperation tasks for adjusting robot's level of autonomy to match the users' needs [17]. The control software provides it with local and global path planning capabilities, which rely on a map of the environment created in a preliminary exploration phase. Algorithms are executed on the Robot Operating System (ROS)-based platform for cloud robotics created by TIM.

Fig. 1. The Virgil robot in a museum installation.

With respect to the original setup, for the purpose of this study, the camera on the robot's head has been replaced by a tablet device on a pan-tilt support, which makes it possible to display at the remote site the face of the operator, thus enhancing the sense of presence.

4   Telepresence Interface

In this section, the telepresence interface considered in this study to both display the different camera configurations and allows human users to teleoperate the robot through the provided navigation modalities is presented.

As illustrated in Fig. 2, it consists of a web-based application with a wide central region occupied by a video window, in which the live stream received from the robot's camera is displayed (a smaller window shows the video captured by a local webcam, which is displayed on the remote tablet mounted on the robot). Right below the video window, there is a colored bar, which is used to visualize the robot's distance from possible obstacles. The bar is split in three regions, which refer to obstacles in front, to the left and the right of the robot. Bar's color changes from green to red based on the actual measurements of the laser sensor. A map showing position and orientation of the robot in real time is also included on the left side of the interface. Robot is represented by a yellow triangle.

In Fig. 2 the interface is showing 3D content generated by the simulation environment, though it can be seamlessly used to control the real robot.

5   Setups

In the following, the different setups considered in this work in terms of camera configurations and navigation modalities (keyboard and point-and-click) will be introduced, by providing also some implementation details.

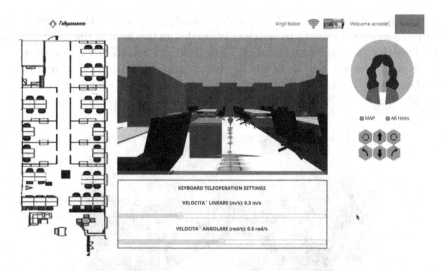

Fig. 2. Telepresence interface. (Color figure online)

Fig. 3. Narrow FOV (NFOV) configuration.

5.1 Camera Configurations

This section describes the three camera configurations that have been studied, which differ in the size of the FOV and the way the user can control the position and orientation of the camera mounted on top of the robot.

In the first configuration, later referred to as *Narrow FOV (NFOV)*, the robot was equipped with a forward-facing camera characterized by a common 45° FOV, as illustrated in Fig. 3.

In the second configuration, a wide-angle perspective camera with a 180° horizontal FOV and pan-tilt capabilities (later abbreviated as *WFOV&PT*) was employed, as shown in Fig. 4. The pan-tilt was introduced in order to overcome the limitation experienced in [1,25], which was due to the fact that users were not able to move the camera to see close obstacles on the floor in the perspective view. The user can issue horizontal or vertical orientation sliding commands by holding down the left button of the mouse to hook the current view and drag it to the desired position (e.g. dragging the view allows the user to look to the right, like in Google Street View[1]).

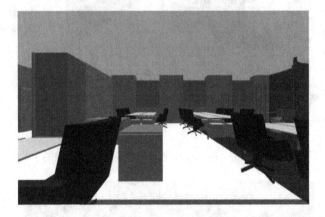

Fig. 4. Wide FOV plus pan-tilt (WFOV&PT) configuration.

Fig. 5. Fisheye FOV (FFOV) configuration.

In the third configuration, a wide-angle fisheye camera with a 180° diagonal FOV (abbreviated as *FFOV*) was exploited, as illustrated in Fig. 5. Since fisheye lens suffer from radially symmetric distortions, a radially symmetric image

---

[1] https://www.google.com/streetview/.

remapping phase was implemented in order to obtain an undistorted (perspectively correct) circular region in the center of the view. As the intrinsic parameters of the camera, as well as its distortion vector, were known, the pixels in the circular area with a given radius could be undistorted, rectified and remapped on the image in order to generate a perspectively correct view inside the circle with the same radius. These steps (excluding the remapping) were also exploited in the point-and-click video navigation modality (described later).

All the cameras transmitted a video stream at approximately 30 frames per second with a resolution of 1024×768 pixels.

5.2   Navigation Modalities

This section describes the approach to robot's teleoperation that has been considered in this study, based on [1], which combines two different navigation modalities, i.e., *keyboard teleoperation* and *point-and-click video navigation*, in order to allow human operators to switch between them when needed [1]. The two modalities have been integrated in the web-based application implementing the user interface, which communicates with the robot and the cloud robotics platform that hosts the navigation algorithms (to this purpose, roslibjs was used, a JavaScript-based library for using ROS on the Web [24]). It is worth recalling that navigation algorithms actually work on a map that was created by using the robot's laser sensor and applying a Simultaneous Localization and Mapping (SLAM) strategy.

In the keyboard teleoperation navigation modality, the operator manually drives the robot throughout the environment by means of directions keys. When the up or down arrow keys are pressed, a ROS linear speed command is sent by making the robot move forward or backward. Similarly, the left and right keys twist the robot by changing its angular velocity. When pressed together, the above keys can be used to make the robot move in the given direction while turning left or right. Augmented reality arrows are displayed on the video stream to provide human operators with a feedback about the command issued and the current robot's direction (Fig. 2). The robot exploits a local path planning algorithm to navigate the environment.

In the point-and-click video navigation modality, the operator issues navigation commands to the robot by clicking on the video stream received by the camera to specify a target destination, as illustrated in Fig. 6. As said, since the intrinsic parameters of the camera and the pan-tilt configuration, when used, are known, the coordinates of the pixel clicked by the operator can be converted to a point on the map by using ray-tracing. In fact, for each (x, y) pixel clicked in the image, a ray can be generated whose intersection with the floor plane at $z = 0$ determines the position in the environment where the robot should move to. The robot exploits a global path planning algorithm to reach the destination in an autonomous way by avoiding both fixed and moving obstacles. The path that is being followed by the robot and the clicked target are overlapped to the video stream using augmented reality (Fig. 2).

Fig. 6. Point-and-click video navigation (Source: [1], p. 50).

6   Experimental Results

In this section, the experiments that were carried out to assess the impact of different camera configurations in remote navigation tasks will be presented.

Experiments involved 10 volunteers (8 males and 2 females) aged between 24 and 32 years (M = 26.60 SD = 2.32), who were recruited among university students from Politecnico di Torino. Participants were told that they would have to navigate within a simulated environment to reach the office of a person they were looking for. This navigation task was specifically designed to be composed by three different subtasks referred to as *T1 - Reach the column, T2 - Reach the room,* and *T3 - Enter/exit the room* in order to test the suitability of the various configurations in the possible scenarios the robot could be involved into when used in an office environment. In particular, T1 was designed to assess the three configurations when driving the robot to a destination that is outside the camera's FOV. T2 was meant to study a scenario in which obstacles are to be avoided. Lastly, T3 was designed to study performance when driving the robot in constrained spaces.

A brief training was delivered in order to instruct participants on the use of the interface for teleoperating the robot with the navigation modalities discussed in Sect. 5.2. Afterwards, participants were invited to perform the three subtasks in sequence by using all the camera configurations. To compensate for possible learning effects, configurations were selected using the Latin Square order.

At the beginning of the experiment, the robot is initially standing in the open space of the office environment to ensure that the camera cannot frame the location to be reached in the first subtask. Robot's position is indicated by the yellow triangle in the map, as illustrated in Fig. 7. Participants have to teleoperate the robot in order to reach the location labeled T1 on the map. A possible path that can be followed is shown by the blue line. In the second task, participants have to drive the robot from location T1 to location T2, which is located in front of the room they were looking for. In this case, they need to avoid the column. A possible path is shown in green on the map. Lastly, in the third sub-task participants have to drive the robot to make it enter the intended room, bring it close to a desk (indicated by label T3), and finally exit the room. A possible path is drawn in red on the map.

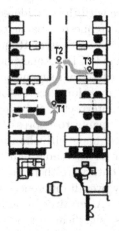

Fig. 7. Map of the environment considered in the experiments: initial position of the robot (yellow triangle), destinations to be reached in the subtasks and possible paths. (Source: [1], p. 51). (Color figure online)

During the experiments, quantitative data about time required to complete the subtasks and number of navigation commands (key presses and/or mouse clicks) were recorded. After having tested a given camera configuration, participants were asked to fill in a NASA Task Load Index (TLX) [19] and a NASA Situation Awareness Rating Technique (SART) [6] questionnaire. These questionnaires were exploited to both evaluate participants' self-assessed mental workload and situation awareness (as done in [9]).

The first questionnaire evaluated participant's perceived mental strain on a six-dimension scale regarding *mental demand, physical demand, temporal demand, performance, effort,* and *frustration.* Each dimension was assigned a score from 0 to 100. A global score was then calculated by using a weighting mechanism to combine the six individual scores.

The second questionnaire evaluated the subjective situation awareness of the participants on a seven-point scale concerning the *demand of attentional resources* (complexity, variability, and instability of the situation), the *supply of attentional resources* (division of attention, arousal, concentration, and spare mental capacity), and the *understanding of the situation* (information quantity, and information quality). Like for the first questionnaire, a global score was then calculated according to [6].

At the end of the experience, each participant was also asked to fill in a usability questionnaire split in three parts.

The first part was created by considering the Usefulness, Satisfaction, and Ease of use (USE) questionnaire [13]. USE requested participants to evaluate the ease of use and the satisfaction of the experimented camera configurations by expressing their agreement on a seven-point scale.

The second part was created by considering the Subjective Assessment of Speech System Interfaces (SASSI) methodology [8] and adapting it to let participants judge the user experience with the considered camera configurations. The (adapted) SASSI questionnaire requested participants to evaluate statements referring to six usability factors, i.e., System Response Accuracy (SRA), Likeability (LIKE), Cognitive Demand (CD), Annoyance (AN), Habitability (HAB) and Speed (SPE) by expressing their agreement on a seven-point scale. For the sake of consistency with other questions, scores for CD and AN were inverted (thus, higher scores have to be interpreted as being more positive).

The third part asked participants to express their preferences by ranking, for each subtask, the experience made with the three camera configurations by providing their judgment both for the three individual subtasks as well as for the task as a whole. Collected data were then analyzed using one-way repeated ANOVA in order to detect any overall differences between the three configurations (significance level of 0.05). Afterwards, a post-hoc analysis was performed using two-tailed paired T-tests (significance level of 0.05) in order to highlight exactly where these differences were actually occurring.

Results obtained in terms of completion time as well as number of interactions required to complete the subtasks are reported in Fig. 8. It is immediately clear that completion time for subtask T1 with the NFOV configuration was largely higher than with the WFOV&PT and FFOV configurations (Fig. 8(a)). Statistical significance validated by both ANOVA and post-hoc analysis confirmed a significant difference between NFOV and FFOV. Results for subtask T2 were not statistically significant. With respect to subtask T3, even though differences between WFOV&PT and both NFOV and FFOV were considerable, they did not reach significance. Average values for the number of interactions (Fig. 8(b)) showed that, for subtask T1 and T3, the NFOV configuration required a larger number of interactions compared to both WFOV&PT and FFOV (this number was much higher in the case of T1). Lower completion time and reduced number of interactions for the WFOV&PT and FFOV configurations were obtained also when summing up results obtained for the task as a whole.

Results obtained in terms of participants' mental workload and perceived situation awareness (Fig. 9) appear to describe an almost comparable situation. In fact, participants judged the NFOV as the most cognitive demanding configuration, followed by WFOV&PT and finally by FFOV. Furthermore, participants judged the WIDE&PT as the configuration providing the highest situation awareness. Therefore, it can be concluded that NFOV was perceived as the most challenging configuration, as it worsened participants' awareness of the operating conditions.

Similar considerations can be made for all the usability factors tackled by the USE and (adapted) SASSI questionnaires. In fact, as shown in Fig. 10, the

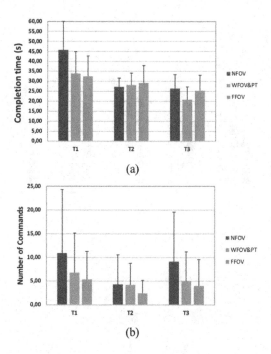

(a)

(b)

Fig. 8. Results in terms of (a) completion time and (b) number of interactions required to complete the three subtasks with each camera configuration. Bar heights report average values (lower is better).

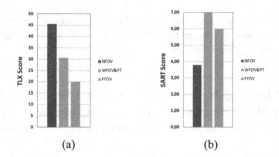

(a)   (b)

Fig. 9. Results concerning (a) mental workload and (b) situation awareness measurements for the three camera configurations. Bar heights report TLX score (lower is better) and SART score (higher is better).

configurations leveraging a wider FOV (WFOV&PT and FFOV) were judged as the more usable, as they performed better for every usability factor. This evidence was also confirmed by ANOVA, as for all the categories statistically significant differences were found. Moreover, it can be observed that the perceived speed (SPE) category was characterized by higher scores for wider FOVs, thus confirming findings obtained in [3] (where it is stated that with wider FOVs,

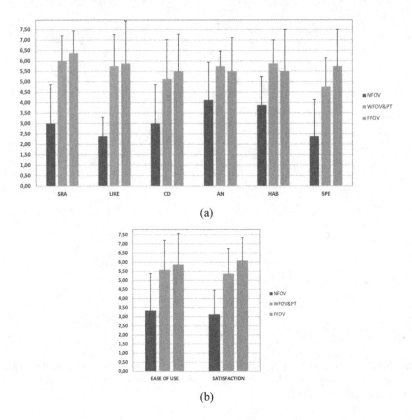

Fig. 10. Results concerning the usability of the three camera configurations for the task as a whole based on (a) adapted SASSI and (b) USE questionnaires. Bar heights report average values (higher is better).

navigation speed tends to be perceived as increased because of the scene compression). It is worth noting also that the cognitive demand (CD) category confirmed results obtained by the NASA-TLX methodology for the mental workload assessment.

Results regarding participants' preferences in using the three camera configurations to perform the individual subtasks as well as the task as a whole are reported in Fig. 11. Considering overall rankings, it appears that the favorite configurations are the FFOV and WFOV&PT. This result is also valid for subtask T1. Considering the other two subtasks, the FFOV configuration was strongly preferred compared to WFOV&PT and NFOV.

Based on the feedback gathered during the experiments, preferences appeared to be mainly motivated by the fact that, as expected, wider FOVs allowed participants to see larger portions of the environment in which the robot was located. This finding can be observed also within results discussed above. In fact, by combining these results with completion times and number of interactions, it is evident that the two configurations with the wider FOVs allowed users to com-

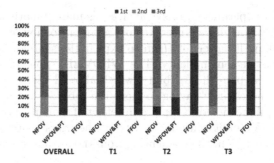

Fig. 11. Number of times the three camera configurations were ranked 1st, 2nd and 3rd for the execution of the task as a whole (overall) and for the execution of individual subtasks.

plete the subtasks in less time by issuing fewer commands. In particular, it can be observed that the FFOV configuration was largely preferred in the execution of subtask T2. This result was reasonably due to the fact that, when obstacles were to be avoided, the wider FOV made it more suited to operate with the semi-autonomous point-and-click video navigation modality, since participants could see more easily the point to click where they wanted to move the robot to. This observation is also confirmed by results concerning mental workload. In fact, the FFOV appeared to be the less cognitive demanding configuration compared to the other ones. It is also worth observing that this result may be also due to the presence of the pan-tilt function of the camera in the WFOV&PT configuration, since the number of commands that participants had to issue for moving the camera was larger than with the FFOV configuration. Concerning the awareness of the robot's surrounding environment, the WFOV&PT configuration was evaluated as the most effective. This result was reasonably due to the fact that the pan-tilt capability of the camera allowed users to better explore the environment without necessarily having to move the robot. Lastly, the radial distortions in the FFOV configuration were judged by participants as altering the perception of the environment on the robot's sides.

7   Conclusions and Future Work

In this paper, a user study was conducted to assess the impact on user experience of different camera configurations (in terms of FOV size and pan-tilt availability) in remote robots navigation tasks, both considering objective and subjective factors. Experimental results in terms of objective observations showed that camera configurations characterized by wider FOVs are more effective, as they allow users to carry out tasks in less time and with fewer navigation commands. Similarly, results obtained through subjective observations suggested that the FFOV was the less cognitive demanding configuration compared to WFOV&PT and NFOV. The WFOV&PT configuration was judged by the users as the configuration providing the highest situation awareness. Based on the preferences expressed after the experiments, this evidence was mainly motivated by the fact the FFOV configuration allowed users to spot a larger portion of the robot's surroundings by making it easier for them to exploit the semi-autonomous point-and-click video navigation modality. The WFOV&PT configuration was preferred because of the pan-tilt capability, which allowed users to better explore the scene without necessarily having to move the robot.

Future works will be aimed to explore the effect of dynamically combining the two wide-angle FOV configurations, by letting the users switch between them depending on the situation, thus benefiting from the advantages offered by both of them.

References

1. Bazzano, F., Lamberti, F., Sanna, A., Paravati, G., Gaspardone, M.: Comparing usability of user interfaces for robotic telepresence. In: Proceedings of the 12th International Joint Conference on Computer Vision, Imaging and Computer Graphics Theory and Applications - Volume 2: HUCAPP, VISIGRAPP 2017, pp. 46–54. INSTICC, SciTePress (2017). https://doi.org/10.5220/0006170300460054
2. Cain, B.: A review of the mental workload literature. Technical report, Defence Research And Development Toronto, Canada (2007)
3. Chen, J.Y., Haas, E.C., Barnes, M.J.: Human performance issues and user interface design for teleoperated robots. IEEE Trans. Syst. Man Cybern. Part C (Appl. Rev.) **37**(6), 1231–1245 (2007)
4. De Barros, P.G., Linderman, R.W.: A survey of user interfaces for robot teleoperation. Technical report Series, WPI-CS-TR-09-12 (2009)
5. Endsley, M.R.: Design and evaluation for situation awareness enhancement. In: Proceedings of the Human Factors and Ergonomics Society Annual Meeting, vol. 32, pp. 97–101. SAGE Publications (1988)
6. Endsley, M.R.: Measurement of situation awareness in dynamic systems. Hum. Factors **37**(1), 65–84 (1995)
7. Giuliano, L., Ng, M.E.K., Lupetti, M.L., Germak, C.: Virgil, robot for museum experience: study on the opportunity given by robot capability to integrate the actual museum visit. In: 7th International Conference on Intelligent Technologies for Interactive Entertainment, INTETAIN, pp. 222–223. IEEE (2015)
8. Hone, K.S., Graham, R.: Towards a tool for the subjective assessment of speech system interfaces (SASSI). Nat. Lang. Eng. **6**(3–4), 287–303 (2000)
9. Johnson, S., Rae, I., Mutlu, B., Takayama, L.: Can you see me now?: How field of view affects collaboration in robotic telepresence. In: Proceedings of the 33rd Annual ACM Conference on Human Factors in Computing Systems, pp. 2397–2406. ACM (2015)
10. Keyes, B.: Evolution of a telepresence robot interface. Ph.D. thesis. Citeseer (2007)
11. Kiselev, A., Kristoffersson, A., Loutfi, A.: The effect of field of view on social interaction in mobile robotic telepresence systems. In: Proceedings of the 2014 ACM/IEEE International Conference on Human-Robot Interaction, pp. 214–215. ACM (2014)
12. Kristoffersson, A., Coradeschi, S., Loutfi, A.: A review of mobile robotic telepresence. Adv. Hum.-Comput. Interact. **2013**, 3 (2013)
13. Lund, A.M.: Measuring usability with the use questionnaire12. Usability Interface **8**(2), 3–6 (2001)

14. Minsky, M.: Telepresence. Omni, pp. 45–51 (1980)
15. Nagahara, H., Yagi, Y., Kitamura, H., Yachida, M.: Super wide view tele-operation system. In: Proceedings of IEEE International Conference on Multisensor Fusion and Integration for Intelligent Systems, MFI 2003, pp. 149–154. IEEE (2003)
16. Nielsen, C.W., Goodrich, M.A.: Comparing the usefulness of video and map information in navigation tasks. In: Proceedings of the 1st ACM SIGCHI/SIGART Conference on Human-Robot Interaction, pp. 95–101. ACM (2006)
17. Potenza, A., Kiselev, A., Loutfi, A., Saffiotti, A.: Towards sliding autonomy in mobile robotic telepresence: a position paper. In: European Conference on Cognitive Ergonomics, ECCE 2017, 20–22 September 2017. Umeå University, Sweden (2017)
18. Rae, I., Venolia, G., Tang, J.C., Molnar, D.: A framework for understanding and designing telepresence. In: Proceedings of the 18th ACM Conference on Computer Supported Cooperative Work & Social Computing, pp. 1552–1566. ACM (2015)
19. Rubio, S., Díaz, E., Martín, J., Puente, J.M.: Evaluation of subjective mental workload: a comparison of SWAT, NASA-TLX, and workload profile methods. Appl. Psychol. **53**(1), 61–86 (2004)
20. Sheridan, T.B.: Teleoperation, telerobotics and telepresence: a progress report. Control Eng. Pract. **3**(2), 205–214 (1995)
21. Shiroma, N., Sato, N., Chiu, Y.h., Matsuno, F.: Study on effective camera images for mobile robot teleoperation. In: 13th IEEE International Workshop on Robot and Human Interactive Communication, ROMAN 2004, pp. 107–112. IEEE (2004)
22. Steinfeld, A., et al.: Common metrics for human-robot interaction. In: Proceedings of the 1st ACM SIGCHI/SIGART Conference on Human-Robot Interaction, pp. 33–40. ACM (2006)
23. Tittle, J.S., Roesler, A., Woods, D.D.: The remote perception problem. In: Proceedings of the Human Factors and Ergonomics Society Annual Meeting, vol. 46, pp. 260–264. SAGE Publications Sage CA, Los Angeles (2002)
24. Toris, R., et al.: Robot Web Tools: efficient messaging for cloud robotics. In: IEEE/RSJ International Conference on Intelligent Robots and Systems, IROS, pp. 4530–4537. IEEE (2015)
25. Vaughan, J., Kratz, S., Kimber, D.: Look where you're going: visual interfaces for robot teleoperation. In: 2016 25th IEEE International Symposium on Robot and Human Interactive Communication, RO-MAN, pp. 273–280. IEEE (2016)
26. Woods, D.D., Tittle, J., Feil, M., Roesler, A.: Envisioning human-robot coordination in future operations. IEEE Trans. Syst. Man Cybern. Part C (Appl. Rev.) **34**(2), 210–218 (2004)
27. Yanco, H.A., Drury, J.: "Where Am I?" Acquiring situation awareness using a remote robot platform. In: 2004 IEEE International Conference on Systems, Man and Cybernetics, vol. 3, pp. 2835–2840. IEEE (2004)

Computer Vision Theory and Applications

One-Shot Learned Priors in Augmented Active Appearance Models for Anatomical Landmark Tracking

Oliver Mothes[(✉)] and Joachim Denzler

Computer Vision Group, Friedrich Schiller University Jena, 07737 Jena, Germany
{oliver.mothes,joachim.denzler}@uni-jena.de
http://www.inf-cv.uni-jena.de

Abstract. In motion science, biology and robotics animal movement analyses are used for the detailed understanding of the human bipedal locomotion. For this investigations an immense amount of recorded image data has to be evaluated by biological experts. During this time-consuming evaluation single anatomical landmarks, for example bone ends, have to be located and annotated in each image. In this paper we show a reduction of this effort by automating the annotation with a minimum level of user interaction. Recent approaches, based on Active Appearance Models, are improved by priors based on anatomical knowledge and an online tracking method, requiring only a single labeled frame. In contrast, we propose a one-shot learned tracking-by-detection prior which overcomes the shortcomings of template drifts without increasing the number of training data. We evaluate our approach based on a variety of real-world X-ray locomotion datasets and show that our method outperforms recent state-of-the-art concepts for the task at hand.

Keywords: One-shot learned detector · X-ray videography ·
Graph-based landmark tracking · Animal locomotion analysis ·
Active appearance models

1 Introduction

The profound investigation of animal locomotion plays an important role in many fields of research, e.g., zoology, biomechanics, and robotics. For those analyses an immense amount of data has to be recorded to be able to derive a model or to refine existing ones. In this context, it is necessary to evaluate the collected data in detail, which requires considerable expenses by biological experts in terms of manually annotating every single measure [1,2]. Therefore, an automation of this task is highly preferable.

Reflective marker-based systems can be used to capture poses of single recorded frames [3]. However, since the animals locomotor system can be hidden by feathers or fur, the analysis of the inner skeleton is ideally more useful. In

© Springer Nature Switzerland AG 2019
A. P. Cláudio et al. (Eds.): VISIGRAPP 2017, CCIS 983, pp. 85–104, 2019.
https://doi.org/10.1007/978-3-030-12209-6_5

(a) C-arm X-ray acquisition system   (b) Acquisition setup

Fig. 1. The animals are recorded by a C-arm X-ray acquisition system while running through a treadmill.

order to analyze the skeletal locomotor system *in vivo*, high-speed X-ray acquisition is applied to obtain a detailed understanding of bone movements which are unseen using a standard RGB camera.

In an usual experimental setup, animals are placed on a treadmill which is enclosed by a C-arm X-ray acquisition system with two perpendicular detectors providing a top view (*dorsoventral* view) as well as a side view (*lateral* view) image of the entire locomotor system. To allow for a detailed biological evaluation, acquisition is performed at a high spatial and temporal resolution (1536 × 1024 pixels at 1000 FPS) on average for 1–2 s, resulting in up to 2000 frames. In Fig. 1 the experimental setup and the C-arm X-ray acquisition system is shown. In order to avoid the time-consuming task of manual annotation of single images [4], an automation of this task at a minimum level of user interaction is of great interest.

Haase and Denzler [5] applied Active Appearance Models (AAM) [6] to several bipedal bird locomotion datasets. One crucial conclusion of this work is that AAMs need substantial constraints from various sources to handle self-occluded anatomical landmark subsets. With the support of additional anatomical knowledge, i.e. body part segmentation, multi-view acquisition, and a local landmark tracking approach, for the animals lower limb system, the resulting Augmented AAM [5] provides robust results for the majority of the processed datasets. However, the applied online local tracking approach [7] suffers from a potential *template drift* caused by severe and even full occlusion of the tracked objects.

Motivated by this shortcoming, we propose in a more detailed elaboration our one-shot learned tracking-by-detection approach [8] which can handle these limitations by a global search. With one representative example of an annotated landmark subset a detector is learned. A two-staged graph-based tracking approach then provides motion trajectories through the whole sequence. Those trajectories are utilized as a prior in the Augmented Active Appearance Model framework together with priors from other sources as illustrated in Fig. 2. In our

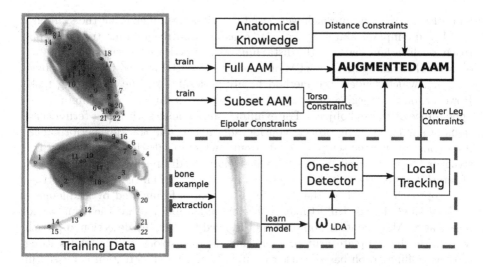

Fig. 2. Based on few annotated biplanar recorded training images an Augmented AAM [5] is trained, consisting of anatomical knowledge, a full multi-view AAM model, an AAM model of the torso landmark subset, epipolar constraints and a local tracking-by-detection prior introduced in [8].

experiments we show that this extension is able to improve previous results by up to 120 pixels in precision.

The remainder of the paper is structured as follows. In Sect. 2 we will give a brief overview of related work, followed by a short introduction to Active Appearance Models in Sect. 3 and its augmentation in Sect. 4. Afterwards, our one-shot learned tracking-by-detection approach will be introduced in Sect. 5. An evaluation of the detection and tracking results is presented in Sect. 6. Finally, Sect. 7 concludes the paper with a short discussion.

2 Related Work and Motivation

For anatomical landmark tracking Haase et al. [9] applied Active Appearance Models [6] to X-ray locomotion scenarios. They showed that this generative model is well suited for the task at hand since training requires only a small amount of low contrast images. However, this approach has its weaknesses for a certain subset of landmarks–primarily landmarks of the lower limb system–undergo severe occlusions. They extended their approach in [10] to multi-view AAMs [11], which is more robust and accurate for torso landmark subsets compared to the single view approach. By concatenating corresponding landmarks of the second view the model became more general. The usage of additional constraints, especially for the distal limb landmarks, supporting the multi-view AAM, leads to a holistic model, referred to as Augmented AAM [5]. Anatomical knowledge, the multi-view information formulated as epipolar geometry, and a local tracking approach were used as priors for augmenting the standard AAM. Subtemplate Matching (STM) [7] as a data-driven online tracking approach localizes landmarks of the distal limb segments. Based on the small number of available training images, STM only needs one initial labeled frame for robust tracking, which renders the method highly preferable for the underlying task. However, online tracking fails in the case of severe occlusions and temporal disappearance of tracked objects. For example, subsequences with long-term occlusions of similar crossing objects considerably affects the tracking performance. As a consequence the template drift occurs, which results in a total loss of the structure to be tracked. Sequences with temporal disappearance of the object of interest produces a similar effect. An extension of STM is a pictorial structure approach [12], where the distal limb system is formulated by a kinematic chain of single bones. Unfortunately, the extended method has the same weaknesses as STM. In contrast, our one-shot learned tracking-by-detection approach will tackle the template drift problem and handles strong texture shifts using a robust offline graph-based tracker even when the patch detection is missed in single frames.

Offline tracking algorithms are used to track objects in sequences [13,14] and they are often formulated as a graph theoretical problem [15–18]. First and foremost, reliable object detections serve as basis for all tracking approaches. Many object detection methods are based on local image features like HOG [19,20] or SIFT [21] to detect objects in every single frame. In order to localize an object of interest a *Support Vector Machine* (SVM) or *Decision Trees* [22] are used for classifying positive and negative image patches in a sliding window manner [20]. However, SVM training is computationally expensive–especially when applying hard negative mining–and need a huge amount of training data.

Based on the fact that the amount of training data in our application scenario is limited, we use Whitened HOG features and an LDA model [23] for detecting landmark subsets, which only needs one single positive example for robust detector training.

More recently, Coarse-to-fine Convolutional Network Cascades [24,25] are designed in a multi-level architecture for facial landmark detection. By fusing the outputs of each level of the multiple networks a robust and accurate estimation is possible. However, the Convolutional Neural Network frameworks have a complex structure and need a lot of data for training which is contrary to our pre-condition of a very limited number of training data.

The main contribution of this paper is a one-shot learned tracking-by-detection approach using a linear detector utilizing *Histogram of Oriented Gradients* (HOG) features and a classifier based on the *Linear Discriminant Analysis* in a sliding-window manner to detect the landmark subset of the lower limb system. The detection method provides two important advantages. On the one hand, many detector models for a sequence can be trained in a very short time and on the other hand the model training requires only one representative positive example which is important for the desired small annotation effort. Additionally, we use smart convolutions to speed up sliding window manner detections.

Subsequently, a two-staged graph-based tracking algorithm is used to determine landmark subset trajectories through the whole sequence. In contrast to STM tracking [7], template drifts are reduced or even eliminated since landmark trajectories are optimized globally. The single landmark tracks of the lower limb system serve as important prior knowledge for the fitting task of an probabilistic Augmented AAM model, trained with only 10 annotated examples.

3   Active Appearance Models

An AAM is a parametric statistical generative model proposed in [26] consisting of a shape component and a shape-free texture component. The interrelationship of shape and texture is used to model visual appearance of different object classes. Object classes, e.g. anatomical structures, represented by a set of landmarks and a spanned texture within these landmarks can be modeled by a AAM. Training data consists of N images $I_1, ..., I_N$ with corresponding landmark annotations $l_1, ..., l_N$ for relevant anatomical structures.

Shape Model

The shape model can be described as the variability of the given landmark coordinates $l_1, ..., l_N$ with $l_n = (x_{n,1}, y_{n,1}, ..., x_{n,L}, y_{n,L})^T \in \mathbb{R}^{2L}$ of the training data. After aligning the N landmark sets via *Procrustes Analysis* [27] to shapes $s_1, ..., s_n$, the variation of the aligned shapes is parameterized by applying *Principle Component Analysis* PCA to the shape matrix $S = (s_1 - \overline{s}, ..., s_N - \overline{s})$ where $\overline{s}$ represents the mean shape with:

$$\overline{s} = \frac{1}{N} \sum_{n=1}^{N} s_n. \tag{1}$$

A shape s can be expressed as a linear shape model with $K \leq rank(S)$ orthonormal shape eigenvectors P_s, a K-dimensional vector of *shape parameters* b_s and the *mean shape* $\overline{s}$ is given by:

$$s \approx \overline{s} + P_s b_s, \quad with \quad b_s = P_s^T (s - \overline{s}). \tag{2}$$

The number of K *shape eigenvectors* is typically chosen between 95% and 98% [28] of the variance of the shapes S.

Texture Model

The texture model of the AAM build the sub-model describing the variation of the shape-free textures of our object class. To guarantee the shape-freeness, each image texture $I_1, ..., I_N$ is warped from its landmark configuration l_n into the mean shape $\overline{s}$. First *Delaunay Triangulation* [29] is used to triangulating the reference shape. Afterwards, a piecewise affine warp based on the landmark triangulation approximates the global warping. The warping process is described in more detail in [30].

To obtain the linear texture model g the very same PCA-based procedure is applied to the mean-centered shape-normalized image vectors of $G = (g_1 - \overline{g}, ..., g_N - \overline{g}) \in \mathbb{R}^{M \times N}$:

$$g \approx \overline{g} + P_g b_g \quad with \quad b_g = P_g^T (g - \overline{g}) \tag{3}$$

with the *texture parameters* b_g, the *texture eigenvectors* P_g and the *mean texture* $\overline{g}$ with

$$\overline{g} = \frac{1}{N} \sum_{n=1}^{N} g_n. \tag{4}$$

As before, the number of covered texture eigenvectors is related to a certain amount of texture variance.

Combined Model

The shape model and the texture model are two independently estimated submodels of an *independent AAM* [30] which can represent a valid object instance. To avoid invalid combinations of shape and texture parameters the *combined AAM* restricts the shape and texture parameter combination to the domains of the training images. By concatenating the variance-normalized shape and texture parameter vectors and applying PCA again, we obtain:

$$c \approx P_c b_c \quad with \quad b_c = P_c^T c, \tag{5}$$

where b_c are the *combined parameters* and P_c are the *combined eigenvectors*. Every mean-free c_n of $C = (c_1, ..., c_N) \in \mathbb{R}^{(K \times K') \times N}$ is denoted like in [6] with:

$$c_n = \begin{pmatrix} b_s \\ w \cdot b_g \end{pmatrix}. \tag{6}$$

The weighting factor w is used to balance the individual influence of shape and texture model. After applying PCA, again, the number of covered combined eigenvectors is related to a certain amount of variance.

Model Fitting

After training, the AAM model can be used to find a best fitting for the model parameter vector $\hat{b}_c$ to a given input image by minimizing the squared distance $\delta g = (g_{image} - g_{model})$ of the given image and the model appearance:

$$\hat{b}_c = \underset{b_c}{\arg\min} \, \delta g^T \delta g, \tag{7}$$

where we make use of a assumed linear relationship [6, 26]

$$\delta b_c = A \delta g. \tag{8}$$

4   Augmented Active Appearance Models

Augmented AAMs (AAAMs) proposed in [5] extend the fitting process of standard AAMs by providing additional prior knowledge. However, the accuracy of standard AAMs is prone to occlusions and unseen cases due to the linear shape and texture modeling. To overcome these limitations prior knowledge from different sources can be incorporated. In addition to multi-view information [10], the authors of [5] use various types of constraints to augment the standard AAM. Constraints like subset AAM, anatomical knowledge, epipolar geometry and a local tracking method [7] for the animals lower limb system are used to increase the fitting performance and overcome the typical AAM weakness based on linear shape and texture modeling. We implement the idea of a combined approach by reformulating the AAM fitting as a maximum *a-posteriori* (MAP) framework as in [5] with a *conditional independent* input image I and every provided fitting constraints π:

$$
\begin{aligned}
\hat{b}_{c,MAP} &= \underset{b_c}{\operatorname{argmax}}\, p(b_c | I, \pi) \\
&= \underset{b_c}{\operatorname{argmax}}\, p(I | b_c) \cdot p(\pi | b_c) \cdot p(b_c).
\end{aligned}
\tag{9}
$$

For input image data I it is sufficient to use only a cropped version g_{image}, defined by the AAM shape configuration. The likelihood can than be modeled as a Gaussian distribution $g_{image} | b_c \sim \mathcal{N}(g_{model}, \Sigma_{g_{image}-g_{model}})$ where $\Sigma_{g_{image}-g_{model}}$ will be estimated in AAM training. The prior term $p(\pi | b_c)$ performs the integration of all the constraints π into the AAM fitting process, where π represents the differences between the given target constraint values and the values based on the AAM parameters b_c. Again a Gaussian distribution $\pi | b_c \sim \mathcal{N}(0, \Sigma_\pi)$ will be assumed. The term $p(b_c)$ can be modeled as *maximum likelihood* estimation using a uniform distribution. For more information about the prior modeling of Augmented AAMs please refer [5].

A serious weakness of standard AAM is tracking landmarks of the lower limbs of the animal locomotor system. To overcome this drawback, a local tracking constraint π_{local} with the results of an online tracking approach [7], localizing those critical landmarks, is included in Augmented AAM framework.

5   One-Shot Learned Tracking Approach

For a reliable data-driven tracking of landmarks of lower limb landmarks, initially, a sophisticated detector is of great importance. As detection of single landmarks is more complicated, a detection of landmark subset patches is of advantage. The landmarks of single bones can be described as such a subset.

In the following sections we introduce a one-shot learned tracking-by-detection approach. In Sect. 5.1 the bone detection method will be discussed, while Sect. 5.2 focuses on bone tracking and landmark retrieval.

5.1 One-Shot Learned Detector

To distinguish positive and negative examples, the combination of HOG features and SVM classification was the most commonly used approach in the past decade [19,20]. Unfortunately, SVM training and testing is computationally expensive, especially when applying hard negative mining with a huge amount of training data.

To overcome this limitation, Hariharan et al. introduces in [23] an object detection approach based on augmented HOG features [20] and a classifier based on linear discriminant analysis (LDA).

Their model relies on the assumption that the distributions of object instances (positives) and background examples (negatives) follow both a Gaussian distribution. Thereby, the major computational effort is caused by the estimation of the background statistics (corresponding to the negative samples). Estimating the covariance matrix Σ_0 and the mean vector μ_0 has to be done only ones.

For every positive class only the respective mean vector μ_1 has to be computed to obtain a discriminative linear separation of the two classes

$$\omega_{LDA} = \Sigma_0^{-1}(\mu_1 - \mu_0). \tag{10}$$

A sliding window-based method and template matching is used to compute similarity scores of a feature vector x by a linear *Whitened Histograms of Orientations* (WHO) detector $f(x) = \langle \omega_{LDA}, x \rangle$. Dense sampling of these features allows for matching the image templates.

To speed up the evaluation the authors of [31] changed the order of computations and reformulated the sampling task as efficient convolutions. The entire set of window patches with D_C feature dimensions in the dense tiled grid of $T \times T$ cells are evaluated by adding D convolutions of 1×1 filters with corresponding feature planes. Consequently, derived from $D = T \cdot T \cdot D_C$, we obtain the feature extraction as efficient convolutions.

The responding normalized similarity scores of every window matching is used as the detection score of a detection hypothesis. Unfortunately, the objects of interest in our application are rotated within a certain range. Accordingly, in the detection process, the input image needs to be rotated. As a result, the detection result at a specific location in the image contains a lot of multiple detections of the same object depending on the used angular resolution. Each detection hypothesis contains position information, a detection angle and a detection score.

For the tracking algorithm the detection results are filtered to obtain more robust object hypotheses. First, the normalized detection maps I_t of every frame t are smoothed by accumulating Gaussian filter kernels $G(x, y, \sigma)$ weighted by the corresponding detection score resulting in a smoothed detection map O_t with

$$O_t(i, j) = \sum_{x=-\frac{m}{2}}^{\frac{m}{2}} \sum_{y=-\frac{n}{2}}^{\frac{n}{2}} I_t(i + x, j + y) G(x, y, \sigma), \tag{11}$$

where $m = n$ describe the filter size of $G(x, y, \sigma)$. In order to extract single detection hypotheses with new detection positions, *Non-Maximum Suppression* is applied to O_t. Based on the assumption that the highest detection score yields the highest similarity with the model, the related detection score and rotation angle result from the rotation angle with the highest detection score within a local neighborhood defined by half the object size around the detection hypotheses is selected. Finally, the detection scores of all frames have to be normalized again.

5.2 Graph-Based Tracking

To associate the detection results of Sect. 5.1 to whole object trajectories, a reliable tracking algorithm is necessary. The graph-based tracking approach inspired by [17] uses the detection results of Sect. 5.1 and is divided into two steps. In the first stage (*tracklet extraction*), the algorithm extracts segments of robust object sub-trajectories by searching similar detected objects of subsequent frames. Afterwards, in second stage (*tracklet linking*), the extracted sub-trajectories are linked to full object trajectories.

Tracklet Extraction. A Directed Acyclic Graph (DAG) $\mathcal{G}$ is formulated where every detection hypothesis represents a node. We define detection hypotheses $H = \{H_0, ..., H_T\}$ with $H_t = \{h_{t,0}, ..., h_{t,K_t}\}$ where $h_{t,i}$ represents the ith detection hypothesis of frame t. Furthermore, we add a virtual source h_{source} and a sink node h_{sink} to $\mathcal{G} = (H, E, d), E \subseteq H \times H$, which are fully connected to all other nodes $h_{t,i}$. The edge weights of the DAG depend on the number of detection feature weights d_p, as for example spatial d_s, temporal d_t and angular distances d_a, but also detection scores or other detection results of adjacent detection hypotheses. These detection feature weights we call detection priors. In Fig. 3 the tracklet extraction graph $\mathcal{G}$ is illustrated.

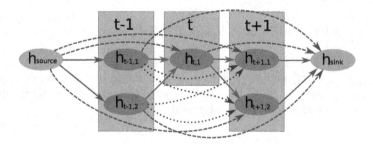

Fig. 3. Sub-trajectories of objects are extracted by formulating the detection hypotheses as a directed acylic graph with edge weights influenced by constrained detection information like spatial, temporal and angular distances between object hypotheses. Applying iteratively a shortest path algorithm extracts robust object sub-trajectories.

However, the non-negative edge cost function $d : \boldsymbol{H} \times \boldsymbol{H}$ with P detection features is calculated unlike [17] as follows:

$$d(\boldsymbol{h}_{t,i}, \boldsymbol{h}_{t+\Delta t,j}) = \sum_{p=0}^{P} \alpha_p \cdot d_p(\boldsymbol{h}_{t,i}, \boldsymbol{h}_{t+\Delta t,j}) \tag{12}$$

$$r.t. \quad \Delta t > 0.$$

The inner weight parameters α_p of the single tracking priors with $\sum_{p=0}^{P} \alpha_p = 1$ regularizes the influence of individual priors. Finding an optimal set of weights automatically is subject of future research. The edge weights between the virtual nodes, $\boldsymbol{h}_{source}$ and $\boldsymbol{h}_{sink}$, result from the temporal distance to the respective node. Before using a shortest path algorithm like *Dijkstra* [32] or *Bellman-Ford* [33], thresholds, θ_{min} and θ_{max}, based on the used tracking priors have to be defined, such that: $\theta_{min} \leq d_p \leq \theta_{max}$. The thresholding sets constraints for the first stage and set edges which do not match the pre-condition to infinity.

Therefore, this constraints guarantee reliable path segments of related detection hypothesis of the same object and prevents mistakenly created shortest paths through the whole graph. In the DAG the edge weights of extracted paths are subsequently set to infinity to avoid multiple extraction of identical tracklets. The tracklet extraction process stops, if no further tracklet can be found, i.e., the tracklet length is smaller than 2.

Tracklet Linking. Afterwards, the extracted tracklets are linked again to whole object trajectories within a second DAG $\mathcal{G}' = (\boldsymbol{H}', \boldsymbol{E}', d')$, $\boldsymbol{E}' \subseteq \boldsymbol{H}' \times \boldsymbol{H}$, where $\boldsymbol{H}' = \{\tau_0, ..., \tau_{K'}\}$ are the estimated tracklet hypothesis and $d' :\subseteq \boldsymbol{H}' \times \boldsymbol{H}'$ a non-negative cost function. In Fig. 4 the tracklet linking graph is illustrated. The weight $d'(\tau_i, \tau_j)$ between the two tracklets τ_i and τ_j is influenced by the spatial and temporal information of the boundary detection hypotheses of the tracklets. Edges between two tracklet nodes become non-infinity when τ_i ends before τ_j starts, more formal:

$$d'(\tau_i, \tau_j) = \begin{cases} d'_{spatial}(\tau_i, \tau_j) + d'_{temporal}(\tau_i, \tau_j) & t_{max}(\tau_i) < t_{min}(\tau_j) \\ \infty & t_{max}(\tau_i) \geq t_{min}(\tau_j), \end{cases} \tag{13}$$

where $d'_{temporal}(\tau_i, \tau_j)$ and $d'_{spatial}(\tau_i, \tau_j)$ is calculated like in d as the temporal and Euclidean distance. Since the single objects in tracklets can have different velocities, this information also can be used in d'.

6   Experiments

In this section we evaluate the performance of the Augmented AAM framework extended by the introduced landmark detection and tracking techniques. We conduct our experiments on five avian locomotion datasets of several bird species with focus on sequences showing long-term object occlusion. The datasets were

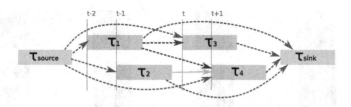

Fig. 4. Another directed acyclic graph is formulated by the extracted tracklets. Applying again a shortest path algorithm extracts full object trajectories.

Table 1. An overview of analyzed datasets [8].

Name	Species	Frames	Labeled frames
Q1	Quail	706	22
Q2	Quail	701	15
T1	Tinamou	776	37
J1	Jackdaw	1201	46
J2	Jackdaw	1051	36

recorded by a high-speed X-ray acquisition system at 1000 Hz with a resolution of 1536×1024 pixels. Table 1 summarizes the analyzed datasets. In Sect. 6.1 we compare different detection methods applied to two selected datasets with considerable self occlusions. Afterwards, results of the graph-based tracking algorithm are shown in Sect. 6.2 which uses the detections retrieved as described in Sect. 6.1. Finally, we use the tracking results in Sect. 6.3 as powerful priors for the Augmented AAM framework.

6.1 Comparison of the Detector Models

In general, detector models are learned from positive object examples. The number and quality of these examples is a crucial factor for their accuracy. However, in our application the number of annotated frames should be as much as necessary, but as few as possible. Another challenge for learning a reliable detector in our application is the visual appearance of the input images. X-ray acquisition systems provide grayscale images of low contrast. Accordingly, the detector has to overcome issues with respect to appearance and amount of positive training examples. Learned detector models using patches around landmarks are not representative enough concerning the high intra-class variability. Figure 5 should illustrate this intra-class variability with the help of visualized HOG features. Instead of using such landmark patches, the usage of subsets of landmarks is highly preferable to obtain a representative robust detector model based on examples with a low intra-class variability. Hence, the usage of corresponding landmarks of the lower limb bones (*proximal* and *distal* landmarks) are used in our application to define subsets and new patches for our detector. This is done by creating rotation normalized bounding boxes around the landmark subset.

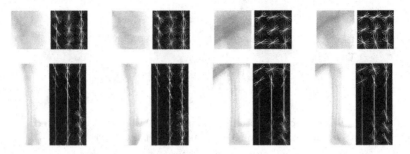

Fig. 5. Image patches of the proximal *Tarsometatarsus* landmark (above) and corresponding bone (below) with visualized HOG features from different time steps of a sequence.

Figure 6 confirms our assumption that using landmark subset patches instead of patches around single landmarks for learning a detector model provides much better detection performance. In our experiments we applied four different detector methods to the mentioned landmark subsets: HOG features trained with a linear SVM using all positive examples, a WHO model trained with all positive examples and as well as a HOG-SVM and a WHO model trained with only one-shot, in other words, one single example (one-shot learning).

HOG. The feature extraction is based on [19] with a gradient quantization to 9 orientation bins, a cell size of 8×8 pixels, a block size of 4×4 cells, and a block spacing stride of 8 pixels. A linear SVM model is trained using all annotated frames (positive bone examples) in the training data. Another SVM model is trained with only one representative example of the training data. To generate negative examples, window patches were clipped around the positive example patches. During detection the image is rotated between $-90°$ and $+90°$ with respect to biological constraints of the bone landmark subsets. For every rotation the detector obtains object hypotheses with information regarding position, detection score, and rotation angle using a sliding window technique. The chosen rotational resolution depends on the patch size. We used a degree step of 1.

WHO. For the WHO model ω_{LDA} the background statistics has to be computed first. Therefore, N_0 randomly unlabeled image patches were selected from the sequence and the mean μ_0 is estimated by computing the mean HOG feature $\mu_0 = \frac{1}{N_0} \sum_{i=0}^{N_0} E[x_i]$. The covariance Σ_0 is estimated using the *spatial autocorrelation function* [23]. With the assumption of independent and identically Gaussian distributed positive and negative examples the model training can be performed using only one positive example. Since the LDA model ω_{LDA} is not rotational invariant, the sliding window technique has to be performed for multiple image rotations, as well. In a further experiment we compare the detection methods for all datasets of Table 1. We compared HOG-SVM models with WHO models. Both are trained with all positive landmark and bone examples. Afterwards, models with only one representative example were trained. Since the detection method of Sect. 5.1 applied to landmark patches yields countless

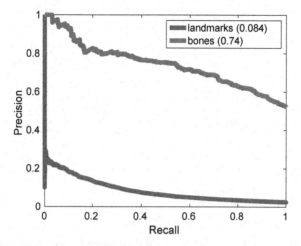

Fig. 6. Detector models were trained for landmark subsets patches (bones) and the single landmark patches of the lower limb landmarks of all datasets of Table 1 [8].

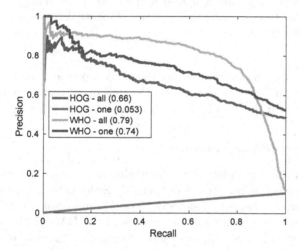

Fig. 7. The Precision-Recall (PR) curve illustrates the performance comparison of the applied detection methods to all datasets of Table 1, respectively [8].

numbers of false positives and missed detections, we use for further experiments only those detection results based on the bone patches. Figure 7 illustrates the comparison of the presented detection methods, which exhibit different detection performances. Both models using WHO features clearly outperform the results using HOG features, because the estimated background statistics Σ_0 has a large influence on the linear separation. Regarding the whitening of the WHO features the performance of trained WHO models are nearly equivalent, regardless of the number of training samples. The poor performance of the model trained with

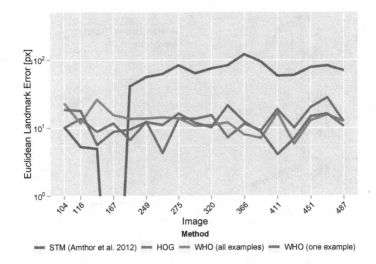

Fig. 8. The detection result for the Q2-dataset from Sect. 6.1 were applied to the two-staged graph-based tracker and compared to the STM approach of [7]. The landmark error observed over time visualizes the drawback of the STM for cases of occlusion and temporal disappearance [8].

one HOG feature example is caused by the weak representation of the class, as a linear separation is nearly impossible. Because of its very poor performance, the one-shot learned HOG-SVM model is ignored for the following experiments.

6.2 Online vs. Offline Tracking

In this section the graph-based tracking algorithm described in Sect. 5.2 is applied to the detection hypotheses of Sect. 6.1. Every detection provides a position information, a detection angle, a detection frame number, and a detection score. Based on this information the weights of the DAG $\mathcal{G}$ are calculated as described in Sect. 5.2, where d_s represents the spatial distance, d_a the angular distance, d_t the temporal distance and d_c the inverted summarized detection scores between two nodes. After normalizing all weights d_p we choose uniform inner weights α_p for the edge cost function d. Additionally, in the second stage (*tracklet linking*), the mean velocity is calculated using position information of all detections covered by the respective tracklets. Based on the anatomical knowledge, especially the length of the extracted bone examples described in Sect. 6.1 and the detection angle information, it is possible to recover the *proximal* and *distal* landmark positions. Figure 8 illustrates the comparison of the STM baseline with our tracking results applied to the Q2-dataset. For all remaining datasets the Euclidean tracking error plots show similar results. The graph of the Euclidean tracking error clearly shows the template drift of the STM algorithm at time step 190 after the initial position at time step 167 where the pixel error was close to 0 pixels. All other graphs show robust trajectories of the

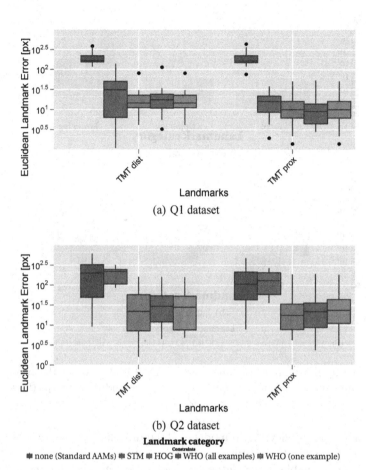

(a) Q1 dataset

(b) Q2 dataset

Landmark category
Constraints
⊞ none (Standard AAMs) ⊞ STM ⊞ HOG ⊞ WHO (all examples) ⊞ WHO (one example)

Fig. 9. Prior for the Augmented AAM: four different local tracking approaches were analyzed with respect to Euclidean landmark errors of the *proximal* and *distal Tarsometatatarsi* landmarks of the lower limb system [8]. The Standard AAM and the Augmented AAM utilizing the STM approach as local prior serve as baseline for the comparison to our approach (see Sect. 6.2).

introduced detection methods with an error of only 10 pixel on average. The trajectories based on the WHO one-shot detector model achieves the nearly same performance like the detectors trained with all positive examples while only one single training example was used.

6.3 A One-Shot Learned Prior for AAAMs

As an extension of the Augmented AAM framework [5], illustrated in Fig. 2, we replaced the utilized local tracking prior π_{local} [7] by our tracking-by-detection approach from Sect. 6.2 which is able to recover lost templates based on global optimization in contrast to [7]. The comparison is conducted for all datasets of

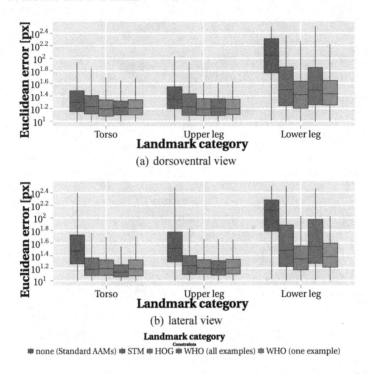

(a) dorsoventral view

(b) lateral view

Landmark category
Constraints
▦ none (Standard AAMs) ▦ STM ▦ HOG ▦ WHO (all examples) ▦ WHO (one example)

Fig. 10. For the five datasets of Table 1 an averaged evaluation of the two different views illustrates the Euclidean landmark error of three landmark groups (torso, upper leg, lower leg) [8].

Table 1. First, a multi-view AAM model of all landmarks and the torso landmark subset were trained with 10 annotated frames and is used as torso constraint. Based on both available views (*lateral* and *dorsoventral*) the epipolar geometry with the help of the Fundamental Matrix is estimated and is used as epipolar constraints. Anatomical knowledge, in terms of biological distance constraints were obtained via image segmentation as proposed in [5]. Together with one of the mentioned tracking approaches as lower leg constraints the AAAM is formulated as in Sect. 4. In our experiments we compared the influence of the different tracking priors. Figure 9 illustrates the Euclidean landmark error of the local tracking approaches of Sect. 6.2 applied to the Augmented AAM framework of [5]. It can be clearly seen that the template drift problem of the Q2-dataset (see Fig. 8) using the STM tracking approach substantially affects the performance of the entire AAAM framework. In contrast, our proposed tracking prior allows for highly accurate results of the combined AAAM approach without the loss of individual landmark subsets. In Fig. 10 the average error over all sequences of Table 1 is shown. It can clearly be seen that our presented tracking-by-detection prior outperforms the online tracking approach even in the case of using only one single example for training. A qualitative comparison can also be seen in Tables 2 and 3.

Table 2. Qualitative results of selected frames of the J2-dataset illustrate the tracked landmarks by the augmented AAM using the STM tracking prior [7] and our one-shot learned tracking-by-detection prior [8].

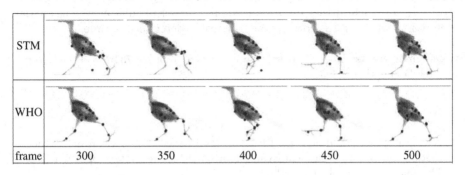

STM					
WHO					
frame	300	350	400	450	500

Table 3. Augmented AAM using the STM tracking approach [7] and our one-shot learned tracking-by-detection method [8] as local tracking prior shows in comparison to each other nearly the same accurate results applied to the T1-dataset.

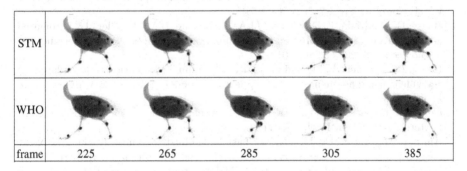

STM					
WHO					
frame	225	265	285	305	385

7 Conclusions

In this paper we proposed a new tracking-by-detection method for anatomical landmark retrieval in animal locomotion analysis. The main contribution is a one-shot learned tracking-by-detection prior supporting an probabilistic Augmented AAM framework. In particular, a linear detector was trained in a very fast manner with only one representative positive example of a desired landmark subset. Afterwards, a two-staged graph-based tracking algorithm generates in two stages whole trajectories of the detected hypotheses and recovers the single landmarks of the subset. Finally, the landmark tracking results are used as a prior for an AAM to support the model-driven baseline algorithm and solve the model fitting task for occluded and temporally disappeared landmark subsets. In our experiments, we compared our approach to an online local tracking method using a frame-by-frame template matching strategy which is very accurate in sequences with partial self occlusion, but fails in case of long-term full occlusions. Additionally, we showed that this extension is able to improve previous results by up to 120 pixels in precision. The tracking precision of the proposed algorithm can reach further improvements, if a higher angular as well as spatial resolution is used, which, however, also increases detection runtime.

Acknowledgments. The research was supported by grant DE 735/8-3 of the German Research Foundation (DFG).

References

1. Nyakatura, J.A., Andrada, E., Blickhan, R., Fischer, M.S.: Avian bipedal locomotion. In: 5th International Symposium on Adaptive Motion of Animals and Machines (AMAM). Elsevier (2011)
2. Andrada, E., Nyakatura, J.A., Bergmann, F., Blickhan, R.: Adjustments of global and local hindlimb properties during terrestrial locomotion of the common quail (coturnix coturnix). J. Exp. Biol. (2013)
3. Sigal, L., Balan, A.O., Black, M.J.: HumanEva: synchronized video and motion capture dataset and baseline algorithm for evaluation of articulated human motion. Int. J. Comput. Vis. **87**(1–2), 4 (2010)
4. Haase, D., Andrada, E., Nyakatura, J.A., Kilbourne, B.M., Denzler, J.: Automated approximation of center of mass position in X-ray sequences of animal locomotion. J. Biomech. **46**, 2082–2086 (2013)
5. Haase, D., Denzler, J.: 2D and 3D analysis of animal locomotion from biplanar X-ray videos using augmented active appearance models. EURASIP J. Image Video Process. (2013)
6. Cootes, T.F., Edwards, G.J., Taylor, C.J.: Active appearance models. IEEE Trans. Pattern Anal. Mach. Intell. (2001)
7. Amthor, M., Haase, D., Denzler, J.: Fast and robust landmark tracking in X-ray locomotion sequences containing severe occlusions. In: International Workshop on Vision, Modelling, and Visualization (VMV). Eurographics Association (2012)
8. Mothes, O., Denzler, J.: Anatomical landmark tracking by one-shot learned priors for augmented active appearance models. In: International Conference on Computer Vision Theory and Applications (VISAPP), pp. 246–254 (2017)
9. Haase, D., Denzler, J.: Anatomical landmark tracking for the analysis of animal locomotion in X-ray videos using active appearance models. In: Heyden, A., Kahl, F. (eds.) SCIA 2011. LNCS, vol. 6688, pp. 604–615. Springer, Heidelberg (2011). https://doi.org/10.1007/978-3-642-21227-7_56
10. Haase, D., Nyakatura, J.A., Denzler, J.: Multi-view active appearance models for the X-ray based analysis of avian bipedal locomotion. In: Mester, R., Felsberg, M. (eds.) DAGM 2011. LNCS, vol. 6835, pp. 11–20. Springer, Heidelberg (2011). https://doi.org/10.1007/978-3-642-23123-0_2
11. Lelieveldt, B., Üzümcü, M., van der Geest, R., Reiber, J., Sonka, M.: Multi-view active appearance models for consistent segmentation of multiple standard views: application to long- and short-axis cardiac MR images. In: International Congress Series (2003)
12. Amthor, M., Haase, D., Denzler, J.: Robust pictorial structures for X-ray animal skeleton tracking. In: International Conference on Computer Vision Theory and Applications (VISAPP). SCITEPRESS (2014)

13. Andriluka, M., Roth, S., Schiele, B.: Monocular 3D pose estimation and tracking by detection. In: 2010 IEEE Conference on Computer Vision and Pattern Recognition (CVPR). IEEE (2010)
14. Li, L., Nawaz, T., Ferryman, J.: Pets 2015: datasets and challenge. In: 2015 12th IEEE International Conference on Advanced Video and Signal Based Surveillance (AVSS). IEEE (2015)
15. Zhang, L., Li, Y., Nevatia, R.: Global data association for multi-object tracking using network flows. In: IEEE Conference on Computer Vision and Pattern Recognition, CVPR 2008. IEEE (2008)
16. Berclaz, J., Fleuret, F., Türetken, E., Fua, P.: Multiple object tracking using k-shortest paths optimization. IEEE Trans. Pattern Anal. Mach. Intell. **33**, 1806–1819 (2011)
17. Jiang, X., Haase, D., Körner, M., Bothe, W., Denzler, J.: Accurate 3D multi-marker tracking in X-ray cardiac sequences using a two-stage graph modeling approach. In: Wilson, R., Hancock, E., Bors, A., Smith, W. (eds.) CAIP 2013. LNCS, vol. 8048, pp. 117–125. Springer, Heidelberg (2013). https://doi.org/10.1007/978-3-642-40246-3_15
18. Dehghan, A., Modiri Assari, S., Shah, M.: GMMCP tracker: globally optimal generalized maximum multi clique problem for multiple object tracking. In: The IEEE Conference on Computer Vision and Pattern Recognition (CVPR). IEEE (2015)
19. Dalal, N., Triggs, B.: Histograms of oriented gradients for human detection. In: IEEE Computer Society Conference on Computer Vision and Pattern Recognition, CVPR 2005. IEEE (2005)
20. Felzenszwalb, P.F., Girshick, R.B., McAllester, D., Ramanan, D.: Object detection with discriminatively trained part-based models. IEEE Trans. Pattern Anal. Mach. Intell. **32**, 1627–1645 (2010)
21. Lowe, D.G.: Distinctive image features from scale-invariant keypoints. Int. J. Comput. Vis. **60**, 91–110 (2004)
22. Breiman, L.: Classification and Regression Trees. CRC Press, Boca Raton (2017)
23. Hariharan, B., Malik, J., Ramanan, D.: Discriminative decorrelation for clustering and classification. In: Fitzgibbon, A., Lazebnik, S., Perona, P., Sato, Y., Schmid, C. (eds.) ECCV 2012. LNCS, vol. 7575, pp. 459–472. Springer, Heidelberg (2012). https://doi.org/10.1007/978-3-642-33765-9_33
24. Sun, Y., Wang, X., Tang, X.: Deep convolutional network cascade for facial point detection. In: 2013 IEEE Conference on Computer Vision and Pattern Recognition (CVPR). IEEE (2013)
25. Zhou, E., Fan, H., Cao, Z., Jiang, Y., Yin, Q.: Extensive facial landmark localization with coarse-to-fine convolutional network cascade. In: 2013 IEEE International Conference on Computer Vision Workshops (ICCVW). IEEE (2013)
26. Cootes, T.F., Edwards, G.J., Taylor, C.J.: Active appearance models. In: Burkhardt, H., Neumann, B. (eds.) ECCV 1998. LNCS, vol. 1407, pp. 484–498. Springer, Heidelberg (1998). https://doi.org/10.1007/BFb0054760
27. Kendall, D.G.: Shape manifolds, procrustean metrics, and complex projective spaces. Bull. London Math. Soc. **16**, 81–121 (1984)
28. Jolliffe, I.: Principal Component Analysis. Springer Series in Statistics. Springer, Heidelberg (2002). https://doi.org/10.1007/b98835
29. Berg, M., Cheong, O., Kreveld, M., Overmars, M.: Computational Geometry: Algorithms and Applications, 3rd edn. Springer, Heidelberg (2008). https://doi.org/10.1007/978-3-540-77974-2
30. Baker, S., Matthews, I.: Lucas-kanade 20 years on: a unifying framework. Int. J. Comput. Vis. **56**(3), 221–255 (2004)

31. Freytag, A., Schadt, A., Denzler, J.: Interactive image retrieval for biodiversity research. In: Gall, J., Gehler, P., Leibe, B. (eds.) GCPR 2015. LNCS, vol. 9358, pp. 129–141. Springer, Cham (2015). https://doi.org/10.1007/978-3-319-24947-6_11
32. Dijkstra, E.W.: A note on two problems in connexion with graphs. Numer. Math. **1**(1), 269–271 (1959)
33. Bellman, R.: On a routing problem. Q. Appl. Math. **16**(1), 87–90 (1958)

Line-Based SLAM Considering Prior Distribution of Distance and Angle of Line Features in an Urban Environment

Kei Uehara[1], Hideo Saito[1(✉)], and Kosuke Hara[2]

[1] Graduate School of Science and Technology, Keio University, Yokohama, Japan
hs@keio.jp
[2] Denso IT Laboratory, Tokyo, Japan
http://hvrl.ics.keio.ac.jp/

Abstract. In this paper, we propose a line-based SLAM from an image sequence captured by a camera mounted on a vehicle in consideration with the prior distribution of line features that detected in an urban environments. Since such scenes captured by the vehicle in urban envirounments can be expected to include a lot of line segments detected from road markings and buildings, we employ line segments as features for our SLAM. We use additional prior regarding the line segments so that we can improve the accuracy of the SLAM. We assume that the angle of the vector of the line segments to the vehicle's direction of travel conform to four-component Gaussian mixture distribution. We define a new cost function considering the prior distribution and optimize the relative camera pose, position, and the 3D line segments by bundle adjustment. The prior distribution is also extended into 2D, the distance and angle of the line segments. In addition, we make digital maps from the detected line segments. Our method increases the accuracy of localization and corrects tilted lines in the digital maps. We apply our method to both the single-camera system and the multi-camera system for demonstrate the accuracy improvement by the prior distribution of distance and angle of line features.

Keywords: Line-based SLAM · Manhattan world assumption · Road markings · Gaussian distribution

1 Introduction

Currently, advanced driver assistance systems (ADAS) has been actively researched. An autonomous car is an example of an ADAS that will enable people to go anyplace without your driving operation. To achieve that, it requires localization to calculate its' trajectory. [12] indicated that the accuracy of the localization required for practical use is from several dozen centimeters to several meters. For localization, one of the main methods is to use GPS. Although POSLV, one of the high-end integrated accurate positioning system, achieves

© Springer Nature Switzerland AG 2019
A. P. Cláudio et al. (Eds.): VISIGRAPP 2017, CCIS 983, pp. 105–127, 2019.
https://doi.org/10.1007/978-3-030-12209-6_6

accuracy within several dozen centimeters using a RTK-GPS receiver, it is not appropriate for use in the autonomous car. One reason is that the cost of RTK-GPS is very high. Another reason is that the GPS system depends on the strength of microwaves from the satellite. Thus, if the vehicle is in the tunnel, it cannot work.

Meanwhile, the visual simultaneous localization and mapping system (SLAM) has extensively been researched and improved for estimating positions and poses for vehicle localization. In visual SLAM, feature points should be detected and tracked from the environment around the vehicle using a camera as an input. If a lot of feature points are detected, SLAM can provide accurate camera positions and poses with 3D map of the target scene in a similar accuracy as a laser range scanner. Since the accuracy of SLAM decreases without enough feature points, a lot of studies have been tried to improve the accuracy for small amount of feature points; for example, studies that uses multi-cameras or researches detect not only points, but also lines. However, using many feature points or lines means an increasing of calculation cost, and it is fatal because the system of the autonomous car requires a real-time calculation. Increasing equipment means increasing of production costs. The less equipment attached to the vehicle, the better it is as long as the accuracy is maintained in the autonomous car.

In this paper, we propose a line-based SLAM considering a prior distribution of line features in an urban environment, which implies the Manhattan world assumption. Based on the fact that a lot of line segments in road markings are parallel or vertical to a vehicle's direction of travel, we define the prior distribution as four-component Gaussian mixture distribution [13]. Then we define a new cost function considering the prior distribution and optimize the relative camera pose, position, and the 3D line segments by bundle adjustment. The prior distribution is also extended into 2D, the distance and angle of the line segments.

To prove our method's effectiveness, we conduct four experiments: (1) single-camera system with line-based SLAM, (2) multi-camera system with line-based SLAM, (3) single-camera system with line-and-point-based SLAM, and (4) multi-camera system with line-and-point-based SLAM. We can achieve a high accuracy of SLAM in all experiments by our method.

In addition, we simultaneously make a digital map. Although, the digital map has been used in ADAS, it must be accurate and up-to-date. Roads and road markings are destroyed frequently, so they must be updated. Our digital map can be generated while driving on streets, and it requires cameras. No other equipment are needed. SLAM often has some intrinsic or extrinsic errors, so the line segments in the map often tilt. However, it is not a problem in our method because the directional distribution is considered.

2   Previous Works

Our goal is to realize SLAM using the distribution of line segments. There are some SLAM works that use line and road markings. Therefore, we discuss line-based SLAM and SLAM using road markings separately in this section.

2.1   Line-Based SLAM

There are previous works on line-based SLAM that have taken different approaches. [10] proposed a real-time line-based SLAM. They added straight lines to a monocular extended Kalman filter (EKF) SLAM, and realized the real-time system using a new algorithm and a fast straight-lines detector that did not insist on detecting every straight line in the frame.

Another approach for the line-based SLAM is using lines and other features. [7] proposed a method of motion estimation using points and lines by stereo line matching. They developed a new stereo matching algorithm for lines that was able to deal with textured and textureless environments.

In addition, [15] proposed a visual 6-DOF SLAM (using EKF) based on the structural regularity of building environments, which is called the Manhattan world assumption [2]. By introducing a constraint about buildings, the system achieved decreasing position and orientation errors.

2.2   SLAM Using Road Markings

There are also previous works using road markings for SLAM for a vehicle. [14] proposed a method for SLAM using road markings that they previously learned. They detected feature points from learned road markings and achieved a high accuracy in estimation of a camera pose.

[4] proposed a method which detects road markings robustly for SLAM. They developed a line detector which did not affected by illumination condition by adapting Otsu thresholding method.

In addition, [11] combined GPS, proprioceptive sensors, and road markings for SLAM.

Jeong et al. [6] proposes a method for SLAM using 3D point cloud of segmented road patterns reconstructed from images, which are also applied to a loopclosure algorithm for improvement of localization.

3   System Overview

We provide an overview of a line-based SLAM considering the distribution of road markings. We implement our method into both a single-camera system and a multi-camera system. We explain the method of the multi-camera system because the radical method for both the single-camera and the multi-camera systems is the almost same.

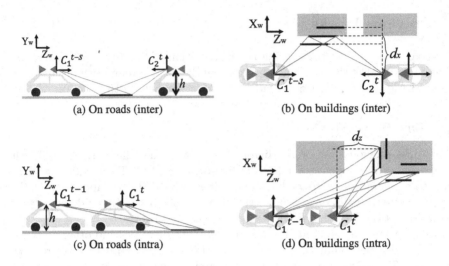

(a) On roads (inter)   (b) On buildings (inter)

(c) On roads (intra)   (d) On buildings (intra)

Fig. 1. Examples of intra- and inter-camera correspondences [13].

As a premise, our SLAM method requires wheel odometry. A relative camera pose and position in each frame are estimated from the data from the wheel sensors. Then, we obtain line segments from input images for each frame t by the line segment detector (LSD) algorithm. To correspond detected line segments, we consider the following three cases: matching between the front images features at frame t and $t-1$, matching between the rear image at frame t and $t-1$, and matching between the rear image at frame t and the front image at frame $t-s$. However, the viewing directions are very different, so it is hard to find matching segments, especially in the case of the third case. For a robust match, we make the feature patches around the line segments warp into other frames. Due to this warping processing, the perspective appearance of the patch resembles a target image. In addition, searching for the appropriate s value for the best match enables us to find the correspondences between a rear image and multiple front images more robustly. As long as corresponding line segments are detected, each line segment can be tracked over. Figure 1 indicates examples of matching.

Using these corresponding line segments, 3D line segments can be initially estimated using a method based on the Manhattan world assumption. After that, bundle adjustment is applied to the relative camera pose, positions and 3D line segments to optimize them. In a cost function of bundle adjustment, which is used for the optimization, we implement a new element considering the distribution of road markings, which is defined by 4-component Gaussian mixture distribution. Due to this element, the accuracy of localization improves and tilted line segments, which include some errors, in the generated map are revised.

The difference between a single-camera system and a multi-camera system is that the former does not consider the third matching case: matching between the rear image at frame t and the front image at frame $t-s$.

4   Notation

We explain the notations briefly before discussing our method in detail. First, we define the four coordinates W, $C_1{}^t$, $C_2{}^t$ and V^t, which indicate the world, front camera, rear camera, and vehicle coordinate systems, respectively. The relative transformations from the world coordinate system to the vehicle coordinates system at frame t are expressed as $\mathbf{R}_{vw}{}^t$, $\mathbf{T}_{vw}{}^t$, and these from the vehicle coordinates system to the front or the rear camera coordinate system are expressed as $\mathbf{R}_{c_1v}$, $\mathbf{T}_{c_1v}$, $\mathbf{R}_{c_2v}$, $\mathbf{T}_{c_1v}$. The relative pose and position of the front and rear cameras are calibrated beforehand. Using these notations, the projections from a world point $\mathbf{p} = (x, y, z)^T$ to camera point $\mathbf{q} = (q_x, q_y, q_z)^T$ are calculated as follows:

$$\mathbf{q}_k = \begin{pmatrix} q_x \\ q_y \\ q_z \end{pmatrix} = \mathbf{R}_{c_k v}(\mathbf{R}_{vw}{}^t \mathbf{p} + \mathbf{T}_{vw}{}^t) + \mathbf{T}_{c_k v} \tag{1}$$

where k denotes camera 1 or camera 2. For this case, $k = 1$ indicates the front camera. Then, projection from a camera point $\mathbf{q}$ to a image point $\mathbf{u} = (u, v)^T$ is calculated as follows:

$$\mathbf{u}_k = \begin{pmatrix} u \\ v \end{pmatrix} = \pi \begin{pmatrix} q_x \\ q_y \\ q_z \end{pmatrix} = \begin{pmatrix} q_x/q_z \\ q_y/q_z \end{pmatrix} \tag{2}$$

Secondly, the 3D line $\mathbf{L}_k$ is expressed as six-vector $(\mathbf{p}_k{}^T, \mathbf{r}_k{}^T)^T$. The three-vectors $\mathbf{p}_k$ is a center point of the 3D line and $\mathbf{r}_k$ is the direction of the 3D line. The 2D line $\mathbf{l}_k$, which is a projection line of $\mathbf{L}_k$ in the image plane, is given as four-vector $(\mathbf{u}_k{}^T, \mathbf{d}_k{}^T)^T$. Point $\mathbf{u}$ is calculated in the same way as the world point $\mathbf{p}$ and the vector $\mathbf{d}$ in the image plane is calculated as follows:

$$\mathbf{D}_k = \begin{pmatrix} D_x \\ D_y \\ D_z \end{pmatrix} = \mathbf{R}_{c_k v} \mathbf{R}_{vw}{}^t \mathbf{r}_k \tag{3}$$

$$\mathbf{d}_k = \begin{pmatrix} d_x \\ d_y \end{pmatrix} = \begin{pmatrix} q_z D_x - q_x D_z \\ q_z D_y - q_y D_z \end{pmatrix} \tag{4}$$

where $\mathbf{D}_k$ is a point of the camera coordinate system. Finally, the wheel odometry $\mathbf{x}$ is expressed as follows:

$$\mathbf{x}^{t+1} = \begin{pmatrix} x^{t+1} \\ z^{t+1} \\ \theta^{t+1} \end{pmatrix} = \mathbf{x}^t + \Delta\mathbf{x}^t + \varepsilon_\mathbf{x}{}^t \tag{5}$$

where $\Delta\mathbf{x}^t$ denotes its relative movement from a previous time and $\varepsilon_\mathbf{x}{}^t$ denotes the noise of $\Delta\mathbf{x}^t$. In the proposed method, we estimate the 3-DOF motion of the vehicle coordinates (x, z, θ) in a 2D-environment. When $\mathbf{x}^0$, which is the initial position of the vehicle, is in the same position as the origin of the world coordinate system, $\mathbf{x}^t$ equals $\mathbf{R}_{vw}{}^t$ and $\mathbf{T}_{vw}{}^t$. We suppose that $\varepsilon_{\mathbf{x}}{}^t$ is zero-mean Gaussian white noise with covariance $\Sigma_{\mathbf{x}}$.

$$\varepsilon_{\mathbf{x}}{}^t \sim \mathcal{N}(0, \Sigma_{\mathbf{x}}) \tag{6}$$

$$\Sigma_{\mathbf{x}} = \begin{pmatrix} \sigma_x{}^2 & 0 & 0 \\ 0 & \sigma_z{}^2 & 0 \\ 0 & 0 & \sigma_\theta{}^2 \end{pmatrix} \Delta t \tag{7}$$

where σ_x, σ_z, and σ_θ denote error variances. The covariance increases in proportion to time, supposing that $\varepsilon_{\mathbf{x}}{}^t$ simply increases.

5   Proposed Method

The purpose of our method is to enhance the accuracy of line-based SLAM by bundle adjustment, which considers the distribution of the line segments. Our system consists of two parts: line matching and bundle adjustment. In this section, we explain how to realize them individually.

5.1   Line Matching

Our method has two matching algorithms: matching inter-camera correspondences and matching intra-camera correspondences as it is also called in [8], the basis of which is warping patches based on the Manhattan world assumption. We explain them individually.

Inter-camera Correspondences. This method of matching is used between the front and the rear images, and is not featured with a single-camera system. The blue-colored rectangle shown in Fig. 2(a) is a patch, which is 20 pixels wide and has a detected red-colored line segment in the center. The patch is transformed into a target image plane by a warp function, which considers the place where the line segments are detected. Conceivable places where they can be detected include front walls of buildings or road surfaces, as shown in Fig. 1(a) and (b). Therefore, two types of warping processing are performed on all line segments in this matching algorithm.

To explain the case of the front walls of building, according to the Manhattan world assumption, a y-coordinate value of all the points in the patch in $C_2{}^t$ is h, which indicates the height of the attached camera. Therefore, the 3D point in the patch is calculated as follows:

$$\mathbf{p}_r = \begin{pmatrix} h(u_{m,2} + \alpha)/(v_{m,2} + \beta) \\ h \\ h/(v_{m,2} + \beta) \end{pmatrix} \tag{8}$$

We define the coordinate of the patch as $\mathbf{u}_{m,2} = (u_{m,2} + \alpha, v_{m,2} + \beta)^{\mathrm{T}}$, where $\mathbf{u}_{m,2}$ denotes the center point of the line segment and α and β are the Euclidean distances from the center point.

In the case of the line segments detected on the road surface, the 3D point in the patch is calculated as follows:

$$\mathbf{p}_{bf} = \begin{pmatrix} d_x \\ d_x(v_{m,2} + \beta)/(u_{m,2} + \alpha) \\ d_x/(u_{m,2} + \alpha) \end{pmatrix} \tag{9}$$

The x-coordinate value of all the points in the patch in $C_2{}^t$ is d_x, which is shown in Fig. 1(b), under the assumption.

(a) Rear image and patch   (b)Warped patch

(c) Front image and a detected line segments

Fig. 2. (a) A rear image with a patch of the red detected line. (b) The warped patch converted from (a). (c) The front image [13]. (Color figure online)

The result of the warping is shown in Fig. 2(b). It shows that the perspective appearance becomes similar to the target image (Fig. 2(c)). Subsequently, we judge whether the warped patch and the line segments in the target image correspond or not with using an error ellipse based on the EKF proposed by

[3]. We use a raster scan of the error ellipse of the warped patch and calculate a zero-mean normalized cross-correlation (ZNCC) score. At the position where the ZNCC is the highest, we calculate two more values: the angle between the warped line segment and the line segments in the target image, and the distances from the endpoints of warped line segments to the line segment in the target image. If these two values are lower than the threshold, they are regarded as the correspondence.

Although we propose this matching method, it has two ambiguous points: one is that we cannot precisely distinguish whether the line segments exist on buildings or the road surface, and the precise value of d_x cannot be calculated. To exclude these ambiguous elements, we test two calculations, for the building and road surface, and change d_x at regular intervals in each experiment. Then we decide the correspondence based on the highest ZNCC score.

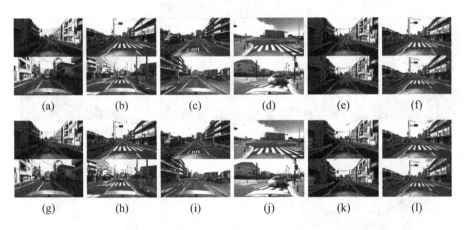

Fig. 3. Examples of matching using our method (a)–(f) and LEHF [5] (g)–(l). (a)–(d) and (g)–(j) are matched pairs of front and rear images. (e) (f), (k), and (l) are matched pairs of front images. The red lines and green lines show correct and incorrect matching, respectively [13]. (Color figure online)

Intra-camera Correspondences. This method of matching is used between pairs of front images or pairs of rear images. There are three conceivable places where the line segments can be detected in this method: two of three are the same as the inter-camera correspondences and the last one is the side wall of buildings, as shown in Fig. 1(c) and (d). The 3D point in the patch is calculated as follows:

$$\mathbf{p}_{bs} = \begin{pmatrix} d_z(u_{m,1} + \alpha) \\ d_z(v_{m,1} + \beta) \\ d_z \end{pmatrix} \tag{10}$$

Under the Manhattan world assumption, z-coordinate of all the 3D points in the patch is d_z, which is shown in Fig. 1(b), so Eq. 10 can be defined. As well as the inter-camera correspondences, we change d_z at regular intervals and find the best one for matching.

The Matching Result. The results of matching are shown in Fig. 3.

Figure 3(a) to (d) indicate intra-matching correspondences with using our method, and Fig. 3(g) to (j) indicate correspondences using LEHF [5]. Although, the enough number of the line segments cannot detected, the accuracy of the matching obviously increases.

Figure 3(e) and (f) indicate inter-matching correspondences with using our method, and Fig. 3(k) and (l) indicate correspondences using LEHF [5]. The accuracy of them is the almost same.

Using our method, we can classify all matched line segments into *on the buildingwalls* or *on the road*, which LEHF cannot do. This detected place data are important for the next step.

5.2 Initial Estimation of 3D Line

We use two methods to estimate the 3D line segments, which will be explained individually in this section.

First, we estimate line segments using a method based on the line of intersection of planes that passes the camera center and the line segment. Figure 4(a) shows examples of road maps generated by the 3D information calculated by this method, although most of them lie wrong place. The reason for this is because when the line segments run parallel to the travel direction, the angle between the planes passing the segments becomes too low. The 3D information create error because of that.

Secondly, we estimate the line segments using Eqs. (8), (9) and (10) as explained in Sect. 5.1. In this method, we can obtain some 3D information per one line segment, because it requires only one line segment to calculate the 3D information and each line segment has some corresponded line segments. Therefore, we choose one line segment by minimum median method. An element used in the minimum median method is the re-projection error, which is calculated from the perpendicular distance from a reprojected 3D line to the endpoints of a detected line in the image plane. This method is widely used and is defined in a paper written by [1]. Figure 4(b) shows a result of this method, which is obviously better than first method.

5.3 Optimization by Bundle Adjustment

We optimize the relative camera pose, position $(\mathbf{R}_{vw}{}^t, \mathbf{T}_{vw}{}^t)$ and the 3D line segments $\mathbf{L}^j$ by bundle adjustment. We define the set of corresponding line segments Ω as:

$$\Omega = \{\omega_i = (t, k, j, p)| \\ t \in \{1, \ldots, T\}, k \in \{1, 2\}, j \in \{1, \ldots, J\} p \in \{1, 2, 3\}\} \tag{11}$$

where the ith line segment indicates that a 3D line is observed in a place p by camera k at frame t. In our method, the objectives are to minimize the reprojection errors of all the line segments and to minimize the angle errors of the line segments observed in the road surface. Then, the cost function is defined as following.

$$E = \mathbf{e}_l + \mathbf{e}_\theta = \frac{1}{2} \sum_i \sum_{n=1}^{2} d^2{}_\perp(\mathbf{g}_n{}^i, \mathbf{l}^i) + \frac{1}{2} \sum_m (e_\theta{}^m)^2 \tag{12}$$

where $d_\perp(\mathbf{a}, \mathbf{b})$ denotes the perpendicular distance from a point $\mathbf{a}$ to a line $\mathbf{b}$ in images, $\mathbf{g}_1{}^i$ and $\mathbf{g}_2{}^i$ denote the endpoints of observed line segments, and e_θ denotes an angle error, which can be calculated using the difference between the travel direction of the vehicle and the vector of the line segments. An objective is to find the best values of $\mathbf{R}_{vw}{}^t$, $\mathbf{T}_{vw}{}^t$, and $\mathbf{L}^j$ to minimize E. We use the iterative non-linear Levenberg-Marquardt optimization algorithm with numerical differentiation based on a method proposed by [9]. We explain the calculation method for the reprojection error and angle error individually.

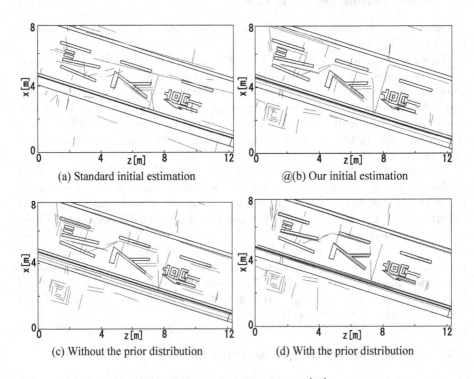

(a) Standard initial estimation

@(b) Our initial estimation

(c) Without the prior distribution

(d) With the prior distribution

Fig. 4. Examples of road maps [13].

Reprojection Error. We use the following equation to calculate $d_\perp(\mathbf{g}_n{}^i, \mathbf{l}^i)$:

$$e_l^i = d_\perp(\mathbf{g}_n{}^i, \mathbf{l}^i) = \frac{d_y(g_x{}^i - u^i) - d_x(g_y{}^i - v^i)}{\sqrt{d_x{}^2 + d_y{}^2}} \tag{13}$$

To solve the bundle adjustment, we make Jacobian matrices made from the result of differentiated Eq. (13) in the relative camera pose, position $(\mathbf{R}_{vw}{}^t, \mathbf{T}_{vw}{}^t)$ and the 3D line segments $\mathbf{L}^j$. The differentiation equations are expressed as follows by conforming to the chain rule:

$$\frac{\partial e_l^i}{\partial \mathbf{R}_{vw}{}^t} = \frac{\partial e_l^i}{\partial \mathbf{q}^i} \frac{\partial \mathbf{q}^i}{\partial \mathbf{R}_{vw}{}^t} \tag{14}$$

$$\frac{\partial e_l^i}{\partial \mathbf{T}_{vw}{}^t} = \frac{\partial e_l^i}{\partial \mathbf{q}^i} \frac{\partial \mathbf{q}^i}{\partial \mathbf{T}_{vw}{}^t} \tag{15}$$

$$\frac{\partial e_l^i}{\partial \mathbf{p}^j} = \frac{\partial e_l^i}{\partial \mathbf{q}^i} \frac{\partial \mathbf{q}^i}{\partial \mathbf{p}^j} \tag{16}$$

$$\frac{\partial e_l^i}{\partial \mathbf{r}^j} = \frac{\partial e_l^i}{\partial \mathbf{D}^i} \frac{\partial \mathbf{D}^i}{\partial \mathbf{r}^j} \tag{17}$$

where $\mathbf{q}$ and $\mathbf{D}$ are defined as Eqs. (1) and (4), respectively.

In addition, we include a geometric constraint into the cost function to enhance the accuracy of the optimization. Under the Manhattan world assumption, y-coordinate of the line segments detected on the road surface is absolutely h, so we keep it constant during the process of bundle adjustment. Since d_x and d_z have ambiguousness, we do not incorporate that constraint. Figure 4(c) and (d) are the result of mapping after bundle adjustment without or with the constraint, respectively. The figures show that the constraint works well.

Angle Error. First, we show that d_θ in Fig. 5 is an angle between the travel direction and the vector of the 3D line segments, and it has either a positive or a negative value; the maximum value is $\frac{\pi}{2}$ and the minimum value is $-\frac{\pi}{2}$. It is calculated as follows:

$$d_\theta = \arctan \frac{F_z}{F_x} - \arctan \frac{r_z}{r_x} \tag{18}$$
$$((F_x \geq 0 \ and \ F_z \geq 0) \ or \ (F_x \leq 0 \ and \ F_z \leq 0))$$

$$d_\theta = \arctan \frac{F_z}{F_x} - \arctan \frac{r_z}{r_x} - \pi \tag{19}$$
$$((F_x \geq 0 \ and \ F_z \leq 0) \ or \ (F_x \leq 0 \ and \ F_z \geq 0))$$

where $\mathbf{F} = (F_x, F_y, F_z)$ denotes the vehicle's direction of travel. To establish the consistency of the sign of d_θ, we take π from d_θ in Eq. (19). In our method, we add a new constraint about d_θ. As I discussed in Sect. 1, we suppose that

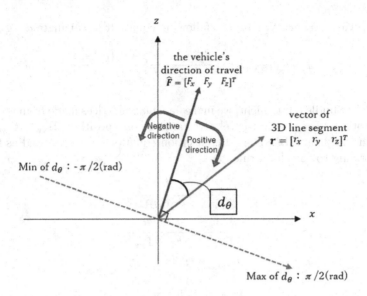

Fig. 5. A schematic diagram of d_θ [13].

most of the road markings are parallel or vertical to the vehicle's direction of travel. Although some markings include diagonal lines, there are many markings that include parallel or vertical lines; for examples, car lanes, and markings at crosswalks.

We compute angle histogram of real road markings based on a road pattern map collected by a road survey company as shown in Fig. 6, which consists of line patterns. The histogram for various d_θ computed from the map is shown in Fig. 7. This histogram suggests that line segments on the road are mostly parallel of vertical with the vehicle driving direction. According to the angle histogram, we consider the prior distribution for the angle d_θ of the line segments as described in the next paragraph.

In the case of the parallel lines to the vehicle driving direction, we assume that d_θ conforms to the Gaussian distribution. In the case of the vertical lines to the vehicle driving direction, we assume that $d_\theta \pm \frac{\pi}{2}$ conforms to the Gaussian distribution. Considering the diagonal lines, we define one more Gaussian distribution. It prevents the diagonal lines from being corrected to the parallel or vertical lines. Figure 8 shows their distribution. The equation for each Gaussian distribution can be expressed as follows:

$$P_1(d_\theta^m | \mu_1 = 0, \sigma_1 = \sigma_\alpha) = \frac{1}{\sqrt{2\pi\sigma_\alpha^2}} exp(-\frac{1}{2\sigma_\alpha^2}(d_\theta^m - \mu_1)^2) \tag{20}$$

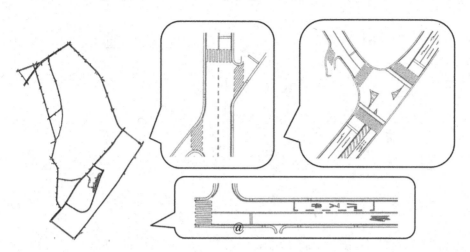

Fig. 6. The road pattern map around JR Shin-Kawasaki Station collected by a road survey company.

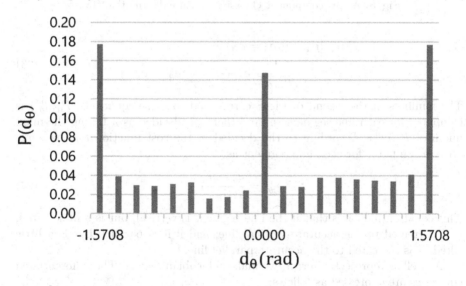

Fig. 7. Histogram of d_θ computed from the road pattern map shown in Fig. 6.

$$P_2(d_\theta^m|\mu_2 = \frac{\pi}{2}, \sigma_2 = \sigma_\alpha) =$$
$$\frac{1}{\sqrt{2\pi\sigma_\alpha^2}}exp(-\frac{1}{2\sigma_\alpha^2}(d_\theta^m - \mu_2)^2) \qquad (21)$$

$$P_3(d_\theta^m|\mu_3 = -\frac{\pi}{2}, \sigma_3 = \sigma_\alpha) =$$
$$\frac{1}{\sqrt{2\pi\sigma_\alpha^2}}exp(-\frac{1}{2\sigma_\alpha^2}(d_\theta^m - \mu_3)^2) \qquad (22)$$

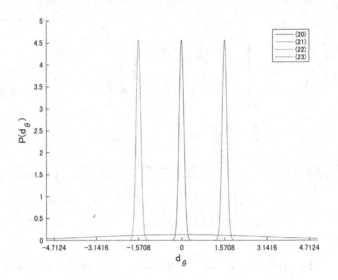

Fig. 8. A four-component Gaussian mixture distribution [13].

$$P_4(d_\theta^m | \mu_4 = 0, \sigma_4 = \sigma_\beta) =$$
$$\frac{1}{\sqrt{2\pi\sigma_\beta^2}} exp(-\frac{1}{2\sigma_\beta^2}(d_\theta^m - \mu_4)^2) \tag{23}$$

The numbers in the legend of Fig. 8 correspond to these equations. $P_n(d_\theta^m)$ is computed for each line segment m, and then n is decided as n taking the maximum of $P_n(d_\theta^m)$. According to the decided n, the cost function for the angle error is computer for each line segment as

$$e_\theta^m = \frac{d_\theta - \mu_n}{\sigma_n} \tag{24}$$

This equation indicates that if the line segment is vertical, but is a little tilted, it is corrected to the accurate vertical line; and if it is parallel, but is a little tilted, it is corrected to the accurate parallel line.

As well as reprojection error, we make a Jacobian matrix. The differentiated equations are expressed as follows:

$$\frac{\partial e_\theta^j}{\partial r} = \left(\frac{\partial e_\theta^j}{\partial r_x} \frac{\partial e_\theta^j}{\partial r_y} \frac{\partial e_\theta^j}{\partial r_z} \right) \tag{25}$$

$$\frac{\partial e_\theta^j}{\partial r_x} = \frac{r_z}{r_x^2 + r_z^2} \tag{26}$$

$$\frac{\partial e_\theta^j}{\partial r_y} = 0 \tag{27}$$

$$\frac{\partial e_\theta^j}{\partial r_z} = -\frac{r_x}{r_x^2 + r_z^2} \tag{28}$$

In addition, we obtain the best value of σ_α and σ_β by changing them at regular intervals for the best optimization in each experiment.

5.4 Extended Prior Distribution

By extending the prior distribution of the line segments for the angle to also the distance from the vehicle, we aim to improve the accuracy of the proposed SLAM. For generating the prior distribution for both angle and distance, we assume that the road patterns consist of the simple road patterns. Then, we generate the prior distribution from the road pattern map collected by a road survey company as shown in Fig. 6 according to the following procedure.

1. Sub-grid division of the road map
2. Extract line segments from the road map and compute the distance ρ and the angle θ
3. Vote for each line segment to generate the histogram in ρ - θ 2D space.
4. Fitting the voted histogram to 2D Gaussians.

In the last step, the voted histogram are fitted to 2D Gaussian of ρ and θ as shown in Fig. 9. The following equations represent the 2D Gaussian distribution for fitting.

$$P_n(\rho^{j,k}, \theta^{j,k} | \mu_{n,\rho}, \mu_{n,\theta}, \sigma_{n,\rho}, \sigma_{n,\theta})$$

$$= \frac{1}{2\pi\sigma_{n,\rho}\sigma_{n,\theta}} exp\left\{ -\frac{1}{2}\left(\frac{(\rho^{j,k} - \mu_{n,\rho})^2}{\sigma_{n,\rho}^2} + \frac{(\theta^{j,k} - \mu_{n,\theta})^2}{\sigma_{n,\theta}^2} \right) \right\}$$

(29)

where n indicate the ID number for Gaussians for fitting. The centroid of each Gaussian $(\mu_{n,\rho}, \mu_{n,\theta})$ is set to the maximum voting position. The standard deviation of each Gaussian $\sigma_{n,\rho}, \sigma_{n,\theta}$ is computed from the distribution of the voted distribution. We limit the number of Gaussian up to 10.

In this case, we extend Eq. (12) as the following Eq. (30) which is optimized for estimating the poses of the camera $(\mathbf{R}_{vw}{}^t, \mathbf{T}_{vw}{}^t)$ and 3D positions of line segment $\mathbf{L}^j$ based on bundle adjustment.

$$E = \mathbf{e}_l + \mathbf{e}_\rho + \mathbf{e}_\theta = \frac{1}{2}\sum_i \sum_{n=1}^2 d^2{}_\perp(\mathbf{g}_n{}^i, \mathbf{l}^i) + \frac{1}{2}\sum_{k=1}^K \sum_j (e_\rho{}^{j,k})^2 + \frac{1}{2}\sum_{k=1}^K \sum_j (e_\rho{}^{j,k})^2$$

(30)

where $\mathbf{e}_l$, $\mathbf{e}_\theta$, and $\mathbf{e}_\rho$ represent the reprojection error, the angle error, and the distance error terms for the line segments, respectively. The reprojection error is defined same as Eq. (13). The angle error and the distance error are defined as follows, where j represents the ID of line segment detected in image frame k.

Distance Error. Distance error of each line segment is computed as the following equation.

$$e_\rho^{j,k} = \frac{\rho^{j,k} - \mu_{n,\rho}}{\sigma_{n,\rho}}$$

(31)

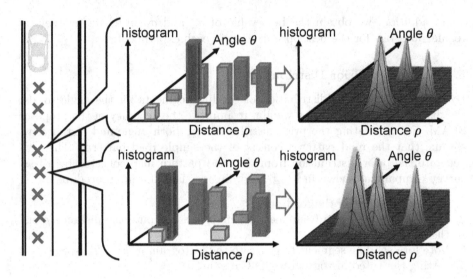

Fig. 9. The flow of computing the prior distribution for the distance and the angle for line segments from the histogram.

In the similar way as the previous section, n is decided as n taking the maximum of Gaussians. The Jacobian for the distance error term can be computed according to the chain rule.

$$\frac{\partial e_\rho}{\partial \mathbf{R}^k_{wv}} = \frac{\partial e_\rho}{\partial \mathbf{L}^{j,k}} \frac{\partial \mathbf{L}^{j,k}}{\partial \mathbf{R}^k_{wv}} \tag{32}$$

$$\frac{\partial e_\rho}{\partial \mathbf{t}^k_{wv}} = \frac{\partial e_\rho}{\partial \mathbf{L}^{j,k}} \frac{\partial \mathbf{L}^{j,k}}{\partial \mathbf{t}^k_{wv}} \tag{33}$$

$$\frac{\partial e_\rho}{\partial \mathbf{L}^j} = \frac{\partial e_\rho}{\partial \mathbf{L}^{j,k}} \frac{\partial \mathbf{L}^{j,k}}{\partial \mathbf{L}^j} \tag{34}$$

$$\frac{\partial e_\rho}{\partial \mathbf{L}^{j,k}} = \left(\frac{\partial e_\rho}{\partial m^{j,k}_x} \; \frac{\partial e_\rho}{\partial m^{j,k}_y} \; \frac{\partial e_\rho}{\partial m^{j,k}_z} \; \frac{\partial e_\rho}{\partial l^{j,k}_x} \; \frac{\partial e_\rho}{\partial l^{j,k}_y} \; \frac{\partial e_\rho}{\partial l^{j,k}_z} \right) \tag{35}$$

$$\frac{\partial \mathbf{L}^{j,k}}{\partial \mathbf{R}^k_{wv}} = \left(\frac{\partial \mathbf{L}^{j,k}}{\partial R^k_x} \; \frac{\partial \mathbf{L}^{j,k}}{\partial R^k_y} \; \frac{\partial \mathbf{L}^{j,k}}{\partial R^k_z} \right) \tag{36}$$

$$\frac{\partial \mathbf{L}^{j,k}}{\partial \mathbf{t}^k_{wv}} = \left(\frac{\partial \mathbf{L}^{j,k}}{\partial t^k_x} \; \frac{\partial \mathbf{L}^{j,k}}{\partial t^k_y} \; \frac{\partial \mathbf{L}^{j,k}}{\partial t^k_z} \right) \tag{37}$$

$$\frac{\partial \mathbf{L}^{j,k}}{\partial \mathbf{L}^j} = \left(\frac{\partial \mathbf{L}^{j,k}}{\partial m^j_x} \; \frac{\partial \mathbf{L}^{j,k}}{\partial m^j_y} \; \frac{\partial \mathbf{L}^{j,k}}{\partial m^j_z} \; \frac{\partial \mathbf{L}^{j,k}}{\partial l^j_x} \; \frac{\partial \mathbf{L}^{j,k}}{\partial l^j_y} \; \frac{\partial \mathbf{L}^{j,k}}{\partial l^j_z} \right) \tag{38}$$

5.5 Angle Error

Angle error of each line segment is computed as the following equation.

$$e_\theta^{j,k} = \frac{\theta^{j,k} - \mu_\theta^{j,k,\alpha}}{\sigma_\theta^{j,k,\alpha}} \tag{39}$$

The Jacobian for the angle error term can be computed according to the chain rule.

$$\frac{\partial e_\theta}{\partial \mathbf{R}_{wv}^k} = \frac{\partial e_\theta}{\partial \mathbf{L}^{j,k}} \frac{\partial \mathbf{L}^{j,k}}{\partial \mathbf{R}_{wv}^k} \tag{40}$$

$$\frac{\partial e_\theta}{\partial \mathbf{t}_{wv}^k} = \frac{\partial e_\theta}{\partial \mathbf{L}^{j,k}} \frac{\partial \mathbf{L}^{j,k}}{\partial \mathbf{t}_{wv}^k} \tag{41}$$

$$\frac{\partial e_\theta}{\partial \mathbf{L}^j} = \frac{\partial e_\theta}{\partial \mathbf{L}^{j,k}} \frac{\partial \mathbf{L}^{j,k}}{\partial \mathbf{L}^j} \tag{42}$$

$$\frac{\partial e_\theta}{\partial \mathbf{L}^{j,k}} = \left(\frac{\partial e_\theta}{\partial m_x^{j,k}} \quad \frac{\partial e_\theta}{\partial m_y^{j,k}} \quad \frac{\partial e_\theta}{\partial m_z^{j,k}} \quad \frac{\partial e_\theta}{\partial l_x^{j,k}} \quad \frac{\partial e_\theta}{\partial l_y^{j,k}} \quad \frac{\partial e_\theta}{\partial l_z^{j,k}} \right) \tag{43}$$

6 Experiment

In this section, we introduce a practical experiment that uses a real vehicle driving in an urban environment. Two cameras and a RTK-GPS, which can get high accuracy of self-position, are attached to the vehicle, shown in Fig. 10. The frame rate of the camera is 3 fps and we prepare two datasets: one is a straight scene that has 72 frames (Dataset 1) and another is curve scene that has 200 frames (Dataset 2). We use the GPS as a ground truth. We evaluate the accuracy of localization and mapping individually. In this experiment, we use a desktop PC with Intel(R) Core(TM) i7-6800K CPU @ 3.40 GHz 3.40 GHz and 64.0 GB RAM. MatLab is used for computation.

Fig. 10. The vehicle for data collection.

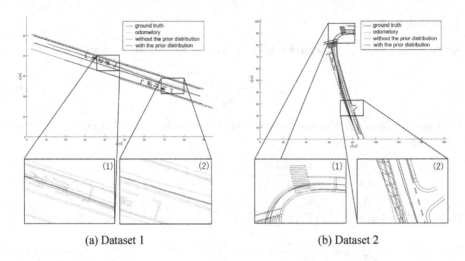

(a) Dataset 1   (b) Dataset 2

Fig. 11. The trajectory results obtained from datasets 1 and 2 in the experiment of line (S). Comparison of the results estimated by ground truth, odometry, optimized data without the prior distribution, and optimized data with the prior distribution [13].

Table 1. Localization error per frame [cm/frame].

	Dataset 1			Dataset 2		
	No prior	Angle	Angle + Distance	No prior	Angle	Angle + Distance
Line (S)	20.93	11.40	13.12	88.05	48.16	55.91
Line (M)	9.40	7.69	5.01	102.8	38.2	72.2
Line-point (S)	13.36	7.06	5.38	90.96	57.03	76.80
Line-point (M)	3.89	2.19	3.63	133.95	54.59	117.3

6.1   Evaluation of Localization

In our experiment, we apply our method to four cases; (1) single-camera system with line-based SLAM (called line (S)), (2) single-camera system with point-and-line based SLAM (point-line (S)), (3) multi-camera system with line-based SLAM (line (M)), and (4) multi-camera system with point-and-line based SLAM (point-line (M)). We check how much the accuracy of localization improves when the directional distribution of road markings is considered in each cases.

Figure 11 shows trajectories of the vehicles in the case of line (S) in two datasets. We compare four types of data in each case; ground truth, odometry, optimized data without the prior distribution, and optimized data with the prior distribution only for angle. A closeup area (1) of Fig. 11(a) and (b) indicates that the optimized data with the prior distribution is the closest to the ground truth and it has higher accuracy than that without the constraint.

Figures 12 and 13 provide a quantitative analysis of the accuracy of localization. They are position errors, which indicate a perpendicular distance to the ground truth. In addition, Table 1 shows the sum of the position errors in each

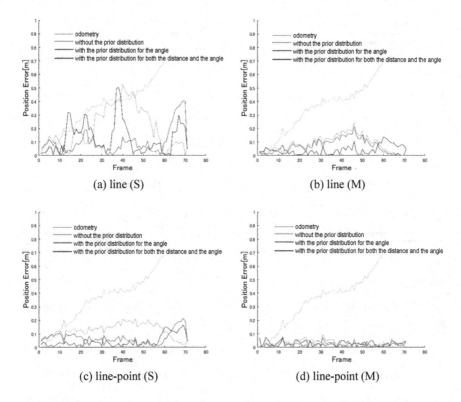

Fig. 12. Comparison of position error in each frame (dataset 1).

case and the rate of improvement in percentage. The accuracy improves in all experiments by considering the prior distribution. For dataset 1, the accuracy improves about 50% in the single-camera experiment. The accuracy of line (S) with the constraint is as well as line (M) without it. For dataset 2, the accuracy improves, especially in the multi-camera experiments. Since our SLAM method is based on the Manhattan world assumption, it is not appropriate for the curving scene because the assumption does not stand up well. However, by using the prior distribution, the error generated in the curving scene is corrected. It may be a reason for the high improvement rate seen in dataset2.

Concerning to the comparison of the error between the previous simple prior distribution and the extended prior distribution, the errors for line (M) and line-point (S) in the dataset 1 are significantly improved, while the error for line (S) and line-point (M) are increased unfortunately. This could be because of the distance error distibution does not work especially for line (S) and line-point (M).

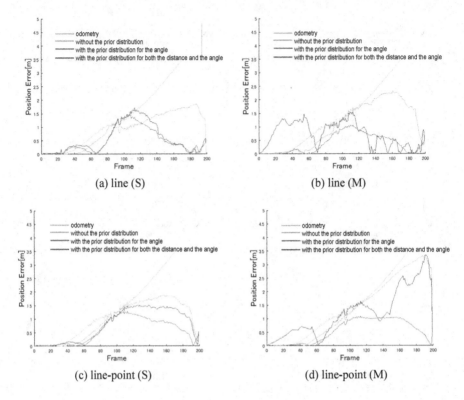

Fig. 13. Comparison of position error in each frame (dataset 2).

Since dataset 2 is curve case, which is not much included in the dataset for generating prior distribution. Therefore, the improvement is not drastic because the prior distribution for distance and angle is mainly for the straight lane.

6.2 Evaluation of Mapping

The detected line segments can be used to make digital maps. Figure 14 show the results of the digital map. To make a quantitative evaluation of the results of the digital map, we compute TPR (True Positive Rate) and PRS (Precision) by comparing with the ground truth map measured by a survey company. TPR shown in Table 2 represents the rate in length of matched line of the ground truth map with the map of the detected lines by the proposed method. The higher TPR means the higher reconstruction rate by the detected line by the proposed method. PRS shown in Table 3 represents the rate in length of correctly detected line segments by the proposed method. The higher PRS means the lower rate of wrongly detected line segments by the proposed method.

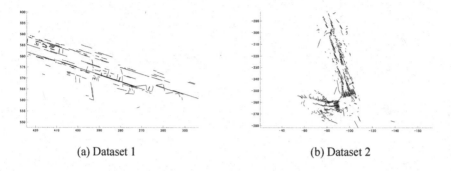

(a) Dataset 1   (b) Dataset 2

Fig. 14. Digital maps made from detected line segments [13].

Both Tables 2 and 3 demonstrate that the prior distribution effectively improve the accuracy of the generated map by the detected line segments in the proposed method. The improvement in dataset 1 is more than that in dataset. The reason is that dataset 2 has more diagonal lines, which are collected to parallel or vertical lines although it does not. Dataset 1 has more vertical and parallel lines, so the rate of inliers increases in any experiment. Figure 15 shows whether the line segments in the digital map are whether inlier or outlier in line (S) of dataset 1. Red lines indicate inlier lines and green lines indicate outlier lines. Tilted lines in Fig. 15(a) is revised, so they change to green lines in Fig. 15(b).

Table 2. TPR (True Positive Rate) [%] represents the rate in length of matched line of the ground truth map with the map of the detected lines by the proposed method.

	Dataset 1			Dataset 2		
	No prior	Angle	Angle + Distance	No prior	Angle	Angle + Distance
Line (S)	28.5	47.5	56.5	40.1	43.7	45.7
Line (M)	35.2	41.6	52.7	39.6	44.0	43.3
Line-point (S)	39.1	49.7	52.5	40.5	43.8	42.6
Line-point (M)	49.6	52.8	55.3	42.2	45.2	44.7

Table 3. PRS (Precision) [%] represents the rate in length of correctly detected line segments by the proposed method.

	Dataset 1			Dataset 2		
	No prior	Angle	Angle + Distance	No prior	Angle	Angle + Distance
Line (S)	28.6	56.2	61.2	38.4	42.4	42.1
Line (M)	41.8	50.6	60.5	33.0	40.8	38.5
Line-point (S)	45.3	64.2	62.2	32.0	44.6	42.1
Line-point (M)	57.5	62.2	66.9	34.9	45.1	38.6

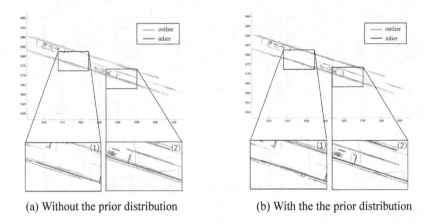

(a) Without the prior distribution   (b) With the the prior distribution

Fig. 15. Mapping results in line (S) Red lines indicate inlier lines and green lines indicate outlier lines [13]. (Color figure online)

7   Conclusions

In this paper, we propose a line-based SLAM from an image sequence captured by a camera mounted on a vehicle in consideration with the prior distribution of line features that detected in an urban environment, which includes a lot of line feature segments on road markings and buildings. We assume the prior distribution can be represented as a combination of Gaussian distributions, and then define a cost function of bundle adjustment based on the prior distribution. We first consider the prior distribution in angle of the line segments, and then extend to make it 2D, the distance and angle of the line segments. In the experiments using image sequences captured with a vehicle running in an urban scenes, we demonstrate that the accuracy of SLAM improves in all cases. The proposed method successfully improves the accuracy of the single-camera SLAM as well as the multi-camera SLAM. We also generate digital maps from the detected line segments, which can also demonstrate the prior distribution contributes to correcting wrong line segments.

References

1. Bartoli, A., Sturm, P.: Structure-from-motion using lines:representation, triangulation, and bundle adjustment. Comput. Vis. Image Underst. **100**, 416–441 (2005)
2. Coughlan, J.M., Yuille, A.L.: Manhattan world: compass direction from a single image by Bayesian inference. In: Proceedings of the Seventh IEEE International Conference on Computer Vision, vol. 2, pp. 941–947 (1999)
3. Davison, A.J., Reid, I.D., Molton, N.D., Stasse, O.: MonoSLAM: real-time single camera SLAM. IEEE Trans. Pattern Anal. Mach. Intell. **29**, 1052–1067 (2007)
4. Hata, A., Wolf, D.: Road marking detection using LIDAR reflective intensity data and its application to vehicle localization. In: 17th International IEEE Conference on Intelligent Transportation Systems, ITSC, pp. 584–589 (2014)

5. Hirose, K., Saito, H.: Fast line description for line-based SLAM. In: Proceedings of the British Machine Vision Conference, pp. 83.1–83.11 (2012)
6. Jeong, J., Cho, Y., Kim, A.: Road-SLAM: road marking based slam with lane-level accuracy. In IEEE Intelligent Vehicles Symposium, IV 2017, pp. 1736–1743 (2017)
7. Koletschka, T., Puig, L., Daniilidis, K.: MEVO: multi-environment stereo visual odometry. In: 2014 IEEE/RSJ International Conference on Intelligent Robots and Systems, pp. 4981–4988 (2014)
8. Lee, G.H., Faundorfer, F., Pollefeys, M.: Motion estimation for self-driving cars with a generalized camera. In: IEEE Conference on Computer Vision and Pattern Recognition, CVPR 2013, pp. 2746–2753 (2013)
9. Madsen, K., Nielsen, H.B., Tingleff, O.: Methods for Non-linear Least Squares Problems, 2nd edn, p. 60. Informatics and Mathematical Modelling, Technical University of Denmark, DTU, Kgs. Lyngby (2004)
10. Smith, P., Reid, I., Davison, A.: Real-time monocular SLAM with straight lines. In: Proceedings of British Machine Vision Conference, pp. 17–26 (2006)
11. Tao, Z., Bonnifait, P., Frémont, V., Ibañez-Guzman, J.: Mapping and localization using GPS, lane markings and proprioceptive sensors. In: 2013 IEEE/RSJ International Conference on Intelligent Robots and Systems, pp. 406–412 (2013)
12. Teramoto, E., Kojima, Y., Meguro, J., Suzuki, N.: Development of the "PRECISE" automotive integrated positioning system and high-accuracy digital map generation. R&D Rev. Toyota CRDL 43, 13–23 (2012)
13. Uehara, K., Saito, H., Hara, K.: Line-based SLAM considering directional distribution of line features in an urban environment. In: Proceedings of the 12th International Conference on Computer Vision Theory and Applications, VISAPP 2017, vol. 6, pp. 255–264 (2017)
14. Wu, T., Ranganathan, A.: Vehicle localization using road markings. In 2013 IEEE Intelligent Vehicles Symposium, IV, pp. 1185–1190 (2013)
15. Zhou, H., Zou, D., Pei, L., Ying, R., Liu, P., Yu, W.: StructSLAM: visual SLAM with building structure lines. IEEE Trans. Veh. Technol. 64, 1364–1375 (2015)

Weak-Perspective
and Scaled-Orthographic Structure
from Motion with Missing Data

Levente Hajder[1,2(✉)]

[1] Department of Algorithms and Their Applications, Eötvös Loránd University,
Pázmány Péter sétány 1/c, Budapest 1111, Hungary
`hajder@inf.elte.hu`
[2] Machine Perception Laboratory, MTA SZTAKI, Budapest, Hungary

Abstract. Perspective n-Point (PnP) problem is in focus of 3D computer vision community since the late 80's. Standard solutions deal with the pinhole camera model, the problem is challenging due to the perspectivity. The well-known PnP algorithms assume that the intrinsic camera parameters are known, therefore, only extrinsic ones are needed to estimate. It is carried out by a rough estimation, usually given in closed forms, then the accurate camera parameters are obtained via numerical optimization. In this paper, we show that both the weak-perspective and scaled orthographic camera models can be optimally calibrated including the intrinsic camera parameters. Moreover, the latter one is done without iteration if the L_2 norm is used. It is also shown that the calibration can be inserted into a structure from motion algorithm. We also show that the scaled orthographic version can be powered by GPUs, yielding real-time performance.

Keywords: Weak-perspective camera model ·
Perpective n-point problem · Structure from motion

1 Introduction

The problem of optimal methods in multiple view geometry [10] is a very challenging research issue. This study deals with camera calibration, a key problem in computer vision. There are well-known solutions [9,36] to calibrate the perspective camera; these methods give a rough estimate of the parameters first, then refine them using numerical optimization, such as the Levenberg-Marquardt iteration. Optimal camera calibrations using the L_2 norm including the popular Perspective n-point Problem (PnP) were published for the perspective camera only if the intrinsic camera parameters are known [12,21,27,37]. The calibration

Supported by EFOP-3.6.3-VEKOP-16-2017-00001: Talent Management in Autonomous Vehicle Control Technologies – The Project is supported by the Hungarian Government and co-financed by the European Social Fund.

A. P. Cláudio et al. (Eds.): VISIGRAPP 2017, CCIS 983, pp. 128–153, 2019.
https://doi.org/10.1007/978-3-030-12209-6_7

can also be solved under the L_∞ norm [16] as well as the Structure from Motion problem [5,19,23]; however, the uncalibrated problem has not been optimally solved yet in the least squares sense to the best of our knowledge.

Weak-Perspective and Scaled Orthographic Camera Calibration. The optimal estimation of the affine calibration is easy since it is a linear problem as it has been shown in several studies, such as that of Shum et al. [28]. The weak-perspective [7] and paraperspective [13] calibration have also been considered, but the proposed algorithms are not optimal since these papers focus on finding the link between para/weak-perspectivity and real projection. Kanatani et al. [17] also dealt with the calibration of different affine cameras, but they did not consider the optimality itself.

The scaled orthographic calibration can optimally be calibrated as discussed in our work [20]. An iteration was proposed by the authors to calibrate the scaled orthographic camera, and it converges to the global minima as proved in [20]. The orthographic camera is not considered separately, but the method can be used for that purpose as well if the scale of the scaled orthographic camera is fixed. Another possible solution [22] for the scaled orthographic calibration is to do an affine calibration and then find the closest scaled orthographic camera matrix to the affine one. However, optimality cannot be guaranteed in this case.

The optimal camera calibration method is proposed for weak-perspective cameras in this paper; it estimates the camera parameters if $3D$–$2D$ point correspondences are known between the points of a 3D calibration object and corresponding locations on the image. The minimization is optimal in the least squares sense.

Structure from Motion. The optimal weak-perspective camera calibration is theoretically very interesting, and it has practical significance as well. We show here that the calibration algorithms can be inserted into 3D reconstruction - also called Structure from Motion (SfM) - pipelines as a substep yielding very efficient weak-perspective reconstruction. Mathematically, the problem is a factorization one: the so-called measurement matrix has to be factorized into the matrices containing camera and structure parameters.

The classical factorization method, when the measurement matrix is factorized into 3D motion and structure matrices, was developed by Tomasi and Kanade [31] in 1992. The weak-perspective extension was published by Weinshall and Kanade [35]. Factorization was extended to the paraperspective [25] case as well as to the real perspective [30] one.

The problem of missing data is also a very important challenge in 3D reconstruction: one cannot guarantee that the feature points can be tracked over the whole image sequence since feature points can appear and/or disappear between frames. The problem of missing data was already addressed by Tomasi and Kanade [31]; however, they use only a naive approach which transforms the missing data problem to the full matrix factorization by estimating the missing entries. Shum et al. [28] gave a method to reconstruct the objects from range images; their method was successfully applied to the SfM problem by Buchanan and Fitzgibbon [4].

The mainstream idea for factorization with missing data is to decompose the rank 4 measurement matrix into affine structure and motion matrices which are of dimension 4. The Shum-method [4,28] also computes affine structure and motion matrices, but the dimension of those matrices is three. This problem can mathematically be solved by Principal Component Analysis with Missing Data (PCAMD) as pointed out by mathematicians since the middle 70's [26]. These methods can be applied directly to the SfM problem as it is written in [4]. Hartley and Schaffalitzky [11] proposed the PowerFactorization method which is based on the Power method to compute the dominant n-dimensional subspace of a given matrix. Buchanan and Fitzgibbon [4] handled the problem as an alternation consisting of two nonlinear iterations to be solved; they suggested the usage of the Damped-Newton method with line search to compute the optimal structure and motion matrices. Kanatani et al. [17] showed that the reconstruction problem can be solved without a full matrix factorization. Marques and Costeira [22] solved the factorization problem considering the scaled orthographic camera constraints; their method was basically an affine factorization, but the camera matrices were refined based on scaled orthographic constraint at the end of each cycle. An interesting approach was also proposed by Whang et al. [34]: their so-called quasi-perspective reconstruction fills the gap between affine and perspective approaches.

One of the aims of this study is to show that SfM algorithms can be run rapidly by utilizing the extreme computational power of the Graphics Processing Unit (GPU). The Bundle Adjustment (BA) method [2] is powered by GPU in several 3D framework, such as that of Choudhary et al. [6]. published There are other kinds of GPU-based 3D reconstruction methods such as [29,33], however, we only concentrate on the SfM problem here.

Contribution. This paper is based on our two conference [8,18] and one journal [20] publications. In the latter one, it was shown that the scaled orthographic camera calibration can be optimally obtained via an iteration. This method was speeded up by GPUs as it written in [18]. The weak-perspective calibration is introduced in 2017 [8], we gave closed-form solution for the problem. Both the weak-perspective and scaled orthographic calibration can be built into Structure from Motion (SfM) pipelines.

This paper summarized the result of these studies [8,18,20]. The methods written here are *interesting theoretically* and *useful practically*. For the latter purpose, we show that the proposed weak-perspective and scaled orthographic factorization can give good initial values for perspective bundle adjustment [2], and it can be inserted into a 3D reconstruction pipeline.

2   Problem Statement

Given the 3D coordinates of the points of a static object and their 2D projections in the image, the aim of camera calibration is to estimate the camera parameters which represent the 3D $\rightarrow$ 2D mapping.

Let us denote the 3D coordinates of the ith point by X_i, Y_i, and Z_i. The corresponding 2D coordinates are denoted by u_i, and v_i. The perspective (pinhole) camera model is usually written as follows

$$\begin{bmatrix} u_i \\ v_i \\ 1 \end{bmatrix} \sim C[R|T_{3D}] \begin{bmatrix} X_i\ Y_i\ Z_i\ 1 \end{bmatrix}^T, \tag{1}$$

where R is the rotation (orthonormal) matrix, and T_{3D} the spatial translation vector between the world and object coordinate systems. These parameters are usually called the extrinsic parameters of the perspective camera. The operator '$\sim$' denotes equality up to an unknown scale. The intrinsic parameters of the camera are stacked in the upper triangular matrix C [9].

If the above equation is multiplied by the inverse of camera matrix C, the following basic camera calibration formula is obtained: $C^{-1}\begin{bmatrix} u_i & v_i & 1 \end{bmatrix} \sim [R|T_{3D}] \begin{bmatrix} X_i\ Y_i\ Z_i\ 1 \end{bmatrix}^T$. If the intrinsic parameters stacked in matrix C and the spatial coordinates in $\begin{bmatrix} X_i\ Y_i\ Z_i\ 1 \end{bmatrix}^T$ are known then the calibration problem is reduced to the estimation of the extrinsic matrix/vector R and T_{3D}. This is the so-called Perspective n-point Problem (PnP). There are several efficient solvers [12,21,27,37] for PnP, however, estimates for the intrinsic parameters of the applied cameras are usually not presented. We deal with this problem, and it is shown here that the weak-perspective camera calibration is possible without the knowledge of any intrinsic camera parameters.

Fig. 1. Pixels for different camera models. Scaled orthographic, weak-perspective and affine camera pixels are equivalent to square, rectangle, and parallelogram, respectively [8].

If the depth of object is much smaller than the distance between the camera and the object, the weak-perspective camera model is a good approximation:

$$\begin{bmatrix} u_i\ v_i \end{bmatrix}^T = [M|t] \begin{bmatrix} X_i\ Y_i\ Z_i\ 1 \end{bmatrix}^T, \tag{2}$$

where M is the motion matrix consisting of two 3D vectors ($M = [m_1, m_2]^T$) and t is a 2D offset vector which locates the position of the world's origin in the image.

Contrary to the affine camera model, the rows of the motion matrix are not allowed to be arbitrary for the weak-perspective projection, they must satisfy the orthogonality constraint $m_1^T m_2 = 0$. A special case of the weak-perspective camera model is the scaled orthographic one, when $m_1^T m_1 = m_2^T m_2$. If the affine camera is considered, there is no constraint: the elements of the motion matrix M may be arbitrary.

The difference between the camera models can be visualized by the shapes of the corresponding camera pixels. Affine camera model is represented by a rectangular pixel: the opposite sides are parallel to each other. The weak-perspective model constraints that the adjacent sides are perpendicular, while the length of the sides are equal for the scaled orthographic camera model. The pixels are pictured in Fig. 1.

The optimal calibration of the affine camera in the least squares sense is relatively simple as the projection in Eq. 2 is linear w.r.t. unknown parameters. The solution can be obtained by the Moore-Penrose pseudo-inverse.

The scaled orthographic camera estimation is a more challenging problem. To the best of our knowledge, there is no closed-form solution. We [20] proved that the optimal estimation can be given via an iteration. However, this method is relatively slow due to the iteration. *One of the main contributions of this paper is that the weak-perspective case is solvable as a root finding problem of a 11-degree polynomial.*

3   Optimal Camera Calibration for Weak-Perspective Projection: The W-PnP Method

In this section, a novel weak-perspective camera calibration is proposed. The goal of the calibration is to minimize the squared reprojection error in the least squares sense. This is written as

$$\frac{1}{2} \sum_{i=1}^{N} \left\| \left[u_i \; v_i \right]^T - [M|t] \left[X_i \; Y_i \; Z_i \; 1 \right]^T \right\|^2, \tag{3}$$

where N is the number of points to be considered in the calibration, and $\|\cdot\|$ denotes the L_2 (Euclidean) vector norm. As Horn et al. [14] proved, the translation vector t is optimally estimated if it is selected as the center of gravity of the 2D points. These are easily calculated as $\tilde{u} = 1/N \sum_{i=1}^{N} u_i$, and $\tilde{v} = 1/N \sum_{i=1}^{N} v_i$.

If the weak-perspective camera model is assumed, the error defined in Eq. (3) can be rewritten in a more compact form as

$$\frac{1}{2} \left\| w_1^T - m_1^T S \right\|^2 + \frac{1}{2} \left\| w_2^T - m_2^T S \right\|^2, \tag{4}$$

where

$$w_1 = [u_1 - \tilde{u}, u_2 - \tilde{u}, \ldots, u_N - \tilde{u}]^T, \tag{5}$$

$$w_2 = [v_1 - \tilde{v}, v_2 - \tilde{v}, \ldots, v_N - \tilde{v}]^T, \tag{6}$$

$$S = \begin{bmatrix} X_1 \; X_2 \ldots X_N \\ Y_1 \; Y_2 \ldots Y_N \\ Z_1 \; Z_2 \ldots Z_N \end{bmatrix}. \tag{7}$$

If the Lagrange multiplier λ is introduced, the weak-perspective constraint can be considered. The error function is modified as follows

$$\frac{1}{2}\left|\left|w_1 - m_1^T S\right|\right|^2 + \frac{1}{2}\left|\left|w_2 - m_2^T S\right|\right|^2 + \lambda m_1^T m_2 \tag{8}$$

The optimal solution of this error function is given by its derivatives with respect to λ, m_1, and m_2:

$$m_1^T m_2 = 0, \tag{9}$$
$$SS^T m_1 - S w_1 + \lambda m_2 = 0, \tag{10}$$
$$SS^T m_2 - S w_2 + \lambda m_1 = 0. \tag{11}$$

m_2 is easily expressed from Eq. (10) as

$$m_2 = \frac{1}{\lambda}\left(S w_1 - SS^T m_1\right). \tag{12}$$

If one substitutes m_2 into Eqs. (11), and (9), then the following expressions are obtained:

$$\frac{1}{\lambda} SS^T \left(S w_1 - SS^T m_1\right) - S w_2 + \lambda m_1 = 0, \tag{13}$$

$$\frac{1}{\lambda} m_1^T \left(S w_1 - SS^T m_1\right) = 0. \tag{14}$$

If Eq. (13) is multiplied by λ, then m_1 can be expressed as

$$m_1 = \left(SS^T SS^T - \lambda^2 I\right)^{-1} \left(SS^T S w_1 - \lambda S w_2\right) \tag{15}$$

where I is the 3×3 identity matrix. Remark that the matrix inversion cannot be carried out if the Lagrange multiplier λ is one of the eigenvalues of the matrix SS^T. If the expressed m_1 is substituted into Eq. (14), the equation from which λ should be determined is obtained:

$$\frac{1}{\lambda} A^T(\lambda) B^{-T}(\lambda) \left(S w_1 - SS^T B^{-1}(\lambda) A(\lambda)\right) = 0 \tag{16}$$

where

$$A(\lambda) = SS^T S w_1 - \lambda S w_2 \tag{17}$$
$$B(\lambda) = SS^T SS^T - \lambda^2 I \tag{18}$$

$A(\lambda)$ and $B(\lambda)$ are a vector and a matrix that have elements containing polynomials of unknown variable λ. Such kind of vectors/matrices is called *vector/matrix of polynomials* in this study. The difficulty is that matrix $B(\lambda)$ should be inverted. This inversion can be written as a fraction of two matrices. $B^{-1}(\lambda)$ can write as

$$B^{-1}(\lambda) = \frac{\text{adj}\left(SS^T SS^T - \lambda^2 I\right)}{\det\left(SS^T SS^T - \lambda^2 I\right)} \tag{19}$$

where adj(.) denotes the adjoint[1] of a matrix. It is trivial that $\det(B(\lambda))$ is a polynomial of λ, while $\mathrm{adj}(B(\lambda))$ is a matrix of polynomials. This expression is useful since the equation can be multiplied by the determinants of $B(\lambda)$.

If one makes elementary modifications, Eq. (16) can be rewritten as

$$\frac{A^T(\lambda)\mathrm{adj}B^T(\lambda)}{\det B(\lambda)}\frac{\det B(\lambda)Sw_1 - SS^T\mathrm{adj}B(\lambda)A(\lambda)}{\det B(\lambda)} = 0. \tag{20}$$

It is also trivial that Eq. (20) is true if the numerator equals zero If the denominator, the determinant of matrix $B(\lambda)$ equals zero, then the problem cannot be solved; in this case, the 3D points in S are linearly dependent, the points in S form a plane, or a line, or a single point instead of a real 3D object. The Lagrange multiplier λ is calculated by solving the following polynomial:

$$A^T(\lambda)\mathrm{adj}B^T(\lambda)\left(\det B(\lambda)Sw_1 - SS^T\mathrm{adj}B(\lambda)A(\lambda)\right) = 0. \tag{21}$$

This final polynomial is of degree 11: $A(\lambda)$, and $B(\lambda)$ have terms of degree 1, and 2, respectively. Therefore, $\mathrm{adj}(B^T(\lambda))$ is of degree 4, while that of $A^T(\lambda)\mathrm{adj}(B^T(\lambda))$ is 5. Since the size of $B(\lambda)$ is 3×3, its determinant has degree $3 \cdot 2 = 6$. Other terms are of lower degree, the degree of the final polynomial comes to $5 + 6 = 11$.

The roots of the polynomial are 11 real/complex numbers, but only the real values have to be considered. The obtained real values of λ should be substituted into Eq. (15) and the obtained m_1 and λ into Eq. (12); then the optimal solution is the one minimizing the reprojection error given in Eq. (3).

We use Joe Huwaldt's Java Matrix Tool[2] to solve the 11-th order polynomial equation. Our implementation uses the Jenkins and Traub root finder [15], and we found that this algorithm is numerically very stable.

A very important remark is that in the case, when the coordinates in vectors w_1 and w_2 are noise-free, it is possible that λ equals zero. Then the camera vectors m_1 and m_2 can be computed as $m_1 = \left(SS^T\right)^{-1}Sw_1$ and $m_2 = \left(SS^T\right)^{-1}Sw_1$.

Minimal Solution. For PnP algorithms, the minimal number of points for the algorithms is also an important issue. The proposed optimization method is based on reprojection error: each point adds two equations to the minimization. The camera matrix consists of eight elements: six for camera pose and scales, two for offset. The pose gives 3 Degrees of Freedom (DoFs), vertical and horizontal scales are two DoFs, while the offset yields another two parameters. In summary, *the problem has 7 DoFs and they can be estimated from at least four 3D → 2D point correspondences.*

---

[1] The transpose of the adjoint is also called the matrix of cofactors.
[2] Available at http://thehuwaldtfamily.org/java/Packages/MathTools/MathTools.html.

4 Structure from Motion with Missing Data

We describe here how the previously discussed optimal calibration method can be applied for the factorization (SfM) problem. Our method allows the points to appear and/or disappear; thus, it can handle the missing data problem.

The proposed reconstruction method is an alternating least squares algorithm to minimize the reprojection error defined as follows

$$\left\| H \odot \left(W - [M|t] \begin{bmatrix} S \\ 1^T \end{bmatrix} \right) \right\|_F^2, \tag{22}$$

where M is the motion matrix consisting of the camera parameters in every frame, and structure matrix S contains the 3D coordinates of the points (points are located in the columns of matrix S). Operator '$\odot$' denotes the so-called Hadamard product[3], and H is the mask matrix. If H_{ij} is zero, then the jth point in the ith frame is not visible. If $H_{ij} = 1$, the point is visible.

Each cycle of the proposed methods is divided into the following main steps:

1. **W-PnP-step.** The aim of this step is to optimally estimate the motion matrix $M = [M_1^T, M_2^T, \ldots, M_F^T]^T$, and translation vector $t = [t_1^T, t_2^T, \ldots, t_F^T]^T$ if S is fixed, where the index denotes the frame number. It is trivial that the estimation of these submatrices are independent from each other if the elements of the structure matrix S are fixed. The optimal solution is given by W-PnP method defined in Sect. 3. Note that missing data should be skipped in the estimation.

2. **S-step.** The goal of S-step is to compute the structure matrix S if the elements of the motion matrix and the translation vector are fixed[4]. The 3D points represented by the columns of the structure matrix must be computed independently (they are independent from each other). Missing data should be considered during the estimation of course. It is a linear problem w.r.t. the coordinates contained by structure matrix S; the optimal method can be obtained using the Moore-Penrose pseudo-inverse as described in [28].

The proposed algorithm iterates the two steps until convergence as overviewed in Algorithm 1. The convergence itself is guaranteed since both steps decrease the non-negative reprojection error defined in Eq. 22. The proposed factorization method requires initial values of the matrices. The key idea for initializing the parameters is that the factorization with missing data can be divided into full matrix factorization of submatrices. If there is overlapping between submatrices, then the computed motion and structure submatrices can be merged if they are rotated and translated with the appropriate rotation matrices and vectors, respectively. We use the method of Pernek et al. [24] for this purpose.

Comparison with Scaled Orthographic Factorization. The scaled orthographic camera calibration [20] is overviewed in Algorithm 2. The main idea of

---

[3] $A \odot B = C$ if $c_{ij} = a_{ij} \cdot b_{ij}$.

[4] This task is usually called triangulation. This term comes from stereo vision where the camera centers and the 3D position of the point form a triangle.

Algorithm 1. Summary of weak-perspective factorization.

$M^{(0)}, t^{(0)}, S^{(0)} \leftarrow$ Parameter Initialization
$k \leftarrow 0$
repeat
    $k \leftarrow k + 1$
    $M^{(k)}, t^{(k)} \leftarrow$ W-PnP-Step($H, W, S^{(k-1)}$)
    $S^{(k)} \leftarrow$ S-Step($H, W, M^{(k)}, t^{(k)}$)
until convergence.

Algorithm 2. Skeleton of Scaled Orthographic Camera Calibration.

repeat
    $w_3 \leftarrow$ Completion($R, t, S, scale$)
    $R, t, scale \leftarrow$ Registration(S, w_1, w_2, w_3)
until convergence.

---

the calibration is as follows: the measured 2D coordinates are completed with a third coordinate that is simply calculated by reprojecting the spatial coordinates with the current camera parameters. Then the registration-step refines the camera parameters, and the completion and registration steps are repeated until convergence. Hajder et al. [20] proved that this iteration converges to the global optimum and this convergence is independent of the initial values of the camera parameters. The completion is simple, easy to implement, however, it is very costly as the calibration algorithm is iterative, closed-form solution is not known.

An alternating-style SfM algorithm can also be formed using the scaled orthographic camera model as it is visualized in Algorithm 3. It has more steps than the weak-perspective SfM method (Algorithm 1) as the completion of the 2D coordinates is required after every other steps. However, the scaled orthographic model can be speeded up by GPU as it is discuss later in this study. GPU-base implementation for weak-perspective model is not possible as the polynomial solver is too complex for a GPU thread.

Comparison with Affine Factorization. As it is discussed before, the estimation of affine camera parameters is a linear problem. There are several methods [4,28] dealing with affine SfM factorization as well. They are relatively fast, but the accuracy of those is lower compared to the scaled orthographic and weak-perspective factorization as the affine camera model enables shearing (skew) of the images that is not a realistic assumption. Remark that the skeleton of the affine SfM methods is the same as that of weak-perspective one defined in Algorithm 1.

Source Code. The proposed weak-perspective SfM algorithm is implemented in Java and available in ResearchGate profile of the author.

Algorithm 3. Summary of scaled orthographic factorization.

$M^{(0)},t^{(0)},S^{(0)} \leftarrow$ Parameter Initialization
$\tilde{H}, \tilde{W}^{(0)}, \tilde{M}^{(0)}, \tilde{t}^{(0)} \leftarrow$ Complete($H, W, M^{(0)},t^{(0)}, S^{(0)}$)
$k \leftarrow 0$
repeat
    $k \leftarrow k + 1$
    $\tilde{M}^{(k)} \leftarrow$ Registration($\tilde{H},\tilde{W}^{(k)},S^{(k-1)}$)
    $\tilde{W}^{(k)} \leftarrow$ Completion(W,$\tilde{H},\tilde{M}^{(k)},S^{(k-1)}$)
    $S^{(k)} \leftarrow$ S-Step($\tilde{H},\tilde{W}^{(k)},\tilde{M}^{(k)}$)
    $\tilde{W}^{(k)} \leftarrow$ Completion(W,$\tilde{H},\tilde{M}^{(k)},S^{(k)}$)
until $\left\| \tilde{H} \odot \left(\tilde{W}^{(k)} - \left[\tilde{M}^{(k)} | t^{(k)} \right] \begin{bmatrix} S^{(k)} \\ 1 \end{bmatrix} \right) \right\|_F^2$ converges.

---

5 Tests on Synthesized Data

Several experiments with synthetic data were carried out to study the properties of the proposed methods. Three methods were compared: (i) **SO** Scaled Orthographic factorization [20], (ii) **WP** proposed Weak-Perspective factorization, and (iii) **AFF**: Affine factorization [28].

We have examined three properties as follows.

1. Reconstruction error: The reconstructed 3D points are registered to the generated (ground truth) ones using the method of Arun et al. [1]. This registration error is called reconstruction error in the tests. The charts show the improvement of the method (in percentage) w.r.t. the original Tomasi-Kanade factorization [31].
2. Motion error: The row vectors of the obtained 3D motion matrix can be registered to that of the generated (ground truth) motion matrix. This registration error is called motion error here. The charts show the improvement in percentage similarly to visualization of the reconstruction error.
3. Time demand: The running time of each algorithm was measured. The given values contain every step from the parameter initialization to the final reconstruction.

To compare the affine method [28] listed above with the other two rival algorithms, the computation of the metric 3D structure was carried out by the classical weak-perspective Tomasi-Kanade factorization [31]. The $2F \times 4$ affine motion was multiplied by the $4 \times P$ affine structure matrix, and a full measurement matrix was obtained. Then this measurement matrix was factorized by the Tomasi-Kanade algorithm [31] with the Weinshall-Kanade [35] extension.

All of the rival methods were implemented in Java. The tests were run on an Intel Core4Quad 2.33 GHz PC with 4 GByte memory.

5.1 Test Data Generation

Generation of Moving Feature Points. The input measurement matrix was composed of 2D trajectories. These trajectories were generated in the following way: (i) Random three-dimensional coordinates were generated by a zero-mean Gaussian random number generator with variance σ_{3D}. (ii) The generated 3D points were rotated by random angles. (iii) Points were projected using perspective projection.[5] (iv) Noise was added to the projected coordinates. It was generated by a zero-mean Gaussian random number generator as well; its variance was set to σ_{2D}. (v) Finally, the measurement matrix W was composed of the projected points. (vi) Motion and structure parameters were initialized as described in Sect. 4. For each test case, 100 measurement matrices were generated and the results shown in this section were calculated as the average of the 100 independent executions.

Generation of Mask Matrix. The mask generator algorithm has three parameters: (i) P: Number of the visible points in each frame, (ii) F: Number of the frames. (iii) O: offset between two neighboring frames. The structure of the mask matrix is the same as in our BMVC 2008 paper [24].

5.2   Test Evaluation

General Remarks. The charts basically show that the **SO** algorithm outperforms the other methods in every test case as it is expected. This is evident since the scaled orthographic projection model is the closest one to real perspectivity. This is true for the reconstruction error as well as the motion error. The second place in accuracy is given to the proposed weak-perspective (**WP**) method which is always better than the affine one, but slightly less accurate than the **SO** method.

Examining the charts of time demand, it is clear that the fastest method is the affine (**AFF**) one; however, the affine algorithm can be very slow as discussed during real tests later if there is a huge amount of input data. It is because a full factorization [31] must be applied after the affine factorization to obtain metric reconstruction, and this can be very slow due to the Singular Value Decomposition. This SVD-step can be faster if only the three most dominant singular values and vectors are computed [17]. Unfortunately, the Java Matrix Package (JAMA) which we used in our implementation does not contain this feature. As shown in [4], there are several methods which implement affine reconstruction. Pernek et al. have shown earlier [24] that the fastest method of those is the so-called Damped-Newton algorithm, which is significantly faster than our affine implementation.

The main conclusion of the tests is that there is a tradeoff between accuracy and time demand. The **SO** factorization is the most accurate but slowest one, while the affine is fast but less accurate. The proposed **WP**-SfM algorithm is very close to **SO** and **AFF** algorithms in accuracy and running time, respectively.

---

[5] We tried the orthographic projection model with/without scale as well, the results had similar characteristics. Only the fully perspective test generation is contained in this paper due to the page limit.

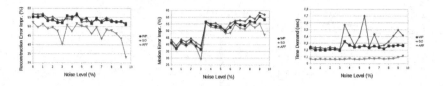

Fig. 2. Improvement of reconstruction and motion errors (left charts) and time demand (right) w.r.t. 2D noise [8].

Error versus Noise (Fig. 2). The methods were run with gradually increasing noise level. The reconstruction error increases approximately in a linear way for all the methods. Therefore, the improvement is approximately the same for all noise levels as the error of the reference factorization [31] increases with regard to noise as well. The test sequence consisted of 20 frames, and $P = 100$ was set. The missing data ratio was 30.6%. The noise level was calculated as $100\sigma_{2D}/\sigma_{3D}$.

The test indicated that the **SO** algorithm outpowered the rival ones, and the **WP** method was better than the affine one as expected; however, **SO** needs the most time to finish its execution, thus the fastest method is the affine one.

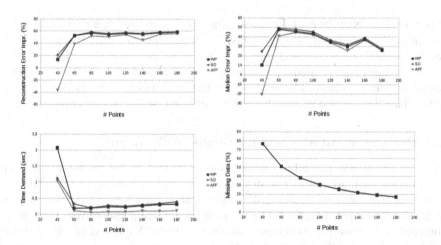

Fig. 3. Improvement of reconstruction and motion errors (top charts) and time demand (bottom left) w.r.t. number of points. Bottom right chart shows the ratio of missing data [8].

Error versus Number of Points (Fig. 3). P increased from 40 to 180 (the missing data rate decreased from approx. 80% to 20%). The noise level was 5%, and the sequence consisted of 100 frames. The conclusion was similar to the previous test case: the most accurate model was given by the **SO** algorithm, the second one was from the **WP** method. The difference was not significant in either accuracy or execution time.

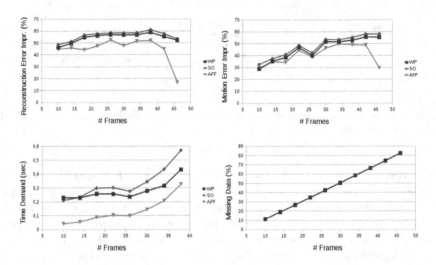

Fig. 4. Improvement of reconstruction and motion errors (top charts) and time demand (bottom left) w.r.t. number of frames. Bottom right chart show the ratio of missing data [8].

Error versus Number of Frames (Fig. 4). F increased from 10 to 46. The corresponding missing data ratio increased from 10% to 80%. The noise level was 5%, and $P = 100$. In each test case, the most accurate algorithm was the one consisting of the scaled orthographic camera model, but this was also the slowest one as expected. The accuracy of the weak-perspective factorization is better than the affine one after both structure and motion reconstruction.

5.3   Parameter Initialization for Bundle Adjustment

As discussed above, the affine, weak-perspective and scaled orthographic SfM method can estimate the 3D structure of the tracked points. In this chapter, we are examining how obtained 3D points can be used as initial parameters for perspective reconstruction. The 3D coordinates are perspectively projected. The applied perspective reconstruction itself is the SBA implementation[6] of the well-known bundle adjustment [2] method.

When the structure matrices have already been computed, the estimation of the 3×4 projection matrices is a camera calibration problem. In our test, the normalized Direct Linear Transformation (DLT) algorithm [9], also known as the 'six-point method', was applied. The projection matrix was then decomposed into camera intrinsic and extrinsic parameters.

We compared the initial parameters of the three compared method. BA cannot guarantee that global optimum is reached through estimation; it is interesting that BA after the *weak-perspective, scaled orthographic and affine parameter initialization usually gives the same results.* The time demand of the two methods

---

[6] http://users.ics.forth.gr/~lourakis/sba/.

differs a bit: the weak-perspective (**WP**) and scaled orthographic (**SO**) methods usually help BA to yield faster convergence than affine (**AFF**) parameterization. We also applied the classical Tomasi-Kanade (**TK**) algorithm [31] for parameter initialization, and that yielded the slowest BA convergence. Moreover, its results were usually less accurate than those of the other three algorithms (**AFF**, **SO**, **WP**); therefore, it seems that BA usually converges to local minima if the initial parameters are obtained by Tomasi-Kanade factorization. Time demand (msec) in our test sequences are listed in Table 1. There is not significant difference between the case when the scaled orthographic or proposed weak-perspective factorization is applied in order to compute initial parameters for perspective BA. Therefore the overall running time of **WP** method is smaller as the **WP** factorization is faster than the **SO** one.

Table 1. Time demand of bundle adjustment. There is not significant difference between the scaled orthographic (**SO**) and weak-perspective (**WP**) values [8].

Test sequence	TK	WP	SO	Aff
Versus noise	1628.35	**986.12**	989.805	1033.27
Versus frames	1649.63	598.93	**582.22**	693.77
Versus points	985.65	452.525	**444.7**	450.4375

The conclusion of the parameter initialization test is that the weak-perspective algorithm gives the fastest results since the time demand for factorization itself is faster than that of rival methods, while the speed of the BA algorithm is approximately the same in the case of **WP** and **SO** parameter initialization; the BA method usually converges to the same 3D reconstructions.

6 Rapid Structure from Motion by GPU

The aim of this section is to show that a rapid implementation of the scaled orthographics SfM can significantly reduce the time demand of the method. Two improvements are introduced: the used linear algorithm methods can be accelerated, and the substeps can be parallelized.

6.1 Faster Matrix Computations

General linear algebra methods in common mathematical software packages operate on arbitrary matrices. By taking advantage of the fact that the dimensions of the matrices in our SfM algorithm are known, the general matrix operations can be accelerated as follows.

Pseudoinverse. In our original implementation, the SVD algorithm applied in the M-step is performed using Java Matrix Package (JAMA)[7]. The pseudoinverse

---

[7] http://math.nist.gov/javanumerics/jama/.

is also calculated using SVD. However, this is not the fastest way. In the S-step, the pseudoinverse of a $3\tilde{F} \times 3$ matrix $\tilde{M}$ is computed, where $\tilde{F}$ is the number of frames in which the processed point is visible. It is well known [3] that the pseudoinverse can be written as

$$\tilde{M}^{\dagger} = (\tilde{M}^{T}\tilde{M})^{-1}\tilde{M}^{T}. \tag{23}$$

The size of matrix $\tilde{M}^{T}\tilde{M}$ is 3×3. Its inverse can be written with the help of the adjoint matrix and the determinant. Therefore, we have implemented a special pseudoinverse algorithm which computes the inverse of matrices with three columns. This simplification reduces the computational load of the method. *According to the tests we executed, our special pseudoinverse implementation is 15–25 times faster than the original one.*

SVD. The SVD implementations in linear algebra software libraries such as JAMA contain iterative solutions [3], because the size of the matrix to be processed is arbitrary. In this SfM algorithm, the SVD is required only for solving the registration problem, and the matrix to be decomposed is always a 3×3 one. The SVD itself has three subproblems: (i) For the calculation of the singular values, the eigenvalues of a 3×3 matrix are required. This calculation is equivalent to finding the three real roots of a 3-degree polynomial. (ii) The calculation of the left and/or right singular vectors are given by determining the null-vectors corresponding to the singular values. In order to solve this homogeneous linear problem, we have used the well-known Gauss-Newton elimination. (iii) If the left/right singular vectors are known, the vectors on the other side are obtained using simple matrix multiplications with normalization. *The computational time of our 3×3 SVD implementation is approximately half of that of the original one.*

6.2   GPU Implementation

The architecture of modern GPUs offers very high computing power to certain algorithms. The main requirement is that the execution be split into branches which are independent and can be executed concurrently. Although our algorithm is iterative and each step must be fully completed before starting the next one, the individual steps themselves are suitable for parallelization and are complex enough for the implementation to benefit from the GPU architecture.

We used OpenCL, a standard for general purpose programming on various devices; it is supported by the modern video card brands of both AMD and NVIDIA. It defines a C-like language for creating so called kernels, functions which are to be executed on the device, and an API for data transfer and execution control. The host code uses this API to access the device, send the input data to the device memory, initiate execution of kernels, and finally read the result data back to the main memory.

After the parameter initialization and completion steps, the GPU implementation of the algorithm transfers all four matrices, M, t, W, and S to the GPU memory. The M-step, the S-step, the Update, and the error computation kernels are executed appropriately, as required by the algorithm. As all four components run on the device, we can avoid most data transfer during the iteration itself. The result is read back to the main memory only when the algorithm terminates.

Parallelism. The key idea in our GPU-based implementation is that most parts of the algorithms can be run in parallel.

S-step. Computation of the 3D coordinates are performed for each point independently, so the S-step translates to the GPU architecture in a straightforward manner. Since the number of points is generally high, and this step requires nontrivial calculations, including a pseudoinverse, we achieved great GPU utilization and performance improvement compared to the traditional implementation.

M-step. The M-step can be executed for each frame concurrently. The number of frames is usually lower than the number of points, but 3D registration is even more computationally intensive than the 3D point estimation of the S-step. For optimal parallel performance, we avoided allocations of large temporary data structures and handled missing data in-place.

Update Step. As it is shown in our previous paper [20], every single projection can be calculated independently.

Computation of Reprojection Error. Although the error of each measured point can be computed independently, summation does not translate to a parallel architecture as it is. In our implementation of this step we first calculate the entire error matrix, then execute a recursive parallel reduction algorithm to produce the sum of more and more elements until the entire matrix is processed. The main benefit of such an implementation is to avoid reading back the matrices to the CPU for the error calculation, as the cost of data transfer is very high.

7   Tests of Time Demand on Synthetic Data

Several experiments with synthetic data have been carried out to study the properties of the reconstruction methods. We focus on the time demand of our following three implementations. **CPU:** Straightforward single-threaded implementation running on an Intel Core4Quad 2.33 GHz CPU with 4 Gbyte memory. **CPU4TH:** The multi-threaded version of the same code using the same CPU. **GPU256TH:** The OpenCL port of the multi-threaded version running on the NVIDIA GTX 285 GPU with only 256 parallel threads.

All three implementations include the faster matrix operations described in Sect. 6.1.

We have tested both the offline and the incremental version of the SfM algorithm.

For the synthetic tests, we have generated the input measurement matrices as follows. (i) A random 3D point cloud has been generated. (ii) Then these points have been rotated randomly and projected into the hypothetic image plane using weak-perspective projection. (iii) Random Gaussian noise has been added to the projections. (iv) Finally, the coordinates have been scaled to the interval $[0, 1000]$.

7.1   Offline SfM

The plots in Fig. 5 show the execution times of the three implementations as a function of the number of points, the number of frames, and the missing data ratio. One of these test parameters was incremented for each graph, the other two were set to a fix value. This value was 1000 for the number of points, 50 for the number of frames, and 50% for the missing data ratio. The termination threshold δ of the iteration was set to 10^{-5} pixel.

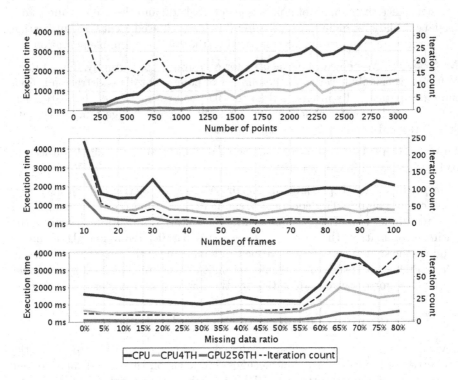

Fig. 5. Time demand and iteration numbers of implementations w.r.t. number of points (top), number of frames (middle), missing data ratio (bottom).

The algorithm is approximately linear in the number of points as it is shown by the first plot. When the number of frames increases (middle chart), the higher computational demand of the steps themselves is balanced by the lower number of iterations required. This can be explained by the initial parameter estimates being of better quality. The bottom graph shows that the missing data ratio has little effect on execution time until about 60%. Then the algorithm starts requiring an increasing number of iterations, and this results in a sharp rise of execution time, even if the less points are visible, the faster each step becomes, since they only use the visible points.

We have performed an additional test with 20000 points, and 500 frames to compare our method to the GPU-powered BA algorithm. The total execution time was 3.8 s. *This is less than the time demand of a single iteration of the GPU-based BA.* The total execution time of BA for this huge amount of data is approximately one day as it is analyzed in [6].

7.2   Incremental SfM

For brevity, and since the incremental variant is aimed for real-time conditions, we only present the results for the GPU version. (The general relationship between the performance of the three implementations is the same as in the offline case.)

In our tests, we used the following parameters by default: 1000 points, 50 frames, 50% missing data ratio, 2.5% noise, an error threshold of $\delta = 10^{-3}$ pixel, and refinement every fifth frame (refinement period of 5).

Figure 6 displays the performance of the algorithm in frames per second (FPS) and the final reprojection error with respect to noise level. The latter is the root mean square (RMS) of the error values. We see that the algorithm becomes faster as the noise increases because less iterations are required altogether. We cannot explain this behavior, but we can clearly state that the reconstruction is real-time. As expected, the error increases with noise.

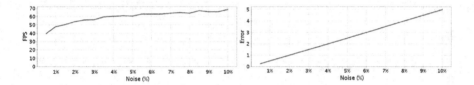

Fig. 6. FPS and final error w.r.t. noise.

In accordance with our expectations, the algorithm becomes slower as the number of points is increased (Fig. 7). The final RMS error is steadily between 1 and 1.3 pixels.

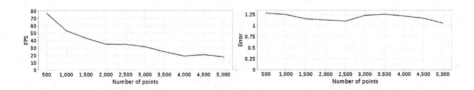

Fig. 7. FPS and final error w.r.t. number of points.

As we increased the total number of images (Fig. 8), the speed of processing increased at first, then it leveled off at around 65 FPS (with error values staying in the 1–1.3 pixel range). This promising result indicates that, although the iterative refinement struggles at the start when few images are available, it can sustain high performance in the long-term.

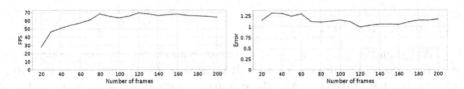

Fig. 8. FPS and final error w.r.t. number of frames.

The missing data chart (Fig. 9) confirms the idea that the more data are available, the less iterations are required to achieve the error threshold. We can even observe a similar jump at 60% missing data as we did in Fig. 5. Also note that for this test sequence we set the number of points to 2500 instead of the default 1000 in order to accommodate to higher ratios of missing data. The error plot shows that missing data ratio has little effect on the final error.

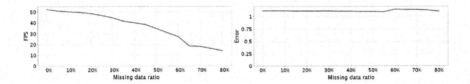

Fig. 9. FPS and final error w.r.t. missing data ratio.

Finally, in Fig. 10, we demonstrate that we can reduce the frequency of iterative refinement during the algorithm to achieve higher throughput without sacrificing accuracy. The RMS reprojection error with respect to the frame number is visualized in Fig. 11. It is clear that the refinement significantly reduces the final error especially when the reconstruction is computed from less frames.

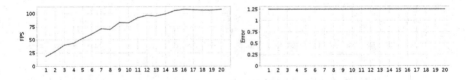

Fig. 10. FPS (left) and iteration number (right) w.r.t. refinement period.

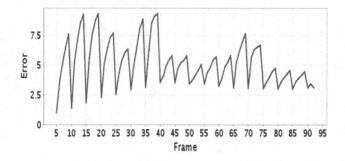

Fig. 11. Error during incremental reconstruction.

8 Tests on Real Data

We tested the proposed algorithm on several real sequences as well.

'Dino' sequence. The 'Dino' sequence, downloaded from the web page of the Oxford University[8], consisted of 36 frames and 319 tracked points. The measurement matrix had a missing data ratio of 77%. Input images are visualized on the left images of Fig. 12. The reconstructed 3D points were computed by the proposed SfM method. The time demand of that was 26 seconds (the affine and scaled orthographic SfM methods have computed the reconstruction in 6 and 34 s, respectively). The results are plotted in the right part of Fig. 12.

Fig. 12. Results on 'Dino' sequence: Left: 2 out of 36 original image and (right) reconstructed point cloud captured from three views [8].

Another interesting examination is to compare the quality of the reconstructed 3D models; the points themselves seem very similar, but the camera positions differs significantly. We compared those after factorization by the original Tomasi-Kanade method to affine, weak-perspective and scaled orthographic improvement as visualized in Fig. 13. The quality of the original factorization method (top-left image) is very erroneous since the cameras should be located at regular locations of a circle. The improvements are significantly better. As expected, the scaled orthographic reconstruction (bottom-right image) serves

---
[8] http://www.robots.ox.ac.uk/~amb/.

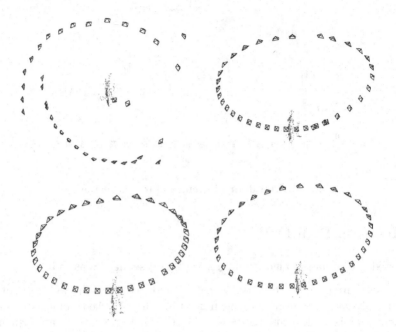

Fig. 13. Reconstructed 'Dino' model with estimated cameras. Top-left: Original Tomasi-Kanade factorization. Top-right: Affine factorization. Bottom-left: Weak-perspective factorization (proposed method). Bottom-right: Scaled orthographic factorization. The cameras should be uniformly located around the estimated point cloud of the plastic dinosaur. The difference between weak-perspective and scaled orthographic camera parameters is not significant [8].

better quality, the proposed weak-perspective (bottom-left) is slightly worse, but it serves acceptable results; the affine refinement (top-right plot) is also satisfactory.

The visualization of the camera optical centers for non-perspective cameras was not trivial. The pose of the cameras were obtained by the factorizations, but the focal length could not be estimated. For this reason, the focal length was set manually.

'Cat' Sequence. We tested the proposed algorithm on our 'Cat' sequence. The cat statuette was rotated on a table and 92 photos were taken by a common commercial digital camera. The regions of the statuette in the images were automatically determined.

Feature points were detected using the widely-used KLT [32] algorithm, and the points were tracked by a correlation-based template matching method. A features point was labeled as missing if the tracker could not find its location in the next image, or the location was not inside the automatically detected region of the object. The measurement matrix of the sequence consisted of 2290 points and 92 frames. The missing data ratio was 82%, that is very high.

Fig. 14. Two images (left) of sequence 'Cat' and the reconstructed points from three views (right). [8].

The 3D reconstructed points are visualized on the right plots of Fig. 14. We tested every possible method and compared the time demand of the methods: the running times of the affine, scaled orthographic, and weak-perspective factorization were 484, 199, and 99 s, respectively.

8.1 GPU-Based Tests on Real Objects

The offline and incremental implementation are compared in this test on two real sequences 'Dino' and 'Cat'.

Offline SfM. We have tested the implementations on two real sequences mentioned above. They have produced identical results, and as expected, the parallel ones were significantly faster than the serial one.

For these tests we used the termination condition $\delta = 10^{-3}$.

'Dino' Sequence. The input images and the reconstructed 3D points are visualized in Fig. 12. The time demands of the CPU, CPU4TH, and GPU256TH implementations were 5.4, 2.4, and 1.3 s, respectively.

'Cat' Sequence. We have tested the implementations on our 'Cat' sequence pictured in Fig. 14 as well. The time demands of the CPU, CPU4TH, and GPU256TH implementations were 14.3, 4.6, and 1.2 s, respectively. The decrease of the RMS reprojection error is pictured in Fig. 15. It is monotonic, as expected, since each substep of the algorithm is optimal.

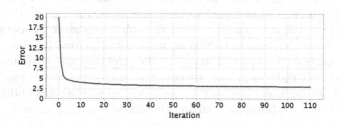

Fig. 15. Error during refinement of the 'Cat' sequence.

8.2   Incremental vs. Offline SfM

Table 2 compares the performance of the incremental and the offline variants of our reconstruction algorithm for the two real sequences. The incremental variant did not reach real-time speed, due to the high missing data ratio; this result is in accordance with the synthetic tests (see Fig. 9). By increasing the termination threshold from 10^{-3} to 10^{-2} (Table 3), both sequences could be processed at over 15 FPS, the speed of conventional web cameras. The cost of this change is quite small with regards to the final reprojection error (for the 'Cat' sequence, the error increased from 3 to 3.5 pixels; and from 1.9 to 2.4 pixels for the 'Dino' sequence).

Table 2. Time demand on real sequences ($\delta = 10^{-3}$).

Sequence	FPS (incr.)	Total (incr.)	Total (offl.)
Dino	11.2	2.7 s	1.3 s
Cat	3.7	23.3 s	1.2 s

Table 3. Time demand on real sequences ($\delta = 10^{-2}$).

Sequence	FPS (incr.)	Total (incr.)	Total (offl.)
Dino	25.9	1.2 s	251 ms
Cat	16.5	5.2 s	482 ms

Still, the offline algorithm, having more data available to it, performs significantly better. These results suggest that the incremental version should only be used when it is important to obtain partial reconstruction results during the process.

9   Conclusion

We have presented the optimal calibration algorithm for the weak-perspective camera model here. The proposed method minimizes the reprojection error of feature points in the least squares sense. The solution is given by a closed-form formula. We have also proposed a SfM algorithm; it is an iterative one, and every iteration consists of two optimal steps: (i) The structure matrix computation is a linear problem, therefore it can be optimally estimated in the least squares sense, while (ii) the camera parameters are obtained by the novel optimal weak-perspective camera calibration method. The introduced SfM approach can also cope with the problem of missing feature points.

The proposed weak-perspective and scaled orthographic SfM algorithms were compared to the affine one. It was shown that weak-perspective SfM is significantly more accurate than the affine one, and usually faster than the scaled orthographic SfM algorithm due to the optimal weak-perspective calibration. We successfully applied the novel method to compute the initial parameters for bundle adjustment-type 3D perspective reconstruction. The (offline) Java implementation of our weak-perspective SfM algorithm can be downloaded from the ResearchGate profile of the author.

Finally, the GPU-based implementation of scaled orthographic SfM is overviewed, and both the offline and incremental variants are compared on real test sequences.

References

1. Arun, K.S., Huang, T.S., Blostein, S.D.: Least-squares fitting of two 3-D point sets. IEEE Trans. PAMI **9**(5), 698–700 (1987)
2. Triggs, B., McLauchlan, P.F., Hartley, R.I., Fitzgibbon, A.W.: Bundle adjustment—a modern synthesis. In: Triggs, B., Zisserman, A., Szeliski, R. (eds.) IWVA 1999. LNCS, vol. 1883, pp. 298–372. Springer, Heidelberg (2000). https://doi.org/10.1007/3-540-44480-7_21
3. Björck, Å.: Numerical Methods for Least Squares Problems. Siam, Philadelphia (1996)
4. Buchanan, A.M., Fitzgibbon, A.W.: Damped Newton algorithms for matrix factorization with missing data. In: Proceedings of the 2005 IEEE CVPR, pp. 316–322 (2005)
5. Bue, A.D., Xavier, J., Agapito, L., Paladini, M.: Bilinear modeling via augmented lagrange multipliers (balm). IEEE Trans. PAMI **34**(8), 1496–1508 (2012)
6. Choudhary, S., Gupta, S., Narayanan, P.J.: Practical time bundle adjustment for 3D reconstruction on the GPU. In: Kutulakos, K.N. (ed.) ECCV 2010. LNCS, vol. 6554, pp. 423–435. Springer, Heidelberg (2012). https://doi.org/10.1007/978-3-642-35740-4_33
7. DeMenthon, D.F., Davis, L.S.: Model-based object pose in 25 lines of code. IJCV **15**, 123–141 (1995)
8. Hajder, L.: W-PnP method: optimal solution for the weak-perspective n-Point problem and its application to structure from motion. In: Proceedings of the 12th International Joint Conference on Computer Vision, Imaging and Computer Graphics Theory and Applications (VISIGRAPP), pp. 265–276 (2017)
9. Hartley, R.I., Zisserman, A.: Multiple View Geometry in Computer Vision. Cambridge University Press, Cambridge (2000)
10. Hartley, R., Kahl, F.: Optimal algorithms in multiview geometry. In: Yagi, Y., Kang, S.B., Kweon, I.S., Zha, H. (eds.) ACCV 2007. LNCS, vol. 4843, pp. 13–34. Springer, Heidelberg (2007). https://doi.org/10.1007/978-3-540-76386-4_2
11. Hartley, R., Schaffalitzky, F.: Powerfactorization: 3D reconstruction with missing or uncertain data (2003)
12. Hesch, J.A., Roumeliotis, S.I.: A direct least-squares (DLS) method for PnP. In: International Conference on Computer Vision, pp. 383–390. IEEE (2011)
13. Horaud, R., Dornaika, F., Lamiroy, B., Christy, S.: Object pose: the link between weak perspective, paraperspective and full perspective. Int. J. Comput. Vis. **22**(2), 173–189 (1997)
14. Horn, B., Hilden, H., Negahdaripourt, S.: Closed-form solution of absolute orientation using orthonormal matrices. J. Opt. Soc. Am. **5**(7), 1127–1135 (1988)

15. Jenkins, M.A., Traub, J.F.: A three-stage variables-shift iteration for polynomial zeros and its relation to generalized Rayleigh iteration. Numer. Math. **14**, 252–263 (1970)

16. Kahl, F., Hartley, R.I.: Multiple-view geometry under the linfinity-norm. IEEE Trans. Pattern Anal. Mach. Intell. **30**(9), 1603–1617 (2008)

17. Kanatani, K., Sugaya, Y., Ackermann, H.: Uncalibrated factorization using a variable symmetric affine camera. IEICE - Trans. Inf. Syst. **E90-D**(5), 851–858 (2007)

18. Kazó, C., Hajder, L.: Rapid weak-perspective structure from motion with missing data. In: ICCV Workshops, pp. 491–498 (2011)

19. Ke, Q., Kanade, T.: Quasiconvex optimization for robust geometric reconstruction. In: Proceedings of the Tenth IEEE International Conference on Computer Vision, ICCV 2005, pp. 986–993 (2005)

20. Hajder, L., Pernek, Á., Kazó, C.: Weak-perspective structure from motion by fast alternation. Vis. Comput. **27**(5), 387–399 (2011)

21. Lepetit, V., Moreno-Noguer, F., Fua, P.: EPnP: an accurate O(n) solution to the PnP problem. Int. J. Comput. Vis. **81**(2), 155–166 (2009)

22. Marques, M., Costeira, J.: Estimating 3D shape from degenerate sequences with missing data. CVIU **113**(2), 261–272 (2009)

23. Okatani, T., Deguchi, K.: On the Wiberg algorithm for matrix factorization in the presence of missing components. IJCV **72**(3), 329–337 (2006)

24. Pernek, A., Hajder, L., Kazó, C.: Metric reconstruction with missing data under weak-perspective. In: BMVC, pp. 109–116 (2008)

25. Poelman, C.J., Kanade, T.: A paraperspective factorization method for shape and motion recovery. IEEE Trans. PAMI **19**(3), 312–322 (1997)

26. Ruhe, A.: Numerical computation of principal components when several observations are missing. Technical report, Umea Univesity, Sweden (1974)

27. Schweighofer, G., Pinz, A.: Globally optimal O(n) solution to the PnP problem for general camera models. In: BMVC (2008)

28. Shum, H.Y., Ikeuchi, K., Reddy, R.: Principal component analysis with missing data and its application to polyhedral object modeling. IEEE Trans. Pattern Anal. Mach. Intell. **17**(9), 854–867 (1995)

29. Stühmer, J., Gumhold, S., Cremers, D.: Real-time dense geometry from a handheld camera. In: Goesele, M., Roth, S., Kuijper, A., Schiele, B., Schindler, K. (eds.) DAGM 2010. LNCS, vol. 6376, pp. 11–20. Springer, Heidelberg (2010). https://doi.org/10.1007/978-3-642-15986-2_2

30. Sturm, P., Triggs, B.: A factorization based algorithm for multi-image projective structure and motion. In: Buxton, B., Cipolla, R. (eds.) ECCV 1996. LNCS, vol. 1065, pp. 709–720. Springer, Heidelberg (1996). https://doi.org/10.1007/3-540-61123-1_183

31. Tomasi, C., Kanade, T.: Shape and motion from image streams under orthography: a factorization approach. Int. J. Comput. Vis. **9**, 137–154 (1992)

32. Tomasi, C., Shi, J.: Good features to track. In: IEEE Conference Computer Vision and Pattern Recognition, pp. 593–600 (1994)

33. Tzevanidis, K., Zabulis, X., Sarmis, T., Koutlemanis, P., Kyriazis, N., Argyros, A.: From multiple views to textured 3D meshes: a GPU-powered approach. In: Kutulakos, K.N. (ed.) ECCV 2010. LNCS, vol. 6554, pp. 384–397. Springer, Heidelberg (2012). https://doi.org/10.1007/978-3-642-35740-4_30

34. Wang, G., Wu, Q.M.J., Sun, G.: Quasi-perspective projection with applications to 3D factorization from uncalibrated image sequences. In: CVPR (2008)

35. Weinshall, D., Tomasi, C.: Linear and incremental acquisition of invariant shape models from image sequences. IEEE Trans. PAMI **17**(5), 512–517 (1995)
36. Zhang, Z.: A flexible new technique for camera calibration. IEEE Trans. PAMI **22**(11), 1330–1334 (2000)
37. Zheng, Y., Kuang, Y., Sugimoto, S., Åström, K., Okutomi, M.: Revisiting the PnP problem: a fast, general and optimal solution. In: ICCV, pp. 2344–2351 (2013)

Spatiotemporal Optimization for Rolling Shutter Camera Pose Interpolation

Philippe-Antoine Gohard[1,2]([⊠]), Bertrand Vandeportaele[1], and Michel Devy[1]

[1] LAAS-CNRS, Toulouse University, CNRS, UPS, Toulouse, France
{philippe-antoine.gohard,bertrand.vandeportaele,michel.devy}@laas.fr
[2] Innersense, Ramonville-Saint-Agne, France

Abstract. Rolling Shutter cameras are predominant in the tablet and smart-phone market due to their low cost and small size. However, these cameras require specific geometric models when either the camera or the scene is in motion to account for the sequential exposure of the different lines of the image. This paper proposes to improve a state-of-the-art model for RS cameras through the use of Non Uniformly Time-Sampled B-splines. This allows to interpolate the pose of the camera while taking into account the varying dynamic of its motion, using higher density of control points where needed while keeping a low number of control points where the motion is smooth. Two methods are proposed to determine adequate distributions for the control points, using either an IMU sensor or an iterative reprojection error minimization. The non-uniform camera model is integrated into a Bundle Adjustment optimization which is able to converge even from a poor initial estimate. A routine of spatiotemporal optimization is presented in order to optimize both the spatial and temporal positions of the control points. Results on synthetic and real datasets are shown to prove the concepts and future works are introduced that should lead to the integration of our model in a SLAM algorithm.

Keywords: Rolling Shutter · Camera geometric model · Bundle adjustment · Simultaneous Localization and Mapping · B-splines interpolation

1 Introduction

In Augmented Reality applications for mobile devices (smartphones and tablets), the real-time localization of the device camera and the 3D modeling of the environment are used to integrate virtual elements onto the images of the real environment. This task is usually performed by algorithms of Structure From Motion (SFM: [1]), and Simultaneous Localization and Mapping (SLAM: MonoSLAM [2], PTAM [3] OrbSLAM [4]). Most existing implementations assume that the cameras are using a Global Shutter (GS), for which all the lines of the image are exposed at the same time, ie. if the integration time is neglected, the whole image is the projection of the scene using a single pose for the camera.

© Springer Nature Switzerland AG 2019
A. P. Cláudio et al. (Eds.): VISIGRAPP 2017, CCIS 983, pp. 154–175, 2019.
https://doi.org/10.1007/978-3-030-12209-6_8

However, more than 90% of mobile devices are equipped with Rolling Shutter (RS) cameras because of their lower cost and smaller size compared with the classic GS cameras. The advantages of RS cameras come with some drawbacks; by the way they are designed, they cause image distortions when observing a dynamic scene or when the camera is moving. In these sensors, all the lines of the image are exposed and transferred sequentially at different times.

More complex geometric models are thus required for RS cameras, to account for the varying pose of the camera. Previous RS Camera model presented in [5,6] are achieving camera pose interpolation using B-splines controlled by Control Points (CP) that are sampled in time with a constant interval. This kind of temporal distribution is referred to as an Uniform Time Distribution (UTD) in the following.

This paper extends these models by using an adaptive Non Uniform Time Distribution (NUTD) for the CP of the B-spline as proposed in [7]. This allows to globally reduce the number of CP required to model a given trajectory with the same accuracy compared with the UTD. The NUTD B-Splines are detailed, alongside a Bundle Adjustment (BA) using this model. The NUTD of the CP allows to optimize the timestamps of the CP, and we demonstrate how it can be used to model trajectories on real datasets.

The paper firstly presents existing SLAM algorithms and exhibits problems arising from the use of images captured with RS cameras. It then presents the theoretical framework used for the modeling of the RS cameras. First, the cumulative B-splines are introduced to allow the interpolation of 6-dof camera pose in continuous time. Second, the pinhole camera model using interpolated poses is derived. Then, the iterative minimization used in the Perspective n-Points and bundle adjustment algorithm is explained. Two methods are briefly exposed to efficiently generate the CP, using either an IMU sensor or multiple iterations of reprojection error minimization. A spatiotemporal optimization approach is then proposed to determine adequate NUTD for the CP. Finally, the proposed PnP and BA implementations using the NUTD B-Splines models are evaluated on synthetic datasets to prove the concept, then the spatiotemporal optimization is tested on real datasets. Future works are then discussed.

2   Related Work for SLAM

2.1   Global Shutter

A monocular visual SLAM algorithm recovers the position and orientation of a mobile camera and dynamically constructs a model of the environment in real-time. In the Augmented Reality context, the camera parameters are used to synthesize images of virtual elements that are rendered coherently over the acquired image, using the reconstructed model of the environment.

Early real-time methods used to solve the SLAM problem in the literature were based on Extended Kalman Filter (EKF) [2,8,9]. The simplicity of this method and it's computing efficiency for small size environment models has made it the most used SLAM method for the past decade.

Other robust and real-time methods based on local BA like PTAM [3] have also been proposed. They minimize the reprojection error over a subset of previously acquired images, called keyframes [4,10], or over a sliding window of frames [11]. They provide improved robustness thanks to the modeling of outliers, and [12] proved the superiority of these BA-based methods over filtering one.

2.2 Rolling Shutter

Using a SLAM method designed for GS camera model with RS camera produces deviations of the estimated trajectory and reconstructed 3D points. These deviations increase with the velocity of the camera. One of the first use of a RS camera model in the SLAM context was the adaptation of PTAM for smartphone [13]. They estimated the angular velocity of the camera at the keyframe using keypoints tracked between the previous and the next frame. This angular velocity was then used to correct the measurements of the points in the image using a first order approximation so they can be used as if they where obtained by a GS camera.

[14] initially used a similar method, and proposed in [15] a BA using a RS camera model. To estimate the varying camera pose inside a frame, they interpolated independently the rotations (using SLERP) and the translations (using linear interpolation).

[16] also used B-splines to have a continuous time representation. In their work, they interpolate rotations and translations by two independent B-splines. Their Cayley-Gibbs-Rodriguez formulation used for the poses had two major issues according to [5]:

- The used Rodrigues parameterization has a singularity for the rotation at π radians.
- The interpolation in this space does not represent the minimum distance for the rotation group hence the generated trajectories can correspond to unrealistic motions.

To address these issues, [5] proposed to use a continuous time trajectory formulation using cumulative B-splines. In precedent works [7], we have shown that the UTD of the B-Splines control poses (CP) leads either to a smoothing of the trajectory or to redundancies. We proposed to use a NUTD of the CP and methods to dynamically generate CP.

This paper is an extension of [7], describing a NUTD B-Spline model suitable for a BA algorithm and proposing a spatiotemporal optimization of the CP. A brief summary of used notations and scientific context is given in the next section.

3   Notations and Scientific Context

In this article, the 6 degrees of freedom associated to the extrinsic parameters of the camera are expressed by a matrix 4×4 corresponding to the transformation from the camera coordinate frame to the world coordinate frame. This matrix $\mathbf{T_w} \in \mathbb{SE}3$ is parameterized by a translation vector $\mathbf{a}$ and a rotation matrix $\mathbf{R}$:

$$\mathbf{T_w} = \begin{pmatrix} \mathbf{R} & \mathbf{a} \\ \mathbf{0}^T & 1 \end{pmatrix}, \mathbf{T_w} \in \mathbb{SE}3, \mathbf{R} \in \mathbb{SO}3, \mathbf{a} \in \mathbb{R}^3 \tag{1}$$

A rigid transformation in the Lie algebra $\mathfrak{se}(3)$ can be expressed by a 6D vector $\xi = [\mathbf{w}, \mathbf{a}]^T \in \mathfrak{se}(3)$ where $\mathbf{w} = [\omega_0, \omega_1, \omega_2]^T$ is the rotation component. Its 4×4 associated matrix can be obtained by applying the wedge operator $[\cdot]_\wedge$ on ξ knowing that $[w]_\times$ is the skew-symmetric matrix 3×3 of w:

$$\Omega = [\xi]_\wedge = \begin{pmatrix} [\mathbf{w}]_\times & \mathbf{a} \\ \mathbf{0}^T & 1 \end{pmatrix}, [\mathbf{w}]_\times = \begin{pmatrix} 0 & -\omega_2 & \omega_1 \\ \omega_2 & 0 & -\omega_0 \\ -\omega_1 & \omega_0 & 0 \end{pmatrix} \tag{2}$$

The logarithmic mapping projects a matrix from $\mathbb{SE}3$ to its tangent space $\mathfrak{se}(3)$ defined locally Euclidean, where compositions of rigid transformations are obtained by additions. The exponential mapping, being the inverse operation of the exponential map, projects back a 6D vector from the tangent space $\mathfrak{se}(3)$ towards $\mathbb{SE}(3)$. These two applications can be resumed (when the magnitude of the angle of rotation is lower than π):

$$\mathbf{T_w} = exp(\Omega)$$
$$\Omega = log(\mathbf{T_w}) \tag{3}$$

3.1   Cumulative B-Splines

As a RS camera exposes its lines at different instants, an estimate of the camera pose for each line is needed to project the 3D points of the observed scene onto the image. This estimate can be obtained with continuous-time modeling of the camera trajectory. To interpolate the camera pose associated with one particular image line, multiple timestamped CP, locally controlling the trajectory, are required, the first of these CP being timestamped at time t_i. The corresponding rigid transformations matrices are defined in the world coordinate system and abbreviated $\mathbf{T_{w,i}}$. Various interpolation methods can be considered (linear, B-Spline, Bézier) according to the final application.

A standard B-spline is defined by constant polynomial basis functions $B_{i,k}$ ($k - 1$ being the degree of the used polynomial) and variable CP $\mathbf{p}_i$. This definition is not suitable for the non euclidean space of rigid body transformation $\mathbb{SE}(3)$ where the elements are composed by matrix multiplication.

In [5], the authors suggest the use of the cumulative form of the B-Splines because of their suitability for the interpolation on the manifold $\mathbb{SE}(3)$ [17]. They chose cubic B-Splines ($k = 4$) for the interpolation to ensure a C^2 continuity of the trajectory, allowing interpolation of velocities and accelerations.

The cumulative basis functions $\tilde{B}(t)_j$ used in cubic cumulative B-Splines are expressed by the jth component of the vector $\tilde{\mathbf{B}}(t)$, starting at index $j = 0$:

$$\tilde{\mathbf{B}}(t) = \frac{1}{6} \begin{pmatrix} 6 & 0 & 0 & 0 \\ 5 & 3 & -3 & 1 \\ 1 & 3 & 3 & -2 \\ 0 & 0 & 0 & 1 \end{pmatrix} \begin{pmatrix} 1 \\ u(t) \\ u(t)^2 \\ u(t)^3 \end{pmatrix} \tag{4}$$

where $u(t) = \frac{t - t_{i+1}}{\Delta t}$ an intermediate time representation such as $0 \leq u(t) < 1$ between the two CP $\mathbf{T}_{\mathbf{w},i+1}$ and $\mathbf{T}_{\mathbf{w},i+2}$ with $t \in [t_{i+1}, t_{i+2}]$. Δt defines the time interval between the CP, which is considered constant for UTD B-Splines.

Interpolation on the $\mathbb{SE}3$ manifold is defined by a composition of CP variations $\boldsymbol{\Omega}_{j-1,j} = log(\mathbf{T}_{\mathbf{w},j-1}{}^{-1}\mathbf{T}_{\mathbf{w},j})$ weighted by basis functions $\tilde{B}(t)_j$ applied to a reference pose $\mathbf{T}_{\mathbf{w},i}$. Thus, in the case of cumulative cubic B-Spline ($k = 4$), the interpolation of the pose $\mathbf{T}_{\mathbf{w}}(t)$ between two CP $\mathbf{T}_{\mathbf{w},i+1}$ and $\mathbf{T}_{\mathbf{w},i+2}$ requires the four neighbor CP $\mathbf{T}_{\mathbf{w},i}$ to $\mathbf{T}_{\mathbf{w},i+3}$. The interpolation function is then expressed as:

$$\mathbf{T}_{\mathbf{w}}(t) = \mathbf{T}_{\mathbf{w},i} \prod_{j=i+1}^{i+k-1} \exp(\tilde{B}(t)_{j-i}\boldsymbol{\Omega}_{j-1,j}) \tag{5}$$

3.2   Non Uniform Time Distribution for B-Splines

This document is an extension of [7], where we suggested to use a NUTD of the CP in order to adjust the distribution to the camera trajectory dynamic. This enables a more efficient modeling of the trajectory, both in terms of computational cost and memory usage.

Using NUTD, the time interval Δ_t between two CP is not constant anymore. Instead, the time interval $\Delta t_{i-1,i}$ is defined as the difference of timestamps between the two CP $\mathbf{T}_{\mathbf{w},i-1}$ and $\mathbf{T}_{\mathbf{w},i}$.

B-Splines whose CP are non-uniformly sampled in time are named NUTD B-Splines in the remainder of this document. For such B-Splines, the basis functions are defined by a recurrence formula slightly different from the standard (UTD) case [18], see [17]:

$$B_{i,k}(t) = \frac{t - t_i}{t_{i+k-1} - t_i} B_{i,k-1}(t) + \frac{t_{i+k} - t}{t_{i+k} - t_{i+1}} B_{i+1,k-1}(t) \tag{6}$$

With the stopping condition defined by:

$$B_{i,1}(t) = \begin{cases} 1 & \text{if } t_i < t < t_{i+1} \\ 0 & \text{otherwise} \end{cases} \tag{7}$$

The recurrence formula allows to compute the basis functions for different degrees. By developing the formula as in [19] or using Toeplitz matrix [20], the basis function can be expressed as a matrix product as in [5] for cubic B-Spline. Unlike the UTD case, the coefficient matrix used in the expression of basis functions is dependent on the CP timestamps. For cubic B-Splines, four CP $\mathbf{T}_{\mathbf{w},i}$ to $\mathbf{T}_{\mathbf{w},i+3}$ and six CP timestamps $\mathbf{T}_{\mathbf{w},i}$ to $\mathbf{T}_{\mathbf{w},i+5}$ are required to interpolate at a time t within $[t_{i+2}; t_{i+3}]$.

The intermediate time representation between the two CP of the considered interpolated section is henceforth given by:

$$u(t) = \frac{t - t_{i+2}}{t_{i+3} - t_{i+2}} \tag{8}$$

The matrix form for the NUTD basis functions are thus expressed by:

$$\mathbf{B}(t) = \mathbf{M} \begin{pmatrix} 1 \\ u(t) \\ u(t)^2 \\ u(t)^3 \end{pmatrix} \tag{9}$$

Details on coefficient matrix $\mathbf{M}$ are given in [19], it is however substantial to note that $\mathbf{M}$ is now relative to the 6 CP timestamps t_i to t_{i+5}.

$\mathbf{C}$ being the cumulative coefficient matrix from $\mathbf{M}$, the cumulative version of the basis functions are now given by:

$$\mathbf{C}_{i,j} = \sum_{l=i}^{k} \mathbf{M}_{l,j} \quad , \quad \tilde{\mathbf{B}}(t) = \mathbf{C} \begin{pmatrix} 1 \\ u(t) \\ u(t)^2 \\ u(t)^3 \end{pmatrix} \tag{10}$$

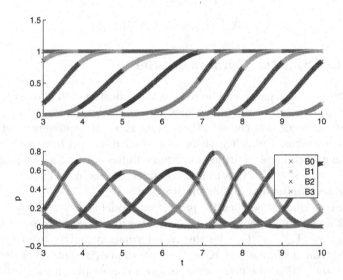

Fig. 1. The evolution of the value of the $k = 4$ cumulative NUTD basis functions $\tilde{B}_{0..k}(t)$(up) and non cumulative $B_{0..k}(t)$(down) w.r.t time. Each basis functions is associated to a color (red, green, blue, cyan), showing the influence of a CP variation(up) or a CP(down) on the interpolated trajectory over time. (Color figure online)

The Fig. 1 shows the value of the 4 NUTD cumulative and non cumulative basis over time. Unlike the UTD case, the basis functions are different for each interpolation section because of the varying time interval between the CP.

The cumulative coefficient matrix $\mathbf{C}$ is invariant with respect to the interpolation time t. For clarity, we redefine $\Omega_j := \Omega_{j-1,j}$. The derivative of the basis functions with respect to t can be retrieved in the same way as UTD B-Splines:

$$\dot{\mathbf{B}}(t) = \frac{1}{\Delta t_{i+2,i+3}} \mathbf{C} \begin{bmatrix} 0 \\ 1 \\ 2u \\ 3u^2 \end{bmatrix}, \ddot{\mathbf{B}}(t) = \frac{1}{\Delta t_{i+2,i+3}^2} \mathbf{C} \begin{bmatrix} 0 \\ 0 \\ 2 \\ 6u \end{bmatrix} \tag{11}$$

The first and second derivatives of the interpolated trajectory are then expressed by:

$$\dot{\mathbf{T}}_w(t) = \mathbf{T}_{w,i} (\dot{\mathbf{A}}_1 \mathbf{A}_2 \mathbf{A}_3 + \mathbf{A}_1 \dot{\mathbf{A}}_2 \mathbf{A}_3 + \mathbf{A}_1 \mathbf{A}_2 \dot{\mathbf{A}}_3) \tag{12}$$

$$\ddot{\mathbf{T}}_w(t) = \mathbf{T}_{w,i} \begin{pmatrix} \ddot{\mathbf{A}}_1 \mathbf{A}_2 \mathbf{A}_3 + \mathbf{A}_1 \ddot{\mathbf{A}}_2 \mathbf{A}_3 + \mathbf{A}_1 \mathbf{A}_2 \ddot{\mathbf{A}}_3) + \\ 2 * (\dot{\mathbf{A}}_1 \dot{\mathbf{A}}_2 \mathbf{A}_3 + \dot{\mathbf{A}}_1 \mathbf{A}_2 \dot{\mathbf{A}}_3 + \mathbf{A}_1 \dot{\mathbf{A}}_2 \dot{\mathbf{A}}_3) \end{pmatrix} \tag{13}$$

$$\mathbf{A}_j = \exp(\tilde{B}(t)_j \boldsymbol{\Omega}_{j+i}) \tag{14}$$

$$\dot{\mathbf{A}}_j = \mathbf{A}_j \dot{\tilde{B}}(t)_j \boldsymbol{\Omega}_{j+i} \tag{15}$$

$$\ddot{\mathbf{A}}_j = \dot{\mathbf{A}}_j \dot{\tilde{B}}(t)_j \boldsymbol{\Omega}_{j+i} + \mathbf{A}_j \ddot{\tilde{B}}(t)_j \boldsymbol{\Omega}_{j+i} \tag{16}$$

4 Rolling Shutter Camera Model

An image from a RS camera can be seen as the concatenation of one dimensional images (rows) exposed at different times as seen in the Fig. 2.

For a static scene and camera, there is no geometric difference between the GS and RS cameras. But when there is a relative motion between the camera and the scene, each line is a projection from a different camera viewpoint. While the camera pose $\mathbf{T} \in \mathbb{SE}3$ is common to all the pixels in a GS image, it varies as $\mathbf{T}(t)$ for each individual line in the RS case.

The pinhole camera perspective projection model is derived below. Let $\mathbf{P}$ be a 3D point defined in homogeneous coordinates in the world coordinate system $\mathbf{w}$. Let $\mathbf{T}_{c,w} = \mathbf{T}_{w,c}^{-1} = \mathbf{T}_w^{-1}$ be the transformation matrix from world $\mathbf{w}$ to camera $\mathbf{c}$ coordinate frame. Let $\mathbf{K}$ be the camera matrix containing the intrinsic parameters and $\pi(.)$ be the perspective projection (mapping from $\mathbb{P}^2$ to $\mathbb{R}^2$). The pinhole model projects $\mathbf{P}$ onto the image plane to $\mathbf{p} = \begin{bmatrix} p_u & p_v \end{bmatrix}^T$ by:

$$\mathbf{p} = \begin{bmatrix} p_u \\ p_v \end{bmatrix} := \pi([\mathbf{K}|\mathbf{0}]\mathbf{T}_{c,w}\mathbf{P}) \tag{17}$$

To model the varying pose, $\mathbf{T}_{c,w}$ is parameterized by t as $\mathbf{T}_{c,w}(t)$. The spline being defined by Eq. (5) in the spline coordinate frame $\mathbf{s}$ (attached to the IMU for

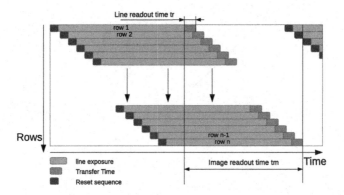

Fig. 2. RS cameras expose the image lines sequentially, thus if the first line is exposed at instant t_0, then the nth line is exposed at $t_0 + n.t_r$ with t_r the readout time of a line. The time taken by the camera to fully expose an image is called the readout time t_m [21]. Image from [7].

instance) different from **c**, a (constant over time) transformation $\mathbf{T_{c,s}}$ is required to obtain $\mathbf{T_{c,w}}(t)$:

$$\mathbf{T_{c,w}}(t) = \mathbf{T_{c,s}}\mathbf{T_{s,w}}(t) \tag{18}$$

The projection is obtained by:

$$\mathbf{p}(t) = \begin{bmatrix} p_u(t) \\ p_v(t) \end{bmatrix} := \pi([\mathbf{K}|\mathbf{0}]\mathbf{T_{c,w}}(t)\mathbf{P}) = \omega(\mathbf{P}, \mathbf{T_{c,w}}(t)) \tag{19}$$

This model does not yet represent the fact that at a given time t corresponds a single line exposure. So the projection $[p_u(t_j)\ p_v(t_j)]^T$ of **P** at time $t = t_j$ will actually be obtained only if the line $p_v(t_j)$ is exposed at time t_j.

[5] expressed the line exposed at a time t as a function of s being the frame start time, e being the end frame time, and h being the height of the image in pixels by:

$$p_v(t) = h\frac{(t - s)}{(e - s)} \tag{20}$$

The Fig. 3 shows plotted in blue the image projections $[p_u(t)\ p_v(t)]^T$ of a single 3D point obtained by Eq. (19) using interpolation of the poses defined in Eq. (5). The value of t is sampled to the different exposure time of each individual row. The green line indicates the row that is actually exposed when the $p_v(t)$ corresponds to the row number and the red cross at the intersection is the resulting projection. For highly curved trajectories, multiple projections of a single 3D point can be observed in a single image.

The projection(s) $[p_u(t)\ p_v(t)]^T$ that is(are) effectively observed by the RS camera is(are) obtained by intersecting the curves corresponding to Eqs. (19) and (20). Determining t is an optimization problem that [5] solves iteratively using first order Taylor expansion of the 2 equations around a time t:

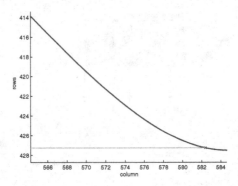

Fig. 3. Projections of a 3D point (in blue) in one image for poses associated to different lines, in the case of a moving camera. The green line shows the exposed rows at the time the 3D point is projected to it. Image from [7]. (Color figure online)

$$p_v(t + \delta t) = h \frac{(t + \delta t - s)}{(e - s)} \tag{21}$$

$$\begin{bmatrix} p_u(t + \delta t) \\ p_v(t + \delta t) \end{bmatrix} = \omega(P, \mathbf{T_{c,w}}(t)) + \delta t \frac{d\omega(P, \mathbf{T_{c,w}}(t))}{dt} \tag{22}$$

This system of equations is reorganized as:

$$\delta t = -\frac{ht + s(p_v(t) - h) - ep_v(t)}{h + (s - e)\frac{d\omega_{p_v}(P, \mathbf{T_{c,w}}(t))}{dt}} \tag{23}$$

By updating t as $t = t + \delta_t$ and iterating, t converges generally in approximately 3 or 4 iterations. Once t is determined, the corresponding projection is obtained using Eq. (19). For slow motions, the initial value for t can be set at the time corresponding to the middle row of the image and the iterative algorithm is very likely to converge. However, for high dynamic motions, the initial value has to be set wisely, as different initial values could lead to different projections that correspond indeed to different actual projections.

4.1   Rolling Shutter PnP

The PnP (perspective-N-Points) algorithm allows to estimate the pose of one or many cameras from n 2D-3D matching between 3D points of the scene $\mathbf{P_k}$ and their observations in the images $\mathbf{p}_{i,k}$.

Having an initial estimate of the camera pose $\mathbf{T_w}$ and a set of 2D-3D matching, a reprojection error can be computed as a function of the image i and point k:

$$Err(i, k) = \mathbf{p}_{i,k} - \pi([K|0]\mathbf{T_w}^{-1}\mathbf{P_k}) \tag{24}$$

This PnP reprojection error function can be extended to RS camera, taking into account the exposure time of the line where the 3D point is projected:

$$Err(i, k) = \mathbf{p}_{i,k} - \pi([K|0]\mathbf{T_w}(t)^{-1}\mathbf{P_k}) \tag{25}$$

In that case, the parameters to optimize θ are the complete set of CP for the B-spline instead of independent camera pose for each image i. Refined parameters $\hat{\theta}$ are obtained by minimizing the sum of squared reprojection error:

$$\hat{\theta} = \underset{\theta}{\operatorname{argmin}} \sum_i \sum_k Err(i, k)^2 \tag{26}$$

4.2   Rolling Shutter Bundle Adjustment

Similarly to the PnP, the BA is an optimization problem that aims to refine a set of parameters by minimizing a cost function but unlike the PnP, it also integrates the 3D points of the scene to the optimization. The parameters to optimize are then defined by $\theta_b = [\theta, P_0..P_M]$, and are refined by minimizing the following reprojection error:

$$\hat{\theta}_b = \underset{\theta_b}{\operatorname{argmin}} \sum_i \sum_k Err(i, k)^2 \tag{27}$$

The minimization can be achieved through Levenberg-Marquardt algorithm, the initial value for θ_b being initialized for instance from a SLAM using a GS camera model. In that case, the CP θ may be initialized directly on the interpolated trajectory.

4.3   Graph Representation

We chose to use a graph representation for the optimization problem and used the g2o library [22] as an open source graph optimization tool and we developed a dedicated C++ solver for both the PnP and BA. The graph representation had to be adapted for the continuous time trajectory model because it is different from the standard formulation where each keyframe corresponds to a single camera pose. In both cases, the observations (2d projections) are represented as edges that connect nodes representing the unknown variables (camera poses and 3D features of the map). In the standard formulation for global shutter cameras, the edges connect two nodes whereas the continuous-time modeling of the camera trajectory requires an observation to be dependent of the 4 neighboring CP and the 6 neighboring timestamps as represented in the Fig. 4. Thus, a multi-edge is used in the graph to model these dependencies between multiple nodes.

Using this multi-edge representation, a single graph for the PnP and BA is created, the values for the X_W parameters being fixed for the PnP while all the parameters have to be estimated for the BA. g2o offers the numeric evaluation of the jacobians by finite differences.

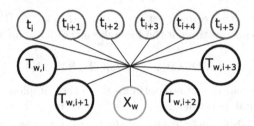

Fig. 4. Graph representation of an observation of a 3D Point $\mathbf{X_w}$ on an image line exposed at time $t_{i+2} < t < t_{i+3}$. The camera pose associated to this line is constrained by the 4 CP $\mathbf{T_{w,i}}$ to $\mathbf{T_{w,i+3}}$ and by the 6 timestamps t_i to t_{i+5}.

5 Non Uniform Time Distribution of the CP

5.1 CP Generation Methods

As our approach uses varying time intervals adapted to the local properties of the motion, it requires the generation of the CP at the right time. We investigated two different approaches involving either an IMU sensor or the analysis of the reprojection error in the images. The first one is better fitted for real-time applications as the CP can be generated online using IMU measurements while the second involves an iterative process that predisposes it for offline computation.

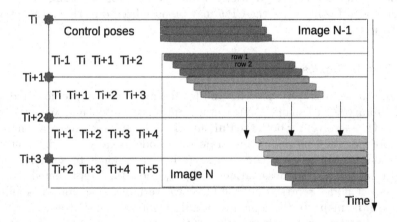

Fig. 5. An example of multiple CP inside a single image, and their influence for interpolating the pose for different rows. 3 CP are time-stamped between the beginning and the end of the image N: $\mathbf{T_{i+1}}$, $\mathbf{T_{i+2}}$ and $\mathbf{T_{i+3}}$. The quartet of CP used for the interpolation of the pose at each row changes three time during the image exposure. Image from [7].

Before providing the details of the CP generation methods, it is worth noting that the NUTD provides the ability to create locally multiple CP inside a single image. This leads to many CP quartets required to interpolate the pose inside different portions of the image (see Fig. 5). As retrieving the CP associated to a time t is an operation that is done thousands of times per frame, some care is required to avoid wasting time searching over all the CP. This is achieved by storing CP indices in a chronologically ordered list and using hash tables for fast access.

CP Generation Based on IMU. An IMU sensor is generally composed of gyroscopes and accelerometers that respectively measure the angular velocities and linear accelerations. On current tablets and smartphones, it generally delivers measurements at about 100 Hz, which is a higher frequency than the frame rate of the camera.

We propose a simple analysis of the measurements done by the IMU to determine when the CP are required. The Fig. 6 shows a generated trajectory (in the two top plots). The left (resp. right) plots corresponds to the translation (resp rotation) components. The data provided by the IMU are plotted in the middle plots. The bottom plots show respectively the norm of the linear accelerations and angular velocities. Different thresholding values (shown in red, blue and black) are used to determine when more CP are required. These threshold values th_i are stored in two (for acceleration and angular velocity) look up table providing $n(th_i)$, the number of CP required per unit of time. These lists of threshold values are generated empirically as a trade-off between accuracy of the motion modeling and computational cost. For instance, if the angular velocity norm is below the threshold th_1, $n(th_1)$ CP per unit of time are used while if its norm rises above th_1 but below th_2, $n(th_2)$ CP per unit of time are used and so on. Once the CP are created, their parameters are optimized using Eq. (26).

CP Generation Based on Reprojection Error. We propose a second method to determine the temporal location of the CP when an IMU in not available or as a post processing step after the application of the IMU based method. This method involves an iterative estimation of the trajectory using initial CP (set for instance with an UTD or with an NUTD obtained from the IMU based method) as shown in Eq. (26). Let $\overline{res_{t_1,\Delta_t}}$ be the mean of the residuals $Err(i,k)$ defined in Eq. (25) between times t_1 and $t_1 + \Delta_t$. The proposed method uses an iterative scheme consisting of the following two steps:

- The residuals are computed along the trajectory and analyzed using a sliding window to measure locally $\overline{res_{t_1,\Delta_t}}$ for varying t_1. Maxima are detected and additional CP are generated at the middle of the two corresponding neighboring CP for time $t_1 + \frac{\Delta_t}{2}$.
- An iterative estimation of the trajectory Eq. (26) is achieved with the added CP to refine the whole set of CP.

The process is iterated until $\forall t_1 : \overline{res_{t_1,\Delta_t}} < threshold$.

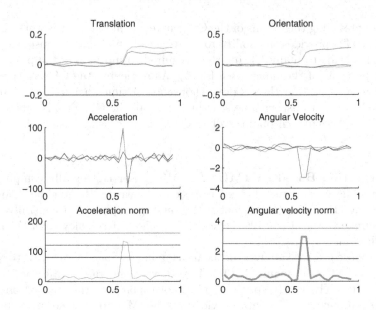

Fig. 6. Determination of the number of required CP per unit of time using IMU measurements analysis (see the text for details). International system of units are used for the axes. Image from [7]. (Color figure online)

These two methods allow to generate new CP specifically on sections of the trajectory that exhibit high dynamic. Despite the fact that the IMU based method is more intuitive because it is based on a physical measurement of the trajectory, the reprojection based method is generally preferable for two main reasons: First, the thresholds in the IMU based method are required to be set cautiously, which is not the case of the reprojection error based method for which the threshold is just expressed in pixel unit. Second, the reprojection error based method uses the same metric than the PnP or BA algorithms, hence it can be efficiently integrated in those contexts.

The Fig. 7 shows one translation component w.r.t time of a simple simulated ground truth trajectory (a) on which the reprojection error method is tested. The UTD interpolation gives poor results (b) and the associated reprojection error (c) is significant when the high dynamic motion occurs ($t \approx 0.5$). By adding a single CP at the right time, the proposed method accurately models the trajectory (d), dividing the reprojection error by approximately fifteen (e)).

5.2   Spatiotemporal Optimisation of the Control Poses

The NUTD B-Splines permit the optimization of the CP timestamps, who only operate on the cumulative coefficient matrix $\mathbf{C}$ (Eq. 10). However, these added parameters have to respect the following constraints to forbid the optimization to diverge, Δt_{min} being the minimum temporal distance between two timestamps and t_{total} being the duration of the whole trajectory:

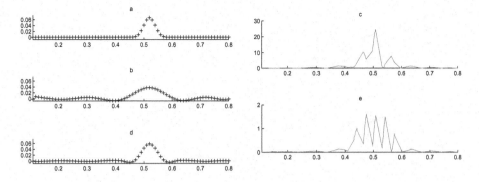

Fig. 7. Results for the reprojection error based method (see text for details).

$$\forall i : \Delta t_{i-1,i} > \Delta t_{min} > 0 \tag{28}$$

$$\sum_i \Delta t_{i-1,i} = t_{total} \tag{29}$$

Starting from a poor estimate, simultaneous optimization of the CP and their timestamps can converge to an erroneous local solution, due to local minima. Trying to overcome this problem, we propose to firstly alternate spatial and temporal only optimizations. A complete spatiotemporal optimization can then be applied to refine the estimated trajectory and adapt the CP time distribution to its actual dynamic.

6   Results

6.1   Synthetic Datasets

Results on simulated dataset are firstly presented to avoid noise induced by image processing (such as corner extraction) and problems arising from erroneous data association (between the extracted corners and 3D map points).

Initially, a set of CP is generated to model different types of reference trajectories and a simple 3D point cloud is used as geometric model of the environment. The Fig. 8 shows an example of generated data. Gaussian noise is added both to these CP and 3D points. The time intervals between the CP are randomly generated to obtain a NUTD and validate the model.

The camera frequency is arbitrary chosen ($fps = 3$), and the start and end exposure time of each image is set accordingly. The camera poses are interpolated using these parameters and the 3D points are projected to the images using the RS projection model. Gaussian noise is then added to these projections to generate the measurements used for the optimization.

To demonstrate the PnP, the interpolated camera poses using the noisy CP are used as initial estimates for the CP to optimize. A hundred camera poses are interpolated from 60 CP and are used to project the 3D point cloud. The

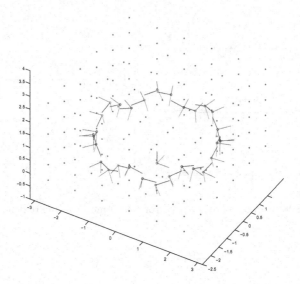

Fig. 8. Example of CP along a circular trajectory, the viewing direction being aligned with the tangent to the circle. An additional sinusoidal translation component is added perpendicularly to the circle plane. The point cloud is displayed in red. (Color figure online)

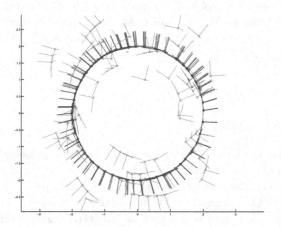

Fig. 9. Illustration of the PnP optimization on a synthetic dataset. Camera poses interpolated from initial CP (green), optimized CP (blue) and the ground truth (red). (Color figure online)

PnP is achieved by our C++ solver and example of results are shown in the Fig. 9. Initial camera poses (green) converge toward the ground truth (red) after optimization (blue). Only 5 iterations were sufficient to refine those camera poses despite significantly noisy initial estimates.

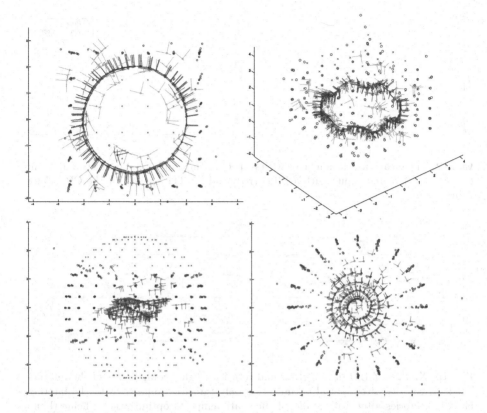

Fig. 10. Different views for the BA using the NUTD model: The initial CP (green), the CP after optimization (blue) and the ground truth (red) are displayed alongside the optimized point cloud (using the same color coding). (Color figure online)

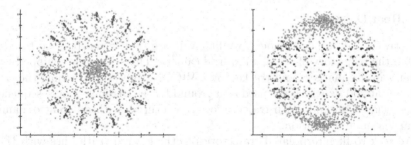

Fig. 11. Different views of the point cloud before (green) and after BA (blue). The ground truth is displayed in red. Only the 3D points that have been observed in the images have been optimized, hence the blue dots do not cover the whole scene. (Color figure online)

The BA is demonstrated with the same synthetic trajectories, but using the noisy point cloud as initial estimate for the map, which is to be refined by optimization. The results are shown in the Figs. 10 and 11.

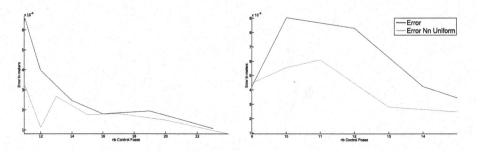

Fig. 12. The mean translation error with respect to the number of CP for two different trajectories (left and right) with a UTD (red) and NUTD (green) for the CP. (Color figure online)

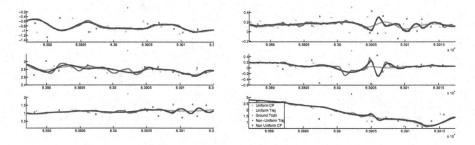

Fig. 13. X, Y, et Z translation (left) and rotation (right) components of the interpolated trajectories after spatial optimization only (green) compared with the interpolated trajectories after 3 iterations of the spatiotemporal optimization scheme (blue) with respect to time. The ground truth is shown in red and is better approximated by the NUTD interpolation (blue) than by the UTD one (green). (Color figure online)

6.2   Real Dataset

To motivate the proposed model, we first validate that it can be used to interpolated the trajectory of a real hand-held camera. This camera is equipped with motion capture markers and tracked by a VICON MOCAP providing the camera poses at 200 Hz which are used as a ground truth. Distinct images sequences and associated ground truth trajectories are captured, with different dynamics in translation and rotation.

We seek to fit interpolated trajectories to the ground truth ones with UTD and NUTD B-Splines model following different optimization schemes. The initial CP are set onto the MOCAP trajectory using UTD. Error $Err_T \in \mathbb{R}6$ between interpolated poses $\mathbf{T_w}(t)$ and the ground truth $\mathbf{T_{GT}}(t)$ is minimized for all timestamps t_j of the samples acquired by the MOCAP:

$$Err_T = \sum_j log(\mathbf{T_{GT}}(t_j)^{-1}\mathbf{T_w}(t_j)) \tag{30}$$

The minimization is achieved using the Levenberg-Marquardt algorithm and jacobians computed by finite differences. This optimization allows to refine spatially the CP. As described earlier, additional CP are iteratively generated between the two CP where surrounding the highest error after each optimization step.

The Fig. 12 shows the mean translation error after spatial optimization with respect to the number of CP, for a UTD (red) and a NUTD (green). As expected, at equal number of CP, the NUTD allows a more accurate modeling of the trajectory than with a UTD, because the algorithm adds CP where required. For a greater number of CP, the UTD and NUTD tend to produce similar results as seen in the left plot, due to the fact that with a sufficient amount of CP, even a UTD accurately represents the trajectory.

It is also important to note that for a greater number of CP, the error (mainly for UTD but also for NUTD) can increase as it is shown in the right plot, because the initial estimates of the CP can be set such that the trajectory cannot be correctly approximated.

The CP generation method adds CP at arbitrary time between the timestamps of the two neighboring CP, basically at $\frac{t_{i+2} + t_{i+3}}{2}$. The time distribution is then refined by optimizing the timestamps of the CP.

The spatiotemporal optimization offers in the majority of the cases a significant reduction of the error. However, better results have been observed by following an alternate optimization scheme. A first spatial optimization is done until it converges. Then these 3 steps are applied n times:

- Temporal optimization
- Adding a CP where the error is maximal
- Spatial optimization.

The Fig. 13 shows the interpolated trajectory components after spatial optimization (green), and after $n = 3$ spatiotemporal optimization cycles (blue), alongside the ground truth (red). The temporal and spatial distributions of the CP are adapted automatically to the trajectory dynamic. This is noticeable on the rotation components (right) and the translation z component (lower left) of the trajectories, where the UTD model fail to model fast oscillations.

Close-up view on different trajectories are given in Figs. 14 and 15 illustrating the final CP distributions. For the NUTD, more CP are used and optimized both temporally and spatially to accurately model fast motions, while less significant motions are smoothed. Note that with additional optimization and CP addition cycles, the CP distribution would adapt to the whole trajectory, however the error reduction would be less significant. There is obviously a trade-off between the increase in accuracy and the induced increase in terms of computational cost.

The Fig. 16 highlights the evolution of the error (red) during the optimization iterations. It is important to note that the plots begin after the convergence of a first spatial optimization. Hence, without the proposed approach, the minimum achievable error through standard spatial optimization corresponds to the first

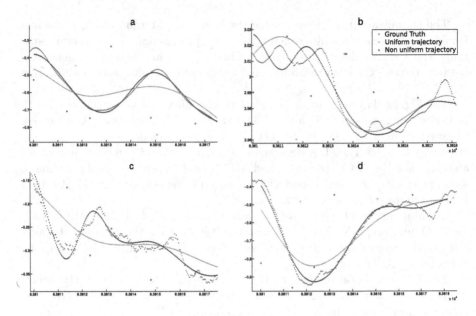

Fig. 14. X translation (a), Y translation (b), X rotation (c) and Y rotation (d) components of the interpolated trajectories in sequence 1.

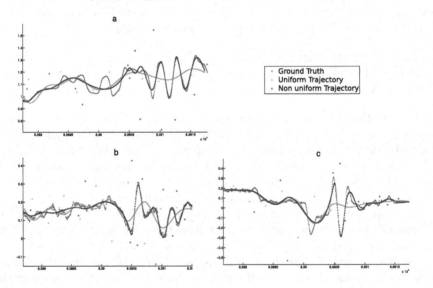

Fig. 15. Z translation (a), X rotation (b) and Y rotation (c) components of the interpolated trajectories in sequence 4.

error displayed in the plots. The temporal optimization allows to reduce this error by a significant factor using either no (a, b) or a low number (c) of additional CP.

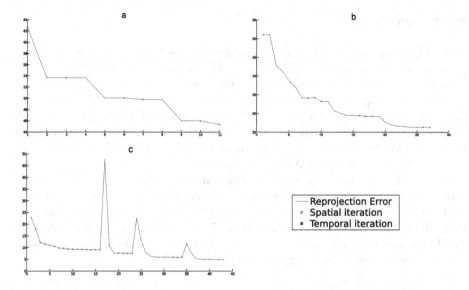

Fig. 16. Evolution of the translation error (red) as a function of space (green) and time (blue) optimization iterations. The optimization follows temporal then spatial optimization steps with without addition of CP in two first cases (a, b) whereas it required additional CP in the third case (c). In this test, the non optimal initial values for the added CP at iterations 16, 24 and 35 are the reason of the temporarily increased error. The error is then minimized, taking into account these added CP. (Color figure online)

7 Future Works

The conducted experiments demonstrated that it is possible to adapt the spatiotemporal distribution of the CP to the dynamic of real trajectories through the proposed optimization process. The used cubic interpolation model allows an accurate modeling of the trajectory. Quadratic or even linear models can be sufficient depending on the type of trajectory, however the availability of interpolated velocities and accelerations can be useful for applications using inertial measurements. The cost function used in our experiments on real datasets is relative to a ground truth that is not available in the case of a SLAM process whereas the available inertial measurements would be compared with the derivatives of the interpolated trajectory. Hence it could be possible to integrate the inertial measurements to the optimization as done in [5], which would allow to recover the metric scale of the scene and to perform auto-calibration.

The presented work is still an early work, and new tests within a complete SLAM process using the NUTD model must be driven on real datasets, involving the complete image processing pipeline. We also plan to integrate other geometric features such as segments, lines and planar patches to describe the environment and adapt their observation models to the RS cameras.

8   Conclusion

A NUTD cumulative B-Spline model maintaining the C^2 continuity of the interpolated trajectory have been presented. This model have been tested to fit interpolated trajectories to real and synthetic ones using different optimization schemes. The improvement offered by the optimization of the CP timestamps have been demonstrated for both simulated datasets and real trajectories. The integration of the model within a BA have been shown for simulated datasets only as it did not involved to operate image processing and because the ground truth for the environment was directly available.

The continuous-time trajectory model using a NUTD for the CP allows a reduction of both the memory usage and the computational cost. For trajectories with large partially linear parts, as encountered in automotive applications, a large amount of camera poses can be efficiently parameterized by a small number of CP. For trajectories with varying dynamics, it is possible to accurately model the high speed motion by locally increasing the CP density.

References

1. Hartley, R.I., Zisserman, A.: Multiple View Geometry in Computer Vision, 2nd edn. Cambridge University Press, Cambridge (2004). ISBN 0521540518
2. Davison, A.J.: Real-time simultaneous localisation and mapping with a single camera. In: 9th IEEE International Conference on Computer Vision (ICCV 2003), 14–17 October 2003, Nice, France, pp. 1403–1410 (2003)
3. Klein, G., Murray, D.: Parallel tracking and mapping for small AR workspaces. In: Proceedings Sixth IEEE and ACM International Symposium on Mixed and Augmented Reality (ISMAR 2007), Nara, Japan (2007)
4. Mur-Artal, R., Montiel, J.M.M., Tardós, J.D.: ORB-SLAM: a versatile and accurate monocular SLAM system. IEEE Trans. Rob. **31**, 1147–1163 (2015)
5. Lovegrove, S., Patron-Perez, A., Sibley, G.: Spline fusion: a continuous-time representation for visual-inertial fusion with application to rolling shutter cameras. In: Proceedings of the British Machine Vision Conference. BMVA Press (2013)
6. Patron-Perez, A., Lovegrove, S., Sibley, G.: A spline-based trajectory representation for sensor fusion and rolling shutter cameras. Int. J. Comput. Vis. **113**, 208–219 (2015)
7. Vandeportaele, B., Gohard, P.A., Devy, M., Coudrin, B.: Pose interpolation for rolling shutter cameras using non uniformly time-sampled B-splines. In: Proceedings of the 12th International Joint Conference on Computer Vision, Imaging and Computer Graphics Theory and Applications, VISAPP, (VISIGRAPP 2017), pp. 286–293. INSTICC, SciTePress (2017)
8. Roussillon, C., et al.: RT-SLAM: a generic and real-time visual SLAM implementation. CoRR abs/1201.5450 (2012)
9. Gonzalez, A.: Localisation par vision multi-spectrale. Application aux systèmes embarqués, theses. INSA de Toulouse (2013)
10. Engel, J., Schöps, T., Cremers, D.: LSD-SLAM: large-scale direct monocular SLAM. In: Fleet, D., Pajdla, T., Schiele, B., Tuytelaars, T. (eds.) ECCV 2014. LNCS, vol. 8690, pp. 834–849. Springer, Cham (2014). https://doi.org/10.1007/978-3-319-10605-2_54

11. Mouragnon, E., Lhuillier, M., Dhome, M., Dekeyser, F., Sayd, P.: Real time local-ization and 3D reconstruction. In: 2006 IEEE Computer Society Conference on Computer Vision and Pattern Recognition (CVPR 2006), vol. 1, pp. 363–370 (2006)
12. Strasdat, H., Montiel, J., Davison, A.J.: Real-time monocular slam: why filter? In: 2010 IEEE International Conference on Robotics and Automation (ICRA), pp. 2657–2664. IEEE (2010)
13. Klein, G., Murray, D.: Parallel tracking and mapping on a camera phone. In: Proceedings Eigth IEEE and ACM International Symposium on Mixed and Aug-mented Reality (ISMAR 2009), Orlando (2009)
14. Hedborg, J., Ringaby, E., Forssén, P.E., Felsberg, M.: Structure and motion esti-mation from rolling shutter video. In: 2011 IEEE International Conference on Com-puter Vision Workshops (ICCV Workshops), pp. 17–23 (2011)
15. Hedborg, J., Forssén, P.E., Felsberg, M., Ringaby, E.: Rolling shutter bundle adjustment. In: 2012 IEEE Conference on Computer Vision and Pattern Recogni-tion (CVPR), pp. 1434–1441 (2012)
16. Furgale, P., Barfoot, T.D., Sibley, G.: Continuous-time batch estimation using temporal basis functions. In: 2012 IEEE International Conference on Robotics and Automation (ICRA), pp. 2088–2095 (2012)
17. Kim, M.J., Kim, M.S., Shin, S.Y.: A general construction scheme for unit quater-nion curves with simple high order derivatives. In: Proceedings of the 22nd Annual Conference on Computer Graphics and Interactive Techniques - SIGGRAPH 1995, pp. 369–376 (1995)
18. de Boor, C.: On calculating with B-splines. J. Approx. Theory **6**, 50–62 (1972)
19. Yang, H., Yue, W., He, Y., Huang, H., Xia, H.: The deduction of coefficient matrix for cubic non-uniform B-spline curves. In: 2009 First International Workshop on Education Technology and Computer Science, pp. 607–609 (2009)
20. Qin, K.: General matrix representations for B-splines. Vis. Comput. **16**, 177–186 (2000)
21. Li, M., Kim, B., Mourikis, A.I.: Real-time motion estimation on a cellphone using inertial sensing and a rolling-shutter camera. In: Proceedings of the IEEE Inter-national Conference on Robotics and Automation, Karlsruhe, Germany, pp. 4697–4704 (2013)
22. Kuemmerle, R., Grisetti, G., Strasdat, H., Konolige, K., Burgard, W.: g2o: a gen-eral framework for graph optimization. In: Proceedings of the IEEE International Conference on Robotics and Automation (ICRA), Shanghai, China, pp. 3607–3613 (2011)

Hierarchical Hardware/Software Algorithm for Multi-view Object Reconstruction by 3D Point Clouds Matching

Ferran Roure[1], Xavier Lladó[2], Joaquim Salvi[2], Tomislav Privanić[3], and Yago Diez[4(✉)]

[1] Eurecat, Technology Center of Catalonia, Barcelona, Spain
[2] ViCOROB Research Institute, University of Girona, Girona, Spain
[3] Faculty of Electrical Engineering and Computing, University of Zagreb, Zagreb, Croatia
[4] Faculty of Science, Yamagata University, Yamagata, Japan
`yagodiezdonoso@gmail.com, yago@sci.lj.yamagata-u.ac.jp`

Abstract. The Matching or Registration of 3D point clouds is a problem that arises in a variety of research areas with applications ranging from heritage reconstruction to quality control of precision parts in industrial settings. The central problem in this research area is that of receiving two point clouds, usually representing different parts of the same object and finding the best possible rigid alignment between them. Noise in data, a varying degree of overlap and different data acquisition devices make this a complex problem with a high computational cost. This issue is sometimes addressed by adding hardware to the scanning system, but this hardware is frequently expensive and bulky. We present an algorithm that makes use of cheap, widely available (smartphone) sensors to obtain extra information during data acquisition. This information then allows for fast software registration. The first such hybrid hardware-software approach was presented in [31]. In this paper we improve the performance of this algorithm by using hierarchical techniques. Experimental results using real data show how the algorithm presented greatly improves the computation time of the previous algorithm and compares favorably to state of the art algorithms.

1 Introduction and Previous Work

The registration or matching of objects represented as 3D point clouds is a widely studied problem in research communities such as Computational Geometry [2,6,15], Computer Vision [10,11,17] and Computer Graphics [4,44]. Its many existing applications touch subjects as diverse as medical imaging [28], road network matching [12] or mobile phone apps [33,41].

The main aim of the 3D point cloud registration problem is to find a rigid transformation[1] $\mu : \mathbb{R}^3 \longrightarrow \mathbb{R}^3$ that brings a point cloud $\mathcal{B}$ close to another point

---

[1] Holding $d(a_i, b_j) = d(\mu(a_i), \mu(b_j)) \forall a_i, b_j \in \mathbb{R}^3$, $d()$ being the euclidean distance.

© Springer Nature Switzerland AG 2019
A. P. Cláudio et al. (Eds.): VISIGRAPP 2017, CCIS 983, pp. 176–191, 2019.
https://doi.org/10.1007/978-3-030-12209-6_9

cloud $\mathcal{A}$ in terms of a designated distance. $\mathcal{A} = \{a_1, \ldots, a_n\}$ with $a_i \in \mathbb{R}^3$ $\forall i = 1 \ldots n$ and $\mathcal{B} = \{b_1, \ldots, b_m\}$ with $b_j \in \mathbb{R}^3$ $\forall j = 1 \ldots m$. We refer the interested reader to [14] for a review of the problem.

The registration process consists of several steps (see Fig. 1).

Fig. 1. Registration pipeline.

As existing devices for data acquisition produce point clouds with a large number of points, first a *Detection* step reduces this data size. Points that are prominent (according to a predefined criterion) are selected. In the second step of the Pipeline values are assigned to the *key-points*. These values characterize the local shape of the object around each key point. This step is named *Description*. This part of the pipeline has been the most active in research for many years. Among the many existing approaches [21,40,42,45] obtained high repeatability scores in studies such as [38,39]. In terms of detector performance, [23,29,42] present very good results in terms of speed and accuracy. However new approaches keep appearing and claiming improved performance in terms of speed and accuracy. See, for example [46,47].

In the subsequent step of the point cloud matching pipeline, *Searching Strategies* are used to identify point correspondences. Once at least three correspondences have been detected it is possible to determine a rigid motion between the two sets that brings corresponding points close together. As this step is potentially computationally very expensive descriptor values are used to prioritize the best apparent correspondences. For most point cloud matching algorithms, the process is divided into two parts. Initially an initial pose for matching is found through *coarse* point correspondences and then an iterative process is used to bring the two sets globally as close together as possible. This last step is called *fine* matching. Perhaps the most significant contributions made recently to the point cloud matching problem correspond to the coarse matching searching strategies presented by [3] and improved in [26]. Efficient coarse matching approaches (also including [18]) are able to deal with large data sets in an efficient manner so the subsequent execution of a fine matching algorithm (usually ICP [7]) converges. Recently, and similar to other research areas, a strong new trend present in all the steps of the matching pipeline is the use of deep learning approaches [16,19,43].

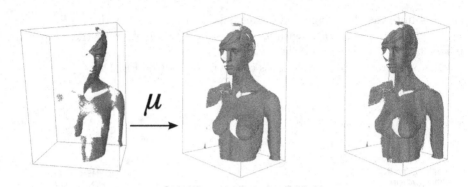

Fig. 2. Registration example, two views from the bust model are brought to the same coordinate system by rigid motion μ. Figure originally appearing in [36].

3D Point Cloud Matching for Object Reconstruction from Multiple Views. A typical instance of the point cloud matching problem in 3D is that of object reconstruction. This requires gathering 3D object information from multiple viewpoints. Acquisition devices are used to capture discrete points in the surfaces of objects which then represented as *point clouds*.

Since every view usually contains 3D data corresponding to a different spatial coordinate system it is necessary to transform the information from all the views into a common coordinate system (see Fig. 2 for a graphical example). From a formal standpoint, two such systems are related through three angles of rotation and a three-dimensional translation vector. In order to register two objects represented as point clouds, a minimum of three point correspondences are needed to determine a 3D rigid motion. Thus, the number of possible correspondences is in $O(n^6)$, making the design of algorithms that can navigate this search space efficiently an important issue. Most existing methods deal with this issue with pure software solutions. By using the discriminating power of shape descriptors For instance, approaches based on shape descriptors determine point correspondences based on local shapes measures (see, for example [27,35] for descriptor comparison). Other strategies include data filtering [13,37] or devising novel searching strategies to speed up the search for correspondences between points [3]. There are methods which expect as the input of the 3D reconstruction system not only 3D point position data, but also the normal vectors of every 3D point [22]. Another generic way to increase the efficiency of any parallelized method is to use GPU implementations [9].

However, the issue of creating fast coarse matching algorithms can also be tackled with the assistance of hardware. At its most basic level, the acquisition system can be upgraded with dedicated parts to gain information on some of the parameters [24,25]. This type of solutions (usually involving the use of robot arms and/or turntables) demands complex installations and are often expensive. A recent trend [33,41] seeks to use sensors from mobile devices in order to help registration. These sensors are commonly available and less expensive, circumventing many of the previous problems. The goal in this case is to propose hybrid 3D registration methods which combine the best features of software and mechanical approaches. Significantly, [31] presented a hybrid algorithm with a hardware part based on smartphone technology that managed to gain access to rotation data that could then be used to search for the remaining translation part of the rigid motion by software means. The idea of separating the rotation and translation part was not new and can be found, for example in [20]. Once the rotation part of the problem is solved (either by using hardware data as in the former reference or by software means as in the later), what remains is determining the translation vectors that brings the two sets being registered closer together. To solve this problem it is enough to find one single correspondence between one point in each set so that the resulting translation brings the sets close enough for a fine registration to succeed. This yields an immediate $O(n)$ asymptotic cost for this version of the problem.

In this paper we present an algorithm that extends the work in [31]. By using the hardware part developed in the mentioned reference, we are able to focus on the software solution of the translation problem. We propose a hierarchical approach that finds a coarse matching solution by selecting one point in one set and determining a correspondence in the other in the following way. First, the search is initialized by using the center of masses of the set. Then, the search proceeds using a regular sample grid. Initially only the overlap between bounding boxes of the sets is considered. Next, the sets are divided in regular cells and the number of points in each cell is considered. Finally, the result of the coarse step of the algorithm is determined by computing the residues considering the points in the sets.

The rest of the paper is organized as follows. Section 2 introduces the papers that motivates this research and provides details on the approach used in the current work. The experiments in Sect. 3 illustrate the validity of our approach and compare it with other registration methods. This comparison includes not only the original algorithm [31] but also two widely used registration methods: (a) The 4PCS method, which is one of the most widely used [3], and (b) its improved version, the super4PCS method [26] which is, to the best of our knowledge, the fastest general-purpose coarse matching algorithm to date. The paper ends with a summary of the findings of the paper with special attention to the most salient results reported in the experiments in Sect. 4. An initial version of this work appeared at [36].

2   Materials and Methods

In this section we start by providing some details on the algorithm that motivates this research. On the second part we provide details on the new approach to the problem.

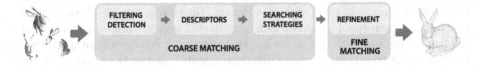

Fig. 3. Detailed registration pipeline. Figure originally appearing in [36].

2.1 Previous Algorithm

A detailed version of the registration pipeline is presented in Fig. 3. As no filtering or detection steps where used (although the algorithm does allow for them) and the searching strategies part was divided in two steps, the algorithm presented in [31] is as a hybrid hardware-software coarse matching algorithm.

- First, the authors roughly determine the sets rotation by using a smartphone providing 3D orientation data (from the accelerometer and magnetometer sensors). The orientation angle outputted by the sensors is used to produce an orientation matrix for the scanning system respect to a certain world reference axis. These orientation matrices are composed to obtain the aforementioned rough rotation correspondence.
- In the second step, translation is determined. As the previous rotational alignment is expected to be noisy, a robust translation matching algorithm is needed. The goal here is to provide a good enough initial pose for the subsequent fine registration algorithm to succeed.

As the data used for the experiments in the reference where made available by the same authors in [34] we can produce reliable comparison results in Sect. 3 as well as focus on the improvement of the translation (software) part of the problem in the current work:

- Once the two sets $\mathcal{A}$ and $\mathcal{B}$ have been registered in terms of rotation, the goal is to find a translation τ such that $\tau(\mathcal{B})$ is close enough to $\mathcal{A}$ in terms of the mean Euclidean distance of the Nearest Neighbouring (NN) point pairs between sets. Close enough in this case stands for a pose that allows the subsequent fine matching algorithm [37] to converge to the best possible alignment without stalling at any local minimum.
- The search is initialized by picking a point in set $\mathcal{A}$ for which a correspondence will be searched for. In this case, the authors choose this point $x_\mathcal{A}$ randomly among the 100 closest points to the center of masses of set $\mathcal{A}$.
- The algorithm then searches for the best correspondence for $x_\mathcal{A}$ among all the points in set $\mathcal{B}$. To do this a grid-based greedy search is performed that tries several possible translations. At every iteration, the best translation is chosen by computing the distance between $\mathcal{A}$ and each of the proposed $\tau(\mathcal{B})$ and choosing the best. This step is commonly referred to as residue computation. The grid is subsequently expanded around the ongoing best point and a new iteration starts. Notice that with this strategy, the number

of points explored in the grid and, thus, the number of residues computed, is constant for all executions. However, for every residue computation, the time needed will vary depending on how close the two sets are. Experimental details of this are presented in Sect. 3.4.

- After finishing the grid-based search, a translation vector is outputted. This data is joined with the rotation estimation obtained from the sensors and the combination becomes the result of the matching algorithm. Then the algorithm proceeds as described in Fig. 3 by running a fine matching algorithm [37].

2.2 Our Approach

We propose to look at the sets being matched in a hierarchical fashion to avoid unnecessary residue computations and save computation time. A graphical overview of our algorithm is presented in Fig. 4.

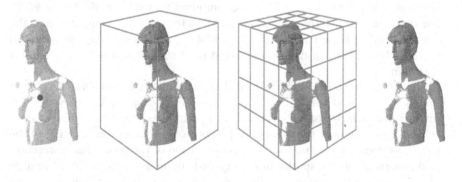

Fig. 4. Hierarchical approach. Successive approximations of the software part of the coarse matching algorithm consider more and more detailed information. First, the algorithm is initialized using centers of masses. Second, the overlap volumes of the bounding boxes of the sets being matched are considered. Third, the number of points contained in a Regular Grid is factored in. Finally, full sets are used. Figure originally appearing in [36].

After obtaining the rotation data, the algorithm needs to find the translation τ that brings the two sets being matched as close as possible. A naive approach would be to choose a point in set $\mathcal{A}$ and try all the possible correspondences with all the points in set $\mathcal{B}$. This would have $O(n)$ cost (with $n=|\mathcal{B}|$) which is already feasible in most cases. The authors in [31] realized how it is not necessary to explore the whole search space and that, by taking samples using a grid it was possible to "zoom in" a good enough coarse solution so the subsequent fine matching algorithm would produce the best possible solution.

However, the algorithm used to explore the grid treated all possible translation equally. The exact same process was undergone by the first translation tested than to the final one (which was much closer to the final solution after having undergone several algorithmic iterations). This resulted in a large number of operations where the distance between two sets had to be computed (residue computations). In our case, we take this into account and look at the sets being matched using varying levels of detail. For the sake of simplicity from now on we will consider that each new iteration increases the level of detail. The resulting algorithm can be described in the following fashion:

- As sets $\mathcal{A}$ and $\mathcal{B}$ have been registered up to rotation the algorithm needs to find the translation τ such that $\tau(\mathcal{B})$ is close enough to $\mathcal{A}$ for the subsequent fine matching algorithm to succeed.
- Our algorithm is stable enough to be initialized directly by using the centers of masses of the two sets (Fig. 4, left). As the following steps optimizes high level (bounding box) overlap between the two sets, we can perform a faster initialization. Consequently, $x_{\mathcal{A}}$ is chosen to be the center of mass of set $\mathcal{A}$ and the search grid of set $\mathcal{B}$ is built around the center of mass of set $\mathcal{B}$.
- In the first iteration of the grid-based search (Fig. 4, middle left), the algorithm only considers a bounding box computed for each set: $\mathbb{B}(\mathcal{A})$ and $\mathbb{B}(\mathcal{B})$. For each grid point b the translation τ_b of vector $b - x_{\mathcal{A}}$ is computed and the volume overlap between $\tau_b(\mathbb{B}(\mathcal{B}))$ and $\mathbb{B}(\mathcal{A})$ is considered. All the points in this first level of the grids are considered until the optimal volume overlap is determined.
- In the second iteration of this search (Fig. 4, middle right), the two sets being matched are stored inside a 3D regular grid. The bounding box of each set is divided in regularly spaced cells and each point is assigned to a cell. For each cell, we annotate only the number of points stored in it as the "weight" of the cell. This stands for a "mid-level" representation of the sets. This representation groups points by spatial proximity and summarizes the set as a number of weighted cubic regions. In this case for each translation τ_b considered we check whether or not there are enough points in the cells intersected by every translated cell. Finding the best score in terms of possibly matched points is the goal in this step. However, the bounding box overlap values are required to remain within a threshold of the value obtained in the previous step.
- In the third and final step of the grid-based search, (Fig. 4, right), all the points in the sets are considered and the residues between the sets are computed. As is usual in this type of computations, a monte-carlo approach is used in order to speed up these computations [13]. As a major difference with [36], in the current work we have used two separate data structures for residue computations to assess their importance in the overall runtime.
- After finishing the grid-based search the algorithm proceeds by running a fine matching algorithm [37].

2.3   Residue Computation

An important issue in point cloud matching problems is how to assess distance between point sets. A commonly used distance is the Root Mean Squared Distance (RMSD). Taking into account the object reconstruction problem, where different views cover different parts of the object with some overlap only a subset of points of a given view is expected to match some points of the other view (partial match). Thus, in order to avoid non-overlapping subsets of points ruining residue computation, only those points a_i whose nearest neighbor $\mu(b_j)$ is closest than a given threshold ε are considered as matched points belonging to the overlapping subset C. A certain percentage of matched points is also required for a motion to be accepted as a solution to the matching problem. The *residue* between sets $\mathcal{A}$ and $\mathcal{B}$ is then defined as:

$$RMSD(\mathcal{A}, \mu(\mathcal{B}), \varepsilon) : a_i, b_j \in C = \sqrt{\frac{\sum_C d(a_i, \mu(b_j))^2}{|C|}} \tag{1}$$

where $\mu(b_j)$ is the nearest neighbor to a_i in $\mathcal{B}$ (euclidean distance d).

Given a set of 3D points $\mathcal{B}$ and a query point $a_q \in \mathbb{R}^3$ RMSD can be computed from finding the point $b_q \in \mathcal{B}$ closest to a_q ($d(a_q, b_q) \leq d(b_i, b_q) \forall i = 1 \ldots n$) or selecting the set of points in $\mathcal{B}$ within a range ε of a_q ($\{b_q \in \mathcal{B} | d(a_q, b_q) < \varepsilon\}$). These approaches are known as *Nearest Neighbor* and *Range Searching* problems, respectively. Hence, in range searching, the residue is computed by discarding points away from ε while in nearest neighbor is computed iterating over the points to minimize ε distance. Both approaches can be solved in linear time by brute-force. Hence, residue computation can be naively achieved in $O(n^2)$. Although this is sometimes done for small data sets, it is time consuming and quickly becomes unacceptable when n increases. Residue computation is crucial in the registration pipeline because it is used for measuring the initial alignment conditions like overlapping ratio, and for the evaluation of final alignment results.

As an improvement to the algorithm presented in [36], in this paper we will study the effect of residue computation in our approach. The previous algorithm used the widely used **KDtrees** [5] from the ANN library [1]. The KDtree is a binary tree where each node represents a hyperplane dividing the 3D space. In each level, a division is made according to one of the 3D axes. The points in the parent node are sorted according to the selected coordinate and the splitting value is used as the division point organizing the points in the left and right son nodes. For a detailed explanation on splitting values see. This operation is repeated with all coordinate axes, until leaf nodes (i.e. nodes with less than a previously fixed number of points) are obtained.

In the current work we improve the performance of the algorithm by using regular Grids to perform range searching residue computations. This data structure, introduced in [13] and used, for example, in [8], stands for a regular 3D grid that divides an axis aligned bounding box into cells each containing a set of unsorted points. A section of each coordinate axis contained in the bounding box is divided into k intervals where $k = \lfloor (\sqrt[3]{n}) \rfloor$. Then the Cartesian product of these intervals is considered and a set of k^3 regular rectangular prism cells is obtained. The goal is to have roughly as many cells as points in the set so each point would correspond to one cell in the best possible distribution of points. This heuristic data structure presents high asymptotic costs when points are not evenly distributed among the cells. However, in practice it obtains good results (details follow in Sect. 3).

3 Experiments

In this section we present experiments with real data that show how the algorithm presented in this paper improves the performance of the algorithm used in [31]. Furthermore, the current work also improves on the preliminary version presented in [36] by studying the effect of residue computation data structures in the performance of the algorithm. We also compare the algorithm presented in this paper to state of the art point set matching algorithms in order to illustrate the efficiency of our approach. The code for all the algorithms considered was implemented in C++. All experiments where run using a 33 MHz processor under a linux Ubuntu operating system.

Some significant improvement in the run-times reported here for the algorithm by [31] and in the original paper can be observed. This is mostly due to code optimization and parameter tuning. Due to the fact that the algorithm presented in this paper extends and improves that in [31] we were able to use some of the profiling information studied to improve our code to also improve that of [31]. In order to keep the comparison fair, we present these improved results in this paper. Additionally, this allows us to show clearly what part of the improvement corresponds to general code optimization and what part related to the use of the hierarchical approach presented in this paper. From now on, an for the sake of brevity, we will refer to the previous algorithm as the *regular grid* algorithm.

3.1 Data Used

The data used in this section corresponds to the "bust" or "mannequin" dataset used in [31] (detailed in [34]). We feel that using the same data makes the comparison more meaningful. This model along with accompanying hardware alignment data can be downloaded from http://eia.udg.edu/3dbenchmark which we also feel helps the reproducibility of results.

The data consist of a 5 views from the mannequin "bust" model (see Fig. 5). This corresponds to a real-sized mannequin of a human body scanned with a 3D structured-light system. See [30,32] for more details on the model and acquisition procedure. Each of the 5 views of the model contain ≈450000 points. No post-processing was performed. This dataset presents quite a lot of noise and the overlap between some of the views is very low (ranging from 60–70% in consecutive views to around 10% for the most distant views). This is a very challenging scenario for any registration method.

We registered the 5 available views each against all different views. This provided us with 20 different registration instances. Amongst these, 4 presented low (around 10%) overlap, 6 presented medium (between 30 and 50%) overlap

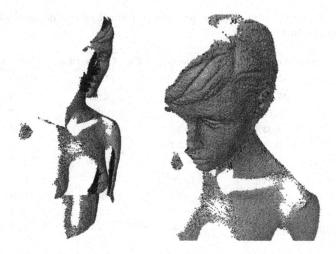

Fig. 5. Left: *bust0* view of bust model. Right: detail of *bust0* view. Figure originally appearing in [36].

and the remaining 10 presented high (approximately between 60 and 85%) overlap. All the results produced in this section were checked manually to ensure correctness and the percentage of overlap obtained were closely monitored.

3.2   Runtime Improvement Due to the Hierarchical Approach

In order to evaluate whether the hierarchical approach described in Sect. 2 improves the run-time performance of the algorithm, the code-optimised version of the regular grid algorithm was compared with the algorithm presented in this work. Table 1 presents results corresponding to five representative registration instances. The first half of the table corresponds to the regular grid method, the second half of the table depicts the results of our new proposal. Within each half of the table, the two initial rows and the final row correspond to sets with high overlap, the third row to sets with low overlap and the fourth to medium overlap.

All registration instances where also checked for correctness manually. All times are presented in seconds. The first column lists the views involved in the registration, the second and third column contains information on the overlap obtained for set $\mathcal{A}$ after coarse and fine alignment respectively. The fourth and fifth column present times for the coarse matching algorithms as well as the total time (which includes the former as well as the time for fine matching).

Table 1 shows how the proposed approach performs faster than the regular grid algorithm. On average (over all views) the time needed by the new algorithm was less than half that of the regular grid algorithm. Notice how the overlap after coarse matching is sometimes higher for the regular grid algorithm.

This happens due to this degree of overlap being the only criteria that is considered while our approach relies on other criteria to speed up the search

Table 1. Details on the runt-time improvement obtained by the hierarchical approach introduced in the current paper.

	Views	Overlap % coarse	Overlap % fine	Coarse time (s)	Total time (s)
Regular grid	0–1	15.30%	86.36%	14.23	17.39
	1–2	17.70%	72.24%	18.52	21.26
	1–4	8.15%	9.87%	19.14	22.17
	2–4	11.03%	43.38%	15.13	17.84
	3–4	19.71%	76.53%	12.55	15.10
Our approach	0–1	11.89%	86.34%	0.087	3.40
	1–2	17.44%	72.28%	0.010	3.87
	1–4	3.81%	9.84%	9.014	12.24
	2–4	11.03%	43.30%	7.63	10.11
	3–4	15.28%	76.58%	3.63	7.13

(such as bounding box overlap or coincidence of points in grid cells). In any case, the small reduction in coarse matching overlap does not affect the success of the subsequent fine matching algorithm as can be seen in the third column of the table.

3.3   Comparison with SOA Methods

In this section we study the performance of our algorithm against state of the art point cloud matching algorithms. Additionally to the algorithm that motivated the current research, [31] two widely used registration methods. The 4PCS method [3] is a widely used general-purpose point cloud matching method that also counts with an improved version called super4PCS [26] which is, to the best of our knowledge, the fastest general-purpose coarse matching algorithm to date.

The first issue that needs to be addressed is that of the nature of the methods being considered. The two grid based methods are hardware-software hybrid methods, so they rely on the fact that they can obtain information on the rotation part of the problem and take advantage of this to make the software part of the algorithm much simpler (they only look for a translation). Conversely the two 4PCS-based methods are actually looking for rotation as well as translation, so they are exploring a larger search space. While we acknowledge this, the point of hybrid methods is actually that the information that they get from hardware provides an advantage over pure software methods. In order to limit this as much as possible, we run the 4PCS-based methods both with the original sets and also with the same rotation-aligned methods used by the hybrid methods. We found out that the algorithms were faster with the rotation aligned sets, so these are the numbers that we report here.

Regarding parameter tuning and precision: Grid based algorithms mainly needed to determine the size of the grid. After trying 10 different grid sizes, we found out that grids with very few points (six grid points per iteration) did miss

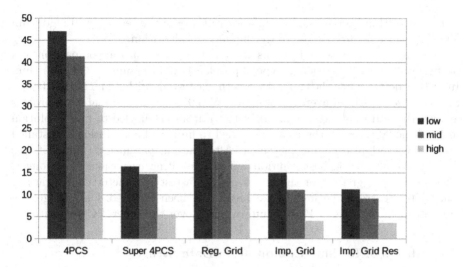

Fig. 6. Run-times for: 4PCS algorithm [3], Super4PCS [26], Regular Grid [31] and Improved Grid (current paper). For the improved grid we present two versions, the first computes residues using a KDtree, the second (Imp.Grid Res. in the graph) computes the residue using regular grids. (Color figure online)

the correct result in some cases. Consequently, we include results corresponding to the fastest results among those grids that produced correct results (this corresponds to grids with 6 points per coordinate for a total of 18 points per grid iteration). Conversely, 4PCS algorithm required quite a lot of parameter tuning and were prone to missing the correct result if the parameters were not set properly. The numbers presented here correspond to the best running time that we could achieve after trying several parameter configurations (so they correspond to different parameter settings).

Figure 6 presents run-times for all the algorithms studied. For each of them, data is separated in registration scenarios with low overlap (first bar, in blue), medium overlap (second bar, in red) and high overlap (third bar, in yellow). All times are presented in seconds. For the rest of this section we will comment on the results obtained by the state of the art methods and the non-optimised (in terms of residue computation) version of our algorithm. Consequently, we will be focusing on the four initial groups of bars in the graph, from 4PCS to Imp. Grid. The impact of residue computation optimization will be addressed in Sect. 3.4.

Results show how the rotation information obtained from hardware sensors allows to make the software part of these algorithms quite fast. Specifically, the previously existing regular grid method outperforms the well-established 4PCS method and is the most robust method overall in the sense that it presents less relative difference in execution times between sets with high and low overlap. The times of the 4PCS algorithm are somewhat skewed by some registrations that are way slower than the others. If we ignore these cases, the running times of this algorithm become slightly inferior to those of the regular grid algorithm although quite far from those of the super4PCS algorithm.

The algorithm presented in this work is the fastest in the comparison and outperforms (for this particular type of problem) even the super4PCS algorithm. In further detail, while the super4PCS is the fastest algorithm in 5 of the 10 high overlap cases (with an average total time of 3.97 s for all the matching process against the 4.01 s average for our algorithm), it also struggled to find a solution in 10 of the 20 cases. In these cases it failed to find the best solution and stalled under 5% overlap after fine matching. After careful parameter tuning, it was possible to obtain the best solution but the resulting executions took longer. The resulting aggregate of the times of the fastest parameter configurations leading to a correct solution is what has finally been reported. On average, the current paper obtained a 19.67% improvement over the super4PCS algorithm.

3.4   Effects of Residue Computation Data Structes

As can be seen in Fig. 6, the optimization of the computation of residues has a significant effect on the performance of the algorithm presented. The improvement depends, as expected, on the weight of the residue computations on the matching algorithms. Subsequently, higher improvement (of up to 32% in one of the cases) is observed for the registration instances with lower overlap. In these cases, more overlap means matching that are easier to find and, thus, less residue computations so the improvement in the sets with higher overlap is smaller (around 10% on average). The fact that using the very simple regular grid data structure achieves a significant improvement over the widely used (although general purpose) ANN KDtree also indicates how it is important to analyze both asymptotic costs as well as practical performance when studying the suitability of a data structure for one particular application.

4   Conclusions

In this paper we have presented a Hybrid hardware/software approach for point cloud matching applied to the problem of reconstructing objects from different views with varying degrees of overlap. Building on the previous algorithm presented in [31] by improving the translation determination part of its software step we managed to cut the average computation time by more than half. The hierarchical approach presented for the new software part of the algorithm is exemplified in Fig. 4.

Results run with real data show (Table 1, second column) how this reduction is achieved at the cost of achieving slightly less overlap after the coarse matching step. This does not, however, reduce the algorithm accuracy after the refinement step as the subsequent (ICP) fine matching algorithm is able to make up for the loss. As providing a sufficient starting step for fine registration is considered the main goal of coarse matching algorithms, the trade-off between speed and overlap percentage is experimentally shown to be acceptable. Additionally, and focusing on time efficiency, we have shown how hybrid algorithms can outperform two well established coarse registration methods including a 19% improvement over the super4PCS [26] algorithm which is, to the best of our knowledge, the best pure-software, general-purpose point cloud registration algorithm to date. Finally, we have shown how the use of dedicated structures for residue computation results in a further improvement (of between 5% and 32%) in runtime. This is achieved by using a regular grid structure for residue computation.

Acknowledgements. We want to thank the authors of the state of the art algorithms considered for making their code publicly available.

References

1. https://www.cs.umd.edu/~mount/ann/
2. Agarwal, P.K., Har-Peled, S., Sharir, M., Wang, Y.: Hausdorff distance under translation for points and balls. In Proceedings of the Nineteenth Annual Symposium on Computational Geometry, SCG 2003, pp. 282–291. ACM, New York (2003)
3. Aiger, D., Mitra, N.J., Cohen-Or, D.: 4-points congruent sets for robust pairwise surface registration. In: SIGGRAPH, vol. 27, no. 3, p. 85 (2008)
4. Andreadis, A., Gregor, R., Sipiran, I., Mavridis, P., Papaioannou, G., Schreck, T.: Fractured 3D object restoration and completion. In: ACM SIGGRAPH 2015 Posters, p. 74. ACM (2015)
5. Arya, S., Mount, D.M.: Approximate nearest neighbor queries in fixed dimensions. In: SODA, vol. 93, pp. 271–280 (1993)
6. Bærentzen, J.A., Gravesen, J., Anton, F., Aanæs, H.: 3D surface registration via iterative closest point (ICP). In: Guide to Computational Geometry Processing, pp. 263–275. Springer, London (2012). https://doi.org/10.1007/978-1-4471-4075-7_15
7. Besl, P.J., McKay, N.D.: A method for registration of 3-D shapes. IEEE Trans. Pattern Anal. Mach. Intell. **14**(2), 239–256 (1992)
8. Buchin, K., Diez, Y., van Diggelen, T., Meulemans, W.: Efficient trajectory queries under the Fréchet distance (GIS Cup). In: Proceedings of the 25th ACM SIGSPATIAL International Conference on Advances in Geographic Information Systems, SIGSPATIAL 2017, pp. 101:1–101:4. ACM, New York (2017)
9. Choi, S., Kim, S., Chae, J.: Real-time 3D registration using GPU. Mach. Vis. Appl. **22**, 837–850 (2011)
10. Choi, S., Zhou, Q.-Y., Koltun, V.: Robust reconstruction of indoor scenes. In: IEEE Conference on Computer Vision and Pattern Recognition, CVPR, pp. 5556–5565. IEEE (2015)
11. da Silva Tavares, J.M.R.: Image processing and analysis: applications and trends. In: 2010 Fifth International Conference on AES-ATEMA# 8217 (2010)
12. Diez, Y., Lopez, M.A., Sellarès, J.A.: Noisy road network matching. In: Cova, T.J., Miller, H.J., Beard, K., Frank, A.U., Goodchild, M.F. (eds.) GIScience 2008. LNCS, vol. 5266, pp. 38–54. Springer, Heidelberg (2008). https://doi.org/10.1007/978-3-540-87473-7_3
13. Díez, Y., Martí, J., Salvi, J.: Hierarchical normal space sampling to speed up point cloud coarse matching. Pattern Recogn. Lett. **33**, 2127–2133 (2012)
14. Díez, Y., Roure, F., Lladó, X., Salvi, J.: A qualitative review on 3D coarse registration methods. ACM Comput. Surv. (CSUR) **47**(3), 45 (2015)

15. Diez, Y., Sellarès, J.A.: Noisy colored point set matching. Discrete Appl. Math. **159**(6), 433–449 (2011)
16. Elbaz, G., Avraham, T., Fischer, A.: 3D point cloud registration for localization using a deep neural network auto-encoder. In: 2017 IEEE Conference on Computer Vision and Pattern Recognition, CVPR, pp. 2472–2481 (2017)
17. Fan, J., et al.: Convex hull indexed Gaussian mixture model (CH-GMM) for 3D point set registration. Pattern Recogn. **59**, 126–141 (2016)
18. Gelfand, N., Mitra, N.J., Guibas, L.J., Pottmann, H.: Robust global registration. In: Eurographics Symposium on Geometry Processing, pp. 197–206 (2005)
19. Jerbić, B., Šuligoj, F., Švaco, M., Šekoranja, B.: Robot assisted 3D point cloud object registration. Proc. Eng. **100**, 847–852 (2015). 25th DAAAM International Symposium on Intelligent Manufacturing and Automation (2014)
20. Larkins, R.L., Cree, M.J., Dorrington, A.A.: Verification of multi-view point-cloud registration for spherical harmonic cross-correl. In: 27th Conference on Image Vision Computing, New Zealand, pp. 358–363. ACM (2012)
21. Lian, Z., et al.: A comparison of methods for non-rigid 3D shape retrieval. Pattern Recogn. (2012)
22. Makadia, A., Patterson, A., Daniilidis, K.: Fully automatic registration of 3D point clouds. In: 2006 IEEE Computer Society Conference on Computer Vision and Pattern Recognition, vol. 1, pp. 1297–1304 (2006)
23. Manay, S., Hong, B.-W., Yezzi, A.J., Soatto, S.: Integral invariant signatures. In: Pajdla, T., Matas, J. (eds.) ECCV 2004. LNCS, vol. 3024, pp. 87–99. Springer, Heidelberg (2004). https://doi.org/10.1007/978-3-540-24673-2_8
24. Martins, A., Bessant, M., Manukyan, L., Milinkovitch, M.: R2OBBIE-3D, a fast robotic high-resolution system for quantitative phenotyping of surface geometry and colour-texture. PLoS One **10**(6), 1–18 (2015)
25. Matabosch, C., Fofi, D., Salvi, J., Batlle, E.: Registration of surfaces minimizing error propagation for a one-shot multi-slit hand-held scanner. Pattern Recogn. **41**(6), 2055–2067 (2008)
26. Mellado, N., Aiger, D., Mitra, N.J.: Super 4PCS fast global pointcloud registration via smart indexing. In: Computer Graphics Forum, vol. 33, no. 5, pp. 205–215. Wiley Online Library (2014)
27. Mian, A., Bennamoun, M., Owens, R.: On the repeatability and quality of keypoints for local feature-based 3D object retrieval from cluttered scenes. Int. J. Comput. Vis. **89**(2), 348–361 (2010)
28. Oliveira, F.P., Tavares, J.M.R.: Medical image registration: a review. Comput. Methods Biomech. Biomed. Eng. **17**(2), 73–93 (2014). PMID: 22435355
29. Pottmann, H., Wallner, J., Huang, Q.-X., Yang, Y.-L.: Integral invariants for robust geometry processing. Comput. Aided Geom. Des. **26**(1), 37–60 (2009)
30. Pribanić, T., Diez, Y., Fernandez, S., Salvi, J.: An efficient method for surface registration. In: VISAPP, no. 1, pp. 500–503 (2013)
31. Pribanić, T., Diez, Y., Roure, F., Salvi, J.: An efficient surface registration using smartphone. Mach. Vis. Appl. **27**(4), 559–576 (2016)
32. Pribanić, T., Mrvoš, S., Salvi, J.: Efficient multiple phase shift patterns for dense 3D acquisition in structured light scanning. Image Vis. Comput. **28**(8), 1255–1266 (2010)
33. ProjectTango: Project tango (2016). https://www.google.com/atap/projecttango/#project. Accessed 20 Sept 2016
34. Roure, F., Díez, Y., Lladó, X., Forest, J., Pribanic, T., Salvi, J.: An experimental benchmark for point set coarse registration. In: International Conference on Computer Vision Theory and Applications (2015)

35. Roure, F., Diez, Y., Lladó, X., Forest, J., Pribanic, T., Salvi, J.: A study on the robustness of shape descriptors to common scanning artifacts. In: 14th International Conference on Machine Vision Applications, MVA, pp. 522–525. IEEE (2015)
36. Roure, F., Llad, X., Salvi, J., Pribanić, T., Diez, Y.: Hierarchical techniques to improve hybrid point cloud registration. In: Proceedings of the 12th International Joint Conference on Computer Vision, Imaging and Computer Graphics Theory and Applications - Volume 4: VISAPP, VISIGRAPP 2017, pp. 44–51. INSTICC, SciTePress (2017)
37. Rusinkiewicz, S., Levoy, M.: Efficient variants of the ICP algorithm. In: IEEE International Conference on 3D Digital Imaging and Modeling, pp. 145–152 (2001)
38. Salti, S., Tombari, F., Stefano, L.D.: A performance evaluation of 3D keypoint detectors. In: IEEE International Conference on 3D Imaging, Modeling, Processing, Visualization and Transmission, pp. 236–243 (2011)
39. Salvi, J., Matabosch, C., Fofi, D., Forest, J.: A review of recent range image registration methods with accuracy evaluation. Image Vis. Comput. **25**(5), 578–596 (2007)
40. Sipiran, I., Bustos, B.: Harris 3D: a robust extension of the Harris operator for interest point detection on 3D meshes. Vis. Comput. **27**(11), 963–976 (2011)
41. StructureSensor: Structure sensor (2016). http://structure.io/. Accessed 20 Sept 2016
42. Sun, J., Ovsjanikov, M., Guibas, L.: A concise and provably informative multi-scale signature based on heat diffusion. In: Computer Graphics Forum, vol. 28, pp. 1383–1392 (2009)
43. Tonioni, A., Salti, S., Tombari, F., Spezialetti, R., Stefano, L.D.: Learning to detect good 3D keypoints. Int. J. Comput. Vis. **126**(1), 1–20 (2018)
44. Yang, J., Li, K., Li, K., Lai, Y.-K.: Sparse non-rigid registration of 3D shapes. In: Computer Graphics Forum, vol. 34, pp. 89–99. Wiley Online Library (2015)
45. Zaharescu, A., Boyer, E., Varanasi, K., Horaud, R.: Surface feature detection and description with applications to mesh matching. In: IEEE Conference on Computer Vision and Pattern Recognition, pp. 373–380 (2009)
46. Zhang, J., Sun, J.: Instance-based object recognition in 3D point clouds using discriminative shape primitives. Mach. Vis. Appl. **29**(2), 285–297 (2018)
47. Zou, Y., Wang, X., Zhang, T., Liang, B., Song, J., Liu, H.: BRoPH: an efficient and compact binary descriptor for 3D point clouds. Pattern Recogn. **76**, 522–536 (2018)

Real-Time HDTV-to-8K TV Hardware Upconverter

Seiichi Gohshi[✉]

Kogakuin University, 1-24-2, Nishi-Shinjuku, Shinjuku-Ku, Tokyo, Japan
gohshi@cc.kogakuin.ac.jp

Abstract. 8K is the pinnacle of the video systems and 8K broadcasting service will be started in December 2018. However, the availability of content for 8K TV is still insufficient, a situation similar to that of HDTV in the 1990s. Upconverting analogue content to HDTV content was important to supplement the insufficient HDTV content. This upconverted content was also important for news coverage as HDTV equipment was heavy and bulky. The current situation for 8K TV is similar wherein covering news with 8K TV equipment is very difficult as this equipment is much heavier and bulkier than that required for HDTV in the 1990s. The HDTV content available currently is sufficient, and the equipment has also evolved to facilitate news coverage; therefore, an HDTV-to-8K TV upconverter can be a solution to the problems described above. However, upconversion from interlaced HDTV to 8K TV results in an enlargement of the images by a factor of 32, thus making the upconverted images very blurry. Super resolution (SR) is a technology to solve the enlargement blur issue. One of the most common SR technologies is super resolution image reconstruction (SRR). However, SRR has limitations to use for the HDTV-to-8K TV upconverter. In this paper an HDTV-to-8K TV upconverter with nonlinear processing SR has been proposed in this study in order to fix this issue.

Keywords: 8KTV · 4KTV · HDTV · Up-convert ·
Super resolution with non-linear processing ·
Super resolution image reconstruction ·
Learning based super resolution · Non-linear signal processing

1 Introduction

Research about HDTV started in the 1960s, and its practical usage began in the late 1990s. The broadcasting service began in 2000 for digital satellite HDTV and in 2003 for terrestrial HDTV, and now both services are offered in multiple countries. More than 30 years of research were required for HDTV to become a practical service, and only 18 years have passed since these services began. However, 4K TV services have been made available via satellite broadcasting and Internet services. The horizontal and vertical resolutions of HDTV are 1,980

© Springer Nature Switzerland AG 2019
A. P. Cláudio et al. (Eds.): VISIGRAPP 2017, CCIS 983, pp. 192–212, 2019.
https://doi.org/10.1007/978-3-030-12209-6_10

pixels and 1,080 pixels, respectively [11], and that of 4K TV are 3,860 pixels and 2,160 pixels, respectively [12]. The 4K TV system has evolved over time and is used for multiple applications such as sports content, cinema and personal videos. 8K TV has a horizontal resolution of 7,680 pixels and a vertical resolution of 4,320 pixels [12], which is four times greater than that of 4K TV and 16 times greater than that of full HDTV (progressive HDTV). Broadcasting HDTV adopts an interlaced video system which contains half the information as that contained by full HDTV. This means that 8K TV content has a resolution 32 times higher than that of the broadcasting HDTV content. The system clock frequencies for broadcasting HDTV, 4K TV and 8K TV are set at 74.25 MHz, 594 MHz and 2,376 MHz (2.376 GHz), respectively. The HD equipment used currently has evolved both in terms of technology and cost effectiveness, and a majority of the video content available, including films, is made in HD. Although the use of commercial 4K TV is practical, its equipment is not commonly available, especially that used professionally, for example, 4K TV professional video cameras. Sony began to release its professional studio cameras in 2014, which are still expensive. Other 4K TV equipment such as professional editing systems, transmission systems and outside broadcasting cars are both technically immature and expensive. All types of 8K TV equipment are currently under development or are being researched; therefore, its practical use is much more difficult to begin than that of 4K TV. However, 8K TV broadcasting strats in December 2018 and is expected to be a highlight of the 2020 Olympic Games. There are a couple of problems that 8K TV services are faced with. First, 8K TV content for broadcasting is crucial but rather insufficient. Second, using 8K TV equipment in news gathering systems such as outside broadcasting cars and helicopters is not currently practical because of the reasons described earlier. The same situation existed for HDTV in the late 1990s, wherein creating HDTV content and gathering news was difficult because of the expensive and bulky equipment. In contrast, analogue TV content was sufficient and the professional equipment required was less expensive and of small size and low weight. Therefore, analogue TV content was upconverted to HDTV content to resolve the problems of insufficient HDTV content and expensive equipment. The HD equipment available currently is sufficiently small to be used for news gathering and outside broadcasting; however, analogue content is still used for HDTV broadcasting with analogue TV-to-HDTV upconversion as much excellent analogue content has been stored and accumulated over time. However, upconverted content is blurry because the images are interpolated. The highest resolution of the original image and the interpolated image remains the same despite using an ideal interpolation filter. The upconverted HDTV content can be immediately recognised as it appears blurry. The resolution ratio of HDTV to analogue TV is 5:1. The same issue will occur if HDTV content is used for upconversion to 8K TV. The accumulated HDTV content is interlaced as the professional equipment used for it is an interlaced system; hence, we need to upconvert this interlaced content to 8K TV content, including that for news gathering and outside broadcasting.

As discussed earlier, the resolution ratio of HDTV to 8K TV is 1:32, whereas that for analogue TV-to-HDTV conversion is 1:5. This shows that HDTV-to-8K TV conversion produces blurrier content than that produced by analogue TV-to-HDTV conversion. Currently the upconversion from the interlaced HDTV to progressive HDTV (full HD) is not so difficult and the full HD equipment such as cameras, recorders and other studio equipment are available. However, the upconversion from full HD to 8K is still 1:16 and it is higher magnifying scale than that of analogue TV to HDTV. Such blurry content does not take advantages of the high resolution screen, which is the most important sales point of 8K TV. Therefore, it is necessary to develop a new technology which can cope with creating such elements that are not available for the current upconverted images [8].

2   Super Resolution (SR)

2.1   Enhancer

For years, TV manufacturers have competed to improve the image quality of their sets, and enhancer (sometimes called "unsharp masking" or "edge enhancement") was the only real-time video enhancement method available [14,20,25]. The enhancer is an effective method for improving image quality; however, it does not truly improve an image's resolution. Rather, it merely amplifies the image's edges, which are detected with a high-pass filter (HPF) prior to being amplified. When enhancer is applied to a blurry image, it does not improve the image quality because there are no edges to be detected.

2.2   SR for Still Image

Methods for creating HRIs from LRIs have been researched for many years. Until the 1990s, a defocused photograph was always the target of such research and the goal was "image restoration". These methods were later extended in scope and their current goal is SR [15,22]. Currently one of the most common SR techniques is super resolution image reconstruction (SRR) [1,3,4,10,13,18,19,28,29].

Although other SR technologies exist [5,26], they do not work in real time. This study discusses real-time video improvement technologies. SRR is, at present, the only SR method among the many proposed to be incorporated into commercial products and to work in real time [16,27]. However, its resulting image quality is inferior to that obtained with conventional enhancers. In fact, subjective tests have shown that the image quality of commercial HDTV sets equipped with SRR is poorer than that of HDTV sets equipped with enhancer technology [7]. Figure 1 shows the basic idea [4]. An HRI is processed with a low-pass filter (LPF) that does not cut all the high-frequency elements. The cut-off frequency of the LPF is higher than the Nyquist frequency of LRIs. Sub-sampling is used to create LRIs from an HRI. All LRIs are different since the sampled pixel phases of each LRI are different. The summation of sampled pixels

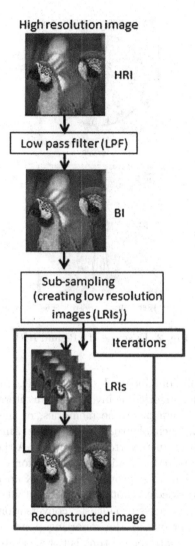

Fig. 1. SRR algorithm.

exceeds all the pixels in the HRI. For example, suppose we want to make 256 ×
256 pixel LRIs from a 512 × 512 pixel HRI. In this case, four LRIs would have
the same number of pixels as the HRI but, in fact, SRR must create more than
four 256 × 256 images to reconstruct the HRI. That is, we need a larger amount
of information than that in the HRI to reconstruct the HRI with SRR.

2.3   SR for HDTV

Super Resolution (SR) is a technology that creates a high-resolution image from
low-resolution ones [4,9,18,19,21,28]. The keyword phrase "Super resolution"

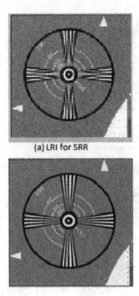

(a) LRI for SRR

(b) Reconstructed HRI with SRR

Fig. 2. Example of LRI and HRI.

gets about 160 million hits on Google. Indeed, there are many SR proposals, but most of them are complex algorithms involving many iterations. If the iterations are conducted for video signals, frame memories, of the same number as the iterations, are required. Such algorithms are almost impossible to work with real-time hardware for the upconverted 8K content. Although non-iterative SR was proposed [24], it only reduces aliasing artifact for a couple of images with B-Splines. It is not sufficient to improve HDTV-to-8K upconverted blurry videos because the upconverted videos do not have aliasing at all. SR for TV should have low delay. Especially in live news broadcasts, conversations between announcers in the TV studio and persons at the reporting point tend to be affected by delays. For viewers, the superimposed time is not accurate on a TV screen if the delay is longer than 60 seconds. For these reasons, complex SR algorithms with iterations cannot be used in TV systems. Although a real-time SR technology for HDTV was proposed [16,27], its resolution is worse than that of HDTV without SR [7]. These iterations are essential for SRR to reconstruct an HRI from LRIs. The result of the iterations must converge to the HRI. However, the result may diverge if the cost or some other function (such as sampling phases) is not appropriate. The number of iterations is also an issue. The time consumed by the iterations is in proportion to their number. A small number is required for practical applications. Yet, although considerable research has gone into finding solutions to these problems, which are called "Fast and Robust Convergence to HRI," other much more important issues remain to be addressed, such as finding the ultimate highest resolution that can be produced with SRR. If the convergence point of SRR is just the HRI in Fig. 1, then SRR cannot improve the resolution beyond that of the original HRI that we began with.

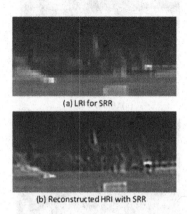

Fig. 3. Example of LRI and reconstructed HRI 1 [28].

2.4 Truth of SRR

All previous studies considering SRR evaluate the peak signal to noise ratio (PSNR) between the HRI and the reconstructed image shown in Fig. 1. They compare their proposed PSNR with previous PSNRs. If their proposed PSNR is better than the previous one, the result is good achievement in SRR research. However, there is a trick in the SRR algorithm shown in Fig. 1. The algorithm shows that the role of the LPF is very important. If the LPF does not exist, then the process is nothing more than the breaking down of the HRI into LRIs and then reconstructing the HRI from those LRIs. In other words, although the LRIs are solved by minimizing the complex cost function, the process is nothing more than creating and then solving a jigsaw puzzle with the LRIs. SRR's resulting resolution depends on the LPF's characteristics, and it is necessary for LRIs to have an aliasing signal, according to the Nyquist sampling theory of LRIs. Aliasing is very important in SRR and appears to be based on the LPF's characteristics in the algorithm shown in Fig. 1. Aliasing does not occur if the LPF's cut-off frequency is sufficiently low. According to the Nyquist sampling theory, the LPF's cut-off frequency prior to sub-sampling should be sufficiently low to not cause aliasing. If the LPF in Fig. 1 is eliminated, aliasing occurs; however, this does not occur in the general combination of LPF and sub-sampling.

Figure 2(a) is an example LRI, and Fig. 2(b) shows an HRI reconstructed from LRIs using SRR. Figure 2(a) has the typical characteristics of LRIs used for SRR; all have aliasing. Figure 2(b) is derived by reducing the aliasing in the LRIs that is used to reconstruct the HRI. This is the truth of SRR. It merely reduces aliasing by using many LRIs. In other words, SRR does not work unless

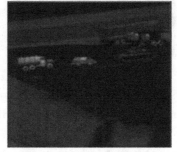

(b) Reconstructed HRI with SRR

Fig. 4. Example of LRI and reconstructed HRI 2 [4].

Fig. 5. Motion blur in video.

LRIs have aliasing. This aliasing, which is good for SRR, is caused by a wide-bandwidth LPF that does not satisfy the Nyquist sampling theory. Aliasing does not exist if there is no HRI. As the PSNR was compared with the HRI and the reconstructed image in previous studies considering SRR, the prepared HRI was automatically accepted. However, previous SRR research merely compared the PSNR with the original image (HRI) and its reconstructed jigsaw puzzle (reconstructed HRI). The SRR algorithm is not logical if the original HRI is not given, which is the case in general applications, implying that SRR does not work for general purposes. SRR has recently been applied to video. Figures 3(a) and 4(b) are examples of video LRIs. The block-wise shapes in those figures are caused by aliasing. Figures 3(b) and 4(b) are reconstructed HRIs with SRR. They were created by simply reducing the aliasing from Figs. 3(a) and 4(b). If there is no aliasing in Figs. 3(a) and 4(a), SRR cannot improve the image quality. Block-shape aliasing does not occur in general broadcasting content because the video camera pixels are too small to show block shapes, which indicates that SRR does not work for broadcasting content.

Fig. 6. Original image.

Figure 5 shows the video frames of a fast-moving bullet train. A general video of such a fast-moving object will have motion blur, as shown in Fig. 5, and none of the aliasing shown in Figures, 2, 3(a), and 4(a). Thus, SRR does not work for general applications. SRR only works for images and videos that have aliasing, such as the aliasing caused by the interlace artifact, which only reduces the vertical resolution. Iterative methods can be used to align the edges of images so that lines with aliasing will be connected across the edges; however, because the interlace artifact only reduces the vertical resolution, the horizontal resolution will not be improved. Furthermore, iterative methods cannot create an HRI from blurry LRIs. If it were possible to create high-frequency elements from low-frequency elements, operas would have no need for soprano singers as a "soprano singer" could be composed from the voices of many bass singers. Yet, the SRR algorithm could have results that are analogous to creating soprano voices from bass voices, although the voices of bass singers will never create a soprano voice. SRR was first proposed for still images. To apply it to a video, the SRR algorithm must treat the video frames as LRIs. However, the SRR algorithm requires one HRI from which LRIs can be created with aliasing [4,19,28]. LRIs with aliasing are created using iterations that are subject to a constraint condition, and the algorithm reconstructs an HRI. Although the reconstruction of an HRI depends on the shot objects and camerawork, video frames are not created from one HRI. Furthermore, although motion vectors are used to adjust the phase of the

Fig. 7. Reconstructed image.

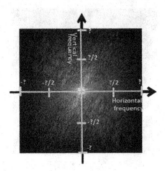

Fig. 8. Tow dimensional spectrum of Fig. 6.

frames, they are different images. If no HRI is available to make the LRIs, there is no guarantee that the LRIs will converge to an HRI. Moreover, SRR cannot create an HRI from LRIs that are all the same. For example, if the camera is completely still and shoots still-life images, SRR cannot create a high-resolution video because every video frame is the same image without noise.

3   Analysis in the Frequency Domain

SRR is usually discussed with regard to the original and reconstructed images. Yet, image quality is very subjective and it is not easy to distinguish image quality with images printed on sheets of paper or in PDF files. In this study, "image quality" refers to that in the frequency domain. Figure 6 shows the original image and Fig. 7 shows the SRR-reconstructed image. Sixteen LRIs that are a quarter of the size of the HRI are used and iteration is conducted 100 times to recreate Fig. 7. This is how SRR signal processing is conducted for still images, which is the best condition for SRR since a still image has sharp edges. Although Figs. 6 and 7 look identical, the two-dimensional Fast Fourier Transform (2D FFT) results shown in Figs. 8 and 9 are different. Figures 7 and 9 show the

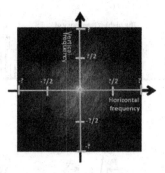

Fig. 9. Tow dimensional spectrum of Fig. 7.

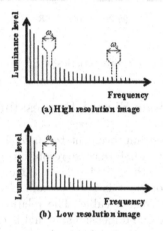

Fig. 10. High and low resolution spectrum of the same video.

2D FFT results of Figs. 6 and 7, respectively. The important points of these Figures are not the strength but how widely the spectrum spreads without spaces. The areas of the spectrum is in proportion to higher resolution and the geometrical spectrum gaps cause artifacts due to the lack of the particular frequencies. In Fig. 9, there is a rectangular-shaped null area that does not appear in Fig. 7. This null area is caused by the size of LRIs and is the Nyquist frequency of LRIs. Figure 7 is reconstructed with 16 LRIs using 100 iterations–ideal conditions for SRR. Yet, despite these ideal conditions, the original image cannot be recreated. The definition used in this study states that SR can create higher frequency elements than those contained within the original image or video [22]. Thus, on the basis of this definition, it is necessary to discuss SR technologies in the frequency domain.

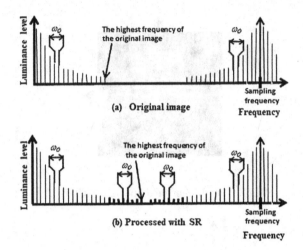

Fig. 11. Frequency characteristics of SR processed video.

4   SR with Non-linear Signal Processing

There are various resolution improvement technologies similar to the one proposed in this paper. Here, we analyze these resolution improvement technologies in the frequency domain. Although video is a three dimensional signal (horizontal, vertical and temporal), it is scanned and can be transmitted as one-dimensional signal with a coaxial cable. The relationship between the three-dimensional signal and the one-dimensional signal is explained in [37]. We will use a one-dimensional frequency model to make the discussion simple. Figure 10 is an illustration of image and video signals having typical line spectrums in the frequency domain. Figure 10(a) shows the spectrum of a high resolution video and Fig. 10(b) shows the spectrum of a low resolution video of the same system of Fig. 10(a). The difference between them is only the resolution. Video signals have special line spectrum characteristics in the frequency domain. The interval between the lines is the same as the fundamental frequency regardless of high or low resolution. The fundamental frequency of video signals is the frame frequency.

The level of the line spectrum attenuates in proportion to the frequency, and the level of it is the maximum at the frequency zero. High-resolution images and video sequences have high-frequency elements. The resolution of the video is in proportion to the highest frequency [37]. The highest frequency of NTSC video is 4.2 MHz and that of HDTV is 24 MHz. Figure 11 shows the performance of SR in the frequency domain. If SR really works, the SR processed video will have high frequency elements that the original image does not have. This is shown in Fig. 11(b), where the bold-lined frequency elements do not exist in Fig. 11(a). The created bold-lined frequency elements in Fig. 11(b) have the same characteristics as the original video and the fundamental frequency of them should be also ω_0.

SR with non-linear signal processing (NLSP) has been proposed as an alternative to the conventional image enhancement methods [6], and it has several advantages compared with conventional SR technologies. Since it does not use iterations or frame memories, it is sufficiently lightweight to be installed in an FPGA (Field Programmable Gate Array) for real-time video processing. Furthermore, it can create frequency elements that are higher than those of the original image, as has been proven by performing two-dimensional fast Fourier transform (2D-FFT) results [6]. However, it has not been used for 8K content because the system clock of 8K is 2.3376 GHz. In this paper, we present real-time HD/8K upconverter with NLSP to improve actual resolution of the content upconverted to 8K from HDTV.

SRNL was proposed to solve the issues that previous SR technologies encountered [21–25]. The basic idea of NLSP is like that of the one-dimensional signal processing shown in Fig. 12 [6]. The input is distributed to two blocks. The upper path creates high-frequency elements that the original image does not have as follows. The original image is processed with a high pass filter (HPF) to detect edges. The output of the HPF is edge information that has a sign, i.e., plus or minus, for each pixel. After the HPF, the edges are processed with a non-linear function (NLF). If an even function such as x^2 is used as the NLF, the sign information is lost. To stop this from happening, the most significant bit (MSB) is taken from the edge information before the NLF and restored after the NLF. Non-linear functions generate harmonics that can create frequency elements that are higher than those of the original image. NLSP using a number of non-linear functions should be able to create high-frequency elements. Here, we propose $y = x^2$ for plus edges and $y = -x^2$ for minus edges.

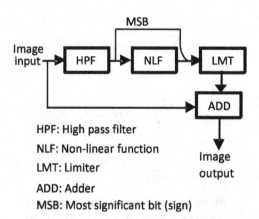

Fig. 12. NLSP algorithm [8].

It is well known that images are expanded in a Fourier series [17]. Here, we take a one-dimensional image $f(x)$ to make the explanation simple. $f(x)$ is expanded as follows.

$$f(x) = \sum_{n=-N}^{+N} a_n \cos(n\omega_0) + b_n \sin(n\omega_0) \tag{1}$$

ω_0 is the fundamental frequency and N means a positive integer. The HPF attenuates low-frequency elements including the zero frequency element (DC). We denote the output of the HPF by $g(x)$ and it becomes as follows.

$$g(x) = \sum_{n=-N}^{-M} a_n \cos(n\omega_0) + b_n \sin(n\omega_0)$$

$$+ \sum_{n=M}^{N} a_n \cos(n\omega_0) + b_n \sin(n\omega_0) \tag{2}$$

M is also a positive integer and $N > M$. The frequency elements from $-M$ to M are eliminated with the HPF. DC has the largest energy in the images, and it sometimes causes saturation whereby the images become either all white or all black. The square function does not cause saturation by eliminating DC, and it has the following effect. Edges are represented with $\sin(n\omega_0)$ and $\cos(n\omega_0)$ functions. The square function generates $\sin^2(n\omega_0)$ and $\cos^2(n\omega_0)$ from $\sin(n\omega_0)$ and $\cos(n\omega_0)$. $\sin^2(n\omega_0)$ and $\cos^2(n\omega_0)$ generate $\sin 2(n\omega_0)$ and $\cos 2(n\omega_0)$. Theoretically it can be explained as follows. Since the most significant bit (MSB) of the $g(x)$ is protected, the input of the LMT for $g(x) > 0$ becomes the Eq. 3 and that of the LMT for $g(x) < 0$ becomes the Eq. 4.

$$(g(x))^2 = \sum_{n=-2N}^{-M} c_n \cos(n\omega_0) + d_n \sin(n\omega_0)$$

$$+ \sum_{n=M}^{2N} c_n \cos(n\omega_0) + d_n \sin(n\omega_0) \tag{3}$$

$$-(g(x))^2 = - \sum_{n=-2N}^{-M} c_n \cos(n\omega_0) + d_n \sin(n\omega_0)$$

$$- \sum_{n=M}^{2N} c_n \cos(n\omega_0) + d_n \sin(n\omega_0) \tag{4}$$

Here, c_n and d_n are coefficients of the expansion of Eq. 2. Although Eqs. 3 and 4 have the high frequency elements from $(N+1)\omega_0)$ to $2N\omega_0)$, they do not exist in the input image, Eq. 1. Since these high frequency elements are created with the non-linear function, some of them are too large and need to be processed with LMT. After LMT processing, the created high frequency elements are added to the input with ADD. These NLFs create frequency elements that are two times higher than the input, and they can be used to double the size of the images horizontally and vertically, such as in the upconversion from HD to 4K.

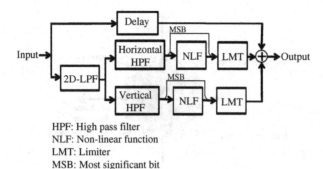

HPF: High pass filter
NLF: Non-linear function
LMT: Limiter
MSB: Most significant bit

Fig. 13. Block diagram of real-time hardware [8].

It is necessary to apply NLSP horizontally and vertically, since images and videos are two-dimensional signals. Figure 13 is a block diagram of the real-time video processing. The input is distributed to two paths. The output of the upper line, the delay path, is the same as the input. The signal is delayed until the signal processing on the other paths ends. The bottom line includes a two-dimensional low pass filter (2D-LPF) and a parallel NLSP part. The 2D-LPF block decreases noise in video because noise has horizontal and vertical high frequency elements. Figure 14 shows the two-dimensional frequency characteristics of the 2D-LPF. 2D-LPF passes the checker marked area and eliminates the diagonal frequency elements, i.e., the four corners shown in Fig. 14. NLSP creates horizontal high frequency elements and vertical high frequency elements. Both horizontal and vertical high frequency, diagonal, elements are processed with horizontal NLSP and vertical NLSP separately. If these frequency elements are processed with NLSP, the diagonal frequency elements are emphasized to excess.

The human visual system is not so sensitive to the horizontal and vertical high-frequency elements, i.e. the four corners shown in Fig. 14 [23]. This means these frequency elements in the NLSP video do not affect the perceived resolution. Thus, to maintain the original diagonal resolution, the original diagonal frequency elements are sent through the delay line and added to the output. After the 2D-LPF the signal is provided into two paths. The upper path is the horizontal NLSP, and the lower path is the vertical NLSP. The three video paths are added together at the end to create the NLSP video. This parallel signal processing is fast. It reduces the delay from input to output, as discussed in Sect. 1, and it can work at 60 Hz. Figure 15 shows the NLSP hardware. It up-converts full to 4K , and it processes the up-converted 4K video with NLSP to increase the resolution at 60 Hz. The NLSP algorithm is installed in the FPGA, which is located under the heat sink. Although there are many parts on the circuit board, most of them are input and output interface devices and electric power devices.

Figure 16 shows an image processed with the NLSP hardware shown in Fig. 15. Figure 16(a) is just an enlargement from HD to 4K, and it looks blurry. Figure 16(b) shows the image processed with NLSP after the enlargement. Its

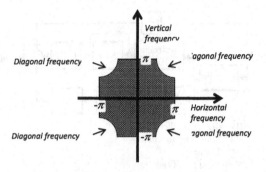

Fig. 14. Characteristics of 2D-LPF [8].

Fig. 15. Appearance of real-time hardware [8].

resolution is clearly better than that of Fig. 16(a). Figure 16(c) and (d) are the 2D-FFT results of Fig. 16(a) and (b) respectively. In Fig. 16(c) and (d), the horizontal axis the the horizontal frequency and the vertical axis the vertical frequency. HD Fig. 16(d) has horizontal and vertical high-frequency elements that Fig. 16(c) does not have. This shows that real-time hardware works and it produced the high frequency elements that the original image does not possess.

5   NLSP Focusing Effect

Focus is an important factor for creating finely detailed content. Professional cameras do not have auto-focus functions because professional camera persons have the ability to adjust the fine focus and use complex focus controls on the HD cameras. It is very difficult to manually adjust the focus of 8K cameras using only a small viewfinder, and if the focus is off, the 8K format cannot live up to its full potential. Because 8K is developed for broadcasting, 8K cameras are equipped with zoom lenses as well as HD cameras. The focus of zoom lenses is less accurate than that of single-focus lenses. A zoom lens makes it more difficult to accurately adjust the focus. HD-to-8K upconverted videos are blurry and

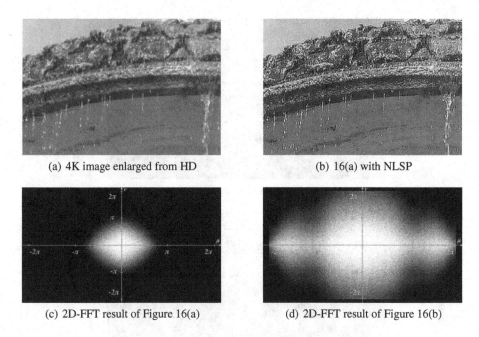

(a) 4K image enlarged from HD

(b) 16(a) with NLSP

(c) 2D-FFT result of Figure 16(a)

(d) 2D-FFT result of Figure 16(b)

Fig. 16. Image processed with real-time NLSP [8].

their characteristics are similar to those of out-of-focus videos. It is important to note that NLSP has a focusing effect. Figure 17(a) shows a blurry image. The original image is crisp (it is part of a test pattern), and a low pass filter (LPF) is used to blur the image. Figure 17(b) shows the result of processing the image in Fig. 17(a) with the NLSP hardware. Comparing these figures, we observe that the resolution of the image in Fig. 17(b) is better than that of Fig. 17(a) and the focus looks adjusted. This effect is owing to the characteristics of NLSP. NLSP can generate high-frequency elements that the original image does not have, and these high-frequency elements have a focusing effect. The focusing effect works for the unconverted blurry 8K to improve the resolution.

6   Real-Time HD-to-8K Upconverter

6.1   HD to 8K Upconverter with NLSP

Figure 18 shows a block diagram of the HD-to-8K upconverter. The input, which is full HD, is shown on the left side and the 8K output is shown on the right side of Fig. 18. The HD-to-8K upconversion is processed in two steps: full HD-to-4K and 4K-to-8K upconversion. The left half of Fig. 18 shows the block diagram of the upconverter from full HD to 4K, which uses two dimensional Lanczos interpolation [2]. The upconverted 4K video from HD is blurry and is processed with NLSP to improve resolution. The real-time hardware for full HD to 4K upconversion with NSLP is shown in Fig. 20.

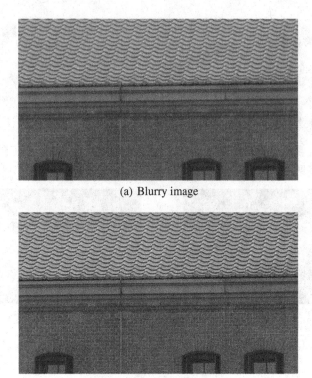

(a) Blurry image

(b) Focused image with NLSP

Fig. 17. Focusing effect [8].

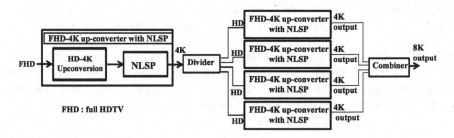

Fig. 18. Block diagram of full HD to 8K upconverter with NLSP [8].

The latter signal processing of the image in Fig. 18 achieved via upconversion from 4K to 8K using NLSP. The upconverted 4K frame comprises four full HD frames, which are divided as shown in Fig. 19. Each HD frame is processed with the same unit shown in Fig. 20, and the four 4K frames with NLSP are created. These 4K frames are combined to create an 8K frame with NLSP. The real-time hardware for the 4K-to-8K upconversion with NLSP is shown in Fig. 22,

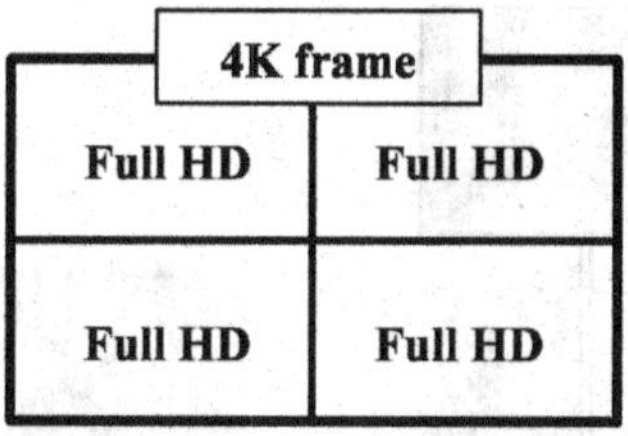

4K frame	
Full HD	**Full HD**
Full HD	**Full HD**

Fig. 19. Divided 4K frame with full HD [8].

Fig. 20. Real-time full HD to 4K upconverter with NLSP [8].

which includes four of the full HD-to-4K upconverter units shown in Fig. 20. The other units are the divider and combiner units shown in Fig. 18.

6.2 Resolution of the 8K Upconverted Image

Figure 21 shows parts of example 8K images upconverted using the real-time hardware shown in Figs. 20 and 22. The images shown in Fig. 21(a) and (c) are blurry because the NLSP option is off. The images in Fig. 21(b) and (d) are created with the NLSP option on. The resolution of these images is better than of the ones in Fig. 21(a) and (c). The only difference between them is whether the NLSP was used or not. Note that NLSP improves the resolution of upconverted 8K content. The focus effect discussed in Sect. 5 works, and it improves the resolution of the blurry image. The discussed hardware can upconvert images from full HD to 8K in real-time and will be useful for 8K broadcasting. It can address the problems of insufficient 8K content and is capable of upconverting HDTV content of varying quality to 8K.

Currently the square function is applied to create the high frequency elements and it works. However, we should continue to try and find a better nonlinear function than the square function to improve image quality. 8K is a broadcasting system and there are various kinds of content such as news, drama, variety shows, sports and others. HDTV-to-8K upconverter have to process this content. Upconversion tests for the various content should be done before 8K broadasting becomes operational.

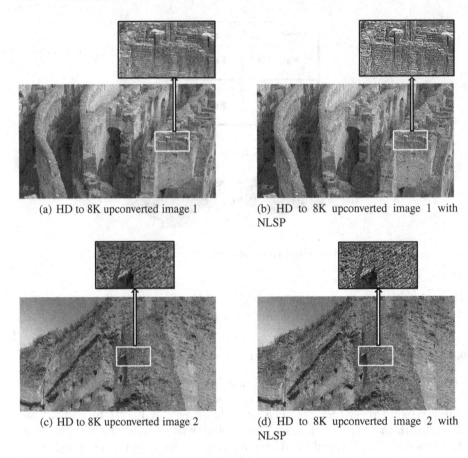

(a) HD to 8K upconverted image 1

(b) HD to 8K upconverted image 1 with NLSP

(c) HD to 8K upconverted image 2

(d) HD to 8K upconverted image 2 with NLSP

Fig. 21. Upconverted images with real-time HD-to-8K upconverter [8].

Fig. 22. Real-time 4K to 8 K upconverter with NLSP [8].

6.3   Result

Upconverted videos are blurry, and this is a serious issue for HD-to-8K conversion. Although SR algorithms have been proposed, they are complex and cannot cope with real-time videos, particularly high-speed 8K videos. An algorithm for an HD-to-8K upconverter with NLSP was proposed and real-time hardware was developed. The converter creates high-frequency elements that the upconverted blurry video does not possess and produces high-resolution 8K content. This converter will be helpful for fixing the problems of insufficient 8K content and mobile news gathering for 8K broadcasting. Searching for a better nonlinear function and testing it with various content should be the primary focus forn the near future.

References

1. Bannore, V.: Iterative-Interpolation Super-Resolution Image Reconstruction (2010)
2. Duchon, C.E.: Lanczos filtering in one and two dimensions. J. Appl. Meteorol. **18**, 1016–1022 (1979)
3. Eekeren, A.W.M., Schutte, K., Vliet, L.J.: Multiframe super-resolution reconstruction of small moving objects. IEEE Trans. Image Process. **19**(11), 2901–2912 (2010)
4. Farsiu, S., Robinson, D., Elad, M., Milanfar, P.: Fast and robust multi-frame super-resolution. IEEE Trans. Image Process. **13**, 1327–1344 (2004)
5. Glasner, D., Bagon, S., Irani, M.: Super-resolution from a single image. International Conference on Computer Vision (ICCV) (2009)
6. Gohshi, S., Echizen, I.: Limitations of super resolution image reconstruction and how to overcome them for a single image. ICETE2013 (SIGMAP), Reykjavik, Iceland (2013)
7. Gohshi, S., Hiroi, T., Echizen, I.: Subjective assessment of hdtv with super resolution function. EURASIP J. Image Video Process. (2014)
8. Gohshi, S., Nakamura, S., Tabata, H.: Development of real-time HDTV-to-8K TV upconverter. In: VISIGRAPP 2017, VISAPP, vol. 4, pp. 52–59 (2017)
9. Houa, X., Liu, H.: Super-resolution image reconstruction for video sequence. IEEE Trans. Image Process. (2011)
10. Huang, J., Mingzhai Sun, J.M., Chi, Y.: Super-resolution image reconstruction for high-density three-dimensional single-molecule microscopy. IEEE Trans. Computat. Imag. **4**(12), 763–773 (2017)
11. ITU-R-HDTV (2015). https://www.itu.int/rec/r-rec-bt.709/en
12. ITU-R-UDTV (2015). https://www.itu.int/rec/r-rec-bt.2020/en
13. Katsaggelos, A.K., Molina, R., Mateos, J.: Super Resolution of Images and Video. Morgan and Claypool Publishers, San Rafael (2007)
14. Lee, J.S.: Digital image enhancement and noise filtering by use of local statistics. IEEE Trans. Pattern Anal. Mach. Intell. **2**, 165–168 (1980)
15. Lucy, L.B.: An iterative technique for the rectification of observed distributions. Astronom. J. **79**(6), 745–754 (1974)
16. Matsumoto, N., Ida, T.: Reconstruction based super-resolution using self-congruency around image edges (in Japanese). J. IEICE **93**, 118–126 (2010)

17. Mertz, P., Gray, F.: A theory of scanning and its relation to the characteristics of the transmitted signal in telephotography and television. IEEE Trans. Image Process. (1934)
18. Panda, S., Prasad, R., Jena, G.: POCS based super-resolution image reconstruction using an adaptive regularization parameter. IEEE Trans. Image Process. (2011)
19. Park, S.C., Park, M.K., Kang, M.G.: Super-resolution image reconstruction: a technical overview. IEEE Signal Process. Mag. **20**, 21–36 (2003)
20. Pratt, W.K.: Digital Image Processing, 3rd edn. Wiley, New York (2001)
21. Protter, M., Elad, M., Takeda, H., Milanfar, P.: Generalizing the nonlocal-means to super-resolution reconstruction. IEEE Trans. Image Process. **18**, 36–51 (2009)
22. Richardson, W.H.: Bayesian-based iterative method of image restoration. J. Opt. Soc. Am. **62**(1), 55–59 (1972)
23. Sakata, H.: Assessment of tv noise and frequency characteristics. J. ITE (1980)
24. Sanchez-Beato, A., Pajares, G.: Noniterative interpolation-based super-resolution minimizing aliasing in the reconstructed image. IEEE Trans. Image Process. **17**(10), 1817–1826 (2008)
25. Schreiber, W.F.: Wirephoto quality improvement by unsharp masking. J. Pattern Recogn. **2**, 111–121 (1970)
26. Shahar, O., Faktor, A., Irani, M.: Space-time superresolution from a single video. In: CVPR f11 Proceedings of the 2011 IEEE Conference on Computer Vision and Pattern Recognition, vol. 19, no. 11, pp. 3353–3360 (2011)
27. Toshiba (in Japanese). https://www.toshiba.co.jp/regza/function/10b/function09.html. Accessed 12 Sept 2016
28. van Eekeren, A.W.M., Schutte, K., van Vliet, L.J.: Multiframe super-resolution reconstruction of small moving objects. IEEE Trans. Image Process. **19**, 2901–2912 (2010)
29. Zhou, F., Xia, S., Liao, Q.: Nonlocal pixel selection for multisurface fitting-based super-resolution. IEEE Trans. Circ. Syst. Video Technol. **24**(12), 2013–2017 (2011)

Non-local Haze Propagation
with an Iso-Depth Prior

Incheol Kim and Min H. Kim[(✉)]

KAIST, 291 Daehak-ro, Yuseong-gu, Daejeon 34141, Korea
minhkim@vclab.kaist.ac.kr

Abstract. The primary challenge for removing haze from a single image is lack of decomposition cues between the original light transport and airlight scattering in a scene. Many dehazing algorithms start from an assumption on natural image statistics to estimate airlight from sparse cues. The sparsely estimated airlight cues need to be propagated according to the local density of airlight in the form of a transmission map, which allows us to obtain a haze-free image by subtracting airlight from the hazy input. Traditional airlight-propagation methods rely on ordinary regularization on a grid random field, which often results in isolated haze artifacts when they fail in estimating local density of airlight properly. In this work, we propose a non-local regularization method for dehazing by combining Markov random fields (MRFs) with nearest-neighbor fields (NNFs) extracted from the hazy input using the Patch-Match algorithm. Our method starts from the insightful observation that the extracted NNFs can associate pixels at the similar depth. Since regional haze in the atmosphere is correlated with its depth, we can allow propagation across the iso-depth pixels with the MRF-based regularization problem with the NNFs. Our results validate how our method can restore a wide range of hazy images of natural landscape clearly without suffering from haze isolation artifacts. Also, our regularization method is directly applicable to various dehazing methods.

Keywords: Dehazing · Non-local regularization · Image restoration

1 Introduction

The atmosphere in a landscape includes several types of aerosols such as haze, dust, or fog. When we capture a landscape photograph of a scene, often thick

The initial version of this manuscript was published in conference proceedings of International Conference on Computer Vision, Theory and Applications (VISAPP 2017) [1]. This paper was invited to be published in the Communications in Computer and Information Science series by Springer afterward. It is a revised and extended version of the conference paper to additionally introduce more scientific analysis and evaluation on the proposed method.

Electronic supplementary material The online version of this chapter (https://doi.org/10.1007/978-3-030-12209-6_11) contains supplementary material, which is available to authorized users.

© Springer Nature Switzerland AG 2019
A. P. Cláudio et al. (Eds.): VISIGRAPP 2017, CCIS 983, pp. 213–238, 2019.
https://doi.org/10.1007/978-3-030-12209-6_11

aerosols scatter light transport from the scene to the camera, resulting in a hazy photograph. A haze-free image could be restored if we could estimate and compensate the amount of scattered energy properly. However, estimating haze from a single photograph is a severely ill-posed problem due to the lack of the scene information such as depth.

An image processing technique that removes a layer of haze and compensates the attenuated energy is known as *dehazing*. It can be applied to many outdoor imaging applications such as self-driving vehicles, surveillance, and satellite imaging. The general dehazing algorithm consists of two main processes. We first need to approximate haze initially by utilizing available haze clues based on a certain assumption on natural image statistics, such as a dark channel prior [2]. In this stage, most of dehazing algorithms tend to produce an incomplete transmission map from the hazy image. Once we obtain rough approximation of haze, we need to propagate the sparse information to the entire scene to reconstruct a dense transmittance map used for recovering a haze-free image.

Difficulty of dehazing arises from the existence of ambiguity due to the lack of the scene information. First, the initial assumption on image statistics on natural colors in particular is insufficient to cover the wide diversity of natural scenes in the real world, resulting in *incomplete* haze estimation. No universal image statistics on natural colors can handle the dehazing problem. Moreover, as shown in Fig. 1, state-of-the-art propagation algorithms with a common grid random field often suffer from *haze-isolation artifacts* [3–5]. Meanwhile, the amount of haze in the atmosphere at each pixel is determined by its depth. In order to handle abrupt changes of haze density, we need the scene depth information, even though it is unavailable in single-image dehazing.

In this paper, we propose a non-local regularization method for dehazing that can propagate sparse estimation of airlight to yield a dense transmission map without suffering from the typical isolation problem (Fig. 1). Our regularization approach is developed by combining Markov random fields (MRFs) with nearest-neighbor fields (NNFs) using the PatchMatch algorithm [6]. Our main insight is that the NNFs searched in a hazy image associate pixels at the similar depth. Since no depth information is available in single-image dehazing, we utilize the NNF information to infer depth cues by allowing non-local propagation of latent scattered light, which is exponentially proportional to depth [7]. To the best of our knowledge, this approach is the first work that combines MRF regularization with NNFs for dehazing. This proposed regularization method can be used with any other dehazing algorithms to enhance haze regularization.

2   Related Work

Previous works on dehazing can be grouped into three categories: multiple image-based, learning-based and single image-based approaches.

Multiple Image-Based Dehazing. Since removing haze in the atmosphere is an ill-posed problem, several works have attempted to solve the problem using

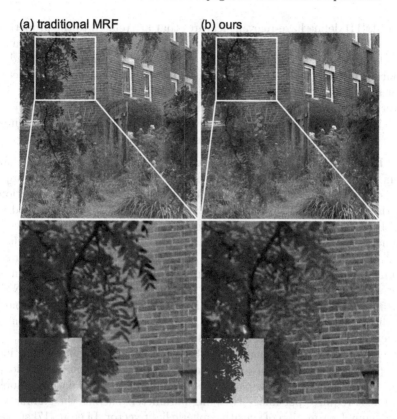

Fig. 1. Comparison of dehazing results using (a) regularization of haze using traditional MRFs commonly used in state-of-the-art dehazing algorithms [3–5] and (b) our regularization using *MRFs with iso-depth NNFs* (Insets: corresponding transmission maps). The proposed method for single-image dehazing can propagate haze more effectively than traditional regularization methods by inferring depth from NNFs in a hazy image. Images courtesy of Kim and Kim [1]. (Color figure online)

multiple input images, often requiring additional hardware. Schechner et al. capture a set of linearly polarized images. They utilize the intensity changes of the polarized lights to infer the airlight layer [8]. Narasimhan et al. [7,9] employ multiple images with different weather conditions to restore the degraded image using an irradiance model. Kopf et al. [10] remove haze from an image with additionally known scene geometry, instead of capturing multiple images. These haze formation models stand on the physics of light transport to provide sound accuracy. However, these applications could be limited at the cost of acquiring multiple input images.

Learning-Based Dehazing. Learning-based methods have been proposed to mitigate the ill-posed dehazing problem using a trained prior knowledge. From training datasets, they attempt to earn a prior on natural image statistics to factorize the haze layer and the scene radiance from the hazy image.

Tang et al. [11] define haze-relevant features that are related to the properties of hazy images, and train them using the random forest regression. Zhu et al. [12] obtain the color attenuation prior using supervised learning. They found that the concentration of haze is positively correlated with the difference between brightness and saturation, and they train a linear model via linear regression. However, no general statistical model can predict the diverse distributions of natural light environments; hence, they often fail to restore hazy-free images that are not similar to the trained dataset.

Single Image-Based Dehazing. Owing to the ill-posedness of the dehazing problem, single image-based methods commonly rely on a certain assumption on statistics of natural images. Most prior works have made an assumption on the statistics of natural *scene radiance* [2,4,13–16]. Tan [13] and Tarel and Hautiere [14] restore visibility by maximizing local contrast, assuming that clean color images have a high contrast, but this causes overly saturated results. He et al. [2] exploit image statistics where a natural image in the sRGB color space should include a very low intensity within a local region. However, it often overestimates the amount of haze if there is a large area having bright pixels. Nishino et al. [15] employ scene-specific priors, a heavy-tailed distribution on chromaticity gradients of colors of natural scenes, to infer the surface albedo, but they also often produce over-saturated results.

Developing the natural image prior further, Fattal [4] assumes that in the sRGB space, the color-line of a local patch within a clear image should pass through the origin of the color space. This can yield a clear and naturally-looking result, but it requires per-image tweaking parameters such as the gamma value and the manual estimation of the atmospheric light vector. Li et al. [17] suggest a nighttime dehazing method that removes a glow layer made by the combination of participating media and light source such as lamps. Recently, a non-local transmission estimation method was proposed by Berman et al. [5], which is based on the assumption that colors of a haze-free image can be approximated by a few hundred distinct colors forming tight clusters in the RGB space.

In addition, an assumption on *light transport* in natural scenes is also used. Fattal assumes that shading and transmission are statistically independent [3], and Meng et al. [18] impose boundary conditions on light transmission. In particular, our airlight estimation follows the traditional approach based on dimension-minimization approach [3], which allows for robust performance in estimating airlight.

Haze Regularization. Most single-image dehazing methods estimate per-pixel haze using a patch-wise operator. Since the operator often fails in a large portion of patches in practice, regularizing sparse haze estimates is crucial to obtain a dense transmission map for restoring a haze-free image. Grid Markov random fields are most commonly used in many dehazing algorithms [3,5,13,15,19], and filtering methods are also used, for instance, matting Laplacian [2], guided filtering [20], and a total variation-based approach [14,18]. These regularization methods only account for local information, they often fail to obtain sharp depth-discontinuity along edges if there is an abrupt change in scene depth.

Recently, Fattal [4] attempts to mitigate this isolation problem by utilizing augmented Markov random fields, which extend connection boundaries of MRFs. However, this method does not search neighbors in every region in an image since only pixels within a local window are augmented. For this reason, the augmented MRFs cannot reflect all non-local information in the image, and in some cases, isolation artifacts still remain. Berman et al. [5] non-locally extend the boundary in estimating haze; however, they still regularize an initial transmission map by using Gaussian MRFs (GMRFs) with only local neighbors. As a result, severe isolation problems occur in a region where there is an abrupt change of scene depth. In our regularization method, we extend neighbors in MRFs with NNFs to allow non-local propagation across iso-depth pixels to obtain sharp edge-discontinuity when inferring latent transmission values.

3 Initial Estimation of Haze

We first estimate the initial density of haze following a traditional dimension-reduction approach using linear subspaces [3,7]. To help readers understand the formulation of the dehazing problem, we briefly provide the foundations of the traditional haze formation model.

Haze Formation Model. Haze is an aerosol that consists of ashes, dust, and smoke. Haze tends to present a gray or bluish hue [7], which leads to decrease of contrast and color fidelity of the original scene radiance. As the amount of scattering increases, the amount of degradation also increases in light transport. This phenomenon is defined as a *transmission* function that represents the portion of light from the scene radiance that is not affected by scattering in participating media.

The relationship between the scattered light and the attenuated scene radiance has been expressed as a linear interpolation via a transmission term commonly used in many dehazing algorithms [3,4,7,9]:

$$I(x) = t(x) J(x) + (1 - t(x)) A, \tag{1}$$

where $I(x)$ is the linear signal intensity at pixel x, $J(x)$ is unknown scene radiance, $t(x)$ is the transmission ratio, describing the portion of remaining light when the reflected light from a scene surface reaches to the observer through the medium, and A is a global atmospheric vector, which is unknown. The atmospheric vector A represents the color vector orientation and intensity of atmospheric light in the linear sRGB color space, and along with the interpolation term $(1 - t(x))$, the right additive term in Eq. (1) defines the intensity of airlight at an arbitrary pixel x. Additionally, the atmospheric vector is independent of scene locations, i.e., the atmospheric light is globally constant.

The amount of scattering is closely related to the distance that light travels, i.e., the longer light travels, the more scattering occurs. Therefore, the transmission decays as light travels. Suppose that haze is homogeneous; this phenomenon then can be written as follows: $t(x) = e^{-\beta d(x)}$, where β is a scattering coefficient of the atmosphere [9] that controls the amount of scattering, and $d(x)$ is the scene depth at the pixel x.

The goal of haze removal is to estimate the transmission ratio t and the atmospheric vector A so that scene radiance J can be recovered from the transmission t and the atmospheric vector A as follows:

$$J(x) = \frac{I(x) - (1 - t(x)) A}{\max(\varepsilon, t(x))}, \tag{2}$$

where ε is a small value to prevent division by zero.

Linear Color Space. As shown in Eq. (1), the hazy image formation is the linear combination of a scene radiance and haze factor. Dehazing is a process to perform subtraction from the input intensity by the amount of haze. The required condition for the process is that the pixel intensity must be linearly proportional to the incident radiance based on physics, which is only valid in the *linear* sRGB color space. However, *gamma correction* is already baked in the pixel intensities in general color images. If one subtracts the haze factor from the original intensity in the nonlinear sRGB space, dehazing results appear inconsistent with different levels of pixel intensities. Consequently, manual tweaking parameters are often required, as in Fattal [4]. Different from existing dehazing methods [2–4, 17], we first perform inverse gamma correction to linearize the pixel values before recovering the scene radiance; i.e., we use a linearized image I_L by applying a power function with an exponent of the standard display gamma to an sRGB value: $I(x) = \{I'(x)\}^\gamma$, where $I'(x)$ is a non-linear RGB value, and γ is a display gamma (e.g., $\gamma = 2.2$ for the standard sRGB display), instead of I during the transmission estimation and regularization processes, and we then perform gamma correction for display.

Haze Estimation. Since airlight is energy scattered in air, airlight tends to be locally smooth in a scene, i.e., local airlight remains constant in a similar depth. In contrast, the original radiance in a scene tend to vary significantly, naturally showing a variety of colors. When we isolate the scene radiance into a small patch in an image, the variation of scene radiances within a patch tends to decrease significantly to form a cluster with a similar color vector, assuming that the real world scene is a set of small planar surfaces of different colors. Then, one can estimate a transmission value with certain natural image statistics within a patch based on the local smoothness assumption on scene depths.

Following this perspective of the traditional approach [3], we also define a *linear subspace* that presents local color pixels in the color space. A linear subspace in each patch comprises two bases: a scene radiance vector $J(x)$ at the center pixel x and a global atmospheric vector A. In this space, a scene depth is piecewise smooth, and the local pixels share the same atmospheric vector. Now we can formulate dehazing as finding these two unknown basis vectors, approximating the transmission value $t(x)$ that is piecewise smooth due to the local smoothness of a scene depth. Figure 2 depicts the estimation process for an overview.

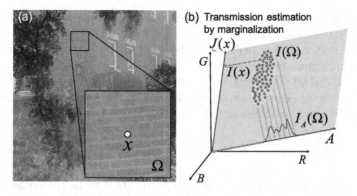

Fig. 2. (a) Extracting a patch from a hazy image. $I(\Omega)$ is a set of linearized color pixels in patch Ω that has a center pixel of x. The white dot indicates the center pixel x. (b) We initially estimate the amount of haze using linear subspaces [3,7]. A is an atmospheric vector of the image (a), $I(x)$ is the linearized center pixel x depicted as the white dot, and $J(x)$ is the scene radiance vector of the pixel $I(x)$. Pixel intensity $I(x)$ is a linear interpolation of the vector A and $J(x)$, and hence lies on the linear subspace [the blue plane in (b)] spanned by those two vectors. The red dots describe pixels extracted from $I(\Omega)$. These pixels are projected onto vector A to obtain a marginal distribution with respect to A. The red arrow from the cluster denotes the amount of airlight that is determined from the minimum value of the marginal distribution. Images courtesy of Kim and Kim [1]. (Color figure online)

Atmospheric Vector Estimation. Airlight is a phenomenon that acts like a light source, which is caused by scattering of participating media in the atmosphere [7]. The atmospheric vector represents the airlight radiance at the infinite distance in a scene, i.e., the color information of airlight itself. Therefore, the atmospheric vector does not include any scene radiance information, and it only contains the airlight component. The region full of airlight is the most opaque area in a hazy image. We follow a seminal method of airlight estimation by He et al. [2]. The atmospheric vector A is estimated by picking up the pixels that have the top 0.1% brightest dark channel pixels and then choosing the pixel among them that has the highest intensity in the input image. However, if there are saturated regions such as sunlight or headlights, maximum filtering of the dark channel could be incorrect since those regions might have the highest (saturated) dark channel. Also, we assume that the most opaque region is the most brightest within an image, and we therefore discard the pixels that are within aforementioned saturated regions. We then select the 0.1% pixels among the rest as He et al. [2]'s method does, so that we can estimate the atmospheric vector consistently. We subsequently average the chosen pixels to reject noise.

Transmission Estimation. We first assume that transmission is piecewise smooth. In Eq. (1), the portion of haze at a pixel x is determined by the term $(1 - t(x))$ that indicates the amount of haze to be removed. We determine the amount of haze from given color signals within a patch. Suppose the given color signals in each patch are linear combinations of two unknown bases, J and A, that form a linear subspace. If we project the given pixels onto the atmospheric vector A, we can estimate the contribution of the haze signal mixed into the input signals in the patch.

Supposing $I_A(\Omega)$ is a set of *scalar projections* of color vectors $I(\Omega)$ onto an atmospheric vector A in patch Ω (Fig. 2), where the pixel x is located at the center, then it can be written as following Fattal's method [3]:

$$I_A(\Omega) = I(\Omega) \cdot \frac{A}{\|A\|}, \quad I_A(\Omega) \in \mathbb{R}^{1 \times |\Omega|}. \tag{3}$$

We assume the airlight within a patch to be constant while the scene radiance might vary. To focus only on the airlight component, it is necessary to obtain a *marginal distribution* of the surrounding pixels with respect to the basis vector A, as shown in Fig. 2(b).

The marginal distribution $I_A(\Omega)$ describes the histogram of airlight components within a patch. This distribution would have had a very low minimum value if it had not been influenced by piecewise constant airlight. However, if we take the minimum projected value, there could be a large chance to take an outlying value as the minimum. We use the i-th percentile value from the projected pixel distribution to reject outliers effectively to achieve robust performance:

$$I_A^{\min}(\Omega) = \underset{k \in \Omega}{P_i}(I_A(k)), \quad I_A^{\min}(\Omega) \in \mathbb{R}^1, \tag{4}$$

where P_i represents an i-th percentile value ($i = 2$).

The minimum percentile scalar projection onto an atmospheric vector corresponds to the amount of haze of a pixel from its patch, and thus the minimum projection corresponds to the haze component part in Eq. (1), which is $(1 - t(x)) \leftarrow I_A^{\min}(\Omega)$.

Additionally, projection onto the atmospheric vector requires two bases (a pixel and an atmospheric vectors) to be orthogonal. However, pixels within a patch are not necessarily orthogonal to the atmospheric vector, so projection needs to be compensated for non-orthogonality. If a color vector has a small angle with its atmospheric vector, then its projection will have a larger value due to the correlation between the two vectors. We attenuate $I_A^{\min}$ by a function with respect to the angle between a pixel vector and an atmospheric vector that is given by

$$t(x) = 1 - f(\bar{\theta}) \cdot I_A^{\min}(\Omega), \tag{5}$$

where $\bar{\theta}$ is a normalized angle between a pixel vector and an atmospheric vector within $[0, 1]$. The attenuation function $f()$ is given by

$$f(\bar{\theta}) = \frac{e^{-k\bar{\theta}} - e^{-k}}{1 - e^{-k}}, \tag{6}$$

where the function has a value of $[0, 1]$ in the range of $\bar{\theta}$. In this work, we set $k = 1.5$ for all cases. This function compensates transmission values by attenuating the value $I_A^{\min}$ since the function has a value close to 1 if $\bar{\theta}$ has a small value. See Fig. 3(c). Figure 4 shows the impact of our attenuation function. Our attenuation prevents over-estimation of transmission where orthogonality between the atmospheric vector and a color vector does not hold: Thus, we can avoid over-saturated dehazed results.

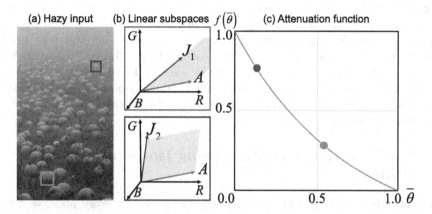

Fig. 3. (a) A hazy input image. (b) Each single pixel from the red and blue boxes is plotted in the RGB space along with the atmospheric vector A. J_1 and J_2 in each plot correspond to the two pixels extracted. (c) The attenuation function defined as Eq. (6) is plotted as above. The red and blue dots indicate the amount of attenuations of the red and blue patches. This plot shows that the amount of attenuation increases as an angle between a color vector and an atmospheric vector decreases. Images courtesy of Kim and Kim [1]. (Color figure online)

The size of a patch is crucial in our method. If the size is too small, then the marginal distribution does not contain rich data from the patch, resulting in unreliable estimation such as clamping. On the contrary, an excessively large patch might include pixels in different scene depth and our estimation stage takes the minimum value in the marginal distribution, and hence the transmission estimate will be overestimated. In our implementation, we use patches of 15-by-15 pixels and it showed consistent results regardless of the size of an image.

Removing Outliers. While our transmission estimation yields reliable transmission estimates in most cases, however, there are a small number of cases that does not obey our assumption. We take them as outliers and mark them as invalid transmission values, and then interpolate them in the regularization stage (see Sect. 4).

Distant regions in an image such as sky, and objects whose color is grayish have a similar color of haze. In the RGB color space, the angle between an atmospheric vector and the color vector of a pixel in those regions is very narrow and the image pixel's luminance is quite high. In this case, unreliable estimation is inevitable since there is a large ambiguity between the color of haze and scene radiance. As a result, unless we do not reject those regions, the transmission estimate will be so small that those regions will become very dim in turn. For this reason, we discard the transmission estimates, where the angle between an image pixel and an atmospheric vector is less than 0.2 rad, the pixel's luminance (L*) is larger than 60 in the CIELAB space, and the estimated transmission value is lower than a certain threshold: 0.4 for scenes having a large portion of distant regions and 0.1 for others.

When estimating an atmospheric light, we assumed that the most opaque region in an image is the brightest area of the whole scene. However, pixels brighter than the atmospheric light can exist due to very bright objects such as direct sunlight, white objects, and lamps in a scene. Those pixels do not obey our assumption above, and hence this leads to wrong transmission estimation. Therefore, we discard pixels whose luminance is larger than the luminance of the atmospheric light.

4   Non-local Regularization Using Iso-Depth Neighbor Fields

Once we calculate the initial estimates of transmission for every pixel, we filter out invalid transmission values obtained from extreme conditions. The transmission estimation and outlier detection stages might often yield incomplete results with blocky artifacts. We, therefore, need to propagate valid transmission values in the image.

MRF Model. As we mentioned above, the transmission is locally smooth. Therefore, in order to obtain a complete transmission map having sharp-edge discontinuities, we need to propagate the incompletely estimated transmission map using Markov random fields. The probability distribution of one node in an MRF is given by

$$p\left(t\left(x\right)\middle|\hat{t}\left(x\right)\right) = \phi\left(t\left(x\right),\hat{t}\left(x\right)\right)\psi\left(t\left(x\right),t\left(y\right)\right), \tag{7}$$

where $t\left(x\right)$ is a latent transmission variable at pixel x, $\hat{t}\left(x\right)$ is an initially estimated transmission value (see Sect. 3), $\phi()$ is the data term of the likelihood between $t(x)$ and $\hat{t}(x)$, and $\psi()$ is a smoothness prior to relate latent transmission $t(x)$ with neighboring transmission $t(y)$, where y is a neighboring pixel of x. While the data term $\phi()$ describes the fidelity of observations by imposing a penalty function between the latent variable and the observed value, the regularization term $\psi()$ enforces smoothness by penalizing the errors between one latent variable and its neighboring variables.

The data term $\phi()$ is given by

$$\phi\left(t\left(x\right),\hat{t}\left(x\right)\right) = \exp\left(-\frac{\left(t\left(x\right) - \hat{t}\left(x\right)\right)^2}{\sigma_{\hat{t}}(\Omega)^2}\right), \tag{8}$$

where $\sigma_{\hat{t}}(\Omega)$ is the variance of observation values $\hat{t}$ within patch Ω that has the center at pixel x. See Fig. 5. The data term models error between a variable and observation with in-patch observation variance noise via a Gaussian distribution. The in-patch variance of observation values implies that the greater the variance of in-patch observation is, the more uncertain the observation values are, resulting in giving less influence from the data term on the distribution.

The regularization term $\psi()$ is written as

$$\psi\left(t\left(x\right),t\left(y\right)\right) = \prod_{y \in N_x} \exp\left(-\frac{\left(t\left(x\right)-t\left(y\right)\right)^2}{\|I\left(x\right)-I\left(y\right)\|^2}\right), \qquad (9)$$

where $I()$ is a linearized pixel intensity of an image, and pixel y is in a set of neighbors N_x of pixel x. The regularization term encourages smoothness among one variable and its neighboring variables by penalizing pairwise distances between them, where the distribution of the distances follows a Gaussian distribution. If $\left(t\left(x\right)-t\left(y\right)\right)^2$ is large, then it indicates that the distance between $t\left(x\right)$ and its neighbor $t\left(y\right)$ is large, and hence the cost from the regularization term will also become large, which enforces strong smoothness between them. $\|I\left(x\right)-I\left(y\right)\|^2$ in the denominator of the prior term controls the amount of smoothness by exploiting information from an input image. This property implies that if two image pixels are similar, then their transmission values are likely to be similar as well. On the contrary, it gives sharp-edge discontinuity in transmission values along edges since the value of the denominator becomes large when the difference between two pixels is large.

In fact, the probability distribution of an MRF over the latent variable t is modeled via the Gaussian distribution. In this case, the MRF is formalized by using a Gauss-Markov random field (GMRF), which can be solved by not only using computationally costly solvers, but also by a fast linear system solver [3, 21].

Finally, we formulate a cost function by taking the negative log of the posterior distribution [Eq. (7)] following Fattal's method [3, 4], which is written by

$$E\left(t\right) = \sum_x \left\{ \frac{\left(t\left(x\right)-\hat{t}\left(x\right)\right)^2}{\sigma_{\hat{t}}(\Omega)^2} + \sum_{y \in N_x} \frac{\left(t\left(x\right)-t\left(y\right)\right)^2}{\|I\left(x\right)-I\left(y\right)\|^2} \right\}. \qquad (10)$$

The regularization process is done by minimizing the cost function, which is solved by differentiating the function with respect to t and setting it to be zero.

Iso-Depth Neighbor Fields. In conventional grid MRFs, a prior term [Eq. (9)] associates adjacent four pixels as neighbors. However, pixels in a patch lying on an edge may be isolated when the scene surface has a complicated shape. In Fig. 5(a), the leaves in the left side of the image have a complicated pattern of edges, and the bricks lie behind the leaves. If we model a grid MRF on the image, then pixels on the tip of the leaves will be isolated by the surrounding brick pixels. In this case, smoothness of the leaf pixels will be imposed mostly by the brick pixels, where there is a large depth discontinuity between them. In other words, a large scene depth discrepancy exists in the patch, and thus if some pixels lying on the edge are only connected to their adjacent neighbors, the

Fig. 4. Impact of our attenuation term in transmission estimation. As the red arrows indicate, our attenuation term prevents over-estimation of transmission which results in over-saturation. (Color figure online)

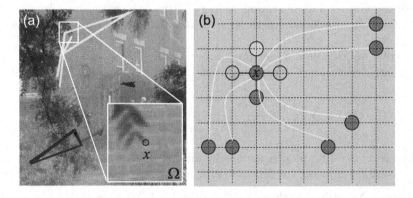

Fig. 5. (a) The picture shows some sampled NNFs that associate pixels having similar scene depths. The line with the same color denotes association of pixels in the same NNF. (b) An MRF model of the node x from the patch in (a) associated with adjacent four neighbors and distant neighbors in the NNF. Since the node x is located in the end point of the leaf, its adjacent pixels have very different transmission values due to a large depth discontinuity. As (a) shows, the neighbors connected with the same NNF have very similar scene depths, and hence they give a more accurate regularization cue than the adjacent neighbors do. Images courtesy of Kim and Kim [1]. (Color figure online)

prior term will enforce wrong smoothness due to the large depth discrepancy. As a result, those regions will be overly smoothed out due to the wrong connection of neighbors.

Algorithm 1. Dehazing via Non-Local Regularization.

Require: an image I
Ensure: a result image J and a transmission map t
  1: $\hat{A} \leftarrow$ ATMOSPHERICVECTORESTIMATE(I)
  2: $\{I_L, A\} \leftarrow$ INVERSEGAMMACORRECT($\{I, \hat{A}\}$)
  3: **for** pixels $x = 1$ to n **do**
  4:      $I_A(\Omega) \leftarrow I_L(\Omega) \cdot \frac{A}{\|A\|}$
  5:      $I_A^{\min}(\Omega) \leftarrow \underset{k \in \Omega}{P_i}(I_A(k))$
  6:      $t'(x) \leftarrow 1 - f(\bar{\theta}) \cdot I_A^{\min}(\Omega)$
  7:      $\hat{t}(x) \leftarrow$ OUTLIERREJECT($t'(x), A, I_L(x)$)
  8: **end for**
  9: $NNF \leftarrow$ PATCHMATCH(I)
10: $t \leftarrow$ REGULARIZE($NNF, \hat{t}, I$)
11: $J_L \leftarrow (I - (1 - t)A)/t$
12: $J \leftarrow$ GAMMACORRECT(J_L)

We investigate neighbors extracted from a nearest-neighbor field (NNF) using the PatchMatch algorithm and found that the NNF associates pixels at similar scene depths. This insightful information gives a more reliable regularization penalty since the neighboring nodes in the NNF are likely to have similar transmission estimates. We validate our method through evaluation using synthetically generated hazy images along with their ground truth depth maps. Figure 6 shows the synthetic hazy scenes and their corresponding depths. We compute the absolute depth difference between a ground truth depth pixel and its iso-depth pixels associated by NNFs. The histograms in Fig. 6 show that the NNFs link one pixel to others having similar depth values. Thus, we add more neighbors belonging to the same NNF to the smoothness term and perform statistical inference on the MRF along with them. We note that these long-range connections in regularization are desirable in many image processing applications, addressed by other works [4,22]. After regularization, we use the weighted median filter [23] to refine the transmission map. Algorithm 1 summarizes our dehazing algorithm as an overview.

5 Results

We implemented our algorithm in a non-optimized MATLAB environment except the external PatchMatch algorithm [6], and processed it on a desktop computer with Intel 4.0 GHz i7-4790K CPU and 32 GB memory. For the case of the house image of resolution 450×440 shown in Fig. 1(b), our algorithm took

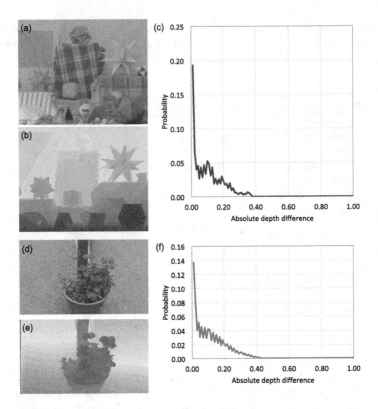

Fig. 6. Images (a) and (d) are synthetically generated hazy scenes, and images (b) and (e) are their ground truth depth maps. We computed the absolute transmission difference between a transmission value of a pixel and its iso-depth pixel's transmission values associated by PatchMatch [6]. Plots (c) and (f) are the distributions of the differences. Plot (c) shows that the portion of the absolute difference below 0.2 occupies 86% of entire NNFs, while Plot (f) shows the case of 81%.

6.44 s for running the PatchMatch algorithm to seek 17 neighbors, 8.32 s to estimate an atmospheric vector, transmission values and rejecting outliers, 43.43 s for our regularization stage, and 0.65 s for running the weighted median filter and recovering the scene radiance, taking approximately 58.84 s in total. We evaluated our algorithm with a large number of outdoor hazy images obtained from Fattal's method [4] to prove robustness, and we also present comparisons with state-of-the-art dehazing methods. Refer to the supplemental materials for more results.

Regularization. We compare results of our method with those of state-of-the-art methods in terms of regularization. Berman's method [5] regularizes initial transmission estimates with a grid GMRF as shown in the second columns in Fig. 7. Due to the lack of non-local information in regularization, certain regions suffer from the haze isolation problem as mentioned above. Other than using a grid MRF, Fattal's method [4] takes an augmented GMRF model for regularization, which extends neighbor fields within a local window. However, it does not connect more neighbors for all pixels due to time complexity. As a result, certain regions are not fully recovered from the haze isolation problem. Figure 7 validates that our method successfully removes haze even from a scene having abrupt depth changes with complicated patterns.

Figure 8 shows the intermediate stages in our regularization process of transmission (d)–(g), along with our result of the house scene (c). We start our regularization from Fig. 8(d) that has outliers [represented as black pixels in Fig. 8(d)]. In particular, Fig. 8(e) and (f) compare the impact of NNFs in the MRF regularization. When we regularize the initial estimate with only GMRFs, certain regions with complex scene structures are over-smoothed due to the wrong smoothness penalty as Fig. 8(e) shows. We account for additional neighbors from NNFs to obtain a clearer transmission map shown in Fig. 8(f). Figure 8(g) shows the final transmission map that we refine with a weighted median filter [23].

We also compare our regularization method with representative matting methods: the matting Laplacian method [24] and the guided filter method [20] in Fig. 9. While we use the guide image as just a guide to smooth and enforce sharp gradient along edges on transmission estimates, both methods are based on the assumption that an output and an input guidance form a linear relationship. As described in Sect. 3, scene radiance varies largely while transmission does the opposite. Consequently, the two methods follow the behavior of the scene radiance, which results in distorting the given estimates. As a result, our regularization method yields an accurate transmission map with clear-edge discontinuities while the others overestimate the transmission estimates in turn.

Qualitative Comparison. Figure 10 qualitatively validates the robust performance in dehazing the common reference dataset of hazy scenes [4]. We compare the performance of our dehazing algorithm with three state-of-the-art methods [2,4,5]. We were motivated to achieve consistent performance of dehazing with less parameter controls like other image processing algorithms [25,26]. Figure 10 shows results using the single set of parameters as described in Sect. 3. Our method shows competitive results to other method [4] that requires manual tweaking parameters per scene to achieve plausible results. For close-up images of the results, refer to the supplemental material.

Time Performance. Table 1 compare the computational performance of our method with traditional grid GMRFs and our iso-depth GMRFs using images shown in Fig. 10. We also shows computational costs of obtaining only NNFs with 17 neighbors using PatchMatch [6] in the third row. Dehazing with iso-depth NNF-GMRFs takes 10.58 times more time; however, iso-depth NNFs give richer information in regularization, resulting in more exact scene radiance recovery.

Fattal14   Berman et al.   ours

Fig. 7. Comparisons of dehazing in terms of regularization. The two columns from left are results from other two methods: Fattal's method [4] using augmented GMRFs and Berman's method [5] using traditional GMRFs, and the third column is our results (Insets: corresponding transmission maps). While other methods often fail to obtain sharp edge-discontinuities in the images, our method yields clear recovered scene radiance maps as shown above. Notable regions are pointed with arrows. Images courtesy of Kim and Kim [1].

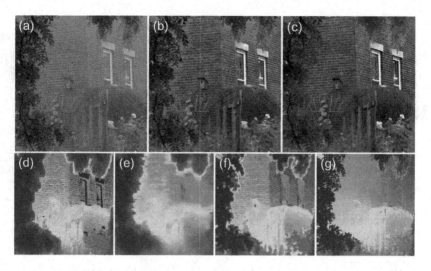

Fig. 8. We present an example before and after applying our dehazing and regularization method. (a) The hazy input image. (b) The recovered scene radiance map with the transmission map regularized by grid MRFs (e). (c) The recovered scene radiance map with the final transmission map (g). Images (d)–(g) compare transmission maps to show the influence of using iso-depth NNFs. All regularizations are done using GMRFs. (d) The initial transmission estimates including discarded pixels (the black pixels). (e) The regularized transmission map without NNFs. (f) The regularized transmission map with NNFs. (g) The final refined map of (f) using the weighted median filter. Images courtesy of Kim and Kim [1].

Quantitative Comparison. We compare our method with the entire synthetic hazy image dataset provided by Fattal [4]. The synthetic hazy images were generated by datasets that contain clear indoor and outdoor scenes, and their corresponding depth maps. Table 2 reports the quantitative comparison of our method with other methods: He et al. [2], Fattal [4], and Berman et al. [5]. Additionally, we present the statistics in Table 2 and Fig. 11. It says that our method shows the best performance in dehazed images, and is strongly competitive to state-of-the-arts in transmission maps. We also show the dehazed images used for the quantitative comparison in Fig. 12. Our method shows competitive and consistent results particularly in dehazed images.

Table 1. Comparison of time performance of dehazing with the traditional grid GMRFs and our GMRFs with iso-depth NNFs (unit: second). Refer to Fig. 10 for processed images. The third row shows computational costs of only seeking NNFs with 17 neighbors using PatchMatch [6] in our method. The table courtesy of Kim and Kim [1].

Dehazing	House	Forest	ny17	Train	Snow	Castle	Cones	Average
With grid GMRFs	6.43	26.55	27.51	7.74	18.88	12.84	6.41	15.19
With NNF-GMRFs	58.84	305.48	305.06	73.06	191.76	129.18	61.12	160.64
(Computing NNFs only)	(6.44)	(31.82)	(28.48)	(7.15)	(18.54)	(11.01)	(7.31)	(15.82)

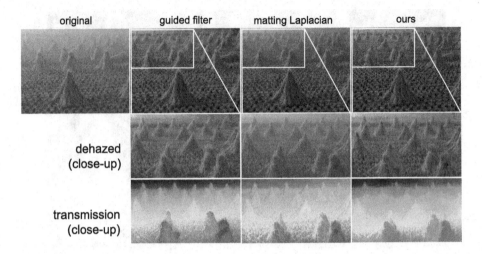

Fig. 9. We compare our regularization with other methods. The leftmost one is the original image of cones. The first row shows dehazed results with our transmission estimation step and each regularization method written at the lower right. We cropped the dehazed images in the first row to highlight the influence of regularization methods in the second row. The third row presents a sequence of cropped transmission maps in the same manner as the second row. Images courtesy of Kim and Kim [1].

Table 2. Quantitative comparisons of our method with other methods [2,4,5]. The error values are computed from the entire synthetic hazy image dataset provided by Fattal [4]. All figures represent mean L_1 error of the estimated transmission t (the left value) and output image J (the right value). Red figures indicate the best results, and blue for the second best. For a fair comparison, parameters for each method, such as display gamma for sRGB linearization and the airlight vector, were optimized for the highest performance. The table courtesy of Kim and Kim [1].

	He [2]	Fattal [4]	Berman [5]	Ours
church	0.0711/0.1765	0.1144/0.1726	0.1152/0.2100	0.1901/0.1854
couch	0.0631/0.1146	0.0895/0.1596	0.0512/0.1249	0.0942/0.1463
flower1	0.1639/0.2334	0.0472/0.0562	0.0607/0.1309	0.0626/0.0967
flower2	0.1808/0.2387	0.0418/0.0452	0.1154/0.1413	0.0570/0.0839
lawn1	0.1003/0.1636	0.0803/0.1189	0.0340/0.1289	0.0604/0.1052
lawn2	0.1111/0.1715	0.0851/0.1168	0.0431/0.1378	0.0618/0.1054
mansion	0.0616/0.1005	0.0457/0.0719	0.0825/0.1234	0.0614/0.0693
moebius	0.2079/0.3636	0.1460/0.2270	0.1525/0.2005	0.0823/0.1138
reindeer	0.1152/0.1821	0.0662/0.1005	0.0887/0.2549	0.1038/0.1459
road1	0.1127/0.1422	0.1028/0.0980	0.0582/0.1107	0.0676/0.0945
road2	0.1110/0.1615	0.1034/0.1317	0.0602/0.1602	0.0781/0.1206
average	0.1181/0.1862	0.0839/0.1180	0.0783/0.1567	0.0836/0.1152

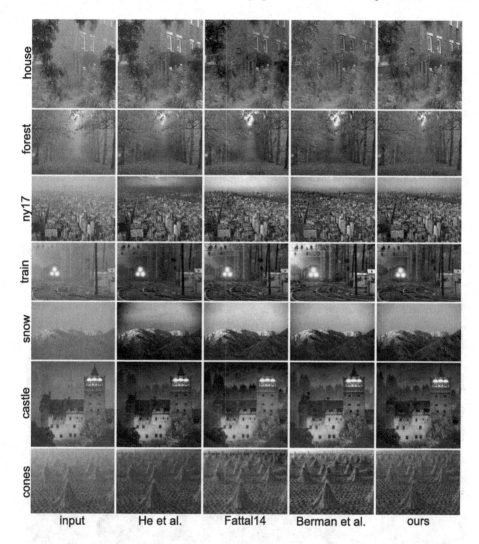

Fig. 10. Validation of consistency of dehazing. The first column shows input images. The second, third, and fourth columns are results from He et al. [2], Fattal [4], Berman et al. [5], respectively. The fifth column presents our method's results. We use the set of parameters as described in Sect. 3. For the images in the third and fifth rows, we only set the threshold of lower bound transmission to 0.4 and the others to 0.1 for removing narrow angle outliers. Our method is competitive to other method [4] that requires with manual tweaking parameters to achieve plausible results. Refer to the supplemental material for more results. Images courtesy of Kim and Kim [1].

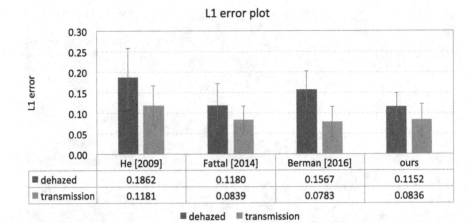

Fig. 11. Mean L1 error plots of 11 pairs of transmission maps and dehazed (Table 2) results, respectively. Our method shows the best performance in dehazed images, and is strongly competitive to state-of-the-arts in transmission maps.

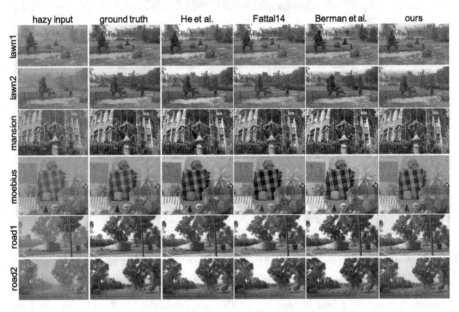

Fig. 12. Dehazed results for the quantitative comparison shown in Table 2. The first column shows synthetic hazy images generated from the ground truth dataset [4] in the second column with their corresponding depth maps. The remaining columns are recovered scene radiance maps by each method. Our method yields consistent results compared with other methods. Parameters for each method were optimized for the highest performance for a fair comparison. Images courtesy of Kim and Kim [1].

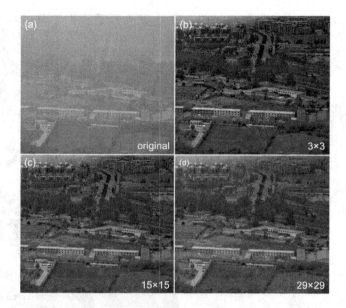

Fig. 13. Comparisons to show the influence of a patch size in estimating transmission. (a) The original canon image. (b) The dehazed image with a patch size of 3×3 where severe color clamping happens. (c) The dehazed image with a patch size of 15×15, which is our choice for all results. (d) The dehazed image with a patch size of 29×29 in which the airlight in distant regions is underestimated. Images courtesy of Kim and Kim [1].

Fig. 14. Validation of our narrow angle outlier rejection method described in Sect. 3. In the second column, the distant region represented as sky has an infinite depth, and hence our transmission estimation stage estimates its transmission as being close to zero, which yields overly saturated results. We obtained consistent results by our outlier rejection stage, as shown in the third column. Images courtesy of Kim and Kim [1].

Fig. 15. Validation of our saturated outlier rejection method described in Sect. 3. The inset is an input hazy image. The first column shows estimated transmission maps without our rejection (upper left) and with our rejection (bottom left). The corresponding dehazed scenes are shown in the second column. The bright regions (the direct light at the upper right and the wall of the castle in the middle) are overly saturated. Our outlier rejection succeeds to produce a consistent result by discarding those regions.

Impact of Patch Size. Figure 13 shows the results of dehazing under varying patch sizes. Image (a) is an input image of canon, the size of which is 600×524. Image (b) is severely over-saturated since the size of patches is so small that each patch cannot contain rich information of scene structures, i.e., the patch failed to reject the influence of highly-varying nature of scene radiance. On the other hand, as shown in image (d), its airlight is underestimated since patches are too large to hold the assumption that transmission is piecewise constant.

This underestimation result is exacerbated in distant regions where their scene depth changes rapidly. In our experiment, we found that the patch size of 15×15 works properly for most scenes, and therefore we take the same patch size for all results in this paper.

Outlier Removal. We validate our outlier-rejection process. Figure 14 shows the regions in infinite scene depths occupy a large portion of the image that is full of airlight in the two input images. In these regions, there is a large ambiguity between airlight and scene radiance, and hence our method fails to produce a naturally looking result as the second column shows. After we discard outliers having a narrow angle between the atmospheric vector and the input color pixel, we could obtain high-quality scene radiance maps in the third column. We also show the influence of saturated intensity outliers as mentioned in Sect. 3. We estimated an atmospheric vector under the assumption that the atmospheric light is the brightest all over a scene. As Fig. 15 presents, without rejecting saturated intensity outliers, transmission of those pixels will be severely overestimated due to their high luminance. We can also reject those regions by increasing a patch size; however, this will cause underestimation of airlight and cannot handle a large area as well.

6   Limitations

While our method produces consistent results for most cases; however, there are a small number of cases where our atmospheric vector estimation stage fails. Figure 16 shows an example of our algorithm's failure in finding the correct atmospheric light. There are clouds in the image that occupy relatively large regions but are not saturated, and therefore in the atmospheric vector estimation stage, our method selects pixels in cloud regions as candidates of the atmospheric light, which is not correct. For this reason, our transmission estimation stage severely overestimates the amount of airlight, particularly in distant regions in the scene as shown in Fig. 16(b). We validate the limitation by picking up the atmospheric vector of the image manually, and our algorithm yields a naturally-looking result, as the Fig. 16(c) presents. In addition, if there is a large region that is grayish and thereby has a narrow angle between an atmospheric vector and the region color, our algorithm fails to find correct transmission estimates since there are too many outliers according to our outlier rejection stage, which leads to unreliable regularization. We leave these problems as future work.

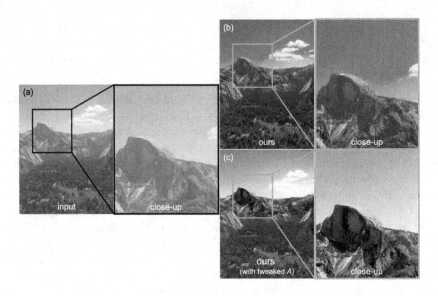

Fig. 16. Our failure case with a landscape image. Image (a) shows the input image, and Image (b) presents our result with the same set of parameters described. Image (c) is our result produced with the manually-tweaked atmospheric vector. (Color figure online)

7   Conclusion

We have presented a single-image dehazing method with our novel non-local regularization using iso-depth neighbor fields. While traditional dehazing methods often suffer from haze isolation artifacts due to improper propagation of the haze cues in the transmission map, our dehazing method can clarify hazy images robustly thanks to our iso-depth regularization approach. Our non-local regularization method infers nonlocal iso-depth cues to obtain more reliable smoothness penalty for better handling the isolation problem even with blunt changes of depth. The proposed iso-depth regularization method is independent of haze-component estimation so that it is directly applicable to any state-of-the-art dehazing methods.

Acknowledgments. Min H. Kim, the corresponding author, acknowledges Korea NRF grants (2016R1-A2B2013031, 2013M3A6A6073718) and additional support by KOCCA in MCST of Korea, Cross-Ministry Giga KOREA Project (GK17P0200), Samsung Electronics (SRFC-IT1402-02), and an ICT R&D program of MSIT/IITP of Korea (2017-0-00072, 2016-0-00018). We also would like to appreciate Seung-Hwan Baek's helpful comments.

References

1. Kim, I., Kim, M.H.: Dehazing using non-local regularization with Iso-depth neighbor-fields. In: Proceedings of International Conference Computer Vision, Theory and Applications (VISAPP 2017), Porto, Portugal (2017)
2. He, K.M., Sun, J., Tang, X.: Single image haze removal using dark channel prior. In: Proceedings of IEEE CVPR, pp. 1956–1963 (2009)
3. Fattal, R.: Single image dehazing. ACM Trans. Graph. **27**, 72:1–72:9 (2008)
4. Fattal, R.: Dehazing using color-lines. ACM Trans. Graph. **34**, 13:1–13:14 (2014)
5. Berman, D., Treibitz, T., Avidan, S.: Non-local image dehazing. In: IEEE CVPR, pp. 1674–1682 (2016)
6. Barnes, C., Shechtman, E., Finkelstein, A., Goldman, D.B.: Patchmatch: a randomized correspondence algorithm for structural image editing. ACM Trans. Graph. **28**, 24:1–24:11 (2009)
7. Narasimhan, S.G., Nayar, S.K.: Vision and the atmosphere. Int. J. Comput. Vis. **48**, 233–254 (2002)
8. Schechner, Y.Y., Narasimhan, S.G., Nayar, S.K.: Instant dehazing of images using polarization. In: Proceedings of IEEE CVPR, pp. I:325–I:332 (2001)
9. Narasimhan, S.G., Nayar, S.K.: Contrast restoration of weather degraded images. IEEE Trans. Pattern Anal. Mach. Intell. **25**, 713–724 (2003)
10. Kopf, J., et al.: Deep photo: model-based photograph enhancement and viewing. ACM Trans. Graph. **27**, 116:1–116:10 (2008)
11. Tang, K., Yang, J., Wang, J.: Investigating haze-relevant features in a learning framework for image dehazing. In: Proceedings of IEEE CVPR, pp. 2995–3002 (2014)
12. Zhu, Q., Mai, J., Shao, L.: A fast single image haze removal algorithm using color attenuation prior. IEEE Trans. Image Process. **24**, 3522–3533 (2015)
13. Tan, R.T.: Visibility in bad weather from a single image. In: Proceedings of IEEE CVPR, pp. 1–8 (2008)
14. Tarel, J., Hautière, N.: Fast visibility restoration from a single color or gray level image. In: Proceedings of IEEE ICCV, pp. 2201–2208 (2009)
15. Nishino, K., Kratz, L., Lombardi, S.: Bayesian defogging. Int. J. Comput. Vis. **98**, 263–278 (2012)
16. Ancuti, C.O., Ancuti, C.: Single image dehazing by multi-scale fusion. IEEE Trans. Image Process. **22**, 3271–3282 (2013)
17. Li, Y., Tan, R.T., Brown, M.S.: Nighttime haze removal with glow and multiple light colors. In: 2015 IEEE ICCV 2015, Santiago, Chile, 7–13 December 2015, pp. 226–234 (2015)
18. Meng, G., Wang, Y., Duan, J., Xiang, S., Pan, C.: Efficient image dehazing with boundary constraint and contextual regularization. In: Proceedings of IEEE ICCV, pp. 617–624 (2013)
19. Carr, P., Hartley, R.I.: Improved single image dehazing using geometry. In: DICTA 2009, pp. 103–110 (2009)
20. He, K., Sun, J., Tang, X.: Guided image filtering. IEEE Trans. Pattern Anal. Mach. Intell. **35**, 1397–1409 (2013)
21. Marroquín, J.L., Velasco, F.A., Rivera, M., Nakamura, M.: Gauss-Markov measure field models for low-level vision. IEEE Trans. Pattern Anal. Mach. Intell. **23**, 337–348 (2001)

22. Li, Y.P., Huttenlocher, D.P.: Sparse long-range random field and its application to image denoising. In: Forsyth, D., Torr, P., Zisserman, A. (eds.) ECCV 2008. LNCS, vol. 5304, pp. 344–357. Springer, Heidelberg (2008). https://doi.org/10.1007/978-3-540-88690-7_26

23. Zhang, Q., Xu, L., Jia, J.: 100+ times faster weighted median filter (WMF). In: CVPR, pp. 2830–2837. IEEE (2014)

24. Levin, A., Lischinski, D., Weiss, Y.: A closed-form solution to natural image matting. IEEE Trans. Pattern Anal. Mach. Intell. **30**, 228–242 (2008)

25. Kim, M.H., Kautz, J.: Consistent tone reproduction. In: Proceedings of the IASTED International Conference on Computer Graphics and Imaging (CGIM 2008), Innsbruck, Austria, pp. 152–159. IASTED/ACTA Press (2008)

26. Kim, M.H., Kautz, J.: Consistent scene illumination using a chromatic flash. In: Proceedings of Eurographics Workshop on Computational Aesthetics (CAe 2009), British Columbia, Canada, Eurographics, pp. 83–89 (2009)

CUDA-Accelerated Feature-Based Egomotion Estimation

Safa Ouerghi[1(✉)], Remi Boutteau[2], Xavier Savatier[2], and Fethi Tlili[1]

[1] Carthage University, SUP'COM, GRESCOM, El Ghazela, 2083 Ariana, Tunisia
{safa.ouerghi,fethi.tlili}@supcom.tn
[2] Normandie Univ, UNIROUEN, ESIGELEC, IRSEEM, 76000 Rouen, France
{Remi.Boutteau,Xavier.Savatier}@esigelec.fr

Abstract. Egomotion estimation is a fundamental issue in structure from motion and autonomous navigation for mobile robots. Several camera motion estimation methods from a set of variable number of image correspondences have been proposed. Seven- and eight-point methods have been first designed to estimate the fundamental matrix. Five-point methods represent the minimal number of required correspondences to estimate the essential matrix. These feature-based methods raised special interest for their application in a hypothesize-and-test framework to deal with the problem of outliers. This algorithm allows relative pose recovery at the expense of a much higher computational time when dealing with higher ratios of outliers. To solve this problem with a certain amount of speedup, we propose in this work, a CUDA-based solution for the essential matrix estimation from eight, seven and five point correspondences, complemented with robust estimation. The mapping of these algorithms to the CUDA hardware architecture is given in detail as well as the hardware-specific performance considerations. The correspondences in the presented schemes are formulated as bearing vectors to be able to deal with all camera systems. Performance analysis against existing CPU implementations is also given, showing a speedup 4 times faster than the CPU for an outlier ratio $\epsilon = 0.5$ which is common for the essential matrix estimation from automatically computed point correspondences, for the five-point-based estimation. More speedup was shown for the seven and eight-point based implementations reaching 76 times and 57 times respectively.

Keywords: Egomotion · Visual odometry · Robotics · CUDA · GPU

1 Introduction

Accurate localization is a fundamental issue in autonomous navigation that has been extensively studied by the Robotics community. First advancements have emerged within the Simultaneous Localization And Mapping (SLAM) approach - the process of generating an internal map using sensor observations while moving through an environment - has received a great deal of attention [1]. Many

© Springer Nature Switzerland AG 2019
A. P. Cláudio et al. (Eds.): VISIGRAPP 2017, CCIS 983, pp. 239–261, 2019.
https://doi.org/10.1007/978-3-030-12209-6_12

sensory devices have been used in SLAM systems including lidar scanners and cameras that have become very popular due to their low-cost, wide availability, passive nature and modest power requirements [2,3]. Vision-based SLAM systems coined Visual SLAM (or v-SLAM) [4–6] may include several modules to concurrently perform the tracking and mapping tasks such as a visual odometry module (VO) [7,8]. This latter is derived from Structure from Motion (Sfm) and refers to the process of incrementally estimating the egomotion of an agent (e.g., vehicle, human and robot) using only the input of a single or multiple cameras attached to it. The feature-based VO for the monocular scheme consists mainly in finding corresponding features in consecutive frames in the video sequence and using the scene's epipolar geometry to calculate the position and orientation changes between the two images. A common way of determining the relative pose using two images taken by a calibrated camera is based on the estimation of the essential matrix that has been studied for decades. The first efficient implementation of the essential matrix estimation is proposed by Nistér in [9] and uses only five point correspondances. The work of Stewenius built upon the work of Nistér uses the Gröbner Basis to enhance the estimation accuracy [10]. Although the essential matrix expresses the epipolar geometry between two views taken by a calibrated camera, a more general relationship can be derived in the case of a non-calibrated camera expressed by the fundamental matrix which is the algebraic representation of epipolar geometry [11]. However, in a real application, wrong matches can lead to severe errors in the measurements, which are called outliers and that occurs during the descriptors matching step. The typical way of dealing with outliers consists of first finding approximate model parameters by iteratively applying a minimal solution in a hypothesize-and-test scheme. This procedure allows us to identify the inlier subset, and then, a least-squares result is obtained by minimizing the reprojection error of all inliers via a linear solution or a non-linear optimization scheme, depending on the complexity of the problem. This scheme is called RANdom Sample Consensus (RANSAC) and has been first proposed by Fischler and Bolles [12]. RANSAC can often find the correct solution even for high levels of contamination. However, the number of samples required to do so increases exponentially, and the associated computational cost is substantial. Especially for robotics systems, the challenges are more acute, due to their stringent time-response requirements. To solve these problems with a certain amount of speedup, the usage of GPU computation is a popular topic in the community. Researchers and developers have become interested in harnessing the Graphics Processing Units (GPUs) power for general-purpose computing, an effort known collectively as GPGPU (for General-Purpose computing on the GPU). The Compute Unified Device Architecture (CUDA) has enabled graphics processors to be explicitly programmed as general-purpose shared-memory multi-core processors with a high level of parallelism [13]. In fact, recently, many problems are being solved using programmable graphics hardware including feature matching and triangulation [14], feature detectors [15], large non-linear optimization problems such as bundle adjustment [16] and learning algorithms [17]. In this paper, we focus on an efficient implementation of a state-of-the-art relative pose estimation based on the computation of the Essential matrix from five correspondances. We consider single GPU implementation and we describe the strategies to map the problem to CUDA architecture. Furthermore, new Kepler and Maxwell architecture features are used and analyzed, such as CUDA Dynamic Parallelism and new CuBLAS batched interfaces. The outline of this paper is as follows: we briefly present the theory underlying the essential and fundamental matrices estimation in Sect. 2. Section 3 details the CUDA based implementation of the essential matrix estimation algorithm within RANSAC from five, seven and eight points. Afterwards, Sect. 4 shows several experiments as examples of the speedup results obtained with our implementation. Finally Sect. 5 gives the conclusion of the paper.

2   Background

The geometric relations between two images of a camera are described by the fundamental matrix and by the essential matrix in case the camera is calibrated. The essential matrix directly holds the parameters of the motion undergone. In this section, we provide an overview of the important background underlying the robust essential matrix estimation as well as the main feature-based methods used to derive the essential matrix and consequently the camera motion.

2.1   Fundamental and Essential Matrices

The epipolar geometry exists between any two camera systems. For a point u_i in the first image, its correspondence in the second image, u'_i, must lie on the epipolar line in the second image. This is known as the *epipolar constraint*. Algebraically, for u_i and u'_i to be matched, the following equation must be satisfied

$$u_i'^T F u_i = 0, \tag{1}$$

where F is the 3×3 fundamental matrix that has seven degrees of freedom because it is of rank 2 (*i.e.* $det(F) = 0$) and is defined only up to a scale. Therefore, at least seven point correspondences are required to calculate it. In fact, each point match gives rise to one linear equation in the unknown entries of F. From all the point matches, we obtain a set of linear equations of the form

$$A F = 0, \tag{2}$$

where A is a 7×9 constraint matrix. If $rank(A) = 8$ when using 8 correspondences, the solution is unique (up to a scale) and can be found by linear methods. However, least squares methods are preferred because of the presence of image noise and quantization effects.

The essential matrix is a 3×3 matrix as well, and can be considered as a special case of the fundamental matrix, satisfying the following relationship

$$x_i'^T E x_i = 0, \tag{3}$$

where x_i and x_i' are normalized image point correspondences (*i.e.* $x_i = \mathbf{K}^{-1} u_i$ and $x_i' = \mathbf{K}^{-1} u_i'$ with $\mathbf{K}$ the intrinsic calibration matrix). The fundamental and the essential matrices are, therefore, related by

$$E = \mathbf{K}^{-1} F \mathbf{K}, \tag{4}$$

where $\mathbf{K}$ is the intrinsic calibration matrix.

Furthermore, if the two views have relative pose $[R|t]$ then

$$E = [t]_\times R, \tag{5}$$

where $[t]_\times$ is the skew-symmetric matrix with the property that $[t]_\times x = t \times x$.

However, from two images alone, the length of t cannot be determined as E is only determined up to a scale.

To directly compute the essential matrix, expanding Eq. 3 is, generally, done which gives a single linear constraint in the nine elements of E for every correspondence. From N correspondences, these equations can be stacked to form a $9 \times N$ matrix which null space obtained by singular value decomposition (SVD) gives a basis for the space in which E lies. The points within this vector space which are essential matrices are those which can be decomposed into a rotation and a translation. E can be decomposed in this way using an SVD decomposition

$$E = U \begin{pmatrix} s\,0\,0 \\ 0\,s\,0 \\ 0\,0\,0 \end{pmatrix} V^T, \tag{6}$$

which is equivalent to the following constraint providing an efficient test whether a matrix is approximately an essential matrix

$$EE^T E - \frac{1}{2} trace(EE^T) E = 0. \tag{7}$$

2.2 Essential Matrix Computation from Feature Correspondences

Computing E from Eight Correspondences. F can only be determined up to a scale, there are, thus, 8 unknowns and at least 8 point matchings are used by the *8-point algorithm*. The constraint matrix A obtained according to Eq. 2 is, therefore, 9×8. The least square solution is the singular vector corresponding the smallest singular value of A, i.e. the last column of V in the SVD where $A = U D V^T$.

Computing E from Seven Correspondences. The matrix of constraints A is constructed from $n = 7$ correspondences and will therefore have a two-dimensional null-space. This latter is derived from the use an SVD decomposition resulting in two independent vectors f_1 and f_2. Taking f as the vector containing the coefficients of the fundamental matrix F,

$$f = (F_{11}\,F_{12}\,F_{13}\,F_{21}\,F_{22}\,F_{23}\,F_{31}\,F_{32}\,F_{33})^T, \tag{8}$$

f can be written as $f = (1 - t) f_1 + t f_2$ with $t \in \mathbb{R}$, solution of $A f = 0$.
The corresponding F-matrices are therefore,

$$F = (1 - t) F_1 + t F_2. \tag{9}$$

The condition $det(F) = 0$ leads to the equation,

$$det((1 - t) F_1 + t F_2) = 0, \tag{10}$$

that is a 3rd degree polynomial in t having at most 3 real roots, *i.e.* one or three solutions are possible. The correct one is obtained after disambiguation to check for the correct fundamental matrix. In our case, we are dealing with normalized data and would, therefore, directly obtain the essential matrix $E = F$. In fact, the essential and fundamental matrices are related as follows:

$$E = K'^T F K. \tag{11}$$

Computing E from Five Correspondances. Several algorithms have been developed to estimate the essential matrix, including, the seven- and eight-point algorithms that are relatively fast [11]. However, for their use within RANSAC, essential matrix computations have relied on minimal subsets, which for essential matrix is five correspondences. Furthermore, Essential matrix estimation from five correspondances have shown a better accuracy than other faster algorithms with more correspondances. In essential matrix estimation, given five correspondences, four basis vectors satisfying Eq. 1 can be computed by SVD. All linear combinations of these basis vectors satisfying Eq. 3 are essential matrices that provide nine cubic constraints in the elements of E. The methods of Nistér [9], and Stewenius et al. [10] both work by solving these nine equations. Stewenius et al. first showed that the equations can be written as

$$M X = 0, \tag{12}$$

where M is a 10×20 matrix.
After gauss-jordan elimination, the system can be written

$$[I\,B]\,X = 0, \tag{13}$$

where I is a 10×10 identity matrix and B a 10×10 matrix.
Stewenius et al. used, subsequently, the action matrix concept to solve the systems in which a Gröbner basis is found. The 10×10 action matrix real eigenvalues and eigenvectors contain, hence, the solutions of polynomial equations.

2.3 Relative Pose Computation from Essential Matrices Solutions.

Once the essential matrices solutions are computed, they have to be decomposed into rotation and translation. In fact, the decomposition follows the normal procedure for the general case [9], giving two possible solutions for the rotation, R_a

and R_b, and two solutions for the translation as well, t_a and t_b, which have the same direction $\hat{t}$ determined up to a scale.

Thus, if $E \sim USV^T$ is the SVD of E, a matrix D is defined as

$$D = \begin{bmatrix} 0 & 1 & 0 \\ -1 & 0 & 0 \\ 0 & 0 & 1 \end{bmatrix}. \tag{14}$$

Then, $R_a = UDV^T$ and $R_b = UD^TV^T$. The solution for the translation direction is $\hat{t} = [U_{13}U_{23}U_{33}]^T$.

Four pose configurations are, therefore, obtained for each essential matrix namely, (R_a, t_a), (R_b, t_a), (R_a, t_b) and (R_b, t_b). Consequently, a disambiguation has to be performed to output the correct movement undergone by the camera.

2.4   Robust Estimation of the Essential Matrix

Even if the underlying dataset is contaminated with outliers, RANSAC estimator can be used to robustly estimate the model parameters. RANSAC uses a randomly chosen subset of the entire dataset to compute a hypothesis. The remaining datapoints are used for validation. Repeating the hypothesis computation and validation with different subsets, the probability of finding a hypothesis that fits the data well increases. For a data set with a given proportion ϵ of outliers, the number of trials N required to give sufficiently high probability p to pick an outlier-free subset consisting of k point correspondences is

$$N = \frac{\log(1-p)}{\log(1-(1-\epsilon)^k)} \tag{15}$$

Since the confidence p is generally chosen to be $p \geq 0.99$, the number of required RANSAC iterations N only depends on the number of parameters k and the assumed ratio of outliers ϵ. Usually, the ratio of outliers ϵ is unknown. Hence, we resort to an adaptive version of RANSAC, where, after each iteration, the number of inliers γ is counted and the outlier ratio is updated according to

$$\epsilon = 1 - \frac{\gamma}{n}, \tag{16}$$

with n equal to the size of the dataset. The number of iterations N is therefore updated based on ϵ.

3   CUDA-Based Relative Motion Estimation from 2-D to 2-D Correspondences

The complexity of implementing existing algorithms on the GPU depends heavily on control flow of the algorithm. In fact, some algorithms (such as basic image processing) can be classified as *embarrassingly parallel* when little effort is required to split up the process into parallel tasks and are often easily ported to the GPU. In contrast, other algorithms are *inherently sequential* which implies unexpected scheduling difficulties that prohibit parallelization on the one hand and greatly increases the effort required to implement an efficient CUDA solution on the other hand. As has been explicited in the previous section, relative motion estimation algorithms generally execute within RANSAC to deal with the problem of outliers. Our parallelization approach is based on performing the required RANSAC iterations in parallel on CUDA to achieve a certain amount of speedup. This level of parallelism suggests the consideration of RANSAC iterations as a batch of parallel computations, each processing a small subset of data. However, RANSAC is inherently sequential which puts an additional complexity on the development process. Furthermore, we have relied on the use of CuBLAS, a high-performance implementation of BLAS-3 routines, for linear algebra computations [18]. As the matrices sizes in our problem are below 32×32, we have particularly exploited the batched interface of the CuBLAS library where many small dense matrices factorizations, to be performed simultaneously, are provided. In this section, we present the implementation details of relative pose estimation from five, seven and eight correspondences using the CUDA programming model.

3.1   CUDA-Based Relative Motion Estimation from Five Correspondences

In this section, we present the implementation details of the essential matrix estimation from five correspondences within RANSAC presented first in [20]. As has been stated before, the eigenvalues of the action matrix contain the essential matrices solutions according to Stewenius's method [10]. However, a device based eigenvalue computation on CUDA doesn't exist yet. Hence, we have relied on the Matlab code provided by Chris Engels, based on the reduction to a single polynomial [21]. This is done through the computation of the action matrix characteristic polynomial roots, equivalent to the action matrix eigenvalues. In total, four kernels have been employed operating at different levels of parallelism. The first, exploits the CuBLAS library batched interface, manages algebraic computations. It employs, therefore, a thread level parallelism and a nested warp level parallelism as it uses dynamic parallelism to call CuBLAS functions from within device. The second employs a straightforward parallelization and works at a thread-level parallelism where each thread manages the remainder computations after the completion of the first kernel, i.e. one thread per RANSAC iteration. The third kernel is used to rate the models outputted by the previous kernel and works at a block level parallelism where each block validates a model relative to one RANSAC iteration. Finally, an additional kernel is used to compute RANSAC's best model and it simply performs a reduction to find the model with maximum number of inliers which represents the best model.

CuBLAS Based Kernel. This kernel is launched with one block and a number of threads equal to the number of required RANSAC iterations. In fact, according to Eq. 15, for a probability of success of 0.99 and a rate of outliers equal to

0.5 the number of RANSAC trials required for a robust estimation based on five points is equal to 145. We assume that the data is contaminated with 0.5% of outliers which is quite common for the essential matrix estimation from automatically computed point correspondences. 145 threads belonging to one block are therefore used. The high level interface exposed by all implementations in this kernel is CuBLAS batched interface for solving a batch of N different systems. Besides the batch size and the matrix dimensions, the functions expect pointers to array of matrices. All arrays are assumed to be stored contiguously with a column major layout and accessed to in global memory through the handle of an array of pointers that we statically allocate as follows:

```
__device__ double* PointersArray[MaxBatchSize]
```

Firstly, a 9×5 hypothesis $A[i]$, $i = 0...batchSize - 1$ is computed from each random five correspondances by each thread. The computed hypotheses are written to global memory and referenced by an array of pointers as indicated above.

Secondly, the null-space of each hypothesis have to be computed by SVD. However, due to the absence of a GPU-based implementation of SVD decomposition, we use instead a QR decomposition to derive the null space. In fact, standard methods for determining the null-space of a matrix are to use a QR decomposition or an SVD. If accuracy is paramount, the SVD is preferred but QR is faster. Using a QR decomposition, if $A^T = QR$, and the rank of A is r, then the last $n - r$ columns of Q make up the null-space for A. This is performed through a call to the cuBLAS built-in function $cublasDqrfBatched$ performing a QR factorization of each $A[i]$ for $i = 0, ..., batchSise - 1$. The decomposition output is presented in a packed format where the matrix R is the upper triangular part of each $A[i]$ and the vectors v on the lower part are needed to compute the elementary reflectors. the matrix Q is, hence, not formed explicitly, but is represented as a product of these elementary reflectors.

As CuBLAS doesn't provide a built-in routine to retrieve Q as Lapack does, we designed a child kernel called from the main kernel to simultaneously calculate the different reflectors and compute their product to retrieve Q.

The number of Thread-blocks in the launch configuration of the child kernel is equal to the $batchSize$, *i.e. iterations*. Each Thread-block computes a single matrix Q and a block-level parallelism is hence applied. The Thread-blocks are designed to be three-dimensional, where the *x-dimension* refers to the number of rows of each reflector, the *y-dimension* to the number of columns and the *z-dimension* to the number of reflectors. This allows each thread to handle one element in shared memory and consequently, ensure a parallel computation of the different reflectors. It is worth noting that this configuration is possible because the matrix sizes in our problem are small (5 refrectors, each of size 9×9) and consequently, all reflectors fit at once in shared memory. The computation consists in loading, first, the $A[blockIdx.x]$, and the array of scalars $Tauarray[blockIdx.x]$ exited by $cublasDqrfBatched$ into shared memory where the matrix Q is also allocated. The vector v_i relative to each reflector q_i is then putted in the required form, where $v_i(1 : i - 1) = 0$ and $v_i(i) = 1$

with $v_i(i + 1 : m)$ on exit in $A[blockIdx.x][i + 1 : m, i]$. Each reflector q_i has the form $q_i = I - Tau[i].v.transpose(v)$, computed for all reflectors by the pseudocode explicited in Fig. 1 and finally, the product of all reflectors is computed to retrieve Q.

Pseudocode1: Q computation in shared memory.

```
int tidx=threadIdx.x;
int tidy=threadIdx.y;
int tidz=threadIdx.z;
int index_A=tidz*9+tidy;
int index_q=tidx*9+tidy+9*9*tidz;
   Q[index_q]=A[index_A];
__syncthreads();
double alpha;alpha=-1;
int index=tidx*9+tidy+9*9*tidz;
   Q[index]= (-Tau[tidz]*Q[index]
                 *(Q[tidxx*9+tidy+9*9*tidz])));
__syncthreads();
```

Fig. 1. Pseudocode of reflectors computation in shared memory.

Once the null-space determined, the second step is to compute a 10×20 matrix M that is accelerated in the provided *openSource* code, through a symbolic computation of the expanded constraints. The matrix columns are then rearranged according to a predefined order. To save execution time and memory usage, we use to rearrange the matrix columns beforehand and to write it in column major for subsequent use of cuBLAS functions. We hence output a permuted 20×10 matrix M.

Subsequently, the Reduced Row Echelon Form (RREF) of M have to be computed through a gauss-jordan elimination, *i.e.* $M = [I \, B]$. Instead of carrying out a gauss-jordan elimination on M, a factorization method may be used to find directly the matrix B from the existant matrix M. In fact, cuBLAS provides several batched interfaces for linear systems factorizations. We exploit the batched interface of LU factorization performing four GPU kernel calls for solving systems in the form $(MX = b)$ as follows:

1. LU decomposition of M $(PM = LU)$.
2. Permutation of the array b with the array of pivots P $(y = Pb)$.
3. Solution of the triangular lower system $(Lc = y)$.
4. Solution of the upper system to obtain the final solution $(Ux = c)$.

With putting b as an array of pointers to null vector, cuBLAS directly provides *cublasDgetrfBatched* for the first step and *cublasDgetrsBatched* for the three other steps. We finally obtain the matrix B in exit of *cublasDgetrsBatched*, solution of the system $MX = 0$.

RANSAC Models Computation Kernel. At this level, the kernel is launched with one CUDA block and *iterations* number of threads. We only use global memory where the computations of the previous kernel are stored and small per thread arrays using registers and local memory.

Each thread computes a 10th degree polynomial using local variables. This is done by extracting from the RREF in global memory the coefficients of two 3rd degree polynomials and a 4th degree polynomial represented by private local arrays for each thread. These polynomials are afterwards convoluted then subtracted and added to generate a single 10th degree polynomial for each thread as explicited in the original Matlab code and which refers to the computation of the determinant of the characteristic polynomial. The convolution is performed in our implementation through a special *device* function presented as a symbolic computation of three polynomials of 3rd, 3rd and 4th degrees respectively.

The key implementation of this kernel is the resolution of a batch of 10th degree polynomials. In fact, we used a batched version of the Durand-Kerner Method in which we assign to each polynomial a thread. We start by giving a brief overview of the Durand-Kerner method, followed by our implementation details.

Durand-Kerner Method. The Durand-Kerner Method allows the extraction of all roots $\omega_1, ..., \omega_n$ of a polynomial

$$p(z) = \sum_{i=0}^{n} a_i z^{n-i}, \tag{17}$$

where $a_n \neq 0$, $a_0 = 1$, $a_i \in \mathbb{C}$.

This method constructs a sequence, $H(z^k) = z^{k+1}$ in $\mathbb{C}^\mathbb{N}$ with $Z^{(0)}$ being any initial vector and H is the Weierstrass operator making $Z_i^{(k)}$ tends to the root ω_i of the polynomial, defined as:

$$H_i(z) = z_i - \frac{P(z_i)}{\prod_{j \neq i}(z_i - z_j)} \qquad i = 1, ..., n \tag{18}$$

The iterations repeat until $\frac{|Z_i^k - Z_i^{k+1}|}{Z_i^k}$ or $|P(z_i^k)|$ is smaller than the desired accuracy.

GPU Version of Batched Durand-Kerner. The implementation of the Durand-Kerner on GPU, is basically sequential where each thread computes the ten complex roots of the 10th degree polynomial. We defined the type COMPLEX denoting structs of complex numbers. We started from an initial complex guess z randomly chosen, and the vector of complex roots R of size the number of roots (10 in our problem) where, $R[i] = z^i$, $i = 1..n - 1$. The function *poly* evaluates at z a polynomial of the form of Eq. 17 where the vector $A = a1, a2, a3, ..., a(n-2), a(n-1), a(n)$ denotes the coefficients of our polynom.

As we are dealing with complex numbers, complex arithmetic has been employed denoted by *compsubtract* for complex numbers subtraction and *compdiv* for complex division. As explicited in the following piece of code, we iterate until obtaining the desired accuracy expressed as a relative error of estimated roots below a predefined value as depicted in Fig. 2.

Pseudocode2: GPU Version of Durand-Kerner method.

```
double maxDiff = 0; int iter=0; int maxIters =30;
for( iter = 0; iter < maxIters; iter++ ) {
  maxDiff = 0;
  for (int j = 0; j < n; j ++) {
    COMPLEX B = poly(A, n, R[j]);
    for (int k = 0; k < n; k++) {
      if (k != j)
          B = compdiv(B,compsubtract(R[j] , R[k]));
      }
      R[j] = compsubtract(R[j],B);
      maxDiff = max(maxDiff, abs(B.x));
  }
  if( maxDiff <= 1e-10)
    break;
  }
```

Fig. 2. Pseudocode of batched Durand-Kerner method on CUDA.

As explicited in Sect. 2.3, an SVD decomposition of the directly obtained essential matrices which are up to 10 (real solutions of 10th degree polynomial) is used to decompose each solution into rotation and translation. This operation can take a significant portion of the computation time and we use, therefore, a specifically tailored singular value decomposition for essential matrices according to Eq. 6, that is proposed in [9] (Appendix B). In our implementation, each thread computes up to 10 essential matrices, and for each, four movement configurations are obtained.

However, in order to deal with all central camera models including perspective, dioptric, omnidirectional and catadioptric imaging devices, image measurements are represented as 3D bearing vectors: a unit vector originating at the camera center and pointing toward the landmark. Each bearing vector has only two degrees of freedom, which are the azimuth and elevation inside the camera reference frame as formulated in [19]. Because a bearing vector has only two degrees of freedom, we frequently refer to it as a 2D information and it is normally expressed in a camera reference frame.

The disambiguation step that has, finally, to be performed by each thread consists in calculating the sum of reprojection error of the triangulated 3D points relative to the corresponding bearing vectors used to compute the model. Finally, a single 4×3 transformation into the world reference frame matrix is returned by each thread referring to the lowest score of reprojection error between all essential matrices and pose configurations (up to 40). The transformation matrix is directly obtained from the already calculated rotation and translation.

Indeed, the triangulation method used in our implementation follows the general scheme employed in [19]. The reprojection error of 3D bearing vectors was proposed in [19] as well, and is computed by considering the angle between the measured bearing vector f_{meas} and the reprojected one f_{repr}. In fact, the scalar product of f_{meas} and f_{repr} directly gives the angle between them, which is equal to $\cos\theta$ as illustrated in Fig. 3. The reprojection error is, therefore, expressed as

$$\epsilon = 1 - f_{meas}^T f_{repro} = 1 - \cos\theta. \tag{19}$$

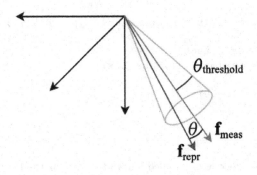

Fig. 3. Reprojection error computation in Opengv (Source: [19]).

RANSAC Rating Kernel. In order to validate each estimated model, we compute a loss value for each datapoint of the dataset. The loss value is used to verify the model by computing the reprojection error of all triangulated bearing vectors of the dataset. Outliers are subsequently found by thresholding the reprojection errors, and the best model refers to the one with the maximum number of inliers. As the entire operation is in 3D, we use the thresholding scheme adopted in the Opengv library [19]. This latter uses a threshold angle $\theta_{threshold}$ to constrain f_{repr} to lie within a cone of axis f_{meas} and of opening angle $\theta_{threshold}$ as depicted in Fig. 3. The threshold error is given by

$$\epsilon_{threshold} = 1 - \cos\theta_{threshold} = 1 - \cos(arctan\frac{\psi}{l}), \tag{20}$$

where ψ refers to the classical reprojection error threshold expressed in pixels and l to the focal length.

The model validation process considers multiple accesses to global memory to evaluate whether each correspondence of the dataset is an inlier or an outlier which is a very time consuming. The shared memory is, hence, used as a cache to accelerate computations. The RANSAC rating kernel employs a block level parallelism and is launched with *iterations* blocks to make each block handle a RANSAC model and $8 \times warpsize$ threads. Since $warpsize = 32$, a total of 256 threads are launched per block and each thread in the block evaluates a point. To load datapoints in shared memory, a buffer is allocated of size $256 \times s$ where s refers to the size of each datapoint. In case of bearing vectors, $s = 6$. Each thread triangulates bearing vector correspondances into a 3D point and computes its reprojection error according to Eq. 19. This latter is, thereafter, compared to the precalculated threshold according to Eq. 20 to decide whether the correspondance refers to an inlier or to an outlier. In our implementation, the number of inliers for 256 values is automatically returned via:

```
inlier_count=__syncthreads_count(
                reproj_error[threadIdx.x]<threshold);
```

The process of loading data into buffer and evaluating 256 reprojection errors is repeated ceil (datasetCount/256) times.

RANSAC Best Model Computation Kernel. This kernel is launched with one block and *itearations* threads and performs a reduction in shared memory to derive the best model which refers to the one with the maximum number of inliers.

3.2 CUDA-Based Relative Motion Estimation from Seven Correspondences

The implementation of the seven-point method relies on many common components with the five-point method presented above. Our parallelization strategy relies on performing the RANSAC iterations in parallel, as well. This suggests redesigning the sequential code as has been done for the five point case. In this section, we will only present the key steps that are different from the previous implementation. We recall that, as has been stated before, the fundamental matrix has 7 degrees of freedom and requires seven correspondences to be estimated. As we are working with normalized bearing vectors on the unit sphere, our data is, therefore, normalized, and we directly obtain the essential matrix. As has been presented in Sect. 2.2, the algorithm requires the computation of the null-space of the constraint matrix formed from 7 correspondences randomly chosen. The null-space is two-dimensional resulting in two independant vectors. These latters lead to a 3rd degree polynomial that has at most 3 real root representing the possible fundamental matrices solutions (or the essential matrices in the calibrated case). This requires the recovery of the null-space and the resolution of a 3rd degree polynomial.

Null-Space Recovery. The constraint matrix, constructed from 7 correspondences is of size 7×9. The null-space recovery is, generally, performed by SVD.

We use instead the same method presented in Sect. 3.1 based on a QR decomposition and use as well the batched interface of the CuBLAS library to simultaneously find the null-spaces of a batch of small matrices, each referring to a RANSAC iteration.

Cubic Polynomial Root Solver. In the 7-point algorithm, finding the fundamental matrices solutions or the essential matrices for the calibrated case is reduced to solving a 3rd degree polynomial in the form of Eq. 10. Several state of the art methods can be used to solve a general polynomial including Durand-kerner method presented in Sect. 3.1. However, as we are dealing with only a cubic degree, we have opted for a direct solver, namely Cardano's Formula [22].

Robust Pose Estimation on GPU. The advantage of the GPU is gained through the execution of the RANSAC iterations in parallel. The RANSAC estimation process consists in two major steps executed by two separate kernels namely, hypotheses computation kernel and loss values computation kernel.

Hypotheses Computation Kernel. This kernel is executed on the CUDA device with a given number of CUDA threads T and CUDA blocks B depending on the number of required iterations as $N = T.B$. We take in general the number of threads T as multiple of warp size. This kernel consists of the steps explained below.

1. At the beginning of each iteration, each thread performs the computation of 7 random numbers that are used to choose the subset for further steps. In our implementation, Marsaglia's random numbers generator has been used to generate random numbers on GPU [23].
2. The second step consists in simultaneously computing the different hypotheses including finding up to 3 possible essential matrices, solutions of the 3rd degree polynomial. Each solution is decomposed, then, into rotation R and translation t and a disambiguation is, subsequently, performed to pick up the right solution. At the end of this stage, transformation matrices (with the form $[R|t]$) are contiguously written in the device's global memory at the number of RANSAC iterations.

RANSAC Rating Kernel. In order to validate each estimated hypothesis obtained on exit of the hypotheses computation kernel, we compute a loss value for each datapoint of the dataset. The loss value is used to verify the hypothesis by computing the reprojection error of all triangulated bearing vectors of the dataset as presented in Sect. 3.1. Outliers are subsequently found by thresholding the reprojection errors, and the best model refers to the hypothesis with the maximum number of inliers.

An additional kernel is, finally, used aiming at determining the best model which refers to the one that has the maximum number of inliers by performing a reduction in shared memory.

3.3   CUDA-Based Relative Motion Estimation from Eight Correspondences

The egomotion estimation using the eight-point algorithm on CUDA follows the same scheme presented in the previous section dealing with seven correspondences. The null-space is obtained via a QR decomposition as has been previously discussed and is one dimensional which gives one essential matrix solution. The implementation mainly involves two kernels, the first for hypotheses computation that is launched with T threads and B blocks to simultaneously compute N RANSAC iterations where $N = T.B$. The second is for rating the RANSAC hypotheses ans is launched with N blocks and 256 threads and involves the bearing vectors rating scheme. Finally, an additional kernel is used to determine the best model which refers to the one that has the maximum number of inliers. However, to avoid the costly iterative SVD, the null-space is determined via QR instead of SVD and the rank 2 constraint that has to be enforced according to Eq. 6 is directly implemented using an SVD computation for 3×3 matrices.

4   Results

In this section we evaluate the speed and accuracy of our CUDA based essential matrix solver within RANSAC and compare it against the CPU based implementation for general relative camera motion provided in the OpenGV library. This latter is an *openSource* library that operates directly in 3D and provides implementations to solve the problems of computing the absolute or relative pose of a generalized camera [19].

4.1   Random Problem Generation

To make synthetic data for our tests, we used the automatic benchmark for relative pose included in the Matlab interface of the OpenGV library. We used the provided experiment to create a random relative pose problem, that is, correspondences of bearing vectors in two viewpoints using two cameras at the number of 1000 correspondences. In fact, the number of 1000 correspondences has been chosen based on an averaged number obtained from real images. The experiment returns the observations in two viewpoints plus the ground truth values for the relative transformation parameters.

4.2   Timing

We have measured the mean time while running on the GPU and CPU (using OpenGV library). To compute the mean time, each estimation is repeated 20 times. The repetition rate is required since a single estimation can be much slower or much faster than the mean due to the randomization. We only present results of computations for single-precision datatype as the precision loss due to single precision doesn't really affect the localization estimation in a real scenario. In addition, visual odometry is generally used with an optimization process to reduce the drift caused by the run-time accumulation error. The system on which the code has been evaluated is equipped with an i7 CPU running at up to 3.5 GHz, the intel i7 CORE. The CUDA device is an NVIDIA GeForce GTX 850M running at 876 MHz with 4096 MB of GDDR5 device memory. The evaluation has been performed with CUDA version 7.5 integrated with VisualStudio 2012.

At the first execution of the estimation, memory allocations have to be performed. This is required only once and takes about 6 ms. To evaluate our implementation, 10 outlier ratios from $\epsilon = 0.05$ to $\epsilon = 0.5$ in steps of $\epsilon = 0.05$ are evaluated. Figure 4 shows the number of required RANSAC iterations for the essential matrix estimation from 5, 7 and 8 correspondences for the 10 outlier ratios.

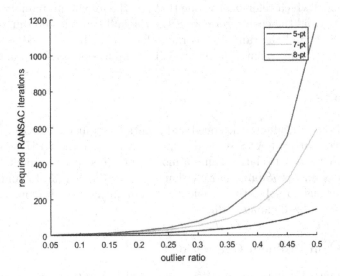

Fig. 4. Required RANSAC iterations vs outlier ratio.

In Fig. 5, we show the performance results of estimating camera relative pose from sets of five 2D bearing vectors correspondences. Firstly, in Fig. 5(a), we compare the mean computation time of CPU and GPU implementations, in single precision. We show a mean computation time even more important for CPU reaching 86 ms for an outlier ratio $\epsilon = 0.5$ against 18 ms for GPU. With an outlier ratio of $\epsilon = 0.5$ which is common for the essential matrix estimation from automatically computed point correspondences, we show in Fig. 5(b) that the speedup is above 4× compared to the CPU implementation. Furthermore, it is useful to visualize the intersection between each CPU and GPU evaluation, *i.e.* the outlier ratio where the speedup is equal to one. Figure 5(b) shows that there is no speedup for lower outlier ratios $\epsilon \leq 0.2$. This is because the needed number of iterations for $\epsilon = 0.2$ is only 12 iterations. However, the minimum number of iterations used in GPU based implementation is 32 iterations referring to the warp size.

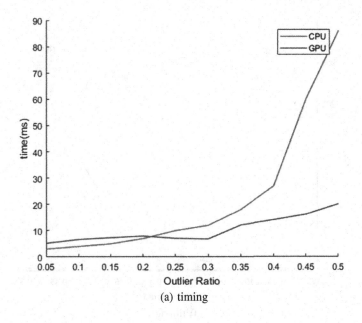

(a) timing

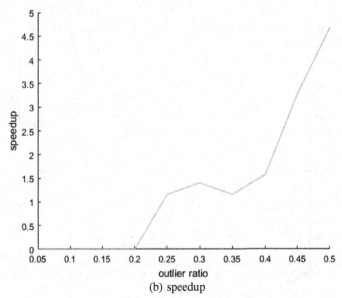

(b) speedup

Fig. 5. Performance of essential matrix estimation with RANSAC from 5 correspondences.

In Fig. 6, we show the performance results of estimating camera relative pose from sets of seven 2D bearing vectors correspondences. In Fig. 6(a), we compare the mean computation time of CPU and GPU implementations, in single precision. We show a mean computation time for CPU reaching 266 ms for

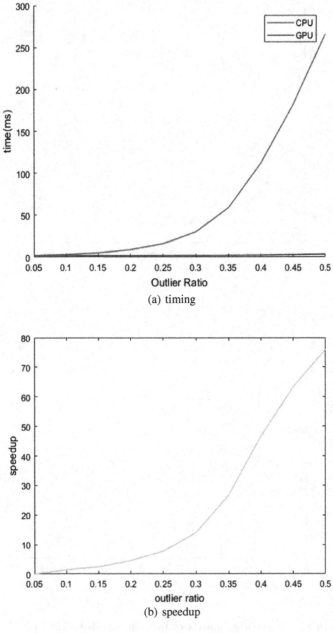

Fig. 6. Performance of essential matrix estimation with RANSAC from 7 correspondences.

an outlier ratio $\epsilon = 0.5$ against 3.5 ms for GPU allowing a highly important speedup of 76× as depicted in Fig. 6(a) and (b) for mean time in ms and speedup respectively.

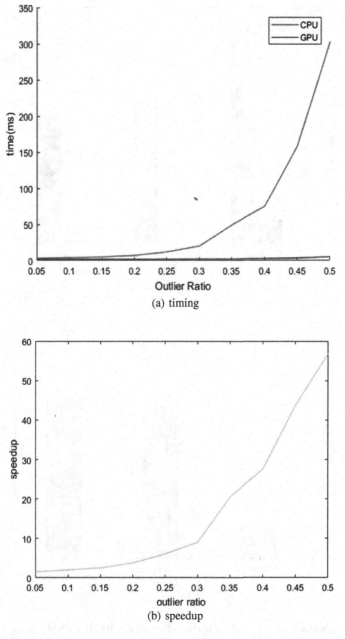

Fig. 7. Performance of essential matrix estimation with RANSAC from 8 correspondences.

In Fig. 7, we show the performance results of estimating camera relative pose from sets of eight 2D bearing vectors correspondences. As shown in Fig. 7(a), a speedup of almost 57× is achieved for an outlier ratio of $\epsilon = 0.5$. In fact,

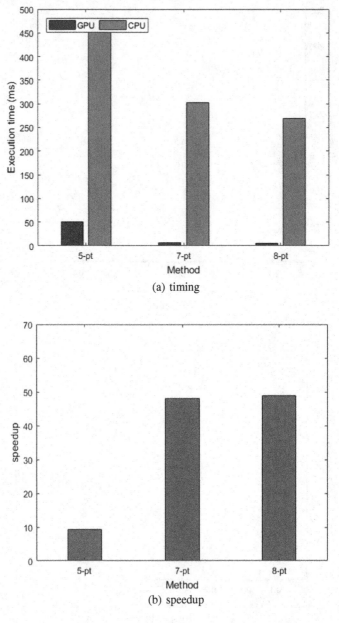

Fig. 8. Performance of essential matrix estimation with RANSAC from 5, 7 and 8 correspondences.

the seven point scheme achieves more speedup as for $\epsilon = 0.5$, 588 iterations are required to attain a probability of 0.99 that the subset is outlier-free against 1177 iterations when relying on eight correspondences.

In a second series of experiments, a fixed number of RANSAC iterations equal to 1024 is used to evaluate the performance of the three egomotion estimation schemes. In fact, a high number of iterations is sometimes needed, priorly determined, in order to estimate the covariance of the data as for instance in [24]. In Fig. 8, we evaluate the time in ms and the speedup of our CUDA-based implementations of essential matrix estimation within RANSAC from five, seven and eight correspondences. Due to the implementations complexities, we only launch 256 parallel threads in the case of *5-pt algorithm* and the kernels are therefore launched 4 times serially by the CPU to perform the 1024 iterations. In the case of the *7-pt algorithm* and *8-pt algorithm*, 512 threads are issued in parallel and the kernels are serially launched 2 times. Figure 8(a) shows an even more important CPU time reaching 464 ms, 303 ms and 269 ms for the *5-pt algorithm*, *7-pt algorithm* and the *8-pt algorithm* respectively against 50.34 ms, 6.31 ms and 5.5 ms for the CUDA-based implementations. This allows to achieve almost $9\times$ speedup for the *5-pt algorithm* and almost $48\times$ speedup for both the *7-pt algorithm* and *8-pt algorithm*.

5   Conclusion

In this paper we presented a CUDA-accelerated 2D-2D feature-based egomotion estimation from five, seven and eight correspondences. Feature-based egomotion is typically used within RANSAC in order to deal with erroneous feature correspondences known as outliers. We presented our parallelization strategy, based mainly on performing the required RANSAC iterations in parallel on the CUDA GPU. We, hence, designed a mapping of the five-point essential matrix using Gröbner basis to CUDA resources and programming model as well as the seven-point and eight-point schemes. Our hardware-specific implementations dealt with multiple CUDA features such as the batched interface of the cuBLAS library and the dynamic parallelism. In addition, in order to deal with all central camera models including perspective, dioptric, omnidirectional and catadioptric imaging devices, we used a novel scheme based on representing feature measurements as bearing vectors. This representation suggested a specific rating measure for RANSAC which is based on the computation of the reprojection error of triangulated 3D points from corresponding bearing vectors. An evaluation of our implementation was presented and the mean computation time of RANSAC for different outlier ratios was measured. For an outlier ratio $\epsilon = 0.5$, common for the essential matrix estimation from automatically computed point correspondences, a speedup of 4 times faster than the CPU counterpart was achieved for the five-point version. Higher speedups were shown for the seven-point and the eight-point versions reaching 76 times and 57 times respectively. The five-point version is known to have a better accuracy at the expense of complexity, whereas the faster seven and eight point versions are preferred when integrating an optimization process aiming at reducing the accumulated run-time error.

References

1. Thrun, S., Leonard, J.J.: Simultaneous localization and mapping. In: Siciliano, B., Khatib, O. (eds.) Springer Handbook of Robotics, pp. 871–889. Springer, Heidelberg (2008). https://doi.org/10.1007/978-3-540-30301-5_38
2. Hager, G., Hebert, M., Hutchinson, S.: Editorial: special issue on vision and robotics, parts I and II. Int. J. Comput. Vis. **74**, 217–218 (2007)
3. Neira, J., Davison, A.J., Leonard, J.: Guest editorial special issue on visual SLAM. IEEE Trans. Robot. **24**, 929–931 (2008)
4. Davison, A.J., Reid, I.D., Molton, N.D., Stasse, O.: MonoSLAM: real-time single camera SLAM. IEEE Trans. Pattern Anal. Mach. Intell. **29**, 1052–1067 (2007)
5. Williams, B., Klein, G., Reid, I.: Real-time SLAM relocalisation. In: Proceedings International Conference on Computer Vision (2007)
6. Newcombe, R.A., Lovegrove, S.J., Davison, A.J.: DTAM: dense tracking and mapping in real-time, November 2011
7. Scaramuzza, D., Fraundorfer, F.: Visual odometry [tutorial]. IEEE Robot. Autom. Mag. **18**, 80–92 (2011)
8. Fraundorfer, F., Scaramuzza, D.: Visual odometry: part II: matching, robustness, optimization, and applications. IEEE Robot. Autom. Mag. **19**, 78–90 (2012)
9. Nistér, D.: An efficient solution to the five-point relative pose problem. IEEE Trans. Pattern Anal. Mach. Intell. **26**, 756–770 (2004)
10. Stewenius, H., Engels, C., Nistér, D.: Recent developments on direct relative orientation. ISPRS J. Photogramm. Remote Sens. **60**, 284–294 (2006)
11. Hartley, R., Zisserman, A.: Multiple View Geometry in Computer Vision, 2 edn. Cambridge University Press, Cambridge (2003)
12. Fischler, M.A., Bolles, R.C.: Random sample consensus: a paradigm for model fitting with applications to image analysis and automated cartography. Commun. ACM **24**, 381–395 (1981)
13. Lindholm, E., Nickolls, J., Oberman, S., Montrym, J.: NVIDIA tesla: a unified graphics and computing architecture. IEEE Micro. **28**, 39–55 (2008)
14. Li, B., Zhang, X., Sato, M.: Pitch angle estimation using a vehicle-mounted monocular camera for range measurement. In: 2014 12th International Conference on Signal Processing (ICSP), pp. 1161–1168 (2014)
15. Yonglong, Z., Kuizhi, M., Xiang, J., Peixiang, D.: Parallelization and optimization of SIFT on GPU Using CUDA. In: 2013 IEEE 10th International Conference on High Performance Computing and Communications 2013 IEEE International Conference on Embedded and Ubiquitous Computing, pp. 1351–1358 (2013)
16. Wu, C., Agarwal, S., Curless, B., Seitz, S.M.: Multicore bundle adjustment. In: CVPR 2011, pp. 3057–3064 (2011)
17. Chang, C.-C., Lin, C.-J.: LIBSVM: a library for support vector machines. ACM Trans. Intell. Syst. Technol. **2**, 27:1–27:27 (2011)
18. NVIDIA documentation, cuBLAS. http://docs.nvidia.com/cuda/cublas/index.html
19. Kneip, L., Furgale, P.: OpenGV: a unified and generalized approach to real-time calibrated geometric vision. In: 2014 IEEE International Conference on Robotics and Automation (ICRA), pp. 1–8 (2014)
20. Ouerghi, S., Boutteau, R., Savatier, X., Tlili, F.: CUDA accelerated visual egomotion estimation for robotic navigation. In: Proceedings of the 12th International Joint Conference on Computer Vision, Imaging and Computer Graphics Theory and Applications, VISAPP, vol. 4, pp. 107–114 (2017)

21. Stewenius, H., Engels, C.: Matlab code for solving the fivepoint problem (2008). http://vis.uky.edu/~stewe/FIVEPOINT/
22. Cardano formula - Encyclopedia of Mathematics. https://www.encyclopediaofmath.org/index.php/Cardano_formula
23. Marsaglia, G.: Random number generators. J. Mod. Appl. Stat. Methods **2**, 2–13 (2003)
24. Ouerghi, S., Boutteau, R., Savatier, X., Tlili, F.: Visual odometry and place recognition fusion for vehicle position tracking in urban environments. Sensors. **18**, 939 (2018)

Automatic Retinal Vascularity Identification and Artery/Vein Classification Using Near-Infrared Reflectance Retinographies

Joaquim de Moura[1,2]([✉]), Jorge Novo[1,2], Marcos Ortega[1,2], Noelia Barreira[1,2], and Pablo Charlón[3]

[1] Department of Computer Science, University of A Coruña, A Coruña, Spain
{joaquim.demoura,jnovo,mortega,nbarreira}@udc.es
[2] CITIC - Research Center of Information and Communication Technologies, University of A Coruña, A Coruña, Spain
[3] Instituto Oftalmológico Victoria de Rojas, A Coruña, Spain
pcharlon@sgoc.es

Abstract. The retinal microcirculation structure is commonly used as an important source of information in many medical specialities for the diagnosis of relevant diseases such as, for reference, hypertension, arteriosclerosis, or diabetes. Also, the evaluation of the cerebrovascular and cardiovascular disease progression could be performed through the identification of abnormal signs in the retinal vasculature architecture. Given that these alterations affect differently the artery and vein vascularities, a precise characterization of both blood vessel types is also crucial for the diagnosis and treatment of a significant variety of retinal and systemic pathologies. In this work, we present a fully automatic method for the retinal vessel identification and classification in arteries and veins using Optical Coherence Tomography scans. In our analysis, we used a dataset composed by 30 near-infrared reflectance retinography images from different patients, which were used to test and validate the proposed method. In particular, a total of 597 vessel segments were manually labelled by an expert clinician, being used as groundtruth for the validation process. As result, this methodology achieved a satisfactory performance in the complex issue of the retinal vessel tree identification and classification.

Keywords: Retinal imaging · Vascular tree · Segmentation · Artery/vein classification

1 Introduction

The retina is the only tissue of the human body where the information of the vascular morphology and structure can be evaluated non-invasively and in vivo [1]. The retinal vasculature is a complex network of blood vessels composed of

© Springer Nature Switzerland AG 2019
A. P. Cláudio et al. (Eds.): VISIGRAPP 2017, CCIS 983, pp. 262–278, 2019.
https://doi.org/10.1007/978-3-030-12209-6_13

arteries, veins and capillaries [2]. In the current clinical practice, optical imaging is widely used in the study, diagnosis, planning, and assessment of the treatment response in a variety of ocular and systemic diseases that affect the retinal vasculature as, for reference, hypertension [3], diabetes [4] or arteriosclerosis [5]. The most common symptoms of those pathologies include micro-aneurysms, vascular tortuosity, arteriovenous nicking or neovascularization.

In many studies, different biomarkers are used to measure the vascular morphology of the retina, particularly between arteries and veins. As reference, we can find the Arterio-Venular-Ratio (AVR) that is defined by the ratio between the arteriolar and the venular diameters [6]. In particular, this biomarker is used by the clinical specialists in the diagnosis of several pathologies as, for example, diabetic retinopathy, which is among the major causes of blindness worldwide [7]. Therefore, an accurate identification of the retinal vasculature structure and its characterization in arteries and veins is essential for the diagnosis and monitoring of the treatment of a variety of retinal pathologies [8].

Nowadays, Computer-Aided Diagnosis (CAD) systems are increasingly being used as auxiliary tools by the expert clinicians for the detection and interpretation of different diseases [9–11]. These independent decision systems are designed to assist clinicians in various tasks, including storage, retrieval, organization, interpretation, and diagnostic output of hypothetical pathological images and data [12], facilitating and simplifying their work.

Optical Coherence Tomography (OCT) is a non-invasive, cross-sectional and high-resolution image modality that allows the acquisition of three-dimensional images of the retinal tissues in real time [13]. This retinal imaging technique uses low-coherence interferometry to obtain a series of OCT histological sections by sequentially collecting reflections from the lateral and longitudinal scans of the ocular tissues of the human eye [14]. The OCT sections are complemented with the corresponding near-infrared reflectance (NIR) retinography image of the eye fundus. Both images are simultaneously captured with the same OCT capture device. Figure 1 shows a representative example of an OCT image composed by the NIR retinography image and a corresponding OCT histological section.

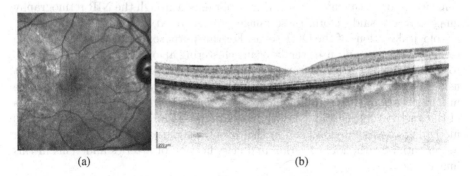

(a)   (b)

Fig. 1. Example of OCT scan. (a) NIR retinography image. (b) OCT histological section.

Given the importance and applicability of the analysis of retinal images, many efforts were done to face the analysis with classical retinographies. Thus, as reference, in the work proposed by Joshi *et al.* [15], a methodology was designed to automatically segment the vascular tree structure using a strategy that is based on graph theory. Then, the blood vessel classification process into arteries and veins is done using properties of color spaces. Dashtbozorg *et al.* [16] proposed an automatic method for the artery/vein classification using a graph-based approach and different machine learning methods. Following a similar strategy, Yang *et al.* [17] proposed a method using a Support Vector Machine (SVM) classifier for the vessels categorization in retinal images. Kondermann *et al.* [18] proposed a method using SVM and Artificial Neural Networks (ANN) in a feature extraction and classification process. Relan *et al.* [19] proposed an unsupervised method of classification based on a Gaussian Mixture Model on small vessel patches to classify the main vessels structures. Welikala *et al.* [21] proposed an automatic methodology using a Convolutional Neural Network (CNN) approach for the automatic classification of arteries and veins in retinal images. The final architecture of this method was composed of six learned layers: three convolutional and three fully-connected. Similarly, Girard *et al.* [22] proposed a method for artery/vein classification combining CNN and graph propagation strategies. In the work of Huang *et al.* [23], the authors proposed a methodology using a set of features that are extracted from the lightness reflection of the blood vessels. Then, a Linear Discriminate Analysis (LDA) learning strategy was used to validate these selected features. In the work proposed by Zou *et al.* [24], a supervised classification method based on feature selection is done. Firstly, the grey-level co-occurrence matrix (GLCM) and adaptive local binary pattern (A-LBP) features are extracted. Then, a Feature-Weighted K-Nearest Neighbors (FW-KNN) algorithm is used to classify the arteries and veins vessels. In the work of Vázquez *et al.* [20], the authors proposed a framework for the automatic classification of the arteries and veins using a k-means clustering. Then, this information is used to calculate the AVR biomarker.

In this work, we present a fully computational method for the automatic extraction of the retinal vascular structure and its classification into arteries and veins using, only, the information that is obtained through the NIR retinography images. As we said before, these images are provided in combination with the histological sections of the OCT scans. For this purpose, the method extracts the retinal vessel tree and uses the k-means clustering algorithm with local features to differentiate the arteries from the veins. A post-processing stage is carried out using the anatomical knowledge of the vessels to identify and correct the possible misclassifications of the individual vessel points. Promising preliminary results of this method were obtained in the work proposed in [25]. In this context, this methodology was extended and further deeply validated in this work, expanding its potential for the identification and classification of arteries and veins in this image modality.

This work is organized as follows: Sect. 2 presents the proposed methodology and the characteristics of all the involved stages. Section 3 details all the experiments that were done to validate the method as well as the discussion about the obtained results. Finally, Sect. 4 includes the conclusions of this proposal as well as the possible future lines of work.

2   Methodology

In this work, the system receives, as input, the NIR retinography image to identify and classify the vascular tree into arteries and veins. The proposed methodology is divided into three main stages: firstly, the entire retinal vascular tree is extracted from the input image; secondly, the region of the optic disc is identified and removed for the posterior analysis; and finally, the remaining identified vessels are analysed and classified into arteries and veins. Figure 2 describes the general scheme of the proposed methodology, from where each stage will be detailed in the following subsections.

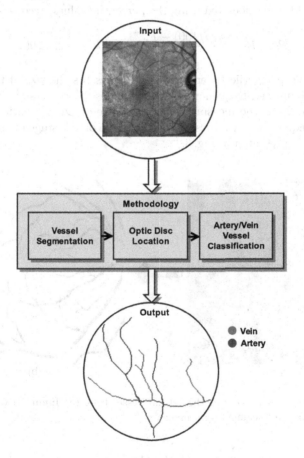

Fig. 2. Main stages of the proposed methodology.

2.1   Vessel Segmentation

The first stage of the classification process faces the segmentation of the retinal vessel tree within the NIR retinography image. For this purpose, we follow the method proposed by Calvo *et al.* [26], given its simplicity and for being a well-established and robust technique that demonstrated its suitability in classical retinographies.

Firstly, an initial segmentation was performed by means of a hysteresis-based thresholding strategy. To achieve this, a hard threshold (T_h) obtains pixels with a high confidence of being vessels while a weak threshold (T_w) keeps all the pixels of the vessel tree, including the spurious ones. The final segmentation is formed by all the pixels that were included by the T_w weak threshold connected to, at least, one pixel obtained by the T_h hard threshold. The values for T_h and T_w are extracted using as reference two metrics that are calculated on the NIR retinography images: the percentage of vascular tree and the percentage of background. These thresholds are calculated using the percentile values, according to Eq. (1).

$$P_k = L_k + \frac{k(n/100) - F_k}{f_k} \times c, \quad k = 1, 2, ..., 99 \tag{1}$$

where L_k is the percentile lower limit k, n represents the size of the data set, F_k is the accumulated frequency for $k-1$ values, f_k depicts the frequency of percentile k and c is the measurement of the size of the percentile interval. In our case, c is equal to 1. A representative example of this stage of the vessel tree segmentation is presented in Fig. 3.

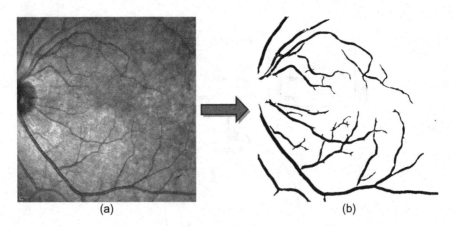

(a)   (b)

Fig. 3. Segmentation process of the retinal vessel tree. (a) Input NIR retinography image. (b) Vessel tree segmentation image.

Next, the vessel centerline is calculated to represent the vasculature as a list of representative segments using as baseline the information that was obtained in the previous segmentation. For this purpose, the implemented strategy was based in the work of Caderno *et al.* [27], where the retinal segments are located by means of the Multi Local Set of Extrinsic Curvature enhanced by the Structure Tensor (MLSEC-ST) operator. The operator detects the tubular structures (ridges or valleys) by means of the analysis of the structure tensor of the segmentation image. And finally, a skeletonization process is done to obtain the representation of the vessel centerline of each vascular segment. Figure 4 presents an example with the result of the centerline identification process.

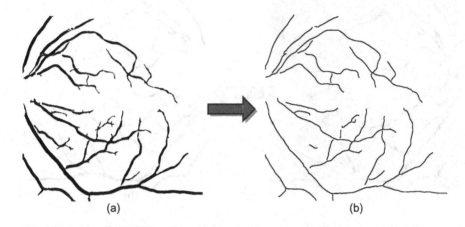

(a)   (b)

Fig. 4. Vessel centerline identification process of the retinal vessel tree. (a) Input vessel tree segmentation image. (b) Vessel tree centerline identification image.

2.2 Optic Disc Location

The optic disc is the region that presents the highest variation of intensities of adjacent pixels in comparison with the rest of the eye fundus. This scenario can disturb the characteristics of the visualization of the vascular structures, a situation that can lead to misclassifications of the surrounding vessel positions and, consequently, of the vessel segments. For that reason, the optic disc region is frequently excluded for the analysis of the retinal vessel tree, as is our case.

To achieve this, we implemented an algorithm based on the work proposed by Blanco *et al.* [28], given its simplicity and the satisfactory results that were obtained for this issue in classical retinographies. Firstly, two Gaussian filters were applied at different scales with a blob operator to identify a region of interest that contains the optic disc. Then, the edges are calculated using the Sobel edge detector [29]. Finally, we extract the optic disc region using the Fuzzy Circular Hough transform [30]. Figure 5(a) shows an example of the optic disc extraction, where r represents the radius of the located optic disc.

In many cases, not only the optic disc but also its contiguous region may include significant intensity changes, being this area of the image biased to bright intensities. As mentioned, this situation can lead to misclassifications of its containing vessels as arteries and veins in posterior stages of the method. To solve this problem, we remove a circular region centered on the optic disc with a radius of $1.5 \times r$ (being r the radius of the identified optic disc), as shown in the example of Fig. 5(b), excluding sufficient region to guarantee the posterior analysis in the desired conditions.

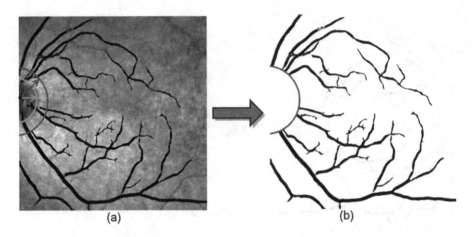

(a)   (b)

Fig. 5. Example of the optic disc location. (a) Optic disc detection, where r represents the radius of the optic disc and $1.5 \times r$ represents the brightness contiguous region to be removed. (b) Removal of the optic disc region in the segmented vasculature image.

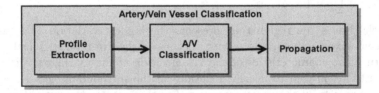

Fig. 6. Steps of the artery/vein vessel classification stage.

2.3 Artery/Vein Vessel Classification

In this stage, we perform the automatic classification of the identified retinal vasculature into arteries and veins. To achieve this goal, we divide this stage into three constituent steps, as represented in Fig. 6. These steps are herein progressively detailed.

Profile Extraction. Firstly, we obtain the vessel profiles in the original NIR retinography image, profiles that are posteriorly used in the process of the blood vessel classification. To achieved that, we based our strategy in the proposal of Vázquez *et al.* [20]. In particular, for each point P of the vessel centerlines, we obtain four equidistant vessel points P_i. These points are used as reference to obtain their corresponding perpendicular lines that are limited by both vessel edges. The vessel intensities over these perpendicular lines determine the vessel profile that is analysed to classify the referenced point, P. This strategy is applied over the entire vascular structure. Figure 7 shows a representative example of the vessel profile extraction, including the representation of the extraction of the perpendicular lines.

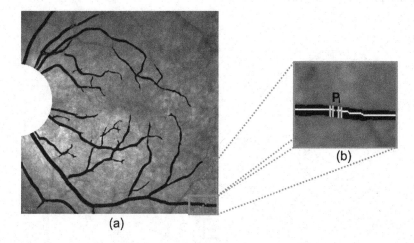

Fig. 7. Example of the vessel profile extraction. (a) Overlap between the result of the vessel segmentation and the NIR retinography image. (b) The four yellow lines, that are perpendicular to the vessel centerlines, identify the vessel profiles at the points that are posteriorly used in the classification process. (Color figure online)

Artery/Vein Classification. In this second step, we use a machine learning approach to discriminate the retinal vessel tree between these two types. Normally, the arteries and veins are distinguished according to its branching pattern and morphology. In this work, the vectors of characteristics are obtained by means of the method proposed by Grisan *et al.* [31] that consist of two components:

- $\mu(H)$ (from HSL color space).
- $\sigma^2(R)$ (from RGB color space).

For the classification task, we selected the k-means clustering algorithm [32], given its simplicity and computational efficiency. This unsupervised learning strategy was used to calculate the centroids for each of the two clusters using the feature vectors as input. As result of this approach, each vascular position of the vessel centerline is categorized as belonging to an artery or vein. In Fig. 8, we explain the result of the classification method where the red points describe arteries whereas blue points indicated veins.

Propagation. In the third and last step, a post-processing strategy is applied using the anatomical knowledge of the retinal vascular structure to identify and correct the possible misclassifications of the individual vessel points. Many times, the vascular points that belong to the same vascular segment can be classified into different categories (see Fig. 9). This particular situation can be caused by possible changes in the brightness profiles, speckle noise or the presence of small capillaries, situations that are frequently present in this type of images and that typically produce these attenuations.

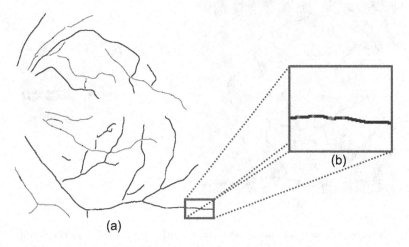

Fig. 8. Example of A/V classification. (a) Results of A/V classification in the entire vascular structure. (b) Red points represent arteries whereas blue points are veins. (Color figure online)

To decrease the influence of these misclassifications, using the context of the classifications, a voting process is carried out in the entire vascular segment. To achieve this, a voting process over each vascular segment is done. Then, the category with the higher number of votes is considered the winning class and, consequently, propagated to all the vessel points of the same vascular segment. In Fig. 10, we can see a representative example of the final classification of the retinal vessels into arteries and veins after using the propagation step.

3   Results and Discussion

The proposed method was tested using a dataset of 30 OCT scans of different patients including their corresponding NIR retinography images. These images

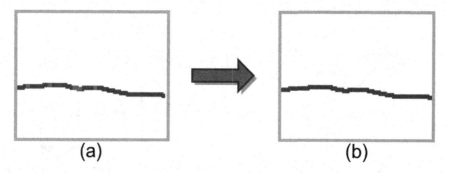

Fig. 9. Example of propagation of the winning class by a majority vote of all the points of the same vascular segment. (a) Vascular segment without propagation. (b) Vascular segment with propagation.

were taken with a confocal scanning laser ophthalmoscope Spectralis® OCT (Heidelberg Engineering). The OCT scans are centered on the macula, from both left and right eyes of healthy patients and presenting a high-resolution. The local ethics committee approved this study, which was conducted in accordance with the tenets of the Helsinki Declaration.

In order to test the performance of the proposed work, the OCT images were manually labelled by an expert clinician, identifying the arteries and veins. The dataset is composed by a total of 597 vascular segments. Next, this dataset was randomly divided in two subsets with the same size, one for training and the other for testing.

The proposed method was evaluated using the following metrics: Accuracy, Sensitivity and Specificity (Eqs. (2), (3) and (4), respectively). These measurements use as reference the true positives (TP), false positives (FP), true negatives (TN), and false negatives (FN) using the artery and vein classifications. In this work, we consider TPs as correctly identified arteries, whereas TNs as correctly identified veins.

$$\text{Accuracy} = \frac{TP + TN}{TP + FP + FN + TN} \qquad (2)$$

$$\text{Sensitivity} = \frac{TP}{TP + FN} \qquad (3)$$

$$\text{Specificity} = \frac{TN}{TN + FP} \qquad (4)$$

Firstly, the classification system before the propagation step was evaluated over all the vessel points of the retinal vessel tree. Figure 11 shows the confusion matrix that is associated with the mentioned manual labelling of the expert clinician. Moreover, Table 1 summarises the performance of the proposed method. As we can see, the results provide a good balance between Accuracy, Sensitivity and Specificity (88.54%, 90.50% and 86.66%, respectively). We also have to consider that these OCT scans are normally taken over the macular region, as is

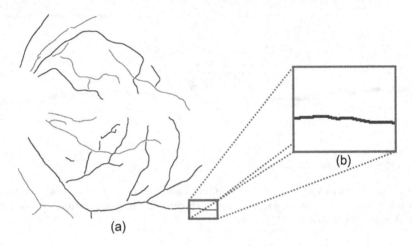

Fig. 10. Final result of the A/V classification stage. (a) Final result of the classification process with propagation applied to all the vascular segments. (b) Final result of a given vascular segment with propagation.

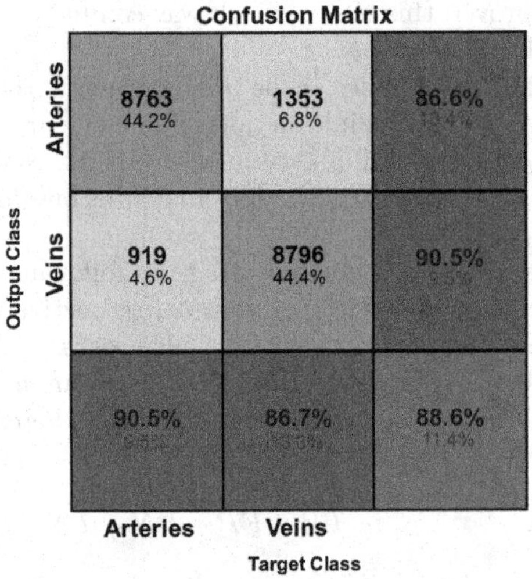

Confusion Matrix

	Arteries	Veins	
Arteries	8763 44.2%	1353 6.8%	86.6% 13.4%
Veins	919 4.6%	8796 44.4%	90.5% 9.5%
	90.5% 9.5%	86.7% 13.3%	88.6% 11.4%

Output Class

Arteries   Veins

Target Class

Fig. 11. Confusion matrix in the A/V classification process without propagation.

the case of all the images of our dataset, region that normally contains smaller vessels in comparison with other parts of the eye fundus, reinforcing the analysis of the obtained performance. Additionally, a ROC curve was performed to compare the results of Sensitivity and Specificity, obtaining an Area Under the Curve (AUC) of 0.886 (see Fig. 12).

Then, the classification approach that includes the propagation stage was evaluated in all the vessel coordinates that were included in the study.

Table 1. Accuracy, specificity and sensitivity results in the A/V classification process without propagation.

Accuracy	Sensitivity	Specificity
88.54%	90.50%	86.66%

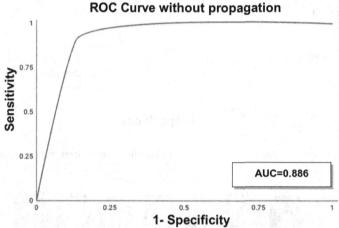

Fig. 12. ROC curve with the results of the classification process without propagation.

As mentioned, the propagation stage identifies and corrects the possible misclassifications of the vessels points in the same vascular segment. Table 2 presents the results of the comparative analysis through Accuracy, Sensitivity and Specificity (90.10%, 91.67% and 88.59%, respectively). As we can see, the results from the proposed method including the propagation step are satisfactory. In addition, Fig. 13 shows the ROC curve obtained by the proposed system, with an area under the curve of 0.901, reinforcing the validity of the designed methodology.

Table 2. Accuracy, specificity and sensitivity results in the A/V classification process with propagation.

Accuracy	Sensitivity	Specificity
90.10%	91.67%	88.59%

Despite the non-existence of any other proposal for the same image modality, we compared the proposed system with other reference approaches of the literature that were proposed for classical retinographies. The results of this comparison are shown in Fig. 14. As we can see, our proposed method offers a competitive performance, outperforming the rest of the strategies, considering that each one was tested in their particular conditions and datasets.

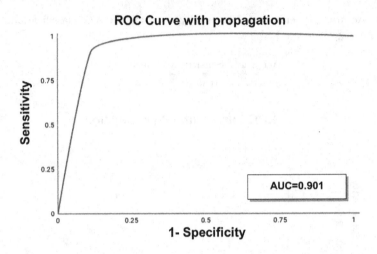

Fig. 13. ROC curve with the results of the classification process using propagation.

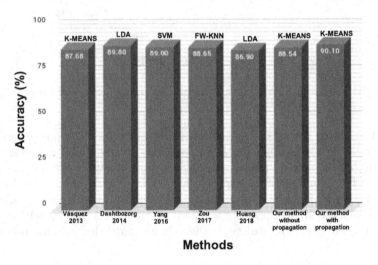

Fig. 14. Vessel classification performance comparative between different techniques of the literature and our proposal.

Figure 15 shows a representative example illustrating the final result of the proposed methodology. As we can see, the method offers accurate results, providing information that can be easily analysed by the experts clinicians in their daily practice.

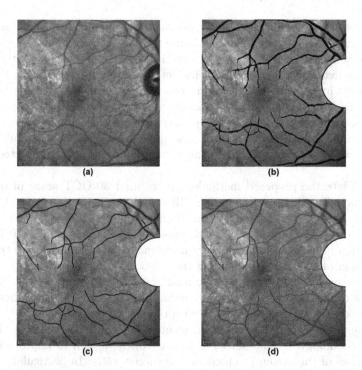

Fig. 15. Example of final result of the proposed methodology. (a) NIR retinography image. (b) Removal of the optic disc region and segmentation of the vasculature image. (c) Vessel tree centerline identification image. (d) Final result of the vascular segment with propagation.

4   Conclusions

The retina is the only tissue of the human body where the morphological information of the blood vessels can be directly obtained non-invasively and in vivo. A precise identification and characterization of the retinal vasculature and potential interesting biomarkers facilitate the diagnose, prevention and treatment of many systemic diseases, such as hypertension, diabetes or arteriosclerosis, among others, that significantly modify and damage the blood vessels architecture.

The CAD systems are increasing its relevance in the daily clinical practice, many of them also including the analysis of many medical image modalities, facilitating the doctor's analysis and diagnosis. Hence, these systems are developed to assist the clinical experts and simplify their work of detection and interpretation of characteristic pathological patterns that are typically present in the medical images of interest.

Among all the modalities, the OCT imaging is a non-invasive medical image modality with a high-speed capture process (being taken in real time) that provides a three-dimensional image of the biological tissues of the eye fundus with micron-level resolution. These specifications enable a precise evaluation and detection of slight modifications in the retinal microcirculation structure.

In this work, we present a new computerized system for the automatic retinal vasculature extraction and classification into arteries and veins using the NIR retinography images. These images are taken in combination with the histological sections in the OCT scans. To identify and classify the vessel structures, the proposed method analyzes the characteristics of each point of the vascular tree structure. The strategy combines the application of the k-means clustering technique with the feature vectors that were obtained from the extracted vessel profiles.

To validate the proposed methodology, we used 30 OCT scans of different patients including their corresponding NIR retinography images. From this OCT image dataset, 597 vessels were identified and manually label by an expert clinician. As result, the proposed method provided an accuracy of a 90.10% in the classification process. This satisfactory performance was achieved with the complete version of the method including the application of the propagation stage. Finally, we performed a comparative analysis with similar proposals that are present in the literature. This review emphasized the relevance and efficiency of the proposed method, comparatively with the rest of the approaches.

Although the favourable obtained results, we expect to reinforce the proposed methodology. In that sense, as future works, we aim to improve the different phases of the method to increase the success rates. In particular, we plan to extend the methodology with the inclusion of a more heterogeneous set of features as well as different testing classifiers to increase the performance of the method. Further, future plans include the design and implementation of an automatic method for the AVR calculation as a relevant biomarker, among others of interest. This way, we take the opportunity of having identified and categorized the arterio-venular tree to derive useful interesting biomarkers for being provided to the specialist. Finally, a CAD system could be developed to combine this methodology with an automatic detection of other eye-related diseases, such as the diabetic retinopathy.

Acknowledgments. This work is supported by the Instituto de Salud Carlos III, Government of Spain and FEDER funds of the European Union through the PI14/02161 and the DTS15/00153 research projects and by the Ministerio de Economía y Competitividad, Government of Spain through the DPI2015-69948-R research project. Also, this work has received financial support from the European Union (European Regional Development Fund - ERDF) and the Xunta de Galicia, Centro singular de investigación de Galicia accreditation 2016-2019, Ref. ED431G/01; and Grupos de Referencia Competitiva, Ref. ED431C 2016-047.

References

1. Eichmann, A., Yuan, L., Moyon, D., Lenoble, F., Pardanaud, L., Breant, C.: Vascular development: from precursor cells to branched arterial and venous networks. Int. J. Dev. Biol. **49**(2–3), 259–267 (2003)
2. de Moura, J., Novo, J., Charlón, P., Barreira, N., Ortega, M.: Enhanced visualization of the retinal vasculature using depth information in OCT. Med. Biol. Eng. Comput. **55**(12), 2209–2225 (2017)
3. Neubauer, A.S., Luedtke, M., Haritoglou, C., Priglinger, S., Kampik, A.: Retinal vessel analysis reproducibility in assessing cardiovascular disease. Optom. Vis. Sci. **85**(4), E247–E254 (2008)
4. Nguyen, T.T., Wong, T.Y.: Retinal vascular changes and diabetic retinopathy. Curr. Diab. Rep. **9**(4), 277–283 (2009)
5. Klein, R., et al.: Are retinal arteriolar abnormalities related to atherosclerosis?: the atherosclerosis risk in communities study. Arterioscler. Thromb. Vasc. Biol. **20**(6), 1644–1650 (2000)
6. Hubbard, L.D., et al.: Methods for evaluation of retinal microvascular abnormalities associated with hypertension/sclerosis in the atherosclerosis risk in communities study1. Ophthalmology **106**(12), 2269–2280 (1999)
7. Bourne, R.R.A., et al.: Magnitude, temporal trends, and projections of the global prevalence of blindness and distance and near vision impairment: a systematic review and meta-analysis. Lancet Glob. Health **5**(9), e888–e897 (2017)
8. MacGillivray, T.J., Trucco, E., Cameron, J.R., Dhillon, B., Houston, J.G., Van Beek, E.J.R.: Retinal imaging as a source of biomarkers for diagnosis, characterization and prognosis of chronic illness or long-term conditions. Br. J. Radiol. **87**(1040), 20130832 (2014)
9. Mookiah, M.R.K., Acharya, U.R., Chua, C.K., Lim, C.M., Ng, E.Y.K., Laude, A.: Computer-aided diagnosis of diabetic retinopathy: a review. Comput. Biol. Med. **43**(12), 2136–2155 (2013)
10. Novo, J., et al.: Hydra: a web-based system for cardiovascular analysis, diagnosis and treatment. Comput. Methods Programs Biomed. **139**, 61–81 (2017)
11. Samagaio, G., Estévez, A., de Moura, J., Novo, J., Isabel Fernandez, M., Ortega, M.: Automatic macular Edema identification and characterization using OCT images. Comput. Methods Programs Biomed. **163**, 47–63 (2018)
12. Liu, D.T., Xu, X.W.: A review of web-based product data management systems. Comput. Ind. **44**(3), 251–262 (2001)
13. Kalev-Landoy, M., Day, A.C., Cordeiro, M.F., Migdal, C.: Optical coherence tomography in anterior segment imaging. Acta Ophthalmol. **85**(4), 427–430 (2007)
14. Michelson, A.A., Morley, E.W.: On the relative motion of the earth and of the luminiferous ether. Sidereal Messenger **6**, 306–310 (1887)
15. Joshi, V.S., Reinhardt, J.M., Garvin, M.K., Abramoff, M.D.: Automated method for identification and artery-venous classification of vessel trees in retinal vessel networks. PloS One **9**(2), e88061 (2014)
16. Dashtbozorg, B., Mendonça, A.M., Campilho, A.: An automatic graph-based approach for artery/vein classification in retinal images. IEEE Trans. Image Process. **23**(3), 1073–1083 (2014)
17. Yang, Y., Bu, W., Wang, K., Zheng, Y., Wu, X.: Automated artery-vein classification in fundus color images. In: Che, W., et al. (eds.) ICYCSEE 2016. CCIS, vol. 623, pp. 228–237. Springer, Singapore (2016). https://doi.org/10.1007/978-981-10-2053-7_21

18. Kondermann, C., Kondermann, D., Yan, M.: Blood vessel classification into arteries and veins in retinal images. In: Medical Imaging 2007: Image Processing, vol. 6512, pp. 651247 (2007)
19. Relan, D., MacGillivray, T., Ballerini, L., Trucco, E.: Retinal vessel classification: sorting arteries and veins. In: 2013 35th Annual International Conference of the IEEE Engineering in Medicine and Biology Society (EMBC), pp. 7396–7399 (2013)
20. Vázquez, S.G., et al.: Improving retinal artery and vein classification by means of a minimal path approach. Mach. Vis. Appl. **24**(5), 919–930 (2013)
21. Welikala, R.A., et al.: Automated arteriole and venule classification using deep learning for retinal images from the UK Biobank cohort. Comput. Biol. Med. **90**, 23–32 (2017)
22. Girard, F., Cheriet, F.: Artery/vein classification in fundus images using CNN and likelihood score propagation. In: 2017 IEEE Global Conference on Signal and Information Processing (GlobalSIP), pp. 720–724 (2017)
23. Huang, F., Dashtbozorg, B., ter Haar Romeny, B.M.: Artery/vein classification using reflection features in retina fundus images. Mach. Vis. Appl. **29**(1), 23–34 (2018)
24. Zou, B.-J., Chen, Y., Zhu, C.-Z., Chen, Z.-L., Zhang, Z.-Q.: Supervised vessels classification based on feature selection. J. Comput. Sci. Technol. **32**(6), 1222–1230 (2017)
25. de Moura, J., Novo, J., Ortega, M., Barreira, N., Charlón, P.: Artery/vein classification of blood vessel tree in retinal imaging. In: VISIGRAPP (4: VISAPP), pp. 371–377 (2017)
26. Calvo, D., Ortega, M., Penedo, M.G., Rouco, J.: Automatic detection and characterisation of retinal vessel tree bifurcations and crossovers in eye fundus images. Comput. Methods Programs Biomed. **103**(1), 28–38 (2011)
27. Caderno, I., Penedo, M., Barreira, N., Mariño, C., González, F.: Precise detection and measurement of the retina vascular tree. Pattern Recog. Image Anal. **15**(2), 523 (2005)
28. Blanco, M., Penedo, M.G., Barreira, N., Penas, M., Carreira, M.J.: Localization and extraction of the optic disc using the fuzzy circular hough transform. In: Rutkowski, L., Tadeusiewicz, R., Zadeh, L.A., Żurada, J.M. (eds.) ICAISC 2006. LNCS (LNAI), vol. 4029, pp. 712–721. Springer, Heidelberg (2006). https://doi.org/10.1007/11785231_74
29. Kittler, J.: On the accuracy of the sobel edge detector. Image Vis. Comput. **1**(1), 37–42 (1983)
30. Philip, K.P., Dove, E.L., McPherson, D.D., Gotteiner, N.L., Stanford, W., Chandran, K.B.: The fuzzy Hough transform-feature extraction in medical images. IEEE Trans. Med. Imaging **13**(2), 235–240 (1994)
31. Grisan, E., Ruggeri, A.: A divide et impera strategy for automatic classification of retinal vessels into arteries and veins. In: Proceedings of the 25th Annual International Conference of the IEEE Engineering in Medicine and Biology Society, 2003, vol. 1, pp. 890–893 (2003)
32. MacQueen, J., et al.: Some methods for classification and analysis of multivariate observations. In: Proceedings of the Fifth Berkeley Symposium on Mathematical Statistics and Probability, vol. 1, 281–297 (1967)

Change Detection and Blob Tracking of Fish in Underwater Scenarios

Martin Radolko[1,2(✉)], Fahimeh Farhadifard[1,2], and Uwe von Lukas[1,2]

[1] Institute for Computer Science, University Rostock, Rostock, Germany
martin.radolko@uni-rostock.de
[2] Fraunhofer Institute for Computer Fraphics Research IGD, Rostock, Germany

Abstract. In this paper, the difficult task of detecting fishes in underwater scenarios is analyzed with a special focus on crowded scenes where the differentiation between separate fishes is even more challenging. An extension for the Gaussian Switch Model is developed for the detection which applies an intelligent update scheme to create more accurate background models even for difficult scenes. To deal with very crowded areas in the scene we use the Flux Tensor to create a first coarse segmentation and only update areas that are with high certainty background. The spatial coherency is increased by the N^2Cut, which is a Ncut adaption to change detection. More relevant information are gathered with a novel blob tracker that uses a specially developed energy function and handling of errors during the change detection. This method keeps the generality of the whole approach so that it can be used for any moving object. The proposed algorithm enabled us to get very accurate underwater segmentations as well as precise results in tracking scenarios.

Keywords: Change detection · Background subtraction ·
Video segmentation · Underwater segmentation · Tracking

1 Introduction

The detection of objects in videos has already a long history in computer vision but still is a very relevant topic today due to new developments such as self-driving cars or robot-aided production which demand a detection in real time and with high precision. In this paper, we address the specific topic of the segregation of a video into two parts, the static background and the moving foreground. This is an important first step in a computer vision pipeline since moving objects are almost always the most interesting part of a scene. In the second part of the paper, a tracking new algorithm is proposed that operates only on the detected foreground blobs and can extract valuable high-level information from the scene.[1]

---

[1] This research has been supported by the German Federal State of Mecklenburg-Western Pomerania and the European Social Fund under grant ESF/IV-BMB35-0006/12.

To detect these moving objects we assume a static camera, so that stationary objects also appear stationary in the video. This makes it possible to create a model of the static background of the scene, e.g. with statistical methods, and every object that does not fit the model is therefore labeled as a moving object. In recent years many of these background modeling and subtraction algorithms have been proposed, but as the tasks and applications of these methods are as plentiful as the suggested algorithms there is still a lot of research to be done.

In this paper, we focus on crowded scenes which pose a particularly difficult task for background subtraction algorithms since the permanent exposure to foreground objects often leads to an adaption of the background model to these foreground objects, especially when they are all similar in color like the fishes in a swarm. To cope with this we introduce pre-segmentations created with a Flux Tensor-based optical flow which are used to exclude parts of the current frame from the updating process of the background model. These parts are very likely to be foreground since they are in motion and therefore excluding them limits the background modeling to the background parts of the scene.

Furthermore, we enhance the Gaussian Switch Model approach proposed in [1] with the Mixture of Gaussian idea, a foreground model and an intelligent updating scheme to make it overall more robust for difficult scenarios. The foreground model proved to be particularly useful with fish swarms because there the difference between the different foreground objects was minor and thereby the time for the model to adapt to a new object was negligible. Lastly, since the approach so far is solely pixel-based, a spatial component was added to make the segmentations coincide with the edges in the frame and better conform to the smoothness of natural images.

To extract more information from the scene, like the directions of movement or speeds of the objects, a tracking algorithm is proposed that uses only the information from the segmenter by applying a special energy function. To account for segmentation errors or (semi-)crowded scenes where fish swim in front of each other, the unification and splitting of these foreground blobs is also considered in the tracking process so that overall very accurate (but not precise) tracking results can be achieved.

2   State of the Art

Background modeling and subtraction has been used in computer vision for a long time already. The first approaches date back to the beginning of the 90ths [2] and commercial applications followed soon. An example is the Patent [3], where background subtraction is used for video compression. The most frequently used approaches in recent years have been statistical methods that use Gaussians to model each pixel of the background. It started with the Single Gaussian approach [4] where one Gaussian distribution is used to describe one pixel-value. They are usually updated with a running Gaussian:

$$m_{t+1} = \alpha m_t + (1 - \alpha)p. \tag{1}$$

Here m_t is the mean of the Gaussian at the time step t, p is the pixel value taken from the current frame and $\alpha \in (0, 1)$ is the update rate.

However, this simple method is not sufficient to model difficult scenes – e.g. permanent exposure to many foreground objects or slightly moving background objects – and therefore in [5] an algorithm was proposed which does not use only one Gaussian but a mixture of several Gaussians. This proved to be a very effective way of modeling the background and is henceforth used with great success in combination with other methods. Together with a Markov Random Field the Mixture of Gaussian (MoG) is used in [6] and can generate great results on the *Wallflower* dataset. In conjunction with an optical flow, the Flux Tensor, it is used in [7] and achieves state of the art results on the *changedetection.net* dataset.

Another approach is to keep a set of samples for each pixel instead of directly modeling a probability distribution. The *ViBe* algorithm in [8] keeps and updates the samples for each pixel randomly so that even old values can have an influence on the current segmentation (although with a decreasing probability). Furthermore, the updating process diverges spatially so that an update of one sample can influence the neighboring samples which makes the model spatially coherent to some degree. The segmentation itself is done by counting the number of values that agree with the current value.

There are also approaches which automatically combine whole segmentations of various methods in a way that the output is better than each individual input. A current approach is [9] which uses the large database of different segmentations of the *changedetection.net* dataset and combines the best performing of them. The fusion process itself is not done by a Bayesian Model, as in the other cases, but with a genetic algorithm. The genetic algorithm has the segmentations and a set of functions it can apply to them and tries to find the best combination. These functions are e.g. morphological erosion or dilation, logical *AND* or *OR* operations or a majority vote on the binary segmentations. In this way, it is possible to improve the already very good results of the top algorithms. However, to run their genetic algorithm ground truth data is necessary and, therefore, they use one video of each category (and the corresponding ground truth data) to find the best combination of segmentations and functions.

After the change detection, the next step is the extraction of valuable information from these results, e.g. about the behavior of fish. To do this it is necessary to associate the detected objects with found objects in the previous (and succeeding) frames. With these associations, a tracking of individual objects can be realized and allows the computation of movement speeds, paths and other valuable higher-level features. Change detection is a very general approach and not limited to a specific object type, nor has it the need for a learning phase for every new object class. Therefore, the tracking approach used should be also very general and not based on any object-specific features (e.g. eyes, faces, colors, etc.). Furthermore, the similarity of the detected fish in a swarm can be a great problem. When humans or cars are tracked there are usually quite notable differences between objects, e.g. in the size (car or truck), color (blue jacket or green jacket) or shape (thin or big). These differences result in distinct features for each object which can then be matched between different frames [10,11]. For different fish of the same species – or even a swarm – these features have to be expected to be very similar and additionally degraded because of the underwater scenario. Another distinguishing attribute which is often used in in-air tracking is depth, however, it is very hard to obtain depth information in underwater scenes because of the refraction and absorption properties of water.

Based on this, the here presented tracking approach will solely rely on the information contained in the segmentation provided by the change detection. This allows a general usage of the approach in underwater scenarios as well as in-air videos to track fish, cars, humans or any other moving object. The strategy used here is in sharp contrast with most other tracking methods where a specific object detector is trained, e.g. [12] uses Haar-like features and an SVM classifier to detect humans. The tracking of any arbitrary foreground detections made by a change detection approach can become extremely difficult, especially when many objects are present in the scene at the same time and overlap each other. However, this strategy preserves the generality of the overall approach and can distinguish even between very similar objects.

3   Change Detection

The proposed change detection method consists of three steps. The first step is the Gaussian Switch Model and its extension (eGSM), afterwards coarse segmentations are derived from the Flux Tensor and used to improve the updating of the eGSM in crowded scenes. The last part is a spatial approach which adapts the segmented objects of the background subtraction to the edges in the image by using a NCut based approach.

3.1   Gaussian Switch Model

The GSM was introduced in [1] and models the background of the scene with two distinct Gaussian models for each pixel in the video. Of these two models, one is updated conservatively (only parts classified as background are updated) and one is updated blindly (the whole image is updated) which allows the method to benefit from the advantages of both strategies.

The conservative strategy has the problem that rapid changes of the background will not get incorporated into the model, an example of this would be a car that parks and therefore, after some time, should become a part of the background model. The blind update strategy has the problem that the foreground objects get included into the background model as well and especially in scenes with a constant presence of foreground objects this can lead to a corrupted background model.

The GSM now has models with both of these updating strategies and normally the one with the conservative updating strategy is used for the background subtraction because it creates a clearer and more accurate background model in most situations. However, scenes in which the conservative update model fails can be detected by a comparison of both models and if such a situation is detected the model is switched to the blindly updated one.

3.2 Extension of the GSM

The extended GSM combines the original approach with the Mixture of Gaussian idea. This increases the accuracy further, especially in difficult situations like the underwater scenes we use for evaluation later, but it also makes the whole approach more complex.

Instead of using two Gaussians we apply two Mixture of Gaussian (MoG) models and update one of them conservatively and one blindly, similar to the GSM. A foreground model was added with a high adaption rate to quickly adjust to different moving objects in the scene. We chose a simple single Gaussian model for this because it should not model different foreground objects at the same time but only the most recent one.

Each of the two MoGs consists of a variable number of Gaussians and each of them is described by three values: mean m, variance v and weight w. The mean and variance describe the shape of the probability distribution and the weight is a measure of how much data supports this Gaussian. To be considered as a part of the background model a minimum weight is necessary, otherwise, the Gaussian is assumed to belong to a foreground object which only appeared shortly in the video. We define the minimum weight as a percentage of the sum over all weights of a MoG and set the percentage to $1/\#\text{Gaussians}$.

The MoGs are updated by first searching for the Gaussian that matches the current data the best and then applying the standard running Gaussian update on them. For a pixel x with pixel-value p_x and update rate α the equations would be the following

$$
\begin{aligned}
v_x &= \alpha \cdot v_x + (1 - \alpha) \cdot (m_x - p_x)^2, \\
m_x &= \alpha \cdot m_x + (1 - \alpha) \cdot p_x, \\
w_x &= w_x + 1.
\end{aligned}
\tag{2}
$$

The α value is specified dynamically according to the weight value of the Gaussian in the following way

$$
\alpha = \frac{1}{w_x}
\tag{3}
$$

but it is capped at 0.5. Furthermore, to prevent an overflow of the weight value and limit the impact of old values on the model, there is a decay of all weight values in the MoG.

Together, this ensures that Gaussians which until now only got very few data points to back them up or only old data points which are not reliable anymore adapt quickly to new values. At the same time, Gaussians which were updated frequently (and therefore have a high weight) will get a low update rate so that they are not strongly affected by outliers. Because of this mechanism, the decay factor strongly impacts the value of α, especially in longer videos, and is, therefore, the most important parameter. Based on empiric values it was set to 0.995 in all following experiments.

A new Gaussian will be created if no matching Gaussian could be found in the existing MoG model, it has the initial values $m_x = p_x$, $v_x = 0.01$ and $w_x = 1$. Should there already exist the maximum number of Gaussians that are allowed, the Gaussian with the lowest weight will be deleted and replaced with the new one. The foreground model is also updated as a running Gaussian but with a fixed α_F value as there is no weight value in the Single Gaussian model. Also, the update rate is higher than in the background models so that it generally adapts quickly to new foreground objects. We set it to $\alpha_F = 0.64$ for our experiments.

Nonetheless, before the updating process of any model starts, the segmentation will be done with the existing model and based on this result the different models will get modified accordingly. The blindly updated MoG is updated every time regardless of the segmentation result. The conservative MoG only gets updated when a pixel was classified as background and the foreground model only when the pixel was marked as foreground. The segmentation itself is created by comparing the current frame with the two MoGs. However, only the Gaussians that have a weight that exceeds the minimum weight are considered part of the background model. If for any of these Gaussians the inequality

$$\exp\left(-\left\|\frac{1}{\beta} \cdot \frac{\bar{p}_x - \bar{m}_x}{\bar{v}_x}\right\|_2^2\right) > 0.5 \tag{4}$$

is true, the pixel value and the MoG are classified as a match. The vectors $\bar{p}_x$, $\bar{m}_x$ and $\bar{v}_x$ contain the values of the three channels of the pixel x and the operations between them are all element-wise. The variance as a divisor makes the thresholding process adaptive so that it is less sensitive if the video contains less noise and vice versa. The value β in the inequality is a parameter controlling the general sensitivity of the approach and we set it with 0.5 quite low since the foreground objects are often quite similar to the background and therefore a high sensitivity is necessary.

If a pixel matches with Gaussians in both MoGs, it will be classified as background. If it only matches with one of them the foreground model is taken as a tiebreaker. The foreground model is compared to the pixel value according to the inequality (4) and if they coincide the pixel marked as foreground, otherwise as background.

Similar to the original GSM algorithm, there is a switching between the conservatively updated MoG and the blindly updated MoG to compensate for the weaknesses of conservative updating scheme. Such an event should occur when there is an area in the scene which is static and constantly classified as foreground, because then an error in the background modeling happened with a high probability and should be corrected.

To detect such an error two conditions are checked. First if the blindly updated MoG and the foreground model are similar as this indicates that the pixel has been classified mainly as foreground in the recent past. If

$$m^{BG,k} - m^{FG} < \frac{v^{FG}}{2} \tag{5}$$

holds for all three channels of a pixel the models are considered similar. Here $m^{BG,k}$ is the mean of the k-th Gaussian of the conservatively updated MoG and it is sufficient if the inequality is true for one of the Gaussians of a pixel. This similarity could also occur when there appear many foreground objects in a short period of time. To filter these events out the variance can be used since foreground objects usually generate higher variations in the image due to their movement. Hence the second conditions is a small variance and the threshold is set to the median of all variances of the completely updated MoG. If both of these conditions are fulfilled (inequality 5 and small variance) an error in the conservatively updated MoG is very probable and therefore the blindly updated MoG is used in these cases.

Lastly, if two Gaussians in one MoG get very similar over time these Gaussians should be unified as they are modeling the same object. The similarity is checked with

$$\|\tilde{m}^{G1} - \tilde{m}^{G2}\|_2^2 < \min(\|\tilde{v}^{G1}\|_2^2, \|\tilde{v}^{G2}\|_2^2) \tag{6}$$

and if the inequality holds, both old Gaussians are deleted and a new Gaussian created with the following values

$$m^{new} = \frac{w^{G1}m^{G1} + w^{G2}m^{G2}}{w^{G1} + w^{G2}},$$
$$v^{new} = \frac{w^{G1}v^{G1} + w^{G2}v^{G2}}{w^{G1} + w^{G2}},$$
$$w^{new} = w^{G1} + w^{G2}. \tag{7}$$

Altogether, this extension of the standard GSM leads to a more robust and accurate model building process since now several different objects can be represented by the model at the same time and the update rate adapts itself automatically based on the confidence the model has in the data. Three examples of modeled backgrounds can be seen in Fig. 1.

3.3   Flux Tensor as a Pre-segmentation

Two-dimensional structure tensors have been widely used for edge and corner detection in images. With computational efficient filters information of derivatives of the image are extracted and used to detect edges or corners. Motion information can be recovered in a similar way, but here a three-dimensional tensor is necessary which is applied on the image volume of a video.

For the location $p = (x, y, t)$ in an image volume the optical flow $v(p) = [v_x, v_y, v_t]$ is usually computed with the formula

$$\frac{\partial I(p)}{\partial x} v_x + \frac{\partial I(p)}{\partial y} v_y + \frac{\partial I(p)}{\partial t} v_t = 0 \tag{8}$$

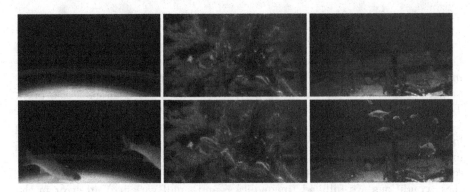

Fig. 1. The top row depicts three background models created with the extended GSM and below that are the corresponding original frames from the video. The background models are visualized by taking the Gaussian with the highest weight of the conservatively updated MoG and displaying the mean of it. (images from [13]).

which leads to an eigenvalue problem that is costly to solve. To extract the valuable motion information without solving the eigenvalue problem the flux tensor was proposed in [14] and is defined by

$$\int_{p \in \Omega} \Big(\frac{\partial^2 I(p)}{\partial x \partial t}\Big)^2 + \Big(\frac{\partial^2 I(p)}{\partial y \partial t}\Big)^2 + \Big(\frac{\partial^2 I(p)}{\partial t \partial t}\Big)^2 dz = \int_{p \in \Omega} \Big\| \frac{\partial}{\partial t} \nabla I(p) \Big\|^2 dz, \quad (9)$$

for the pixel p and a small area Ω around it. By computing the Flux Tensor, one value per pixel is obtained which represents the magnitude of motion in that area (but not the direction of the movement) and this can be thresholded to get a binary segmentation.

However, the Flux Tensor has difficulties segmenting the interior of the objects that are uniform and often only detected the edges. To cope with this behavior a density-based spatial clustering is applied after the thresholding and then a convex hull created around these clusters of foreground detections. Overall, moving objects are detected quite reliable but their shapes are not very accurate (see Fig. 2).

Despite this lack in accuracy, the flux tensor has the advantage to be available without a learning phase. The eGSM has an elaborated learning algorithm but there still exist problems in very crowded scenes. The cause for this is inherent in the modeling of the background: it works under the assumption that the background objects are visible most of the time and will, therefore, adapt to the objects that appear the most.

This assumption is true in almost all of the background subtraction scenarios and works very well. However, in some of our scenes, there is a fish swarm in a certain area so that in the majority of the time fishes are visible there and not the real background. Therefore, the background model would adapt to the color of the fishes and not to that of the background. To solve this problem areas with high movement (detected by the Flux Tensor) are masked for the updating of the

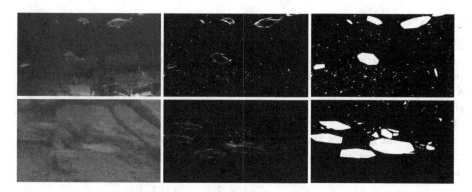

Fig. 2. The Flux Tensor on two examples. The image in the middle shows the result of the Flux Tensor, higher intensities depict higher movement. On the right side is the segmentation after clustering and building a convex hull around the foreground clusters. The noise is due to the Marine Snow (small floating particles). The images are taken from [13].

background model. Thereby, areas with a high probability of being foreground are not updated since it would only train the model with false information.

The principle is similar to that of the conservative updating scheme which excluded pixels that are classified as foreground from the updating. However, this does only work if the background model is already accurate and a good segmentation can be provided. The pre-segmentations now help with the initial creation of an accurate background model since they do not need any training phase. An example of this effect can be seen in Fig. 3.

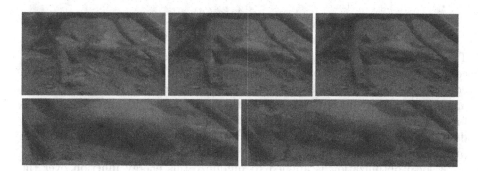

Fig. 3. Effect of the Flux Tensor on the background modeling. In the top row (left to right): the original frame and the visualizations of the two background models with and without pre-segmentation. The next row shows a close up in an area where many fishes were passing by. The model created with pre-segmentations (left) has clearly less artifacts of fishes and is also not as blurry. (images from [13]).

3.4   N²Cut

The whole approach to this point is completely pixel-wise and only uses the temporal changes to detect foreground objects. However, natural images have spatial properties that can be used to further improve the derived segmentations, e.g. a certain degree of smoothness is always present and edges in the segmentation should be aligned to edges of the frame since they often represent borders of objects.

The N²Cut from [15] tackles this problem. It is based on a GraphCut with a special energy function derived from the NCut energy function which is defined as

$$NCut(A, B) = \frac{Cut(A, B)}{Assoc(A)} + \frac{Cut(A, B)}{Assoc(B)},$$

$$Assoc(A) = \sum_{i \in A, j \in A \cup B} w_{ij},$$

$$Cut(A, B) = \sum_{i \in A, j \in B} w_{ij}, \tag{10}$$

where A and B are the sets of foreground and background pixels and w_{ij} is a weight function. The weight between two pixel i and j is defined by the sum over the three color channels

$$w_{ij} = |r_i - r_j| + |g_i - g_j| + |b_i - b_j|. \tag{11}$$

If the pixels are not neighbors the weight is 0. Based on this, the N²Cut is defined as

$$N^2Cut(A, B) = \frac{Cut(A, B)}{nAssoc(A)} + \frac{Cut(A, B)}{nAssoc(B)},$$

$$nAssoc(A) = \frac{Assoc(A) + 1}{\sum_{i \in A, j \in A \cup B, \exists e_{ij}} 1 + 1}. \tag{12}$$

The Cut and $Assoc$ values are here normalized by the number of elements that contribute to them. Thereby, it still favors segmentations that are aligned with edges in the image, similar to the NCut, but also is free of any bias for a certain amount of background or foreground in the segmentation. The NCut has a bias for segmentations with an equal amount of fore- and background which is not desirable for video segmentation where often no foreground objects at all are present in the scene.

A local optimization is applied to minimize this energy function over the already existing segmentation derived from the background subtraction. A single pixel d at the border between foreground and background is located and its classification is changed. The new N²cut value, after changing d from set A to B (or vice versa), can be computed very efficiently with just a few additions and subtractions by using the following formulas

$$Cut(A \setminus \{d\}, B \cup \{d\}) = Cut(A, B) + \sum_{i \in A \,\wedge\, i \in N(d)} w_{id} - \sum_{j \in B \,\wedge\, j \in N(d)} w_{jd}, \tag{13}$$

$$Assoc(A \setminus \{d\}) = Assoc(A) - \sum_{i \in B \, \wedge \, i \in N(d)} w_{id}, \tag{14}$$

$$Assoc(B \cup \{d\}) = Assoc(B) + \sum_{i \in A \, \wedge \, i \in N(d)} w_{id}. \tag{15}$$

Here $N(d)$ is the four connected neighborhood region of d. Thereby, the N^2cut value and the segmentation can be gradually improved without the high computational cost of the global optimization of a cut value over a whole image. To increase the range/effect of the minimization we apply it over several scales of the image, starting with the smallest size and using the result from there as a starting segmentation for the next scale. Overall, this proved to be an efficient way to smooth the segmentation derived from the background subtraction and align it to the edges of objects in the frame. An example is depicted in Fig. 4.

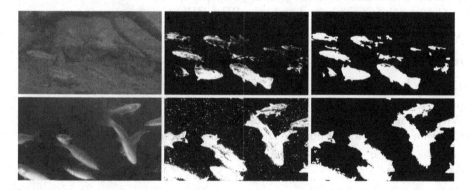

Fig. 4. The effect of the N^2Cut method. On the left are the original images, in the middle the segmentations after background subtraction and on the right is the result after applying the N^2Cut. (images from [13]).

4 Underwater Blob Tracking

To extract valuable information from the segmentations derived with change detection, e.g. about the behavior of fish, it is necessary to associate the detected objects with found objects in the previous and succeeding frames. With these associations, a tracking of individual objects can be realized and allows the computation of movement speeds, paths and other valuable higher-level features. The first step in the building of this tracking method is a matching function that evaluates how similar two foreground detections are.

4.1 Matching Function

At first, all components in the binary segmentations must be extracted so that they can then be matched against each other. For this, a random foreground pixel is chosen in the segmentation as the start of a new component. Then all neighboring foreground pixels are added to this component and this is repeated for all newly added foreground pixels until no further foreground pixels can be added and then a new, so far unused, pixel is chosen to start the next component. These components will be called connected components since each pixel in it can be connected to each other pixel in that component by a path. Each of these connected components has a list of properties that is used to compare them against each other, these properties are:

- Height and width of the bounding box in pixels – BBh, BBw
- Number of pixels that belong to that connected component – NoP
- Coordinates of the centroid of the connected component – (Cx, Cy)
- Velocity in pixels per frame (of the whole component) – Vel
- Direction of movement (of the centroid) – (Dx, Dy)
- Growth rate: change of the NoP in pixels per frame – GR
- Center point of the bounding box – BBx, BBy

All properties that rely on a trend/history are initialized as zero (velocity, growth rate) except the direction of movement which is initialized as $Dx = \sqrt{\frac{1}{2}}$ and $Dy = \sqrt{\frac{1}{2}}$. Between two matched components these values can then be computed, e.g. the GR is defined as the change in the NoP between two components. With this information, the properties get updated in the fashion of a running Gaussian with each new match. The GR will be updated in the following way

$$GR_n = \alpha \cdot GR_{n-1} + (1 - \alpha) \cdot NoP_n - NoP_{n-1}, \tag{16}$$

with α chosen as 0.9. In this way, one wrong detection of a component does not completely change these parameters, but they can still quickly adapt to changes (in around 5 to 10 frames).

The other values can be directly inferred from the connected component itself. With these properties, a measure of similarity between two components can be derived which will be called Connected Component Similarity Measure ($CCSM$) in the following. To compute the CCSM it is assumed that two connected components (CC_1 and CC_2) are from consecutive frames. The lower the $CCSM$ value, the more likely it is that these components represent the same object of the scene and vice versa. The first part of the $CCSM$ is defined as

$$CCSM_a = |BBh_1 - BBh_2| + |BBw_1 - BBw_2| \quad + \sqrt{|(NoP_1 + GR_1) - NoP_2|} \tag{17}$$

$$+ |(Cx_1 + Dx_1 \cdot Vel_1) - Cx_2| \quad + |(Cy_1 + Dy_1 \cdot Vel_1) - Cy_2| \tag{18}$$

$$+ |(BBx_1 + Dx_1 \cdot Vel_1) - BBx_2| \quad + |(BBy_1 + Dy_1 \cdot Vel_1) - BBy_2|. \tag{19}$$

In 17 the sizes of the different bounding boxes are compared under the assumption that they should be very similar if the connected components are representing the same object in consecutive frames. In the next line, the number of pixels is evaluated where $NoP_1 + GR_1$ is the estimated number of pixels in the next frame and should, therefore, be close to NoP_2. Then the 2nd root is taken of that value because it describes a two-dimensional property (the pixels can lie in x- and y-direction) whereas the other values describe one-dimensional values (e.g. length of the bounding box in x-direction). In 18 the positions of the Centroids are compared and $Cx_1 + Dx_1 \cdot Vel_1$ is the estimated x-coordinate in the next frame which is compared to Cx_2. It should be noted that the direction of movement is always scaled so that $\|(Dx, Dy)\|_2 = 1$ and therefore $Dx \cdot Vel$ is the estimated movement in x-direction in pixels per frame. A similar comparison is done in 19 with the middle point of the bounding box.

One important aspect that is missing from the CCSM so far is the shape of the detected foreground object. For this, the bounding box of the connected component is taken and its coordinate system is transferred to polar coordinates in a new frame with a fixed size of 360×360. For this, the center of the bounding box is taken and from there the image is sampled in 360 different angles with a sampling rate of 360.

In order to compare the shapes of two connected components, both are transferred to polar coordinates and then five different scores are computed. These scores work under the assumption that the same detected foreground object in two consecutive frames has a barely changed 3D rotation and pixel size, that means, for example, that the distance and angle to the camera are similar in both frames. Therefore, the aim of this shape comparison is not to be rotational and size invariant in contrast to most of the recent work in shape recognition where exactly this is the objective [16,17]. In this scenario, since fish have very similar shapes, especially if they are of the same species, the rotation of the fish in the scene can be an important indicator to differentiate between fish in an underwater scene and should be used.

The first shape feature that is computed is the percentage of detections (or non-detections) that do not match in both polar images and it can be seen as a general measure of the similarity of the two detected objects. Let PI^1 and PI^2 be the binary polar images of two connected components and $PI_{(\xi,l)}$ the value at angle ξ and length l, the shape feature is then defined as

$$Sh_a = 1 - \left[\sum_{\xi=1}^{s} \sum_{l=1}^{s} g(PI^1_{(\xi,l)}, PI^2_{(\xi,l)}) \right] / s^2, \tag{20}$$

with

$$g(x,y) = \begin{cases} 1 & \text{if } x = y \\ 0 & \text{else} \end{cases} \quad \text{or} \quad g(x) = \begin{cases} 1 & \text{if } x = 255 \text{ (foreground)} \\ 0 & \text{else} \end{cases}. \tag{21}$$

The s in the equation comes from the size of the polar images and is 360 since the polar images are sampled to be 360×360. The second feature is based on a comparison of the number of foreground pixels per angle of the two frames. Since no rotation is assumed the same object should have a similar extension in each angle in both frames, this is checked with:

$$Sh_b = \sum_{\xi=1}^{s} \left| \sum_{l=1}^{s} g(PI^1_{(\xi,l)}) - \sum_{l=1}^{s} g(PI^2_{(\xi,l)}) \right| / s^2 \tag{22}$$

The third and fourth features are similar but evaluate each pixel separately and give them different weights based on their distance to the center of the original detection. The third feature focuses on pixels close to the center and the fourth on pixels at the outside. Furthermore, the standard Euclidean metric is applied so that outliers have a stronger impact.

$$Sh_c = \sum_{\xi,l=1}^{s} \left| \frac{l}{s} \cdot g(PI^1_{(\xi,l)}) - \frac{l}{s} \cdot g(PI^2_{(\xi,l)}) \right| / \sum_{l=1}^{s} l \tag{23}$$

$$Sh_d = \sum_{\xi,l=1}^{s} \left| \frac{s-l}{s} \cdot \left(g(PI^1_{(\xi,l)}) - g(PI^2_{(\xi,l)}) \right) \right| / \sum_{l=1}^{s} l \tag{24}$$

The last shape feature compares the contours of both connected components. First, both polar images are reduced to their edges. The result of this is the binary contour/edge images $Cont^1$ and $Cont^2$ with the same dimensions as PI^1. Afterwards, the contours are compared by computing for each angle the minimal distance in pixels from a contour pixel in one of the connected components to any contour pixel in the same angle in the other connected component. It is computed in the following way

$$She = \frac{1}{2s} \sum_{\xi,l=1}^{s} g(Cont^1_{(\xi,l)}) \min_{\substack{l_2=-s...s \\ g(Cont^2_{(\xi,l_2)})>0}} |l-l_2| + g(Cont^2_{(\xi,l)}) \min_{\substack{l_2=-s...s \\ g(Cont^1_{(\xi,l_2)})>0}} |l-l_2|, \tag{25}$$

where first $Cont^1$ is compared with $Cont^2$ and then the other way around. The term $g(Cont^1_{(\xi,l_2)}, 1)$ is just a check whether the binary contour image is true or false at that position. Furthermore, there appear negative length values in this expression and they imply that the original connected component is scanned in the opposite angle and therefore:

$$Cont_{(\xi,-l)} = Cont_{(\beta,l)} \quad \text{with} \quad \beta = (\xi + 180) \mod 360. \tag{26}$$

Finally, with these five shape features the shape component of the CCSM can be easily derived,

$$CCSM_b = \sqrt{\sum_{k \in \{a,b,c,d,e\}} Sh_k^2}. \tag{27}$$

After the first two components that compared general properties and the shapes, the third and last component of the CCSM focuses on outlier detection. It prevents the matching of connected components that are e.g. in completely different parts of the frame or have very different sizes but are otherwise very similar. This is done by using the exponential function so that a large disparity in one parameter dominates the whole CCSM value. Otherwise the computation is resembling calculation of the first component ($CCSM_a$) with the Eqs. 17 to 19. It is defined as

$$CCSM_c = \tag{28}$$
$$\exp\left(|Cx_1 + Dx_1 \cdot Vel_1 - Cx_2| - z\right) \qquad + \exp\left(|Cy_1 + Dy_1 \cdot Vel_1 - Cy_2| - z\right) \tag{29}$$
$$+ \exp\left(|BBh_1 - BBh_2| - z\right) \qquad + \exp\left(|BBw_1 - BBw_2| - z\right) \tag{30}$$
$$+ \exp\left(|BBx_1 + Dx_1 Vel_1 - BBx_2| - z\right) \quad + \exp\left(|BBy_1 + Dy_1 Vel_1 - BBy_2| - z\right) \tag{31}$$
$$+ \exp\left(|(NoP_1 + GR_1) - NoP_2|\right), \tag{32}$$

where z is a parameter that was set empirically and is based on the image size

$$z = \frac{\sqrt{FrameHeight \cdot FrameWidth}}{25}. \tag{33}$$

The subtraction of z in conjunction with the exponential function ensures that only properties which are very different (outliers) contribute substantially to the $CCSM_c$ component. For example, if the heights of the bounding boxes are less than z pixels apart, the element 30 will contribute less than 1 to the overall sum. However, if the disparity is larger than z it will increase very quickly so that basically all connected components where the difference is greater than z will be rejected. The same applies to all the components of the $CCSM_c$ in the lines 29 to 31 and in 32 it is checked whether the overall number of pixel is not changing by more than 15% in consecutive frames. With these three components, the final $CCSM$ is computed in the following way

$$CCSM = CCSM_b \cdot CCSM_a + CCSM_c. \tag{34}$$

The multiplication of the values $CCSM_a$ and $CCSM_b$ ensures that both values are important for the matching, even though the $CCSM_b$ is usually much smaller than the $CCSM_a$. The $CCSM_c$ should always be very small for correct matches and its only purpose is the rejection of wrong matches.

4.2   Optimal Match Finding

To now compute the best matches between the connected components of two frames according to the $CCSM$, the first step is the creation of a list of all connected components for each of the two frames. However, it has to be considered that two connected components in on frame can merge into one larger component in the next or vice versa. This can be caused by two or more fish swimming in front or behind each other but also by segmentation errors of the change detection approach, two examples of this can be seen in Fig. 6. To take this into account, not only the single connected components are considered but also the unifications of two or more connected components that are close to each other. This means that if three connected components are near to each other, that the three single components would be considered for matching but also the three possible different unions of two of them as well as the union of all three of them.

There exist methods for the task of computing the best overall matchings between two frames, e.g. the Hungarian Method which was originally introduced by Kuhn in [18] and is still often used today [19]. However, since the matching method applied here should also take unions and splits of connected components into consideration, it cannot be used. To find the globally best matching between two frames gradually matching components (e.g. greedy approach) will not be enough, the algorithm must look at all objects and their possible matches at the same time. When splits and unions are allowed this becomes extremely difficult since each component can be a part of many splits and/or unions. Therefore, an adaption of this method that takes unions and splits into account is probably not feasible. The here presented method focuses on finding a local optimum in a shorter runtime.

Considering the possibility of unions of separate connected components makes the handling of splits and merges more accurate but can also be very computational intensive when many smaller components are close to each other. For n components the number of possible combinations is

$$\sum_{k=1}^{n} \binom{n}{k} = \sum_{k=1}^{n} \frac{n!}{(n-k)! \cdot k!}, \tag{35}$$

which means e.g. 15 combinations for $n = 4$ or 31 for $n = 5$. If many small objects are expected in a scene and time is a concern, it is, therefore, advisable to limit the number of possible unions, e.g. by only considering unions of at most two or three components. To be considered for a union the connected components must be close enough together. Here the minimal distance between the borders is important since that is the region where a split or merge would most likely happen. Therefore, to be considered close, two pixels have to exist (one from each connected component) that have a distance of less than T_{CCdist} pixels between them. The threshold is dependent on the resolution of the video and, therefore, it is set to $T_{CCdist} = z$ (compare with Eq. 33).

A union of two or more connected components consists of all the pixels that belong to each of the connected components which are combined. Therefore, the same properties can be derived as for a connected component, e.g. bounding box, number of pixels and so on. Values like the growth rate, direction of movement or velocity are averaged over all connected components weighted by their size. For example, the velocity of a union of t connected components would be

$$Vel_{union} = \frac{1}{\sum_{s=1}^{t} NoP_s} \cdot \sum_{k=1}^{t} NoP_k \cdot Vel_k. \tag{36}$$

With these properties defined, the unions can be compared to connected components or other unions by using the $CCSM$. The only new thing about the unions is that they also have a list of all old connected components they are composed of. This is important in case the union splits later again so that the old connected components can be matched correctly again.

When for each of the two frames (between which the matches have to be found) a list of all connected components and possible unions is created the actual matching can start. For this, the $CCSM$ is computed for every possible match. That means if the list for the first frame has length t and for the second frame length s, a $t \times s$ Matrix of CCSM values is created. Now, let the entry (k, u) be the lowest value in the whole matrix, this means that the connected components k (from frame one) and u (from frame two) are the best possible match at the moment and will be assigned to each other. These two values and all unions that include one of them – or, if they are unions already themselves, all connected components that belong to them and unions that include at least one of them – have to be deleted from the matrix and then the process can be repeated. This is depicted in Fig. 5 where the row and column corresponding to the element (k, u) get deleted and two other elements – indicated in dashed lines – also get deleted because the corresponding elements contain the just matched elements k and l and therefore a matching in the next step is not possible.

By repeating this process all connected components from frame one can be matched with corresponding components in frame two and then the elements in frame two can be similarly matched with the components found in the next frame (frame three) and so on. By choosing the relatively simple greedy approach the time for the optimization, after computing the CCSM values, is neglectable. More elaborated optimization approaches would have to take into account the overall matching costs for all connected components between several frames at the same time. This optimization would be computationally very expensive, require the processing of whole batches of frames (which prohibits any online usage) and promises little accuracy improvement since parameters that include combined information from several frames are already included in the CCSM (e.g. velocity or direction of movement).

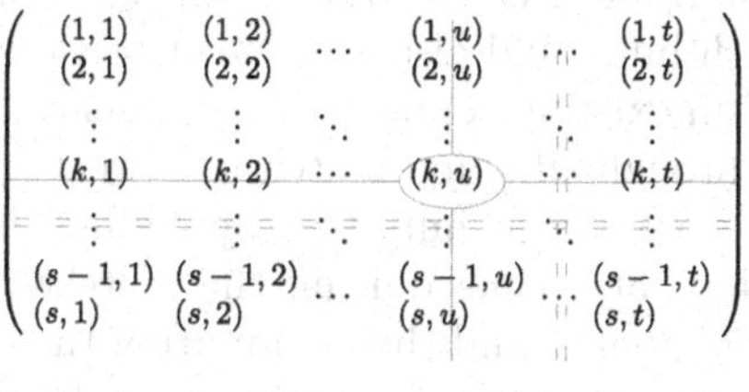

$$
\begin{pmatrix}
(1,1) & (1,2) & & (1,u) & & (1,t) \\
(2,1) & (2,2) & \cdots & (2,u) & \cdots & (2,t) \\
\vdots & \vdots & \ddots & \vdots & \ddots & \vdots \\
(k,1) & (k,2) & \cdots & (k,u) & \cdots & (k,t) \\
\vdots & \vdots & \ddots & \vdots & \ddots & \vdots \\
(s-1,1) & (s-1,2) & \cdots & (s-1,u) & \cdots & (s-1,t) \\
(s,1) & (s,2) & & (s,u) & & (s,t)
\end{pmatrix}
$$

Fig. 5. A correlation matrix between the s elements in frame one and t elements in frame two, that means at position (i, j) is the value $CCSM_{(i,j)}$. The element (k, u) has the lowest value (is the best match) and for any further matching all components that include elements from k or u have to be deleted.

In normal situations, this matching works very well but specific situations can be problematic, e.g. if a new fish appears it cannot be matched since there are no prior detections and hence the connected component of that fish has to be treated differently. In the following, these special cases and their handling are discussed.

4.3   Special Cases

A different number of connected components in two consecutive frames does not yet mean that a new fish appeared or an old one disappeared; sometimes a bad segmentation splits a fish in two and thereby generates two connected components instead of one or two fish swim close to each other so that their connected components merge to one. These cases can usually be handled by the algorithm already because it tries to match also unions of connected components that are close by or expects a split of a connected component that was the result of a merge in the past. However, if at the end there are still elements left over which cannot be matched, they are handled as follows:

Leftover Elements in Frame One - Disappearance of an Existing Fish. If an element in frame one is left over it will most likely correspond to a fish that disappeared, e.g. by swimming out of the scene or swimming so far away from the camera that it cannot be distinguished anymore from the background. To avoid errors (e.g. by a missed detection), these elements will not immediately be forgotten but especially tagged and added to the list of connected components for frame 2. As it could not be matched it will not be shown as an element in the result of frame two, but in the next step, there will be a trial to match this connected component to a component in the following frame. Only if the connected component could not be matched in five consecutive frames will it be completely forgotten. This ensures that the disappearance of a fish is not just a short time error in the segmentation but consistent over several frames.

Leftover Elements in Frame Two - Appearance of a New Fish. If a connected component in frame 2 is left over, it will most likely correspond to the appearance of a new fish but could also be a misdetection (e.g. of a shadow) or an unfortunate split of an existing connected component. The last aspect will be checked first by going through all found matches between frame one and two and checking if the CCSM score can be improved by adding the leftover component to any of the matches. That means uniting the matched component in frame two with the leftover component and then computing the CCSM value with this new component. Most of these unions are already evaluated in the first step of the matching but sometimes the split of a connected component can happen so awkwardly or the objects move so fast that the resulting new components are already far away from each other and therefore a union of these two elements was not checked in the previous step (because they were farther away than T_{CCdist}).

If an existing match could be improved by adding the leftover component, the component will be added to that match and everything is done. Otherwise, a new detection has to be assumed and will be added to the list of components in frame 2. However, similar to the previous case, this component will be tagged as new and not shown in the results at first. It will only be fully accepted as an object that has to be tracked if the connected components could be matched for five consecutive frames. This makes the whole approach more resistant to errors in the segmentation which is especially necessary since the wrong addition of only one new component can strongly affect the tracking accuracy of the already tracked objects in the scene.

Leftover Elements in Both Frames. If both events happen simultaneously, an old connected component disappears and a new one appears, completely false matches can occur since at the end a connected component in frame one that has no true match is left over and also one component in frame two that has no true match. To avoid that these two are matched falsely a threshold for the CCSM has to be set so that all matches above this threshold will be rejected. Since the CCSM score already entails an effective outlier detection (see Eqs. 29 to 32) this threshold can be set quite high. The CCSM value, in this case, is dominated by the exponential functions in the outlier detection which are depending on the image size and, therefore, the threshold is set to

$$T_{CCSMmax} = \exp z, \tag{37}$$

where z is also depending on the resolution of the frame (compare with Eq. 33). If the CCSM score exceeds $T_{CCSMmax}$ no matching will occur and instead the remaining components will be handled separately as discussed in the previous two paragraphs.

5 Results

As before, the results section is subdivided into two parts. First, the change detection results will be evaluated on a special underwater dataset and compared against similar methods. Afterwards, the described tracking algorithm will be performed on these results. As there is no underwater dataset with tracking data available we had to resort to in-air datasets for a quantitative comparison with other approaches. On the underwater dataset, only a qualitative evaluation was possible.

5.1 Segmentation

For the evaluation of the segmentation we took the dataset and numbers presented in [23]. It is the only underwater change detection dataset so far and includes five videos of different scenes with fishes as moving foreground objects. For each video the first 1000 frames are used as a learning phase and are followed

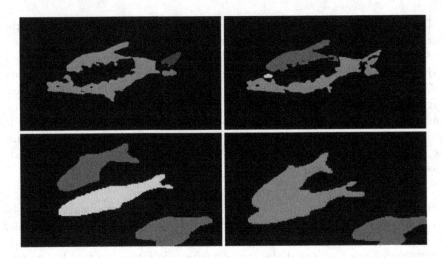

Fig. 6. In the top row are two segmentations of a fish with a low accuracy. This causes the connected components to merge and split frequently although they all belong to the same foreground object. In the bottom row are two fish which are accurately segmented but their paths cross which causes the connected components to merge into one single component. Both situations are very difficult for the tracking approach and have to be handled with care.

by 100 frames to which hand segmented ground truth images are available for the evaluation. The dataset features typical underwater challenges like blur, haze, color attenuation, caustics and marine snow which all complicate the background modeling process.

A comparison between the proposed algorithm, the original GSM and other background subtraction algorithms is given in Table 1. It shows that the extended GSM is a substantial improvement to the original GSM on each of the five videos and also outperforms the other methods on the whole dataset. In Fig. 8 some results of our algorithm are depicted.

In the *Fish Swarm* video we could achieve the largest improvement, mainly because of the pre-segmentations which enabled us to build a far better background model of that scene. The main problem with this video is that there are always fishes in the middle of the scene which are also all quite similar to each other as well as the background. Therefore, a normal background modeling algorithm would take the fishes as part of the background and only the exclusion of moving objects from the updating process with the pre-segmentations could rectify that (see Fig. 3).

Nonetheless, not all fishes in the *Fish Swarm* video could be detected since some of them barely move or are almost indistinguishable from the background. In the other four videos of the dataset the fishes can be detected very reliable by the proposed approach and the problems there mostly consist of false detections of shadows caused by the fishes or caustics on the water surface. It is a complicated task to avoid these errors since the algorithm needs to be very sensitive to detect fishes even when they are similar to the background which then causes these false detections.

Table 1. The results of our and four different background subtraction methods on the underwater change detection dataset. The first one is the original GSM algorithm, the next two are MoG approaches and the last one is a background modeling method based on K-nearest neighbors. Shown are the F1-Scores for the individual video and the total dataset.

Algorithm	Video					
	Fish swarm	Marine snow	Small aquacul.	Caustics	Two fishes	Total
[1]	.569	.836	.773	.549	.789	.731
[20]	.303	.818	.738	.738	.793	.703
[21]	.056	.648	.431	.674	.757	.451
[22]	.590	.824	.882	.753	.706	.767
Proposed	.845	.910	.933	.671	.824	.878

Fig. 7. Example of the S2.L1 Video of the PETS 2009 dataset. The bounding box of the detection of the proposed algorithm is shown in purple and in blue and pink are the provided ground truth bounding boxes. Both humans were accurately detected but considered as one blob and therefore the detection accuracy (MOTP value) for both human is each time below 40%. (Color figure online)

5.2   Tracking

For a meaningful assertion of the quality of different tracking algorithms a quantitative evaluation of the errors against ground truth data created by experts is necessary. The scoring of the results against such ground truth data is not as simple as for the change detection task because many different kinds of errors are possible and have to be reflected all in the metrics. This cannot be done by one measure alone and therefore several metrics will be used here that focus on different aspects. In [24] two measures especially created for the evaluation of tracking algorithms are presented, the Multiple Object Tracking Precision (MOTP) focuses the precision of the tracking approach and the Multiple Object Tracking Accuracy (MOTA) on the accuracy. We will use both of them for the evaluation to get a broader picture over the strengths and weaknesses of the different methods.

PETS 2009 Dataset. To compare various methods based on these metrics the video S2.L1 of the PETS 2009 Benchmark[2] [25] is chosen although it features a normal in-air scene because no ground truth data or tracking results of other approaches are available for underwater scenarios. For this video ground truth data is available[3] and several different algorithms have already been tested on it so that a meaningful evaluation is possible. A comparison of five different algorithms with the proposed algorithm can be seen in Table 2. The metrics MOTP and MOTA show that the proposed algorithm has a high tracking accuracy and a below average precision. Both of these results come at least partially from the combination of change detection with a blob tracker. The extended GSM background subtraction delivers very accurate detection results so that hardly any misses occur. Only when a person was mainly occluded by the sign in the middle of the scene did the algorithm fail to detect this person occasionally (compare Fig. 9). However, this detection accuracy comes with the price that no single humans are detected but only moving foreground blobs which consequently makes the tracking more difficult (splitting and merging of blobs) and also reduces the accuracy of the detection since often humans that are close together are detected and tracked together (see Fig. 7).

Table 2. Results of different tracking approaches on the S2.L1 Video of the PETS 2009 dataset. The data is taken from [26]. The results show that the proposed approach is very good at accurately detecting and matching objects in the scene (MOTA). However, it fails in precision (MOTP) since objects that are close together are often not separated and treated as only one object.

Algorithm	MOTP	MOTA
[26]	**0.788**	0.608
[27]	0.563	0.797
[28]	0.538	0.759
[29]	0.600	0.660
[30]	0.761	0.814
Proposed approach	0.550	**0.885**

---

[2] http://www.cvg.reading.ac.uk/PETS2009/a.html.
[3] http://www.milanton.de/data.html.

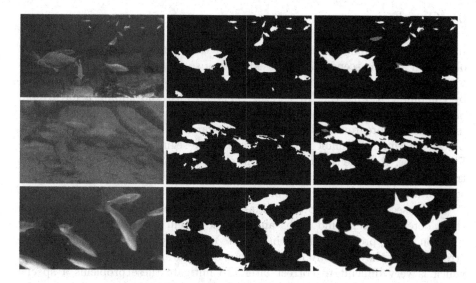

Fig. 8. One frame of three of the five videos of the Underwater Change Detection dataset. Shown are (top to bottom) the videos: *Marine Snow, Fish Swarm* and *small Aquaculture.* In the middle column is the segmentation of the proposed approach and in the right the ground truth data.

Fig. 9. Shown are results of the proposed tracking algorithm in combination with the eGSM background subtraction on the S2.L1 Video of the PETS 2009 dataset. On the top are the pure detection and tracking results of the proposed method and on the bottom the results are interposed with the actual frame and the ground truth bounding boxes which are shown in black. In the left frame it can be noticed that the person in the middle behind the pole is not detected correctly because he is mainly occluded. In the other images it can be seen how the persons tracked as light blue, green and yellow are tracked correctly although the pass and occlude each other. (Color figure online)

6 Conclusion

In this paper, a comprehensive approach for the detection and tracking of any objects in a static scene was proposed, with a special focus on crowded underwater videos. In the first part, the GSM background modeling was enhanced by combining it with the Mixture of Gaussian idea and adding a foreground model. The foreground model is especially accurate and useful in scenes with many similar foreground objects, e.g. fish swarms. Furthermore, the updating process was further enhanced by the usage of pre-segmentation created with the Flux Tensor. To make the segmentations spatially coherent, which simplifies the tracking process later enormously, the N^2Cut approach was applied to adapt the segmentation to the smoothness of natural images.

In the second part, a novel tracking approach was presented that works on these detected foreground blobs and matches them based on a novel energy function. A big problem is false, inaccurate or missing detections because these errors, even if they are only present in one or two frames, lead to a false match which is very difficult to correct later. To mitigate these problems a special handling of merging, splitting, missing and new blobs is integrated into the algorithm.

The segmentation approach was evaluated on a new Underwater Change Detection dataset to test it in difficult situations and scenarios with many foreground objects. Especially on the crowded scenes, the algorithm showed great improvements compared to other methods because of the pre-segmentations but also on the other videos a continuous improvement to the normal GSM could be achieved. The tracking algorithm was evaluated against previous papers on a video from the PETS 2009 dataset and could achieve a high accuracy but low precision in comparison to the other approaches because of the unique technique of this algorithm.

References

1. Radolko, M., Gutzeit, E.: Video segmentation via a Gaussian switch background-model and higher order Markov random fields. In: Proceedings of the 10th International Conference on Computer Vision Theory and Applications, vol. 1, pp. 537–544 (2015)
2. Shelley, A.J., Seed, N.L.: Approaches to static background identification and removal. In: IEE Colloquium on Image Processing for Transport Applications, pp. 6/1–6/4 (1993)
3. Gardos, T., Monaco, J.: Encoding video images using foreground/background segmentation. US Patent 5,915,044 (1999)
4. Wren, C., Azarbayejani, A., Darrell, T., Pentland, A.: Pfinder: real-time tracking of the human body. IEEE Trans. Pattern Anal. Mach. Intell. **19**, 780–785 (1997)
5. Stauffer, C., Grimson, W.: Adaptive background mixture models for real-time tracking. In: Proceedings 1999 IEEE Computer Society Conference on Computer Vision and Pattern Recognition, vol. 2, pp. 246–252 (1999)

6. Schindler, K., Wang, H.: Smooth foreground-background segmentation for video processing. In: Narayanan, P.J., Nayar, S.K., Shum, H.-Y. (eds.) ACCV 2006. LNCS, vol. 3852, pp. 581–590. Springer, Heidelberg (2006). https://doi.org/10.1007/11612704_58

7. Wang, R., Bunyak, F., Seetharaman, G., Palaniappan, K.: Static and moving object detection using flux tensor with split Gaussian models. In: 2014 IEEE Conference on Computer Vision and Pattern Recognition Workshops, pp. 420–424 (2014)

8. Barnich, O., Droogenbroeck, M.V.: ViBe: a universal background subtraction algorithm for video sequences. IEEE Trans. Image Process. **20**, 1709–1724 (2011)

9. Bianco, S., Ciocca, G., Schettini, R.: How far can you get by combining change detection algorithms? CoRR abs/1505.02921 (2015)

10. Xiao, Q., Liu, X., Liu, M.: Object tracking based on local feature matching. In: 2012 Fifth International Symposium on Computational Intelligence and Design, vol. 1, pp. 399–402 (2012)

11. Camplani, M., et al.: Multiple human tracking in RGB-depth data: a survey. IET Comput. Vis. **11**, 265–285 (2016)

12. Shu, G., Dehghan, A., Oreifej, O., Hand, E., Shah, M.: Part-based multiple-person tracking with partial occlusion handling. In: 2012 IEEE Conference on Computer Vision and Pattern Recognition, pp. 1815–1821 (2012)

13. Radolko, M., Farhadifard, F., von Lukas, U.F.: Change detection in crowded underwater scenes - via an extended Gaussian switch model combined with a flux tensor pre-segmentation. In: Proceedings of the 12th International Joint Conference on Computer Vision, Imaging and Computer Graphics Theory and Applications (VISIGRAPP 2017), VISAPP, vol. 4, pp. 405–415 (2017)

14. Bunyak, F., Palaniappan, K., Nath, S.K., Seetharaman, G.: Flux tensor constrained geodesic active contours with sensor fusion for persistent object tracking. J. Multimedia **2**, 20–33 (2007)

15. Radolko, M., Farhadifard, F., Gutzeit, E., von Lukas, U.F.: Real time video segmentation optimization with a modified normalized cut. In: 2015 9th International Symposium on Image and Signal Processing and Analysis (ISPA), pp. 31–36 (2015)

16. Wang, B., Gao, Y.: Structure integral transform versus radon transform: a 2D mathematical tool for invariant shape recognition. IEEE Trans. Image Process. **25**, 5635–5648 (2016)

17. Abukhait, J., Abdel-Qader, I., Oh, J.S., Abudayyeh, O.: Road sign detection and shape recognition invariant to sign defects. In: 2012 IEEE International Conference on Electro/Information Technology, pp. 1–6 (2012)

18. Kuhn, H.W.: The Hungarian method for the assignment problem. Nav. Res. Logist. Q. **2**, 83–97 (1955)

19. Luetteke, F., Zhang, X., Franke, J.: Implementation of the Hungarian method for object tracking on a camera monitored transportation system. In: 7th German Conference on Robotics, ROBOTIK 2012, pp. 1–6 (2012)

20. Zivkovic, Z.: Improved adaptive Gaussian mixture model for background subtraction. In: 17th International Conference on Proceedings of the Pattern Recognition, ICPR 2004, vol. 2, pp. 28–31 (2004)

21. KaewTraKulPong, P., Bowden, R.: An improved adaptive background mixture model for real-time tracking with shadow detection. In: Remagnino, P., Jones, G.A., Paragios, N., Regazzoni, C.S. (eds.) Video-Based Surveillance Systems, pp. 135–144. Springer, Boston (2002). https://doi.org/10.1007/978-1-4615-0913-4_11

22. Zivkovic, Z., Heijden, F.: Efficient adaptive density estimation per image pixel for the task of background subtraction. Pattern Recogn. Lett. **27**, 773–780 (2006)

23. Radolko, M., Farhadifard, F., von Lukas, U.F.: Dataset on underwater change detection. In: OCEANS 2016 - MONTEREY, pp. 1–8 (2016)

24. Bernardin, K., Stiefelhagen, R.: Evaluating multiple object tracking performance: the clear mot metrics. J. Image Video Process. 1–10

25. Ferryman, J., Shahrokni, A.: Pets 2009: dataset and challenge. In: 2009 Twelfth IEEE International Workshop on Performance Evaluation of Tracking and Surveillance, pp. 1–6 (2009)

26. Jiang, X., Rodner, E., Denzler, J.: Multi-person tracking-by-detection based on calibrated multi-camera systems. In: Bolc, L., Tadeusiewicz, R., Chmielewski, L.J., Wojciechowski, K. (eds.) ICCVG 2012. LNCS, vol. 7594, pp. 743–751. Springer, Heidelberg (2012). https://doi.org/10.1007/978-3-642-33564-8_89

27. Breitenstein, M.D., Reichlin, F., Leibe, B., Koller-Meier, E., Gool, L.V.: Online multiperson tracking-by-detection from a single, uncalibrated camera. IEEE Trans. Pattern Anal. Mach. Intell. **33**, 1820–1833 (2011)

28. Yang, J., Vela, P.A., Shi, Z., Teizer, J.: Probabilistic multiple people tracking through complex situations. In: Performance Evaluation of Tracking and Surveillance workshop at CVPR 2009, Miami, Florida, pp. 79–86 (2009)

29. Berclaz, J., Fleuret, F., Fua, P.: Robust people tracking with global trajectory optimization. In: 2006 IEEE Computer Society Conference on Computer Vision and Pattern Recognition (CVPR 2006), vol. 1, pp. 744–750 (2006)

30. Andriyenko, A., Schindler, K.: Multi-target tracking by continuous energy minimization. In: CVPR 2011, pp. 1265–1272 (2011)

Optimizing Phoneme-to-Viseme Mapping for Continuous Lip-Reading in Spanish

Adriana Fernandez-Lopez and Federico M. Sukno[✉]

Department of Information and Communication Technologies,
Pompeu Fabra University, Barcelona, Spain
`federico.sukno@upf.edu`

Abstract. Speech is the most used communication method between humans and it is considered a multisensory process. Even though there is a popular belief that speech is something that we hear, there is overwhelming evidence that the brain treats speech as something that we hear and see. Much of the research has focused on Automatic Speech Recognition (ASR) systems, treating speech primarily as an acoustic form of communication. In the last years, there has been an increasing interest in systems for Automatic Lip-Reading (ALR), although exploiting the visual information has been proved to be challenging. One of the main problems in ALR is how to make the system robust to the visual ambiguities that appear at the word level. These ambiguities make confused and imprecise the definition of the minimum distinguishable unit of the video domain. In contrast to the audio domain, where the phoneme is the standard minimum auditory unit, there is no consensus on the definition of the minimum visual unit (the viseme). In this work, we focus on the automatic construction of a phoneme-to-viseme mapping based on visual similarities between phonemes to maximize word recognition. We investigate the usefulness of different phoneme-to-viseme mappings, obtaining the best results for intermediate vocabulary lengths. We construct an automatic system that uses DCT and SIFT descriptors to extract the main characteristics of the mouth region and HMMs to model the statistic relations of both viseme and phoneme sequences. We test our system in two Spanish corpora with continuous speech (AV@CAR and VLRF) containing 19 and 24 speakers, respectively. Our results indicate that we are able to recognize 47% (resp. 51%) of the phonemes and 23% (resp. 21%) of the words, for AV@CAR and VLRF. We also show additional results that support the usefulness of visemes. Experiments on a comparable ALR system trained exclusively using phonemes at all its stages confirm the existence of strong visual ambiguities between groups of phonemes. This fact and the higher word accuracy obtained when using phoneme-to-viseme mappings, justify the usefulness of visemes instead of the direct use of phonemes for ALR.

Keywords: Automatic Lip-Reading · Visual speech recognition · Phoneme-to-viseme mapping

© Springer Nature Switzerland AG 2019
A. P. Cláudio et al. (Eds.): VISIGRAPP 2017, CCIS 983, pp. 305–328, 2019.
https://doi.org/10.1007/978-3-030-12209-6_15

1   Introduction

Speech perception is inherently a multimodal phenomenon which involves acoustic and visual cues. McGurk and McDonald demonstrated the influence of vision in speech perception in [1], where it was experimentally shown that when observers were presented with mismatched auditory and visual cues, they perceived a different sound from those presented in the stimulus (e.g. audio "ba" + visual "ga" = perceived "da"). Many authors have subsequently demonstrated that the incorporation of visual information into speech recognition systems improves robustness [2].

Audio signals are in general much more informative than video signals, although it has been demonstrated that visual information (lip-reading) is used by most people to better understand speech. Despite the common intuition that speech is something that we hear, there is overwhelming evidence that the brain treats speech as something that we hear, see, and even feel [3]. Visual cues are often used unconsciously and to a different extent for different individuals, depending on aspects such as the hearing ability [4], or the acoustic conditions, e.g. the visual channel becomes more important in noisy environments or when someone is speaking with a heavy foreign accent [5–8]. Furthermore, the visual channel is the only source of information to understand the spoken language for people with hearing disabilities [2,9,10].

In the literature, much of the research has focused on Automatic Speech Recognition (ASR) systems, treating speech primarily as an acoustic form of communication. Currently, ASR systems are able to recognize speech with very high accuracy when the acoustic signal is not degraded. However, when the acoustic signal is corrupted, the performance of ASR drops and there is the need to rely also on the information provided by the visual channel, which relates to the movement of the lips, teeth, tongue, and other facial features. This has led to research in Audio-Visual Automatic Speech Recognition (AV-ASR) systems, which try to balance the contribution of the audio and the visual information channels to develop systems that are robust to audio artifacts and noise. AV-ASR systems have been shown to significantly improve the recognition performance of audio-based systems under adverse acoustic conditions [2,11].

On the other hand, in the last decades there has been an increased interest in decoding speech exclusively using visual cues, leading to Automatic Lip-Reading (ALR) systems [11–20]. Nonetheless, ALR systems are still behind in performance compared to audio- or audio-visual systems. This can be partially explained by the greater challenges associated to decoding speech through the visual channel, when compared to the audio channel. Specifically, one of the key limitations in ALR systems resides on the visual ambiguities that arise at the word level due to homophemes, i.e. characters that are easily confused because they produce the same or very similar lip movements.

Keeping in mind that the main objective of speech recognition systems is to understand language, which is structured in terms of sentences, words and characters, going from larger to smaller speech entities. More precisely, the standard minimum unit in speech processing is the *phoneme*, defined as the minimum distinguishable sound that is able to change the meaning of a word [21]. Similarly, when analyzing visual information many researchers use the *viseme*, which is defined as the minimum distinguishable speech unit in the video domain [22]. However, due to visual ambiguities the correspondence between both units is no one-to-one and not all the phonemes that are heard can be distinguished by observing the lips. There are two main types of ambiguities: (*i*) there are phonemes that are easily confused because they are perceived visually similar to others. For example, the phones /p/ and /b/ are visually indistinguishable because voicing occurs at the glottis, which is not visible. (*ii*) there are phonemes whose visual appearance can change (or even disappear) depending on the context (co-articulated consonants). This is the case of the *velars*, consonants articulated with the back part of the tongue against the soft palate (e.g.: /k/ or /g/), because they change their position in the palate depending on the previous or following phoneme [23]. Thus, visemes have usually been defined as the grouping of phonemes sharing the same visual appearance [24–26]. Nonetheless, there is no consensus on the precise definition of the different visemes nor on their number, or even on their usefulness [22,25–27]. There are discrepancies on whether there is more information in the position of the lips or in their movement [24–26] and if visemes are better defined in terms of articulatory gestures (such as lips closing together, jaw movement, teeth exposure) which relates the use of visemes as a form of model clustering that allows visually similar phonetic events to share a common model [7,22,26].

Then, when designing ALR systems, one of the most important challenges is how to make the system robust to visual ambiguities. Consequently several different viseme vocabularies have been proposed in the literature typically with lengths between 11 and 15 visemes [2,28–30]. For instance, [31] trained an initial set of 56 phones and clustered them into 35 visemes using the Average Linkage hierarchical clustering algorithm. [32] defined a phoneme-to-viseme mapping from 50 phonemes to 11 visemes in the English language (11 visemes plus *Silence*). [30] investigated the design of context questions based on decision trees to reveal similar linguistic context behavior between phonemes that belong to the same viseme. For the study, based on linguistic properties, they determined seven consonant visemes (bilabial, labiodental, dental, palato-velar, palatal, velar, and two alveolars), four vowels, an alveolar-semivowel and one silence viseme (13 visemes in total). [33] proposed a phoneme-to-viseme mapping from 46 American English phones to 16 visemes to achieve natural looking lip animation. They mapped phonetic sequences to viseme sequences before animating the lips of 3D head models. [34] presented a text-to-audiovisual speech synthesizer which converts input text into an audiovisual speech stream. They started grouping those phonemes which looked similar by visually comparing the viseme images. To obtain a photo-realistic talking face they proposed a viseme vocabulary with 6 visemes that represent 24 consonant phonemes, 7 visemes that represent the 12 vowel phonemes, 2 diphthong visemes and one viseme corresponding to the silence.

In this work, we propose to automatically construct a phoneme-to-viseme mapping based on visual similarities between phonemes to maximize word recognition. We investigate the usefulness of different phoneme-to-viseme mappings, obtaining the best results for intermediate vocabulary lengths. We evaluate an ALR system based on DCT and SIFT descriptors and Hidden Markov Models (HMMs) in two Spanish corpora with continuous speech (AV@CAR and VLRF) containing 19 and 24 speakers, respectively. Our results indicate that we are able to recognize 47% (resp. 51%) of the phonemes and 23% (resp. 21%) of the words, for AV@CAR and VLRF. We also show additional results that support the usefulness of visemes. Firstly, we show qualitative results by comparing the average lip-images per subject and phoneme of several subjects from both databases, which clearly illustrate the difficulty to perceive differences between phonemes that are known to produce visual ambiguities. Secondly, we also analyze the results by looking at the confusion matrices obtained with our system trained with and without using visemes as an intermediate representation. Experiments on a comparable ALR system trained exclusively using phonemes at all its stages confirm the existence of strong visual ambiguities between groups of phonemes. This fact and the higher word accuracy obtained when using phoneme-to-viseme mappings, justify the usefulness of visemes instead of the direct use of phonemes for ALR. This paper is an extended and revised version of a preliminary conference report that was presented in [35].

2   ALR System

ALR systems typically aim at interpreting the video signal in terms of visual units, and usually consist of 3 major steps: (1) Lips localization, (2) Extraction of visual features, (3) Classification into sequences. In this section we start with a brief review of the related work and then provide a detailed explanation of our method.

2.1   Related Work

Much of the research on ALR has focused on digit recognition, isolated words and sentences, and only more recently in continuous speech.

For Letter and Digit Recognition: [9] centred their experiments in comparing different image transformations (Discrete Cosine Transform (DCT), Discrete Wavelet Transform (DWT), Principal Component Analysis (PCA), Linear Discriminant Analysis (LDA), and Fast Discrete Curvelet Transform (FDCT)) combined with HMMs using the XM2VTS database [36]. Similarly, [37] presented a system that combines DCT features and HMMs, but it was evaluated in another database, the CUAVE database. On the other hand, both architectures presented by Papandreou et al. [38,39] were evaluated in the CUAVE database, but used a different system based on AMM features and HMMs. In contrast, [15] presented a feature learning method using Deep Boltzmann Machines that recognizes simple sequences of isolated words and digit utterances and evaluated it in the AusTalk database [40]. Their method used both acoustic and visual information to learn features, except for the test stage where only the visual information was used to generate the features. On the other hand, [41] and [42] proposed two different systems to lipread digits in another language. Specifically, they used the CENSREC-1-AV Japanase database [43] to evaluate their systems. [41] proposed a system that combines a general and discriminating feature (GIF) with HMMs, in contrast to [42] who presented a system that combines Deep Bottleneck Features and multi-stream HMMs. For all these methods evaluated in different databases but tackling digit or alphabet recognition, the word accuracy obtained was between 50% and 85%.

For Word and Phrase Recognition: [44] used a subset of 15 speakers of the GRID corpus and centered their experiments in comparing different features such as DCT, Sieve, PCA and AAM. They used one HMM per word for decoding the message, 52 HMMs in total (51 words plus silence). Similarly, [45] proposed a model composed of DCT features and one HMM per word, but using the full set of speakers of the GRID corpus. More recently, [20] compared PCA and HOG using SVM as classifier also in the GRID corpus. In contrast, [46] proposed a spatiotemporal version of the LBP features and used an SVM classifier to recognize isolated phrase sequences from the OuluVS database [46]. In a different approach, [47] used a latent variable model that identifies two different sources of variation in images, speaker appearance and pronunciation, and tried to separate them to recognize 10 short utterances from the OuluVS database (e.g. *Excuse me, Thank you,...*). Also in the OuluVS database, [48] presented a random forest manifold alignment (RFMA) and applied it to lip-reading in color and depth videos. More recently, [20] presented a pipeline based on Long Short-Term Memory (LSTM) recurrent networks and compared it with two systems not using deep learning with the GRID corpus. Similarly, [49] proposed LIPNET, an end-to-end neural network architecture that maps variable length sequences of video to text sequences, and performs sentence-level classification in the GRID database. All these methods addressed word or phrase recognition. It is important to mention that, for word or phrase recognition tasks, the output of the system is restricted to a pre-defined set of possible classes (either words or whole phrases), which is quite different to natural speech. Systems addressing these tasks reported word accuracy between 40% and 97%, with large variations depending on the test database.

For Continuous Speech Recognition: [2] applied fast DCT to the mouth region and trained an ensemble of 100 coefficients. To reduce the dimensionality they used an intraframe linear discriminant analysis and maximum likelihood linear transform (LDA and MLLT), resulting in a 30-dimensional feature vector. To capture dynamic speech information, 15 consecutive feature vectors were concatenated, followed by an interframe LDA/MLLT to obtain dynamic visual features of length 41. They tested their system using the IBM ViaVoice database and reported 17.49% word accuracy in continuous speech recognition. In contrast, Thangthai et al. [50] proposed an ALR systems using AAM features and HMM classifiers. Specifically, they trained Context-Independent HMMs

(CI-HMM) and Context-Dependent HMMs (CD-HMM), but instead of directly constructing word models, they defined phoneme models. They only report tests on single-speaker experiments in the RM-3000 dataset. A different approach was presented in [26], who used a database with short balanced utterances to define a viseme vocabulary able to recognize continuous speech using the VIDTIMIT database. They based their feature extraction on techniques such as PCA or Optical flow, taking into account both the movement and appearance of the lips. On the other hand, [51] used Convolutional Neural Networks (CNNs) to extract high-level features and a combination of HMM to predict phonemes in spoken Japanese. In yet another work, [52] presented a system based on a set of viseme level HMMs. Concretely, they used Active Appearance Model parameters transformed using LDA as visual features to train their models. They trained 14 HMMs corresponding to 13 visemes plus *Silence* to recover the speech. They tested their method in their own database composed of 1000 words, obtaining 14.08% word accuracy for continuous speech recognition. More recently, [16] collected a very large audio-visual speech database (+100,000 utterances), the Lip Reading Sentences (LRS) database, and proposed a sequence-to-sequence model based solely on CNNs and LSTM networks. They achieved the most significant performance to date in lipreading with 49.8% word accuracy.

We can see that the recognition rates for continuous lip-reading are rather modest in comparison to those achieved for simpler recognition tasks, which can be explained due to the visual ambiguities that appear at the word level. Moreover, continuous lip-reading systems must be able to decode any word of the dictionary and process sentences that contain an arbitrary number of words with unknown time-boundaries, not just pre-defined classes, as is the case when addressing digit-, or word-, or sentence-recognition (at least in the cases in which the targeted classes are a fixed set of predefined phrases).

As mentioned before we are interested in continuous speech recognition because it is the task that is closer to actual lip-reading as done by humans. The available databases for lip-reading in Spanish contain around 600 sentence utterances (+1,000 different words) [53,54]. Even though results are often not comparable because they are usually reported in different databases, with variable number of speakers, vocabularies, language and so on, we can consider for comparison to our work, those ALR systems trained with databases with similar amount of data [2,15,20,48,50–52]. However, focusing only on those that address continuous lip-reading (e.g. [2,52]) we find that word accuracy is typically below the 20%, making evident the big challenges that still remain in this field.

2.2 Our System

In this section, each step of our ALR system is explained (Fig. 1). We start by detecting the face and extracting the region of interest (ROI) that comprises the mouth and its surrounding area. Appearance features are then extracted and used to estimate visemes, which are finally mapped into phonemes with the help of HMMs.

Lips Localization. The location of the face is obtained using invariant optimal features ASM (IOF-ASM) [55] that provides an accurate segmentation of the face in frontal views. The face is tracked at every frame and detected landmarks are used to fix a bounding box around the lips (ROI) (Fig. 2(a–b)). At this stage, the ROI can have a different size in each frame. Thus, ROIs are normalized to a fixed size of 48 × 64 pixels to achieve a uniform representation.

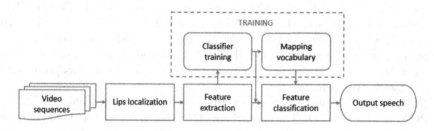

Fig. 1. General process of an ALR system.

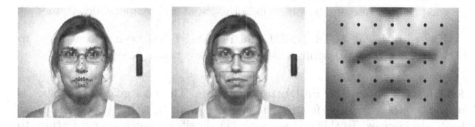

Fig. 2. (a) IOF-ASM detection, the marks in yellow are used to fix the bounding box; (b) ROI detection, each color fix a lateral of the bounding box; (c) Keypoints distribution. (Color figure online)

Feature Extraction. After the ROI is detected a feature extraction stage is performed. Nowadays, there is no universal feature for visual speech representation in contrast to the Mel-Frequency Cepstral Coefficients (MFCC) for acoustic speech. Thus, we look for an informative feature invariant to common video issues, such as noise or illumination changes. We analyze three different appearance-based techniques:

- *SIFT*: SIFT was selected as high level descriptor to extract the features in both the spatial and temporal domains because it is highly distinctive and invariant to image scaling and rotation, and partially invariant to illumination changes and 3D camera viewpoint [56]. In the spatial domain, the SIFT descriptor was applied directly to the ROI, while in the temporal domain it was applied to the centred gradient. SIFT keypoints are distributed uniformly around the ROI (Fig. 2(c)). The distance between keypoints was fixed to half of the neighbourhood covered by the descriptor to gain robustness (by overlapping). As the dimension of the final descriptor for both spatial and temporal domains is very high, PCA was applied to reduce the dimensionality of the features. Only statistically significant components (determined by means of Parallel Analysis [57]) were retained.

- *DCT*: The 2D DCT is one of the most popular techniques for feature extraction in ALR [13,44]. Its ability to compress the relevant information in a few coefficients results in a descriptor with small dimensionality. The 2D DCT was applied directly to the ROI. To fix the number of coefficients, the image error between the original ROI and the reconstructed was used. Based on preliminary experiments, we found that 121 coefficients (corresponding to 1% reconstruction error) for both the spatial and temporal domains produced a satisfactory performance.

- *PCA*: Another popular technique is PCA, also known as *eigenlips* [13,26,44]. PCA, similar to 2D DCT is applied directly to the ROI. To decide the optimal number of dimensions the system was trained and tested taking different percentages of the total variance. Lower number of components would lead to a low quality reconstruction, but an excessive number of components will be more affected by noise. In the end 90% of the variance was found to be a good compromise and was used in both spatial and temporal descriptors.

The early fusion of DCT-SIFT and PCA-SIFT has been also explored to obtain a more robust descriptor (see results in Sect. 3.3).

Feature Classification and Interpretation. The final goal of this block is to convert the extracted features into phonemes or, if that is not possible, at least into visemes. To this end we need: (1) classifiers that will map features to (a first estimate of) visemes; (2) a mapping between phonemes and visemes; (3) a model that imposes temporal coherency to the estimated sequences.

1. **Classifiers:** classification of visemes is a challenging task, as it has to deal with issues such as class imbalance and label noise. Several methods have been proposed to deal with these problems, the most common solutions being Bagging and Boosting algorithms [58–61]. From these, Bagging has been reported to perform better in the presence of training noise and thus it was selected for our experiments. Multiple LDA was evaluated using cross validation. To add robustness to the system, we trained classifiers to produce not just a class label but to estimate also a class probability for each input sample.

   For each bagging split, we train a multi-class LDA classifier and use the Mahalanobis distance d to obtain a normalized projection of the data into each class c:

   $$d_c(x) = \sqrt{(x - \bar{x}_c)^T \cdot \Sigma_c^{-1} \cdot (x - \bar{x}_c)} \tag{1}$$

   Then, for each class, we compute two cumulative distributions based on these projections: one for in-class samples $\Phi(\frac{d_c(x)-\mu_c}{\sigma_c})$, $x \in c$ and another one for out-of-class samples $\Phi(\frac{d_c(x)-\mu_{\tilde{c}}}{\sigma_{\tilde{c}}})$, $x \in \tilde{c}$, which we assume Gaussian with means μ_c, $\mu_{\tilde{c}}$ and variances σ_c, $\sigma_{\tilde{c}}$, respectively. An indicative example is provided in Fig. 3. Notice that these means and variances correspond to the projections in (1) and are different from $\bar{x}_c$ and Σ_c.

We compute a class-likelihood as the ratio between the in-class and the out-of-class distributions, as in (2) and normalize the results so that the summation over all classes is 1, as in (3). When classifying a new sample, we use the cumulative distributions to estimate the probability that the unknown sample belongs to each of the viseme classes (3). We assign the class with the highest normalized likelihood L_c.

$$F(c \mid x) = \frac{1 - \Phi(\frac{d_c(x) - \mu_c}{\sigma_c})}{\Phi(\frac{d_c(x) - \mu_{\tilde{c}}}{\sigma_{\tilde{c}}})} \tag{2}$$

$$L_c(x) = \frac{F(c \mid x)}{\sum_{c=1}^{C} F(c \mid x)} \tag{3}$$

Once the classifiers are trained we could theoretically try to classify features directly into phonemes, but as explained in Sect. 1, there are phonemes that share the same visual appearance and are therefore unlikely to be distinguishable by a ALR system. Thus, such phonemes should be grouped into the same class (visemes). In the next subsection we will present a mapping from phonemes to visemes based on the grouping of phonemes that are visually similar.

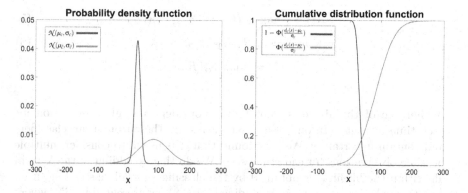

Fig. 3. (a) Probability density functions for in-class (green) and out-of-class (red) samples; (b) Cumulative distributions corresponding to (a). Notice than for in-class samples we use the complement of the cumulative distribution, since lower values should have higher probabilities. Reprinted from [35]. (Color figure online)

2. **Phoneme-to-viseme Mapping:** to construct our phoneme to viseme mapping we analyze the confusion matrix resulting by comparing the ground truth labels of the training set with the automatic classification obtained from the

previous section. We use an iterative process, starting with the same number of visemes as phonemes, merging at each step the visemes that show the highest ambiguity. The method takes into account that vowels cannot be grouped with consonants, because it has been demonstrated that their aggregation produces worse results [26, 28].

The algorithm iterates until the desired vocabulary length is achieved. However, there is no accepted standard to fix this value beforehand. Indeed, several different viseme vocabularies have been proposed in the literature typically with lengths between 11 and 15 visemes. Hence, in Sect. 3.3 we will analyse the effect of the vocabulary size on recognition accuracy. Once the vocabulary construction is concluded, all classifiers are retrained based on the resulting viseme classes.

3. **HMM and Viterbi Algorithm:** to improve the performance obtained after feature classification, HMMs of one state per class are used to map: (1) visemes to visemes; (2) visemes to phonemes. An HMM $\lambda = (A, B, \pi)$ is formed by N states and M observations. Matrix A represents the state transition probabilities, matrix B the emission probabilities, and vector π the initial state probabilities. Given a sequence of observation O and the model λ our aim is to find the maximum probability state path $Q = q_1, q_2, ..., q_{t-1}$. This can be done recursively using Viterbi algorithm [62, 63]. Let $\delta_i(t)$ be the probability of the most probable state path ending in state i at time t (4). Then $\delta_j(t)$ can be computed recursively using (5) with initialization (6) and termination (7).

$$\delta_i(t) = \max_{q_1, ..., q_{t-1}} P(q_1...q_{t-1} = i, O_1, ..., O_t | \lambda) \tag{4}$$

$$\delta_j(t) = \max_{1 \leq i \leq N} [\delta_i(t-1) \cdot a_{i,j}] \cdot b_j(O_t) \tag{5}$$

$$\delta_i(1) = \pi_i \cdot b_i(O_1), 1 \leq i \leq N \tag{6}$$

$$P = \max_{1 \leq i \leq N} [\delta_i(T)] \tag{7}$$

A shortage of the above is that it only considers a single observation for each time instant t. In our case observations are the output from classifiers and contain uncertainty. We have found that it is useful to consider multiple possible observations for each time step. We do this by adding to the Viterbi algorithm the likelihoods obtained by the classifiers for all classes (e.g. from equation (3)). As a result, (5) is modified into (8), as presented in [35], where the maximization is done across both the N states (as in (5)) and also the M possible observations, each weighted with its likelihood estimated by the classifiers.

$$\delta_j(t) = \max_{1 \leq O_t \leq M} \max_{1 \leq i \leq N} [\delta_i(t-1) \cdot a_{i,j}] \cdot \hat{b}_j(O_t) \tag{8}$$

$$\hat{b}_j(O_t) = b_j(O_t) \cdot L(O_t) \tag{9}$$

The short-form $L(O_t)$ refers to the likelihood $L_{O_t}(x)$ as defined in (3). The Viterbi algorithm modified as indicated in (8) is used to obtain the final viseme sequence providing at the same time temporal consistency and tolerance to classification uncertainties. Once this has been achieved, visemes are mapped into phonemes using the traditional Viterbi algorithm (5). Experimental results of this improvement can be found in [35].

3 Experiments

3.1 Databases

AV@CAR Database. [53] introduced AV@CAR as a free multi-modal database for automatic audio-visual speech recognition in Spanish, including both studio and in-car recordings. The Audio-Visual-Lab dataset of AV@CAR contains sequences of 20 people recorded under controlled conditions while repeating predefined phrases or sentences. There are 197 sequences for each person, recorded in AVI format. The video data has a spatial resolution of 768×576 pixels, 24-bit pixel depth, and 25 fps and is compressed at an approximate rate of 50:1. The sequences are divided into 9 sessions and were captured in a frontal view under different illumination conditions and speech tasks. Session 2 is composed of 25 videos/user with phonetically-balanced sentences. We have used session 2 splitting the dataset into 380 sentences (19 users × 20 sentences/user) for training and 95 sentences (19 users × 5 sentences/user) to test the system. Table 1 shows 5 samples sentences and their corresponding phonetic transcription.

VLRF Database. [54] introduced VLRF in 2017 as a free multi-speaker database for automatic audio-visual speech recognition in Spanish. The Audio-Visual data contains sequences of 24 people (15 hearing; 9 hearing-impaired) repeating up to three-time sets of 25 sentences selected from a pool of 500 phonetically-balanced sentences (10,000+ word utterances in total). The video data has a spatial resolution of 1280×720 pixels and 50 fps. We have used the first repetition of each sentence per speaker by splitting the dataset into 480 sentences (24 users × 20 sentences/user) for training and 120 sentences (24 users × 5 sentences/user) to test the system. Table 1 shows 5 samples sentences and their corresponding phonetic transcription.

3.2 Phonetic Vocabulary

SAMPA is a phonetic alphabet developed in 1989 by an international group of phoneticians, and was applied to European languages as Dutch, English, French, Italian, Spanish, etc. We based our phonetic vocabulary in SAMPA because it is the most used standard in phonetic transcription [64,65]. For the Spanish language, the vocabulary is composed by the following 29 phonemes: /p/, /b/, /t/, /d/, /k/, /g/, /tS/, /jj/, /f/, /B/, /T/, /D/, /s/, /x/, /G/, /m/, /n/,

/J/, /l/, /L/, /r/, /rr/, /j/, /w/, /a/, /e/, /i/, /o/, /u/. The phonemes /jj/ and /G/ were removed from our experiments because these databases did not contain enough samples to consider them. Table 1 shows 10 samples of phonetic transcriptions.

Table 1. Sample sentences for each database and their corresponding phonetic transcription using SAMPA.

AV@CAR
Francia, Suiza y Hungría ya hicieron causa común.
f4'an-Tja sw'i-Ta j uN-g4'i-a jj'a i-Tj'e-4oN k'aw-sa ko-m'un.
Después ya se hizo muy amiga nuestra.
des-pw'ez jj'a se 'i-To mw'i a-m'i-Ga nwes-t4a.
Los yernos de ismael no engordarán los pollos con hierba.
loz jj'e4-noz De iz-ma-'el n'o eN-go4-Da-4'an los p'o-Los kon jj'e4-Ba.
Me he tomado un café con leche en un bar.
me 'e to-m'a-Do 'uN ka-f'e kon l'e-tSe en 'um b'a4.
Guadalajara no está colgada de las rocas.
gwa-Da-la-x'a-4a n'o es-t'a kol-G'a-Da De laz r'o-kas.

VLRF
Una sexóloga les ayudó a salvar su relación.
'u-na sek-s'o-lo-Ga les a-jju-D'o a sal-B'a4 su re-la-Tj'on.
Es muy fácil convivir con mis compañeros de piso.
'ez mw'i f'a-Til kom-bi-B'i4 kom mis kom-pa-J'e-4oz De p'i-so.
Cuando tenia quince años fui a mi primer campamento.
kwan-do t'e-nja k'in-Te 'a-Jos fw'i a mi p4i-m'e4 kam-pa-m'en-to.
A las ocho de la mañana estaba haciendo pasteles.
a las 'o-tSo De la ma-J'a-na es-t'a-Ba a-Tj'en-do pas-t'e-les.
El amanacer es uno de los momentos más bonitos del día.
el a-ma-na-T'e4 'es 'u-no De loz mo-m'en-toz m'az Bo-n'i-toz Del d'i-a.

3.3 Results

In this section, we show the results of our experiments. In particular, we show the comparison of the performances between the different vocabularies and the different features.

Experimental Setup. We constructed an automatic system that uses local appearance features based on the early fusion of DCT and SIFT descriptors (this combination produced the best results in our tests, see below) to extract the main characteristics of the mouth region in both spatial and temporal domains. The classification of the extracted features into phonemes is done in two steps. Firstly, 100 LDA classifiers are trained using bagging sequences to be robust under label noise. Then, the classifier outputs are used to compute the globally normalized likelihood, as the summation of the normalized likelihood computed by each classifier divided by the number of classifiers (as explained in Sect. 2). Secondly, at the final step, one-state-per-class HMMs are used to model the dynamic relations of the estimated visemes and produce the final phoneme sequences.

Feature Comparison. To analyze the performance of the different features, we extracted DCT, PCA and SIFT descriptors and compared their performance individually and combining DCT-SIFT and DCT-PCA. We used these features as input to 100 LDA classifiers, generated by means of a bagging strategy, and performed a 4-fold cross-validation on the training set. Figure 4 displays the results obtained for these experiments on a vocabulary of 20 visemes, which was the optimal length in our experiments, as shown in the next section.

Comparing the features independently, DCT and SIFT give the best performances. When combined together, the fusion of both features produced an accuracy of 0.58 for visemes, 0.47 for phonemes.

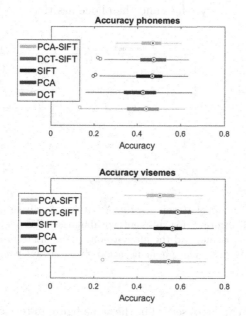

Fig. 4. Comparison of features performance. Reprinted from [35].

Comparison of Different Vocabularies. In this section, we investigate the automatic construction of phoneme-to-viseme mappings with the goal to maximize word accuracy. Our system uses these mappings as an intermediate representation which is hypothesized to facilitate the classification of the visual information, given that viseme classes are visually less ambiguous than phoneme classes. At the final step, our system uses HMMs to model the temporal dynamics of the input stream and disambiguate viseme classes based on the sequence context, always producing a final output in terms of phonemes, regardless of the length of the intermediate viseme-based representation.

To evaluate the influence of the different mappings, we analyzed the performance of our system in the AV@CAR database in terms of viseme-, phoneme-, and word-accuracy using viseme vocabularies of different lengths. Our first observation, from Fig. 5, is that the viseme accuracy tends to grow as we reduce the vocabulary length. This is explained by two factors: (1) the reduction in number of classes, which makes the classification problem a simpler one to solve; (2) the fact that visually indistinguishable units are combined into one. The latter helps to explain the behavior observed in terms of phoneme accuracy. As we reduce the vocabulary length, phoneme accuracy firstly increases because we eliminate some of the ambiguities by merging visually similar units. But if we continue to reduce the vocabulary, too many phonemes (even unrelated) are mixed together and their accuracy decreases because, even if these visemes are recognized better, their mapping into phonemes is more uncertain. Thus, the optimal performance is obtained for intermediate vocabulary lengths, because there is an optimum compromise between the visemes and the phonemes that can be recognized.

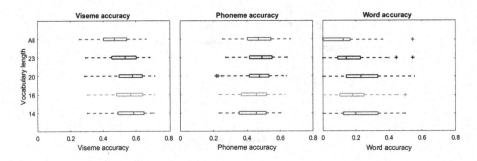

Fig. 5. Boxplots of system performance the AV@CAR database in terms of viseme-, phoneme- and word accuracy for different vocabularies. We analyze the one-to-one mapping phoneme-to-viseme, and the many-to-one phoneme-to-viseme mappings with 23, 20, 16 and 14 visemes. The phoneme accuracy is always computed from the 28 phonemes.

A similar effect can be observed in the same figure in terms of words. Firstly, we see that the one-to-one mapping between phoneme and visemes (e.g. using the 28 phonemes classes directly, without merging them into visemes) produces the lowest word accuracy. In contrast, intermediate vocabulary lengths show higher word accuracy, with the maximum obtained for 20 classes, supporting the view that the many-to-one mapping from phonemes to visemes is useful to optimize the performance of ALR systems.

Interestingly, while our results support the advantage of combining multiple phonemes into visemes to improve performance, the number of visemes that we obtain are comparatively high with respect to previous efforts. In our case, the optimal vocabulary length for Spanish reduced from 28 phonemes to 20 visemes (including *Silence*), i.e. a reduction rate of about 3 : 2. In contrast, previous efforts reported for English started from 40 to 50 phonemes and merged them into just 11 to 15 visemes [26], which implies reduction rates from 3 : 1 to 5 : 1. It is not clear, however, if the higher compression of the vocabularies obeys to a difference inherent to language or to other technical aspects, such as the ways of defining the phoneme-to-viseme mapping.

Indeed, language differences make it difficult to make a fair comparison of our results with respect to previous work. Firstly, it could be argued that our viseme accuracy is comparable to values reported by [26]; however they used at most 15 visemes while we use 20 visemes and, as shown in Fig. 5, when the number of visemes decreases, viseme recognition accuracy increases but phoneme accuracy might be reduced, making more difficult to recover the spoken message. Unfortunately, [26] did not report phoneme or word accuracy.

Speaker Variability. In the literature, it has been proved that different individuals vocalize in different and unique ways, which results in considerable variability in the difficulty to lip-read across subjects. Thus, it is interesting to compare the performance of the system using different viseme-vocabularies with respect to the different subjects of the database. In Fig. 6 we show the performance of the phoneme-to-viseme mappings analyzed in the previous section for each of the speakers of the AV@CAR database. We see that, indeed, some speakers are more difficult to lip-read than others, but the relative performance of the different phoneme-to-viseme mappings varies only marginally. Specifically, it can be observed that the 20-visemes vocabulary obtains the highest word accuracy for the majority of speakers in the database.

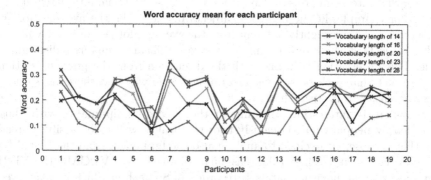

Fig. 6. Comparison of system performance in the AV@CAR database in terms of word accuracy for the different vocabularies and participants.

4   Discussion

Visual ambiguities have been one of the most investigated problems in ALR. In Sect. 1, we described the minimum auditory units (phonemes) and their visual equivalent (visemes), as well as their many-to-one relation. Focusing on visemes, there exist two different points of view in the literature: (i) researchers that defend their utility and proposed several phoneme-to-viseme mappings [7,22,26, 28,35]; (ii) researchers that debate their actual usefulness and existence [16,19, 25,49].

In this work, we proposed to automatically construct a phoneme-to-viseme mapping based on visual similarities between phonemes to maximize word accuracy. Thus, we investigated the usefulness of different phoneme-to-viseme mappings, obtaining the best results for intermediate vocabulary lengths. However, it is also interesting to analyze additional qualitative and quantitative results, such as lip crops and confusion matrices.

Firstly, we can find intuitive support to the existence of visemes by visually analyzing the lips of subjects when pronouncing different phonemes. In Table 2 we show examples of the average lip-images per subject and phoneme for 5 subjects from the AV@CAR database. That is, each cell of the table contains the average of all frames for which a given subject was uttering a certain phoneme. Looking at the examples, we can clearly see strong visual similarities between some of the phonemes. For example, it would be arguably difficult to distinguish between the averages from /a/ and /e/, or between /m/, /p/ and /B/, which correlates well with the proposed viseme mappings. On the other hand, even when there exist visual similarities between /o/ and /u/, we can observe that for /u/ there appears to be a smaller hole inside the lips than for /o/ in most of the cases. The latter suggests that these two phonemes might actually be visually separable, but in our experiments the classification results showed considerable confusion between them (see also Fig. 7) and the best performance was obtained with a vocabulary in which /o/ and /u/ were merged into the same viseme.

Another interesting observation from Table 2 is the variability between subjects. For example, in the first two subjects in the table, the averages for the phoneme /tS/ seem slightly different from the averages for /t/ and /s/; while the other subjects show extremely similar averages, that are arguably indistinguishable. This observation is in line with the discussion from the previous section, i.e. the fact that each person vocalizes in a unique way and there are subjects that are easier to lip-read than others.

Thus, it is interesting to compare the preceding lip-images with those recorded by people who consciously tries to vocalize well to be easily lip-read. For this purpose, we decided to analyze also the lip-images from the Visual Lip Reading Feasibility (VLRF) database [54]. Similarly to AV@CAR, the VLRF database is an audiovisual database recorded in Spanish in which speakers were recorded while reading a series of sentences that were provided to them. However, while in AV@CAR subjects were speaking naturally, in the VLRF database speakers were instructed to make their best effort to be easily understood by lip-reading. Hence, we could hypothesize that, if it were true that all phonemes are visually distinguishable (which would imply that there is no need for visemes) then the VLRF would be ideal corpus to visualize this.

To test the above hypothesis, we replicated our experiments in the VLRF database to make them directly comparable to those from the AV@CAR

Table 2. Average lip-images per user and phoneme of 5 subjects of the AV@CAR database. Each row shows a sample subject. For each subject, every column shows the average of all the frames in which the subject uttered a specific phoneme. The vertical lines separate the phonemes that belong to different visemes according to our mapping. The last row shows the average when considering all the users together.

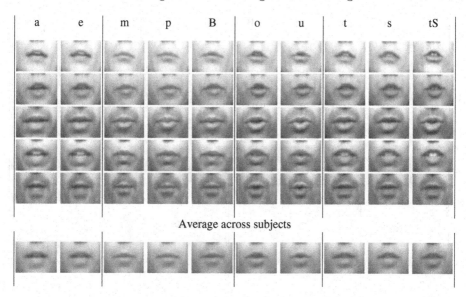

database. We start by showing the obtained results in Table 4 while Table 3 shows examples of the average lip-images per subject and phoneme for 5 subjects from the VLRF database. Compared to those in Table 2, we still observe the same visually similar units, that correlate with our mappings. However, looking separately at each speaker (e.g. each row of the table), we also observe that some of the phonemes seem now more likely to be distinguished. For example, even though phonemes /a/ and /e/ produce very similar lip-images, in /a/ the mouth seems more open vertically while in /e/ the mouth seems widened (more horizontal opening). It is also possible to find differences between /t/, /s/ and /tS/, e.g. /t/ seems to be more opened with visibility of the tongue and /tS/ seems to be pronounced joining the lips more strongly. However, this is not true for all phonemes, e.g. the differences between /m/, /p/ and /B/ are still visually imperceptible. Moreover, the differences between phonemes from the same speaker do not necessarily generalize across multiple speakers, as we can see in the last row of Table 3: the lip-images averaged across multiple speakers are again extremely similar, reflecting the visual ambiguities that justify the mapping of groups of phonemes into the same viseme. As a result, even in a dataset in which subjects were trying to vocalize clearly to facilitate lip-reading, the visual ambiguities between phonemes are still very difficult to distinguish and additional information related to the context would be required to disambiguate them.

Table 3. Average lip-images per user and phoneme of 5 subjects of the VLRF database. Each row shows a sample subject. For each subject, every column shows the average of all the frames in which the subject uttered a specific phoneme. The vertical lines separate the phonemes that belong to different visemes according to our mapping. The last row shows the average when considering all the users together.

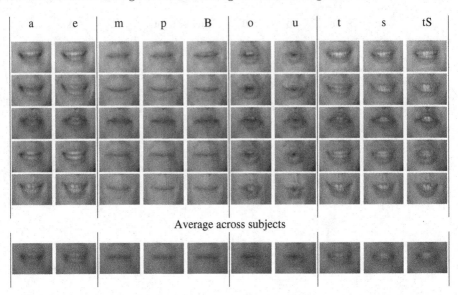

| a | e | m | p | B | o | u | t | s | tS |

Average across subjects

Table 4. System performance in the VLRF database in terms of viseme-, phoneme- and word accuracy for the vocabularies of 20 and 28 classes.

Vocabulary length	Viseme accuracy	Phoneme accuracy	Word accuracy
20	56.07%	51.25%	20.76%
28	51.78%	51.78%	18.17%

A similar conclusion is achieved when we analyze the results in quantitative terms, by looking at the confusion matrices obtained with and without using visemes as intermediate representation. Specifically, Fig. 7 shows the confusion matrices of our ALR system trained in two ways: firstly, using a viseme vocabulary of 20 visemes (found to be optimal experimentally), and the second one trained using a one-to-one mapping between phonemes and visemes (i.e. without visemes). Notice, however, that in both cases we evaluate the confusion at the final stage of the system, which always produces phoneme estimates. Thus, both confusion matrices show the performance of the system in terms of phonemes. A notable observation from these two matrices is that there is high confusion between phonemes that map into the same viseme. This behaviour would be expected in the first matrix, as it corresponds to a system trained based on such phoneme-to-viseme mappings. However, we also see that a very similar confusion

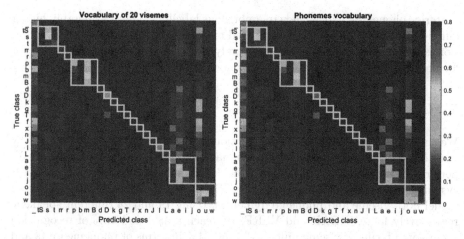

Fig. 7. (a) Resulting confusion matrix from a system trained in VLRF using 20 visemes (many-to-one phoneme-to-viseme mapping). (b) Resulting confusion matrix from a system trained in VLRF using 28 visemes (one-to-one phoneme-to-viseme mapping). Additionally, we highlighted in yellow, the phonemes that share the same viseme in the proposed vocabulary to a clearer comprehension.

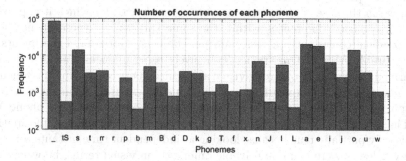

Fig. 8. Frequency of appearance of each phoneme in the VLRF database.

appears also in the second matrix, even when the system was trained directly on phonemes in all its stages.

Detailed analysis of Fig. 7 highlights a few other interesting points. Firstly, in some cases the confusion between groups of phonemes are not symmetric, e.g. although the phonemes /s/ and /t/ are visually similar, the system outputs /s/ more often than /t/, probably because the first one has a higher frequency of appearance in the training set (see Fig. 8). Secondly, there is a huge confusion between several consonants that are very often missclassified as vowels by the system. This type of confusion does not seem directly related to visual similarities, but to difficulties in labeling phoneme transitions and to class imbalance. On the one hand, it is very difficult to precisely define the boundaries between consecutive phonemes and, additionally, these can be influenced by previous and posterior phonemes, which leads to ambiguous labelling. The considerably higher number of vowel samples when compared to consonants explains why the confusion is not symmetric and vowels are rarely missclassified as consonants, except for phonemes with comparably high number of samples, e.g. /s/, /m/, /n/.

5   Conclusions

We investigate the automatic construction of optimal viseme vocabularies by iteratively combining phonemes with similar visual appearance into visemes. We perform tests on the Spanish databases AV@CAR and VLRF using an ALR system based on the combination of DCT and SIFT descriptors and HMMs to model both viseme and phoneme dynamics. Using 19 and 24 different speakers, respectively for AV@CAR and VLRF, we reach a 58% and 56% of recognition accuracy in terms of viseme units, 47% and 51% in terms of phoneme units and 23% and 21% in terms of words units.

Our experiments support the advantage of merging groups of phonemes into visemes. We find that this is the case of both for phonemes that are visually indistinguishable (e.g. /b/, /m/ and /p/) as well as for those in which it is possible to perceive subtle but insufficient differences. The latter occurs, for example, in the case of the phonemes /s/, /t/ and /tS/, for which it is possible to identify visual differences within the same subject but these do not seem to reproduce consistently across multiple subjects. Moreover, experiments on a comparable ALR system trained exclusively using phonemes at all its stages confirmed the existence of strong visual ambiguities between groups of phonemes. This fact and the higher word accuracy obtained when using phoneme-to-viseme mappings, justify the usefulness of visemes instead of the direct use phonemes.

Thus, even though going through visemes may seem like a loss of information, this is only partially true because looking at independent time instants (or small time windows) there is no perceivable difference, in visual terms, between some phonemes. Therefore, training a classifier to predict phonemes based on such information seems like an ill-posed problem, since mistakes between arguably non-separable classes (phonemes within the same viseme) contribute to the loss function as much as those from separable ones (different visemes). Once we estimate the viseme classes, we can disambiguate them into phonemes by means of word or sentence context (e.g. by using HMMs or, more recently, Recurrent Neural Networks).

Acknowledgements. This work is partly supported by the Spanish Ministry of Economy and Competitiveness under project grant TIN2017-90124-P, the Ramon y Cajal programme, the Maria de Maeztu Units of Excellence Programme, and the Kristina project funded by the European Union Horizon 2020 research and innovation programme under grant agreement No. 645012.

References

1. McGurk, H., MacDonald, J.: Hearing lips and seeing voices. Nature **264**, 746–748 (1976)
2. Potamianos, G., Neti, C., Gravier, G., Garg, A., Senior, A.W.: Recent advances in the automatic recognition of audiovisual speech. Proc. IEEE **91**, 1306–1326 (2003)
3. Rosenblum, L.D.: Speech perception as a multimodal phenomenon. Curr. Dir. Psychol. Sci. **17**, 405–409 (2008)
4. Chiţu, A., Rothkrantz, L.J.: Automatic visual speech recognition. In: Speech Enhancement, Modeling and Recognition-Algorithms and Applications, pp. 95–120 (2012)
5. Erber, N.P.: Auditory-visual perception of speech. J. Speech Hear. Disord. **40**, 481–492 (1975)
6. Sumby, W.H., Pollack, I.: Visual contribution to speech intelligibility in noise. J. Acoust. Soc. Am. **26**, 212–215 (1954)
7. Hilder, S., Harvey, R., Theobald, B.J.: Comparison of human and machine-based lip-reading. In: Proceedings of Conference on Auditory-Visual Speech Processing, pp. 86–89 (2009)
8. Ronquest, R.E., Levi, S.V., Pisoni, D.B.: Language identification from visual-only speech signals. Atten. Percept. Psychophys. **72**, 1601–1613 (2010)
9. Seymour, R., Stewart, D., Ming, J.: Comparison of image transform-based features for visual speech recognition in clean and corrupted videos. J. Image Video Process. **2008**, 14 (2008)
10. Antonakos, E., Roussos, A., Zafeiriou, S.: A survey on mouth modeling and analysis for sign language recognition. In: Proceedings of Conference on Automatic Face and Gesture Recognition, vol. 1, pp. 1–7 (2015)
11. Dupont, S., Luettin, J.: Audio-visual speech modeling for continuous speech recognition. IEEE Trans. Multimedia **2**, 141–151 (2000)
12. Nefian, A.V., Liang, L., Pi, X., Xiaoxiang, L., Mao, C., Murphy, K.: A coupled HMM for audio-visual speech recognition. In: Proceedings of Conference on Acoustics, Speech, and Signal Processing, vol. 2, pp. 2013–2016 (2002)
13. Zhou, Z., Zhao, G., Hong, X., Pietikäinen, M.: A review of recent advances in visual speech decoding. Image Vis. Comput. **32**, 590–605 (2014)
14. Yau, W.C., Kumar, D.K., Weghorn, H.: Visual speech recognition using motion features and hidden Markov models. In: Kropatsch, W.G., Kampel, M., Hanbury, A. (eds.) CAIP 2007. LNCS, vol. 4673, pp. 832–839. Springer, Heidelberg (2007). https://doi.org/10.1007/978-3-540-74272-2_103
15. Sui, C., Bennamoun, M., Togneri, R.: Listening with your eyes: towards a practical visual speech recognition system using deep Boltzmann machines. In: Proceedings of IEEE International Conference on Computer Vision, pp. 154–162 (2015)
16. Chung, J.S., Senior, A., Vinyals, O., Zisserman, A.: Lip reading sentences in the wild. In: Proceedings of Conference on Computer Vision and Pattern Recognition, pp. 3444–3453 (2017)
17. Petridis, S., Pantic, M.: Deep complementary bottleneck features for visual speech recognition. In: Proceedings of Conference on Acoustics, Speech and Signal Processing, pp. 2304–2308 (2016)
18. Almajai, I., Cox, S., Harvey, R., Lan, Y.: Improved speaker independent lip reading using speaker adaptive training and deep neural networks. In: Proceedings of Conference on Acoustics, Speech and Signal Processing, pp. 2722–2726 (2016)

19. Chung, J.S., Zisserman, A.: Lip reading in the wild. In: Proceedings of Asian Conference on Computer Vision, pp. 87–103 (2016)
20. Wand, M., Koutník, J., Schmidhuber, J.: Lipreading with long short-term memory. In: Proceedings Conference on Acoustics, Speech and Signal Processing, pp. 6115–6119 (2016)
21. Twaddell, W.F.: On defining the phoneme. Language 11, 5–62 (1935)
22. Fisher, C.G.: Confusions among visually perceived consonants. J. Speech Lang. Hear. Res. 11, 796–804 (1968)
23. Moll, K.L., Daniloff, R.G.: Investigation of the timing of velar movements during speech. J. Acoust. Soc. Am. 50, 678–684 (1971)
24. Luettin, J., Thacker, N.A., Beet, S.W.: Visual speech recognition using active shape models and hidden Markov models. In: Proceedings of Conference on Acoustics, Speech, and Signal Processing, vol. 2, pp. 817–820 (1996)
25. Sahu, V., Sharma, M.: Result based analysis of various lip tracking systems. In: Proceedings of Conference on Green High Performance Computing, pp. 1–7 (2013)
26. Cappelletta, L., Harte, N.: Viseme definitions comparison for visual-only speech recognition. In: Proceedings of Conference on Signal Processing, pp. 2109–2113 (2011)
27. Chung, J.S., Zisserman, A.: Lip reading in profile. In: Proceedings of British Machine Vision Conference (2017)
28. Bear, H.L., Harvey, R.W., Theobald, B.-J., Lan, Y.: Which phoneme-to-viseme maps best improve visual-only computer lip-reading? In: Bebis, G., et al. (eds.) ISVC 2014. LNCS, vol. 8888, pp. 230–239. Springer, Cham (2014). https://doi.org/10.1007/978-3-319-14364-4_22
29. Hazen, T.J., Saenko, K., La, C.H., Glass, J.R.: A segment-based audio-visual speech recognizer: data collection, development, and initial experiments. In: Proceedings of Conference on Multimodal Interfaces, pp. 235–242 (2004)
30. Neti, C., et al.: Audio visual speech recognition. Technical report, IDIAP (2000)
31. Goldschen, A.J., Garcia, O.N., Petajan, E.: Continuous optical automatic speech recognition by lipreading. In: Proceedings of Conference on Signals, Systems and Computers, vol. 1, pp. 572–577 (1994)
32. Jeffers, J., Barley, M.: Speechreading (Lipreading). Charles C. Thomas Publisher, Springfield (1980)
33. Bozkurt, E., Erdem, C.E., Erzin, E., Erdem, T., Ozkan, M.: Comparison of phoneme and viseme based acoustic units for speech driven realistic lip animation. In: Proceedings of Signal Processing and Communications Applications, pp. 1–4 (2007)
34. Ezzat, T., Poggio, T.: MikeTalk: a talking facial display based on morphing visemes. In: Proceedings of Conference on Computer Animation, pp. 96–102 (1998)
35. Fernandez-Lopez, A., Sukno, F.M.: Automatic viseme vocabulary construction to enhance continuous lip-reading. In: Proceedings of Conference on Computer Vision Theory and Applications, vol. 5, pp. 52–63 (2017)
36. Messer, K., Matas, J., Kittler, J., Luettin, J., Maitre, G.: XM2VTSDB: the extended M2VTS database. In: Proceedings of Conference on Audio and Video-Based Biometric Person Authentication, vol. 964, pp. 965–966 (1999)
37. Estellers, V., Gurban, M., Thiran, J.P.: On dynamic stream weighting for audio-visual speech recognition. IEEE-ACM Trans. Audio Speech Lang. Process. 20, 1145–1157 (2012)
38. Papandreou, G., Katsamanis, A., Pitsikalis, V., Maragos, P.: Adaptive multimodal fusion by uncertainty compensation with application to audio-visual speech recognition. In: Proceedings of Multimodal Processing and Interaction, pp. 1–15 (2008)

39. Papandreou, G., Katsamanis, A., Pitsikalis, V., Maragos, P.: Adaptive multimodal fusion by uncertainty compensation with application to audiovisual speech recognition. IEEE-ACM Trans. Audio Speech Lang. Process. **17**, 423–435 (2009)
40. Estival, D., Cassidy, S., Cox, F., Burnham, D.: AusTalk: an audio-visual corpus of Australian English. In: Proceeding of Conference on Language Resources and Evaluation (2014)
41. Ukai, N., Seko, T., Tamura, S., Hayamizu, S.: GIF-LR: GA-based informative feature for lipreading. In: Proceedings Conference on Signal and Information Processing Association Annual Summit and Conference, pp. 1–4 (2012)
42. Ninomiya, H., Kitaoka, N., Tamura, S., Iribe, Y., Takeda, K.: Integration of deep bottleneck features for audio-visual speech recognition. In: Proceedings of Interspeech, pp. 563–567 (2015)
43. Tamura, S., et al.: CENSREC-1-AV: an audio-visual corpus for noisy bimodal speech recognition. In: Proceedings of Conference on Auditory-Visual Speech Processing (2010)
44. Lan, Y., Harvey, R., Theobald, B., Ong, E.J., Bowden, R.: Comparing visual features for lipreading. In: Proceedings of Conference on Auditory-Visual Speech Processing, pp. 102–106 (2009)
45. Kolossa, D., Zeiler, S., Vorwerk, A., Orglmeister, R.: Audiovisual speech recognition with missing or unreliable data. In: Proceedings of Conference on Auditory-Visual Speech Processing, pp. 117–122 (2009)
46. Zhao, G., Barnard, M., Pietikainen, M.: Lipreading with local spatiotemporal descriptors. IEEE Trans. Multimed. **11**, 1254–1265 (2009)
47. Zhou, Z., Hong, X., Zhao, G., Pietikäinen, M.: A compact representation of visual speech data using latent variables. IEEE Trans. Pattern Anal. Mach. Intell. **36**, 1 (2014)
48. Pei, Y., Kim, T.K., Zha, H.: Unsupervised random forest manifold alignment for lipreading. In: Proceedings of the IEEE International Conference on Computer Vision, pp. 129–136 (2013)
49. Assael, Y.M., Shillingford, B., Whiteson, S., de Freitas, N.: LipNet: sentence-level lipreading. In: Proceedings of GPU Technology Conference (2017)
50. Thangthai, K., Harvey, R., Cox, S., Theobald, B.J.: Improving lip-reading performance for robust audiovisual speech recognition using DNNs. In: Proceedings of Conference on Auditory-Visual Speech Processing (2015)
51. Noda, K., Yamaguchi, Y., Nakadai, K., Okuno, H.G., Ogata, T.: Lipreading using convolutional neural network. In: Proceedings of Interspeech, pp. 1149–1153 (2014)
52. Lan, Y., Harvey, R., Theobald, B.J.: Insights into machine lip reading. In: Proceedings of Conference on Acoustics, Speech and Signal Processing, pp. 4825–4828 (2012)
53. Ortega, A., et al.: AV@CAR: a Spanish multichannel multimodal corpus for in-vehicle automatic audio-visual speech recognition. In: Proceedings of Conference on Language Resources and Evaluation (2004)
54. Fernandez-Lopez, A., Martinez, O., Sukno, F.M.: Towards estimating the upper bound of visual-speech recognition: the visual lip-reading feasibility database. In: Proceedings of Conference on Automatic Face and Gesture Recognition (2017)
55. Sukno, F.M., Ordas, S., Butakoff, C., Cruz, S., Frangi, A.F.: Active shape models with invariant optimal features: application to facial analysis. IEEE Trans. Pattern Anal. Mach. Intell. **29**, 1105–1117 (2007)
56. Lowe, D.G.: Distinctive image features from scale-invariant keypoints. Int. J. Comput. Vis. **60**, 91–110 (2004)

57. Franklin, S.B., Gibson, D.J., Robertson, P.A., Pohlmann, J.T., Fralish, J.S.: Parallel analysis: a method for determining significant principal components. J. Veg. Sci. **6**, 99–106 (1995)
58. Khoshgoftaar, T.M., Van Hulse, J., Napolitano, A.: Comparing boosting and bagging techniques with noisy and imbalanced data. IEEE Trans. Syst. Man Cybern.-Part A: Syst. Hum. **41**, 552–568 (2011)
59. Verbaeten, S., Van Assche, A.: Ensemble methods for noise elimination in classification problems. In: Windeatt, T., Roli, F. (eds.) MCS 2003. LNCS, vol. 2709, pp. 317–325. Springer, Heidelberg (2003). https://doi.org/10.1007/3-540-44938-8_32
60. Frénay, B., Verleysen, M.: Classification in the presence of label noise: a survey. Neural Netw. Learn. Syst. **25**, 845–869 (2014)
61. Nettleton, D.F., Orriols-Puig, A., Fornells, A.: A study of the effect of different types of noise on the precision of supervised learning techniques. Artif. Intell. Rev. **33**, 275–306 (2010)
62. Rabiner, L.R.: A tutorial on hidden Markov models and selected applications in speech recognition. Proc. IEEE **77**, 257–286 (1989)
63. Petrushin, V.A.: Hidden Markov models: fundamentals and applications. In: Proceedings of Conference on Online Symposium for Electronics Engineer (2000)
64. Wells, J.C., et al.: SAMPA computer readable phonetic alphabet. In: Handbook of Standards and Resources for Spoken Language Systems, vol. 4 (1997)
65. Llisterri, J., Mariño, J.B.: Spanish adaptation of SAMPA and automatic phonetic transcription. Reporte técnico del ESPRIT PROJECT, vol. 6819 (1993)

A Context-Aware Method for View-Point Invariant Long-Term Re-identification

Athira Nambiar[✉] and Alexandre Bernardino

Institute for Systems and Robotics, Instituto Superior Técnico,
Av. Rovisco Pais, 1, 1049-001 Lisbon, Portugal
{anambiar,alex}@isr.tecnico.ulisboa.pt

Abstract. In this work, we propose a novel context-aware framework towards long-term person re-identification. In contrast to the classical context-unaware architecture, in this method we exploit contextual features that can be identified reliably and guide the re-identification process in a much faster and accurate manner. The system is designed for the long-term Re-ID in walking scenarios, so persons are characterized by soft-biometric features (*i.e.*, anthropometric and gait) acquired using a Kinect^{TM} v.2 sensor. Context is associated to the posture of the person with respect to the camera, since the quality of the data acquired from the used sensor significantly depends on this variable. Within each context, only the most relevant features are selected with the help of feature selection techniques, and custom individual classifiers are trained. Afterwards, a *context-aware ensemble fusion strategy* which we term as 'Context specific score-level fusion', merges the results of individual classifiers. In typical 'in-the-wild' scenarios the samples of a person may not appear in all contexts of interest. To tackle this problem we propose a cross-context analysis where features are mapped between contexts and allow the transfer of the identification characteristics of a person between different contexts. We demonstrate in this work the experimental verification of the performance of the proposed context-aware system against the classical context-unaware system. We include in the results the analysis of switching context conditions within a video sequence through a pilot study of circular path movement. All the analysis accentuate the impact of contexts in simplifying the searching process by bestowing promising results.

1 Introduction

We present a context-aware ensemble fusion framework based on soft-biometric features, for long term person re-identification (Re-ID) in-the-wild[1] surveillance scenarios. In particular, a biometric enabled person Re-ID system, leveraging two kinds of soft biometric features *i.e.*, anthropometric and gait features, is proposed. Since biometric feature extraction is strongly influenced by the view-point, we associate context to the viewing direction, and choose the best features

---

[1] 'in-the-wild' refers to the unconstrained settings.

A. P. Cláudio et al. (Eds.): VISIGRAPP 2017, CCIS 983, pp. 329–351, 2019.
https://doi.org/10.1007/978-3-030-12209-6_16

for each viewpoint (context). This is an extended version of the study the authors conducted in our previous work [1]. Building upon the same, we extrapolate the idea of '*view-point context*' analysis to the case where persons samples are non uniformly distributed in the gallery set by proposing a cross-context analysis. We also include the analysis of the challenging case of switching of contexts when walking paths change direction with respect to the camera, a condition not previously addressed in the literature.

In our approach, we use Kinect^{TM} sensor as the indoor Re-ID data acquisition device. Albeit some similar Kinect based Re-ID systems have been reported in the literature leveraging soft-biometric cues, [2–4] they are view-point dependent *i.e.*, data acquisition and the algorithm verification were carried out in a single direction (view-point) with respect to the camera. Such settings do not clearly represent general scenarios, where people walk in different directions. Hence, in order to assess the impact of view-point on Re-ID performance, as well as to use view-points as the contexts, we couldn't depend upon any of such existing datasets.

To tackle this issue, we collected a new set of data, where people were asked to walk in various directions (left lateral, left diagonal, frontal, right diagonal and right lateral) in front of Kinect. Along with this article, we also release the dataset named "KS20 VisLab Multi-View Kinect skeleton dataset", publicly available for research purposes[2]. We consider that some landmarks in an indoor space, (e.g., door entry/exit, lift location, printing and coffee machines etc.) determine the primary walking directions rather than random walking patterns. We term such predefined directional view-points as 'contexts', in this study. We hypothesize that this knowledge of strategic directions and the assignment of contexts are of great interest within the scope of Re-ID, since the camera positioning and gallery preparation. Benefit a lot from them in a realistic Re-ID surveillance scenario. In addition to that, not all the features are equally relevant in all contexts, because the characteristics of a person that best correlate to its identity depend strongly on the view point. For instance, a person with a short stride gait is better perceived from a lateral view, whereas a person with a large chest is more distinct from a frontal view. Hence, the selection of the relevant features according to the context is also yet another interesting problem. Based on these two hypotheses, we redefine the classical Re-ID strategy by means of a novel '*context-aware ensemble fusion Re-ID framework*', where we explicitly evaluate a context-specific feature matching criteria in Re-ID, and verify its experimental validity in a realistic scenario.

After studying the impact of context based Re-ID with baseline assumptions (equal gallery samples in all contexts as done in [1]), we further extend this study onto more realistic cases, where the gallery samples within the contexts vary. Such instances of data deficiency in some view-points are frequent in 'in-the-Wild' Re-ID scenarios. In many cases of practical interest, the number of samples per person will vary in different view-points. For example in a long

---

[2] More details on KS20 VisLab Multi-View Kinect skeleton dataset is available in the laboratory website http://vislab.isr.ist.utl.pt/vislab_multiview_ks20/.

corridor, the data acquisition will capture more samples of the person, whereas in an entry/exit point, this number may be smaller. Thus, a test sample from corridor sequence will have a large number gallery samples to match against, whereas for a test sample from the door sequence, the number of gallery samples will be very few. Hence, in order to cope with this issue and to find a solution by exploiting also the samples from other contexts, we propose a methodology called *'cross-context'*, wherein a learned feature mapping among various contexts can improve the results.

We include in this work the analysis of the challenging case of *'switching of contexts'* where the direction of person's walk keeps varying in the video sequence. We analyse a circular path movement as an instance of such a context-switching scenario. Detailed analysis of all these topics will be explained in the forthcoming sections. The major contributions of the paper are enumerated as follows:

- Public release of a new dataset with 20 people walking in 5 different directions acquired from Kinect™ v.2, suitable for long-term pose-invariant Re-ID, named "KS20 VisLab Multi-View Kinect skeleton dataset".
- Proposal of a 'Context-aware ensemble fusion Re-ID framework' where different context specific classifiers are trained via adaptive selection of the potentially relevant features in each context.
- Proposal of 'Cross-context analysis', in order to cope with data deficient cases in the gallery contexts, and to improve the Re-ID performance via feature mapping.
- A pilot study of the 'context-switching' test case, by experimenting people walking along circular path (changing contexts) and conducting Re-ID trained with KS20 dataset.

The rest of the paper is organized as follows. The related works are described in Sect. 2. The proposed methodology is explained in Sect. 3, *i.e.* feature extraction method, Context-aware ensemble fusion framework and Cross-context analysis via feature mapping. In Sect. 4, our dataset and experimental results are discussed in detail. Finally, the summary of the paper and some future plans are enumerated in Sect. 5.

2   Related Works

Many Kinect based Re-ID works were reported in the literature in the last few years. The major advantage of such proposals were the incorporation of soft-biometric cues by exploiting the depth info and skeleton joints. This enabled the Re-ID paradigm to extend towards long term scenarios, from the traditional short-term scenarios which leverage primarily appearance cues (colour or texture).

One of the earlier works [2], proposed a specific signature to be built for each subject from a composition of several soft biometric cues (*e.g.*, skeleton and surface based features) extracted from the depth data. Then, Re-ID was accomplished by matching these signatures against the gallery samples. Kinect based person re-identification from soft biometric cues was also addressed in another work by [5], leveraging skeleton descriptors (by computing several limb lengths and ratios) and shape traits (using point cloud shape). In some other recent works in [3] and [4], both static anthropometric features and dynamic gait features were employed towards Re-ID tasks. Nevertheless, in all of those methodologies, data acquisitions were conducted in a constrained manner *i.e.*, in a particular view-point. In this work, we build upon the aforementioned state-of-the-art works but in less constrained conditions by imposing an 'in-the-wild' indoor Re-ID scenario with various viewpoints and by exploiting relevant features in each of those view-points (contexts).

Many definitions of context were encountered in the literature, depending on the field of application. The dictionary definition of context is *"the surroundings, circumstances, environment, background or settings that determine, specify, or clarify the meaning of an event or other occurrence"* [6]. In our work, we deem context as the view-point setting, under which features are computed. The concept and application of context were reported in various fields, for instance, in customer behaviour applications [7], where the context was viewed as the intent of a purchase (*e.g.* context of a gift). In [8], subject re-identification has been conducted exploiting instant messaging in a web surfing navigation. The context used in that work was the special characteristics of chatting text (*e.g.* content, syntax and structural based features). In [9] context (time of the day/location where digital data created) was used for online customer re-identification towards customer behaviour model analysis. The concept of context in terms of predictable and unpredictable image quality characteristics was presented in the traffic monitoring research area in [10]. In [11], both the scene context (environment of the subject at global and local levels) and group context information (activity interaction of subject with group members) were exploited towards activity recognition.

In the person Re-identification paradigm, few works addressed the concept of context. The work of [12] proposed a Re-ID paradigm which leveraged heterogeneous contextual information together with facial features. In particular, they used clothing, activity, human attributes, gait and people co-occurrence as various contexts, and then integrated all of those context features using a generic entity resolution framework called RelDC. Some other recent Re-ID works utilized context as a strategy for refining the classical Re-ID results via re-ranking technique [13,14]. In those works, in addition to the content information of the subjects, they also leveraged context information (k-common nearest neighbors) to fine tune the Re-ID results. From our literature review, context is found to be a new tool whose effectiveness in Re-ID applications is yet to be completely explored.

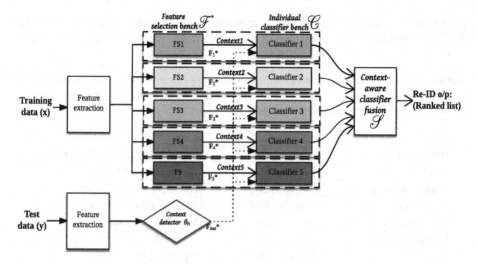

Fig. 1. Context-aware ensemble fusion system consist of a feature extraction module, feature selection context bench, individual classifier bench, a context detector module and a classifier fusion module. The individual classifiers for each context are trained using individual feature subspace ensembles $\mathbf{F}_j^*$, obtained for each context. When the test data enters, context detector identifies the context and activates the corresponding ensemble classifiers. Then, the context-aware classifier fusion strategy finally combines the results of those ensemble classifiers to produce the global result.

3 Methodology

In this section, we explain the proposed methodology *i.e.*, various stages of data analysis including feature extraction, context-aware ensemble fusion framework and cross-context mapping.

3.1 Feature Extraction

Two kinds of features were extracted: *(i)* Anthropometric features *i.e.*, the static physical features defining the body measurements and *(ii)* Gait features *i.e.*, dynamic features defining the kinematics in walking. See Table 1 for the list of features we used. Under the anthropometric feature set, body measurements defining the holistic body proportions of the subject such as height, arm length, upper torso length, lower torso length, upper to lower ratio, chest size, hip size were collected. Similarly, under the gait features, the behavioural features deriving from the continuous monitoring of joints during the gait were collected. In particular, mean and standard deviation of the various measurements during a gait cycle were collected *i.e.*, (i) the angles at various body joints; (ii) the distance between various right-left limbs and; (iii) the relative position of body joints.

Also three scalar features related to walking, *viz.*, stride length, stride time and the speed of walking, are computed within the gait features. Hence, the feature set contains a total of 7 anthropometric features and 67 gait features. In Table 1, the dimension of features derived are shown within parenthesis.

Table 1. List of anthropometric and gait features used in our experiments. L&R correspond to 'left and right' and x&y correspond to 'along x and y axes'. The numbers of features derived are shown within parenthesis.

Anthropometric features	Gait features	
Height-(*1*)	Hip angle(L&R)-(*4*)	Hip position(L&R)(x&y)-(*8*)
Arm length-(*1*)	Knee angle(L&R)-(*4*)	Knee position(L&R)(x&y)-(*8*)
Upper torso-(*1*)	Foot distance-(*2*)	Ankle position(L&R)(x&y)-(*8*)
Lower torso-(*1*)	Knee distance-(*2*)	Hand position(L&R)(x&y)-(*8*)
Upper-lower ratio-(*1*)	Hand distance-(*2*)	Shoulder position(L&R)(x&y)-(*8*)
Chestsize-(*1*)	Elbow distance-(*2*)	Stride-(*1*)
Hipsize-(*1*)	Head position(x&y)-(*4*)	Stride length-(*1*)
	Spine position(x&y)-(*4*)	Speed-(*1*)

3.2 Context-Aware Ensemble Fusion

One key contribution of our work is the proposal of context-aware ensemble fusion Re-ID framework. As mentioned earlier, we experiment the impact of the different data features along different contexts *i.e.*, view-points, and then employ a context-based fusion method to obtain the final Re-ID result. We refer the work on feature subspace ensembles [15] to be a motivation to the authors to come up with a homogeneous ensemble fusion strategy. That work presented an approach to execute multiple parallel feature selection stages leveraging different training conditions, so as to obtain the best features, by using majority voting of the feature ensembles.

Our proposed framework is shown in Fig. 1. After the feature extraction is carried out, four further modules constitute the system: (i) *Feature selection Context bench* (ii) *Individual classifier bench*, (iii) *Context detector module* and (iv) *Context-aware classifier fusion module*.

Feature Selection Context Bench. Refering to Fig. 1, we illustrate our method with five context view-points as *Context1, ..., ContextN*, with $N = 5$. After the features are extracted from the training data within the feature extraction module, the feature descriptors are customized for individual contexts. This usage of 'right-data in the right context' is one of the main advantage of our framework in contrast to the classical approaches. This enables the data to be split and stored in an organized manner (according to context) within the gallery.

Each context module is internally built of a feature selection bench and an individual classifier bench. The former module analyses the feature vectors entered into each context, by means of a feature selection scheme and retain only the most discriminative and relevant features. Specifically, we use the popular Sequential Forward Selection (SFS) algorithm [16] as an instance of Feature Selection (FS). It works iteratively by adding features to an initial subset, seeking to improve the Re-ID measurement. Suppose, $\mathbf{X} = \{x_1, \cdots, x_n\}$ denotes a set of n samples represented in a d-dimensional space, each with a d-dimensional feature set $\mathbf{F} = (f_1, \cdots, f_d)$. FS analyses this d-dimensional space in order to identify the potentially relevant features $f_i \subset \mathbf{F}$, and discard the rest according to some feature subspace evaluation criteria J and ultimately derive $\mathbf{FS}_j^*$, which is the set of most relevant features for context j. Thus, the outputs of the Feature selection context bench consists of an ensemble of feature subspace $i.e.$, the features selected for each particular context $\mathcal{F}^* = (\mathbf{FS}_1^*, \cdots, \mathbf{FS}_5^*)$.

Specifically, the Sequential Forward Selection (SFS) algorithm works as following: It begins from an empty feature set $\mathbf{FS}_{t=0}^*$. At each step, $\mathbf{FS}_{t+1}^*$ all possible super-spaces containing the most relevant feature subspace in the previous step, $\mathbf{FS}_t^*$, and one from the remaining features $f_i \in \mathbf{F}\backslash\mathbf{FS}_t^*$ are formed and evaluated by J. This iterative search will proceed until a stopping criteria is met, for which we considered the degradation of J $i.e.$, if any super-space formed at a given step $\mathbf{FS}_{t+1}^*$ does not improve J, the search stops and the subspace $\mathbf{FS}_t^*$ is considered as the best feature subset. At last, the outputs of the Feature selection context bench consist of an ensemble of feature subspaces $i.e.$, the features selected for each particular context $\mathcal{F}^* = (\mathbf{FS}_1^*, \cdots, \mathbf{FS}_5^*)$. For the implementation of the algorithm, the authors used SFS package[3] [17]. We used 1NN classifier with an Euclidean neighborhood metric in the SFS scheme.

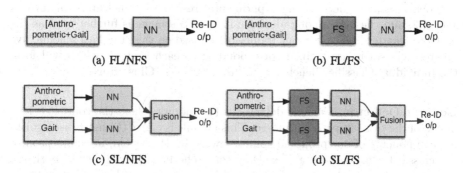

Fig. 2. Various fusion-feature selection schemes employed in this work. Top and bottom rows represents feature-level and score-level fusion strategies respectively. Feature selection (FS) is not used in case studies (a) FL/NFS and (c) SL/NFS, whereas (b) FL/FS and (d) SL/FS shows the inclusion of FS module.

---

[3] http://users.spa.aalto.fi/jpohjala/featureselection/.

Individual Classifier Bench. After the feature selection phase, the selected most relevant features were leveraged to train each individual classifier. These sets of potential features consist of both anthropometric and gait features. In order to understand how to fuse all these various features during the training of classifiers, we use two popular traditional approaches *viz.*, feature level fusion and score level fusion. Also, the impact of feature selection module is verified at this stage by enabling and disabling the FS bench. Hence, four fusion-feature selection case studies are carried out: (i) Feature-level fusion without FS (FL/NFS), (ii) Score-level fusion without FS (SL/NFS), (iii) Feature-level fusion with FS (FL/FS) and (iv) Score-level fusion with FS (SL/FS). The schematic representations of all these cases are depicted in Fig. 2.

In feature level fusion (see Fig. 2 top row), the biometric sets of the same individual are concatenated after an initial normalization (Min-max) scheme. This way, we concatenate our 7D anthropometric features and 67D gait features in order to make a 74D feature vector. Then, the concatenated feature vector is used in the classifier in order to represent the identity of an individual. Instead, in score level fusion (see Fig. 2 bottom row), the fusion is carried out at the score level. The matching scores of each biometric sets are determined independently using two different classifiers and the matching scores at their outputs are fused in order to provide an aggregate score result. As explained in [18], normalized distance scores obtained at each individual classifiers can be fused using some combination rule such as sum, product, min, max or median. In our approach, we adopted sum rule as the classifier combination rule.

In all the case studies mentioned here, a leave one out evaluation strategy is performed within each context, with a Nearest neighbour (NN) classifier using euclidean distance metric. The experimental results obtained are explained in Sect. 4.2, and the best among all those fusion-FS scheme is further used as the *de facto* standard scheme in our framework. Based on this standard scheme, five different classifiers are trained corresponding to each context, which will form the Individual Classifier bench $\mathcal{C} = [\textbf{Classifier1}, \cdots, \textbf{Classifier5}]$.

Context Detector. Context detector is the module where the context (viewpoint) of the test sample is estimated. This module is one of the most distinguishing components of our proposed context-aware Re-ID system, in comparison to the classical context-unaware Re-ID system. The holistic overview of both the classical vs. proposed systems is depicted in Fig. 3. In the classical approaches, no notion of *Context* is enabled, so that all the data in the gallery has to be used in the person matching procedure. Instead, in our proposed context-aware system, data are organised according to context. In addition to that, the *Context-detector* module determines the context of the probe sample and thus redirects the system to the corresponding gallery context in order to facilitate a faster and more accurate person matching.

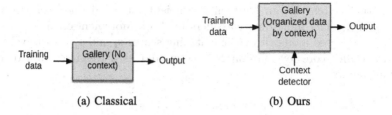

Fig. 3. Classical (context-unaware) vs. proposed context-aware systems.

The design of the context detector module was carried out by analysing any torso joint over a gait cycle[4]. Then, the direction of walking is estimated by analysing the direction of the joint vector. Suppose h_{begin} and h_{end} denote the position of the joint in the first frame and last frame respectively. Then the directional vector among these frames $h = <h_x, h_y, h_z>$ is obtained as follows:

$$h = h_{end} - h_{begin}, \tag{1}$$

The y component h_y is only related to the vertical direction and hence is ignored. Then, the angular direction θ_h made by h can be determined by measuring the inverse tangent of h_z/h_x.

$$\theta_h [\text{degrees}] = \tan^{-1}(h_z/h_x) * 180/\pi \tag{2}$$

Whenever a test data $y \in \mathbb{R}^{1 \times d}$ enters into the system, its context is estimated using (1) and (2), and the corresponding ensemble classifiers are activated in order to proceed with context-aware classifier fusion.

Context-Aware Classifier Fusion. Classifier fusion module performs a context-specific adaptive fusion of the results obtained at the outputs of individual classifiers $\mathcal{C} = [\textbf{Classifier1}, \cdots, \textbf{Classifier5}]$, based on the result from context detector. We propose a score-level fusion based on context termed as '*Context-specific score level fusion*', which can be considered homologous to the concept of user-specific score-level fusion in multibiometric systems, where user-specific weights were assigned to indicate importance of individual biometric matchers [18]. In a similar way, in our proposal, we endorse adaptive weights to the scores from different classifiers according to its context, in order to increase the influence of more reliable context. We employed linear interpolation technique as an instance of the adaptive weighting scheme.

Consider a test sample y, at an arbitrary view-point context v_{test}, is entering into the system. The context is detected using the context-detector module.

---

[4] We used 'SpineShoulder' *i.e.*, the base of the neck refering to joint number 20 of Kinect[TM] v.2 (https://msdn.microsoft.com/en-us/library/microsoft.kinect. jointtype.aspx) as the torso joint towards context detection, since it remains more or less stable while walking.

Suppose the context lies in between two neighbour pre-defined context views *i.e.*, $\mathbf{v_i}$ and $\mathbf{v_j}$. The individual classifiers for both aforementioned contexts $\mathbf{C_i}$ and $\mathbf{C_j}$ are selected alongwith their matching scores $\mathbf{s_i}$ and $\mathbf{s_j}$ respectively. The context-specific score level fusion S is computed as a weighted sum of those scores as follows:

$$S = \eta * \mathbf{s_i} + (1 - \eta) * \mathbf{s_j}, \tag{3}$$

where $\eta \in [0, 1]$. The weight η is computed via linear interpolation of the two contexts *i.e.*, $\eta = |\mathbf{v_j} - \mathbf{v_{test}}|/|\mathbf{v_j} - \mathbf{v_i}|$. The special case where only a single context is activated, η of the nearest context turns to be 1, and all the others will be 0. Various case studies on this concept are analysed in detail, in the experimental Sect. 4.3.

3.3   Cross-Context Analysis

After proposing our 'Context-aware ensemble fusion framework', we also propose a special case of the scenario, where the number of subject samples varies among different contexts. This can be considered as an extended case of the baseline contextual analysis, where, in addition to the training of individual contexts, we also train combination of contexts. In detail, in the baseline scenario, we assume equal number of samples per person per view-point. This always enables the context-aware system for a particular test sequence, to search for the matching gallery sample in the very same context. However, in practical scenarios, the gallery samples differ among various contexts. In order to overcome such situations, we propose 'Cross-context analysis'. Here, even if the system lacks gallery samples of the test person in the very same context, it can search at other contexts as well, where the number of gallery samples are higher than the same context. This is realized via a feature mapping technique. Feature mapping learns the set of relevant features in a particular gallery context, given the same/different context as the test context. Based on this idea, we analyse which are the features of interest in Context B, given the test sample in Context A. Feature mapping among 5 contexts results in 25 various FS sets. A pictorial representation of the proposal is shown in Fig. 4.

In order to better understand the proposed concept, we conducted mainly three case studies: (i) 5 cross-context case known as *Full cover gallery* (ii) 4 cross-context case known as *Sparse cover gallery* and (iii) 1 cross-context case known as *Single cover gallery*.

- **5 cross-context (Full cover gallery)** is the case where all contexts of all subjects are represented in the gallery. Or in other words, we have the probe person in all the five context galleries.
- **4 cross-context (Sparse cover gallery)** is the case, where each subject is represented in many contexts but not exactly the one of the test. In other words, we remove the test person from the same context and thus only the matching person data samples available in the gallery are from other 4 different contexts.

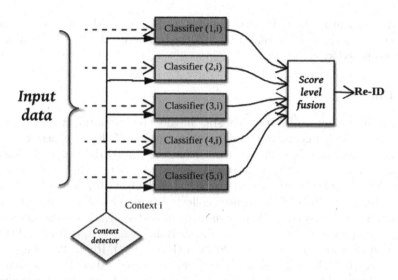

Fig. 4. A schematic overview of cross-context analysis. Individual cross-context classifiers are trained based on the learned feature mapping between the probe context i, and the gallery context of interest. Then, based on score level fusion overall Re-ID result is given as output.

– **1 cross-context (Single cover gallery)** is the case where each subject appears in a single context in the gallery, different from the probe *i.e.*, we remove the test person samples from all the contexts except a random context (other than the probe context).

4 Experiments and Results

In this section, we describe the various experiments conducted as a part of this study, and the results and related observations are explained in detail. First of all, we present our new dataset which we collected in connection with this study, named 'KS20 VisLab Multi-View Kinect skeleton dataset'[5]. We make it publicly available to the community for extending this line of works. Further, we present the performance analysis of our context-aware system and its extension towards cross-context analysis. Four major experiments were carried out in this regard. *(A) Training of the individual context-specific classifiers*, where each classifier model is learned based on respective context; *(B) Contextual analysis*, where the Re-ID system takes into account the context information of the scenario and thus significantly reduces the search space, *(C) Cross-context analysis*, where the issue of sample deficiency in the same context is tackled also by leveraging different

---

[5] KS20 VisLab Multi-View Kinect skeleton dataset: http://vislab.isr.ist.utl.pt/ vislab_multiview_ks20/. Access to the Vislab Multi-view KS20 dataset is available upon request. Contact the corresponding author if you are interested in this dataset.

contexts via feature mapping technique, *(D) Switching of contexts*, wherein a circular path walking test scenario is analysed to verify the Re-ID performance of our proposed system.

4.1 Dataset

In order to employ Re-ID in a realistic 'in-the-wild' scenario, it is essential to have a challenging unconstrained dataset, comprised of the sequences of people walking in different directions. Since a Kinect^{TM} based dataset with different viewangles was unavailable, we acquired our own dataset, in the host laboratory, named 'KS20 Vislab Multi-view Kinect Skeleton dataset'. It is a set of multi-view Kinect skeleton (KS) data sequences collected from 20 walking subjects using Kinect V.2., in the context of long-term person re-identification using biometrics. Multiple walking sequences along five different directions *i.e.*, Left lateral (LL at ~0°), Left diagonal (LD at ~30°), Frontal (F at ~90°), Right diagonal (RD at ~130°) and Right lateral (RL at ~180°) were collected. Altogether we have 300 skeleton image sequences comprising 20 subjects (3 video sequences per person in a particular viewpoint) in the aforementioned directions.

Regarding the data acquisition, the Kinect sensor was kept at a height of an average human (See Fig. 6(a) for the data acquisition system). This simulates a normal video surveillance environment as well as changes in the position of camera over time, as in a long term 'in-the-wild' person Re-ID scenario. The position of camera as well as the walking directions of subjects were deliberately altered in order to ensure a typical surveillance scenario. 20 people within the age group 23–45, including 4 ladies and 16 men participated in the data collection. The statistical details of the people *i.e.*, age, gender, height and weight are highlighted in the Table 2. All of them were asked to walk in their natural gait, in front of the camera three times each along each direction. No markers were provided to determine the path, instead only approximate direction was instructed. The visualization of the existing five contexts in our dataset is given in Fig. 5 by plotting how the actual view-points spread within each contexts. Based on this study, we could observe that five contexts $v_1, ..., v_5$ are spread around their respective cluster means $\mu = [1.67, 35.63, 92.83, 130.70, 180.17]^{\top}$ degrees with standard deviations $\sigma = [3.64, 4.90, 3.29, 5.34, 3.99]^{\top}$ degrees. Different walking directions and sample video frames extracted from our dataset, are shown in Fig. 6.

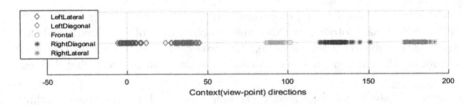

Fig. 5. Distribution of the contexts in the dataset (note: directions are in degrees.).

Table 2. Characteristics of people involved in KS20 Vislab Multiview Kinect Skeleton dataset. This table contains the statistics of 18 people, since two people were reluctant to provide the details.

	Mean	Standard deviation	Minimum	Maximum
Age	31.72	6.08	23	45
Height (cm)	174.78	8.17	160	185
Weight (kg)	72.11	11.60	51	95

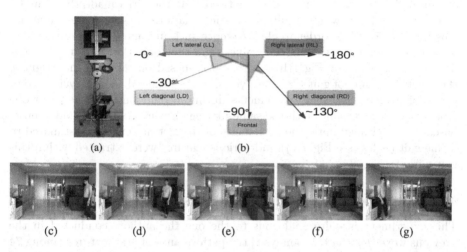

(a) (b)

(c) (d) (e) (f) (g)

Fig. 6. Data acquisition: (a) subject walking directions in front of the camera system (direction angles are defined with respect to the image plane.) (b) Data acquisition set up (c–f) sample frames from our data acquisition, in five different directions- left lateral ($\sim$0°), left diagonal ($\sim$30°), frontal ($\sim$90°), right diagonal ($\sim$130°) and right lateral ($\sim$180°) respectively.

Kinect^{TM} sensor device is composed of a set of sensors, which is accompanied with a Software Development Kit (SDK), and can track movements from users by using a skeleton mapping algorithm that provides the 3D information related to the movements of body joints[6]. We acquired all the three available data *i.e.* skeleton, colour and depth. The skeleton data contains the position and orientation of 25 joints of the human body and was captured at the full frame rate of the sensor @ 30 fps. Colour and depth information are employed for appearance based features, which generally require single frame, and hence was captured at 1 fps. However, these were not used in the current work[7].

---

[6] For body joint types and enumeration, refer to the link: https://msdn.microsoft.com/en-us/library/microsoft.kinect.jointtype.aspx.

[7] In the publicly available dataset also, only the skeleton data is provided. Nevertheless, color and depth information can be made available on demand.

Prior to the analysis, we had to pre-process the data to remove the noise contents in the data. We had discussed the preprocessing and feature extraction phases in detail in the prior work [19]. Usually, the primary effect of noise are jerks/abnormalities in the skeleton data, during the sequences. In addition to that, the skeleton is not detected in some frames, especially in the boundary of the kinect range. In order to tackle such situations, we use a semi-automatic approach to select the best frames to retain in the video sequence. By empirically analysing the evolution of lower body angles over time, we cleared the unwanted jerks in the signals. In particular, by observing the measurements of hip angle over the sequences, we noticed that the jerks made these angles increase abnormally, which results in drastic variations in the corresponding signals (see Fig. 7(a)). In order to clean/remove such unwanted frames, we assign some thresholds upon the angular values, and thus only the valid data signals are being selected (see Fig. 7(b)). Afterwards, based on those cleaned signals, the functional units of gait *viz.*, gait cycles, were estimated. A gait cycle is comprised of sequence of events/movements during locomotion from the point one foot contacts the ground until the same foot again contacts the ground. Hence, based on the cleaned data, the periodicity of the feet movement is estimated to define gait cycles (see Fig. 7(c)) and various features were extracted within this gait period.

4.2   Training of the Individual Context-Specific Classifiers

This experiment is quite analogous to the one the authors conducted in the previous work [1], where we analysed the performance of best features among 74 features *i.e.*, feature subset selected via feature selection. Albeit we carried out similar analysis in the aforementioned paper, herein we have used some different features *i.e.*, relative joint positions instead of absolute joint positions. Based on all these 74 features, we conduct an extensive analysis of various fusion-Feature selection schemes, as mentioned in Sect. 3.2: (a) FL/NFS, (b) FL/FS, (c) SL/NFS and (d) SL/FS, leveraging both feature level/score level fusion and without/with FS. The resulting Re-ID performance as well as the corresponding cumulative matching rank scores (showing overall CMC rank-1) are shown in Fig. 8 and Table 3 respectively.

Results highlight that: (i) Feature selection (FS) outperforms the cases without FS (NFS). (ii) Score-level fusion performs better than the feature level fusion in Re-ID. (iii) SL/FS is found to be the best among the group and thus is considered as the '*de-facto*' in our context-aware ensemble fusion framework, at the individual classifier bench.

Thus, we choose SL/FS as the feature selection scheme for the remaining of this work. This context-aware feature selection criteria resulted in the selection of best features in respective contexts as shown in Table 4. From those customized features, we can observe that some global discriminative anthropometric features such as height, arm length, chest size are highly relevant in almost all the contexts. However, certain features clearly show its affinity towards certain contexts, for e.g., vertical movements of joints associated to gait features

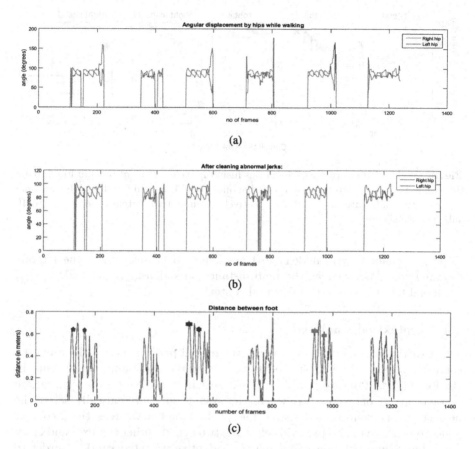

(a)

(b)

(c)

Fig. 7. (a) The abnormal transients at the ends of each sequence are due to the jerks of skeleton occurring at its respective frames; (b) after obtaining the cleaned frames, by filtering the abnormal frames; (c) gait cycle estimation. Three consecutive peaks (two adjacent markers) within a sequence, represent a gait cycle.

Table 3. Chart showing the Re-ID accuracy rates for five contexts at rank-1 CMC. The highest and second highest Re-ID rates observed are highlighted in **bold** and *italic* letters, respectively.

Context	FL/NFS	FL/FS	SL/NFS	SL/FS
Left lateral	68.33	**90.00**	83.33	*88.33*
Left diagonal	55.00	76.67	**81.67**	*78.33*
Frontal	81.67	91.67	*93.33*	**95.00**
Right diagonal	65.00	*81.67*	78.33	**85.00**
Right lateral	68.33	*86.67*	86.67	**88.33**
Average for all contexts	67.66	*85.34*	84.6	**86.99**

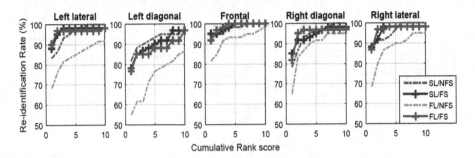

Fig. 8. The Re-ID performances of various fusion-FS schemes mentioned in Fig. 2 along five contexts *viz.*, left lateral (∼0°), left diagonal (∼30°), frontal (∼90°), right diagonal (∼130°) and right lateral (∼180°) respectively. Cumulative matching scores up to 10 subjects are shown.

(hipY$_{\mu,SD}$, handY$_{\mu,SD}$, ankleY$_{\mu,SD}$) are found to be selected in the lateral/ diagonal contexts, whereas the limb distances (handDist$_{\mu,SD}$, elbowDist$_{\mu,SD}$) are found to be selected in the frontal context.

4.3   Contextual Analysis

This experimental analysis is to verify the overall performance of the proposed context-aware system against the baseline classical context-unaware systems. In the former *i.e.*, *Context-aware*, 1-context scenario and 2-contexts scenario are carried out. 1-context case is where the system will automatically select the nearest gallery context and search for the best match whereas the 2-context scenario is where the system will select the two neighbouring contexts and carry out a linear interpolation technique (via adaptive weighted sum), in order to re-identify the person. (see Sect. 3.2 for further details on Context-aware Re-ID paradigm). The latter case is the baseline scenario *i.e.*, *Context-unaware*, where we disable the context detector module, and hence no notion of the probe context is available to the system. We call this case as *'Pure'* baseline, since no notion of context has been considered even during the classifier training phase. Instead, feature selection has been done globally irrespective of any context, and the same features got selected globally thus making the FS in all the samples context-unaware. Then, the test sample is matched against all those gallery samples.

The results are presented in Table 5. Results clearly shows the outper- formance of the *Context-aware* system against *Context-unaware* system. It is notable that context-aware methods (either by using a single or two contexts) bestow high performance level about 88%, whereas Context-unaware approaches 78%. Also, context-aware systems performed faster (6–11 s) compared to the context-unaware system (20 s), since the notion of Context helped the reduction of the search space and speed up the matching process. Hence, the knowledge of context is found to be vital in augmenting the performance of a Re-ID system in terms of both speed and accuracy.

Table 4. Context-specific features selected via SL/FS scheme, during the training of individual context classifiers.

Feature	LL	LD	F	RD	RL
height	✓	✓	✓	✓	✓
arm	✓	✓	✓	✓	
upper	✓		✓		
lower		✓		✓	✓
ULratio		✓		✓	
chestsize		✓	✓	✓	✓
hipsize	✓		✓	✓	
kneeAngle		✓		✓	
kneeDist$_{\mu,\mathrm{SD}}$	✓	✓	✓	✓	
elbowDist$_{\mu}$			✓	✓	
elbowDist$_{\mathrm{SD}}$	✓	✓		✓	
headY$_{\mu}$		✓		✓	
headY$_{\mathrm{SD}}$	✓				
rhipY$_{\mu,SD}$	✓	✓		✓	
lhipY$_{\mu,SD}$	✓	✓			✓
lkneeY$_{\mu}$					✓
ankleY$_{\mu,SD}$	✓			✓	
lhandY$_{\mu}$		✓			
lhandY$_{\mathrm{SD}}$	✓			✓	
rhandY$_{\mu,SD}$					✓
lshouldY$_{\mu}$		✓			
handDist$_{\mu,\mathrm{SD}}$		✓			
lshouldY$_{\mathrm{SD}}$		✓			

Table 5. Results of classifier fusion showing our proposed context-aware classifier fusion against context-unaware baseline case studies. In context-aware cases, context detector module is enabled, whereas in the context-unaware cases, context detector module is disabled.

	Context-unaware	Context-aware	
	No context (pure baseline)	1 context (binary weights)	2 contexts (adaptive weights)
Anthropometric	60.33%	68.67%	68.00%
Gait Re-ID	72.33%	80.67%	80.67%
Overall Re-ID	78.33%	88.00%	88.67%
Processing time	25.14 s	6.176 s	11.63 s

4.4   Cross-Context Analysis

Refering to Sect. 3.3, we also conduct an extension of the baseline context-aware framework, with the difference that the number of subject sample varies among different contexts. We carried out three case studies: (i) 5 cross-context case known as *Full cover gallery*, where the test sample is compared against all the remaining 299 data samples in all the 5 contexts, (ii) 4 cross-context case known as *Sparse cover gallery*, where each test will be compared against 297 data samples in the gallery, and (iii) 1 cross-context case known as *Single cover gallery*, where the test sample has to be matched against 288 samples.

Now, for each of the aforementioned cases, five matching techniques are performed: (a) No FS (b) Pure baseline (c) 1-nearest context (d) 2 neighboring contexts and (e) Cross-contexts. Method 'no FS' doesn't consider any Feature selection criteria, thus the matching will be the basic feature matching of 74D feature vectors in all the gallery contexts. The second method (Global FS) conducts feature selection globally upon the whole set of data. This is the pure baseline analysis mentioned in Table 5. Then, upon the selected feature set, it carries out the feature matching. Since both of these cases don't consider the notion of context, they are categorized under *Context-unaware* paradigms. The latter ones *i.e.* (c) 1-nearest context (d) 2 neighboring contexts and (e) Cross-contexts, execute feature selection and context-aware Re-ID. In both (c) and (d), baseline context-aware framework is considered whereas in (e), the cross-context technique is exploited.

Table 6. Chart showing the Re-ID accuracy rates of cross-context analysis. Full, sparse and single cover gallery cases with different feature selection schemes *i.e.*, no FS, Global FS and Customized FS are shown. The accuracy rates shown in each cell represents Rank-1 CMC rate (in percentage).

	Context-unaware		Context-aware		
	No FS	Global FS	1-context	2 contexts	Cross-context
(i) Full cover (5 contexts)	74.67	78.33	88.00	88.67	82.33
(ii) Sparse cover (4 contexts)	28.00	41.67	x	x	44.33
(iii) Single cover (1 context)	8.33	12.67	x	x	18.33

The results for the aforementioned cases are reported in Table 6. The primary observation made out of the results is that the context-aware cases always outperforms the context-unaware cases[8]. We can observe the improvement in Re-ID performance by incorporating feature selection scheme as well as context framework. It is notable that 'Pure baseline' (global FS) could improve the results compared to the 'no FS'. While exploiting contextual analysis, the best performance is reported (they are applicable only in the full-cover scenarios).

---

[8] 1-context and 2-contexts work only for the full cover scenario, and hence other sparse cover and single cover scenarios for the same are represented via crossmark, refering 'Not Applicable'.

However, Cross-context outperforms both 'no FS' and 'Pure baseline', in all the three gallery cover scenarios. Thus, it is confirmed that when the relevant features are selected according the context by learning the mapping of features among various contexts, it can improve the result of Re-ID. Since deficiency of samples in some viewpoints are a big challenge in realistic practical scenarios, such cross-context customized FS approach is of great interest.

The best Re-ID performance among the 3 cases of gallery settings was observed in the Full-cover gallery context $i.e.$, 5 contexts. This may be due to the fact that there are more and better examples to match to the test sample. Sparse cover produces a bit worse results compared to the former since there is no availability in the very same context, instead it searches and finds the best matching in the four other different contexts. The worst case is where only a single cover gallery (other than the test context) is provided, where always the matching is poor in terms of the number of samples and quality of data, but still outperforms the context-unaware case.

4.5 Switching of Contexts

Yet another experiment we conducted as a part of this study was that of switching of contexts. This is a scenario where the person continuously changes his direction of walk, and hence the context ($i.e.$, view point) also continuously changes. We analyze this issue by considering a circular path walking. This is a pilot study in order to understand the feasibility of applying our system towards 'Context-switching' scenarios. Hence, we acquired new circle path data from two people (who belong to Vislab Multiview KS20 dataset), and try to match them against the KS20 dataset sequences which where collected almost one year before. Two advantages of such an acquisition were: (i) This makes a perfect long-term Re-ID validation system since collected with a gap of long duration and (ii) good for the analysis of varying context scenario.

In this experiment, we asked the people to walk in front of Kinect sensor in circular paths. Either three or four complete walking sequences were recorded. For the processing, we cleaned the data, and then segmented the data to separate gait cycles, as described in Sect. 4.1, with the assumption that, within a gait cycle, the person is walking in a linear path. Hence, a complete circular path contains five or six gait cycles. Note here that, since in our training of the data we used only the directions towards the camera, we ignore the gait cycles where the person is walking away from the camera. Thus, out of a single circular path walking, we extract either 2 or 3 gait cycles. Ultimately, we succeeded in making 7 gait cycles extracted out of whole sequences of walking.

We show the results of Re-ID performance of switching contexts in 2 mode settings of the gallery samples: (i) Complete gallery and (ii) Incomplete gallery. In the former, gallery is provided with sufficient set of samples, and thus we analyse the Re-ID as we conducted Contextual analysis (Sect. 4.2). In the latter, we assume the practical scenario of deficiency of gallery samples, and thus we analyse Re-ID as we conducted Cross-contextual analysis (Sect. 4.3). The corresponding results are shown in Fig. 9. Each diagram shows the k-th rank

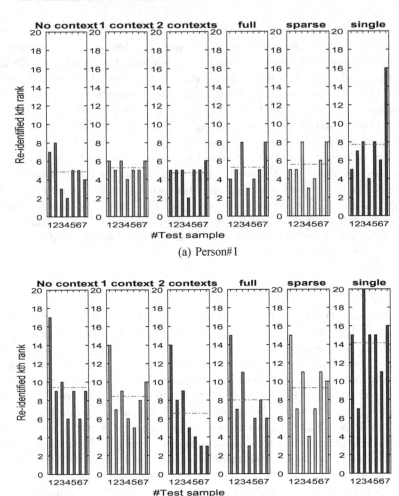

(a) Person#1

(b) Person#2

Fig. 9. A case study of "switching the context", carried out upon two persons are depicted above. In each row, first three diagrams result from contextual analysis (complete gallery samples) and the last three diagrams result from cross-contextual analysis (incomplete gallery samples). The mean k-Rank in each case is marked via dash-dot lines. The best results (lower mean k-Rank) were found in 2-Contexts case scenario, in both persons.

at which the person is correctly re-identified, hence, lower the rank, better the performance. We can observe in both cases that, the Contextual analysis outperforms the Cross-contextual analysis, which clearly accentuates the importance of having good enough number of samples in the gallery set. Within the contextual analysis, the best Re-ID performance is reported in 2-context case, exploiting linear interpolation technique(adaptive weighted sum). Person#1 and #2 are respectively a woman and a man. Considering the relative population of women and men in the dataset (16 men and 4 ladies), better Re-ID was observed for Person#1 (lower k-th rank), implying that Re-ID of the lady candidate was much easily done compared to the man candidate.

5   Conclusions

In this work, a context-aware person re-identification system named 'Context-aware ensemble fusion Re-ID framework', and its extension towards Cross-context analysis have been discussed. As a part of the study, we acquired a new multi-view Kinect skeleton (KS) dataset, containing 300 data sequences collected from 20 subjects, using Kinect^{TM} v.2. We make the dataset publicly available to the research community as one of the contributions of this paper, under the name '*KS20 VisLab Multi-View Kinect skeleton dataset*'.

We conducted extensive study on the impact of various anthropometric and gait features upon person Re-ID. Since certain features have upperhand in specific view-points, we associate context to the viewing direction of walking people in a surveillance scenario and choose the best features for each case. Such a Context-aware proposal exploiting view-point as the contexts is one of the very first of that kind in the Re-ID literature. Building upon our previous works in the same area [1], we analysed various fusion schemes (Score level vs. Feature level) and feature selection (Sequential Forward Selection), we could observe the *Score level fusion with Feature Selection* schemes works the best among all of them and is selected as the de-facto standard for our framework. Other major contributions of the framework are context detection module and context-aware classifier fusion technique. The experimental results of the holistic Re-ID system performance shows that Context-aware system works faster (upto 4 times) and accurate (up to 10% point better) compared to the context-unaware system.

Some other major extension studies were also conducted in this work. First one was cross-context analysis, in order to overcome the practical limitation of gallery data deficiency in the same context. The proposed cross-contextual paradigm enables a feature mapping technique with which the best features could be learned among different contexts, and hence the probe can search and find the best matching even in different contexts. Results show that cross-context beats context-unaware cases. Among the context aware methods, the cross-context is the only applicable to cases of incomplete gallery, eventhough the 1 context and 2 context methods are the best in the full gallery cases. Another very interesting experiment was the context-switching, where the person keeps on changing the direction. In order to validate Re-ID in such scenarios, we exploited a circular path walking for 2 people as a pilot study, and tested against KS20 data gallery. Among various cases, 2-neighboring context (context-aware Re-ID) method performed the best. In the future works, we envisage to incorporate multiple contextual features (*i.e.*, view-point, distance to the camera, occurrence of face, person co-occurrence etc.), as well as to learn contexts automatically (e.g., data clustering).

References

1. Nambiar, A., Bernardino, A., Nascimento, J.C., Fred, A.: Context-aware person re-identification in the wild via fusion of gait and anthropometric features. In: B-Wild Workshop at 12th IEEE International Conference on Automatic Face & Gesture Recognition, pp. 973–980 (2017)
2. Barbosa, I.B., Cristani, M., Del Bue, A., Bazzani, L., Murino, V.: Re-identification with RGB-D sensors. In: Fusiello, A., Murino, V., Cucchiara, R. (eds.) ECCV 2012. LNCS, vol. 7583, pp. 433–442. Springer, Heidelberg (2012). https://doi.org/10.1007/978-3-642-33863-2_43
3. Gianaria, E., Grangetto, M., Lucenteforte, M., Balossino, N.: Human classification using gait features. In: Cantoni, V., Dimov, D., Tistarelli, M. (eds.) International Workshop on Biometric Authentication, pp. 16–27. Springer, Cham (2014). https://doi.org/10.1007/978-3-319-13386-7_2
4. Andersson, V.O., de Araújo, R.M.: Person identification using anthropometric and gait data from kinect sensor. In: AAAI, pp. 425–431 (2015)
5. Munaro, M., Fossati, A., Basso, A., Menegatti, E., Van Gool, L.: One-shot person re-identification with a consumer depth camera. In: Gong, S., Cristani, M., Yan, S., Loy, C.C. (eds.) Person Re-Identification. ACVPR, pp. 161–181. Springer, London (2014). https://doi.org/10.1007/978-1-4471-6296-4_8
6. Context definition. https://en.wiktionary.org/wiki/context
7. Palmisano, C., Tuzhilin, A., Gorgoglione, M.: Using context to improve predictive modeling of customers in personalization applications. IEEE Trans. Knowl. Data Eng. **20**, 1535–1549 (2008)
8. Ding, Y., Meng, X., Chai, G., Tang, Y.: User identification for instant messages. In: Lu, B.-L., Zhang, L., Kwok, J. (eds.) ICONIP 2011. LNCS, vol. 7064, pp. 113–120. Springer, Heidelberg (2011). https://doi.org/10.1007/978-3-642-24965-5_13
9. Panniello, U., Hill, S., Gorgoglione, M.: Using context for online customer re-identification. Expert Syst. Appl. **64**, 500–511 (2016)
10. Alldieck, T., Bahnsen, C.H., Moeslund, T.B.: Context-aware fusion of RGB and thermal imagery for traffic monitoring. Sensors **16**, 1947 (2016)
11. Wei, L., Shah, S.K.: Human activity recognition using deep neural network with contextual information. In: International Conference on Computer Vision Theory and Applications, pp. 34–43 (2017)
12. Zhang, L., Kalashnikov, D.V., Mehrotra, S., Vaisenberg, R.: Context-based person identification framework for smart video surveillance. Mach. Vis. Appl. **25**, 1711–1725 (2014)
13. Leng, Q., Hu, R., Liang, C., Wang, Y., Chen, J.: Person re-identification with content and context re-ranking. Multimedia Tools Appl. **74**, 6989–7014 (2015)
14. Garcia, J., Martinel, N., Micheloni, C., Gardel, A.: Person re-identification ranking optimisation by discriminant context information analysis. In: Proceedings of the IEEE International Conference on Computer Vision, pp. 1305–1313 (2015)
15. Silva, H., Fred, A.: Feature subspace ensembles: a parallel classifier combination scheme using feature selection. In: Haindl, M., Kittler, J., Roli, F. (eds.) MCS 2007. LNCS, vol. 4472, pp. 261–270. Springer, Heidelberg (2007). https://doi.org/10.1007/978-3-540-72523-7_27
16. Whitney, A.W.: A direct method of nonparametric measurement selection. IEEE Trans. Comput. **C-20**(9), 1100–1103 (1971)
17. Pohjalainen, J., Räsänen, O., Kadioglu, S.: Feature selection methods and their combinations in high-dimensional classification of speaker likability, intelligibility and personality traits. Comput. Speech Lang. **29**, 145–171 (2015)

18. Ross, A.A., Nandakumar, K., Jain, A.: Handbook of Multibiometrics, vol. 6. Springer, Heidelberg (2006). https://doi.org/10.1007/0-387-33123-9
19. Nambiar, A., Bernardino, A., Nascimento, J.C., Fred, A.: Towards view-point invariant person re-identification via fusion of anthropometric and gait features from Kinect measurements, pp. 108–119 (2017)

On Using 3D Support Geometries for Measuring Human-Made Corner Structures with a Robotic Total Station

Christoph Klug[1], Dieter Schmalstieg[2], Thomas Gloor[3], and Clemens Arth[2(✉)]

[1] VRVis, Donau-City-Strasse 11, 1220 Vienna, Austria
klug@icg.tugraz.at
[2] Institute for Computer Graphics and Vision (ICG), Graz University of Technology,
Inffeldgasse 16/II, 8010 Graz, Austria
arth@icg.tugraz.at
[3] Hilti Corporation, Feldkircher Strasse 100, 9494 Schaan, Liechtenstein
thomas.gloor@hilti.com
https://www.vrvis.at/, https://www.hilti.com/

Abstract. Performing accurate measurements on non-planar targets using a robotic total station in reflectorless mode is prone to errors. Besides requiring a fully reflected laser beam of the electronic distance meter, a proper orientation of the pan-tilt unit is required for each individual accurate 3D point measurement. Dominant physical 3D structures like corners and edges often don't fulfill these requirements and are not directly measurable.

In this work, three algorithms and user interfaces are evaluated through simulation and physical measurements for simple and efficient construction-side measurement correction of systematic errors. We incorporate additional measurements close to the non-measurable target, and our approach does not require any post-processing of single-point measurements. Our experimental results prove that the systematic error can be lowered by almost an order of magnitude by using support geometries, *i.e.* incorporating a 3D point, a 3D line or a 3D plane as additional measurements.

1 Introduction

Robotic total stations (RTS) are commonly used in surveying and building construction for measuring 3D points with high precision and accuracy [1]. These devices use an electronic distance meter (EDM) for accurate distance measurements, angle sensors and actors for EDM pose definition, and RGB cameras for tele-operation of the system. Modern devices support measuring retro-reflective and natural targets. In the simplest case, an RTS defines a spherical coordinate system with no parallax effects between the coordinate systems of sensors and actors. An exemplary geometric model is shown in Fig. 1. In practice, more complete geometric models are used, which allow for better calibration between

© Springer Nature Switzerland AG 2019
A. P. Cláudio et al. (Eds.): VISIGRAPP 2017, CCIS 983, pp. 352–374, 2019.
https://doi.org/10.1007/978-3-030-12209-6_17

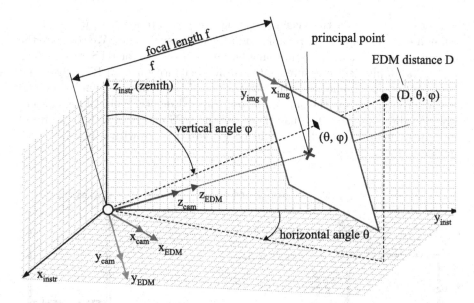

Fig. 1. Conceptual Drawing of a simplified geometric model for a calibrated RTS with azimuth angle θ, polar angle ϕ and radial distance D, as described in Klug *et al.* [7]. The coordinate system of the EDM is aligned with the camera coordinate system and with the spherical coordinate frame RTS. Real-world devices require six degrees of freedom (DOF) pose conversations between the coordinate frames as well as further corrections.

the individual components. Details about RTS models, environmental influences and their calibration can be found in [1–6].

Common natural targets in surveying and building construction are corners and edges of human-made structures. These targets have a high recall value, but are also prone to distance measurement errors. By definition, the laser of the EDM should be fully reflected by a planar surface. However, the laser beam divergence of the EDM renders the direct measurement of such targets critical; it increases the measurement uncertainty, and decreases the measurement reliability. Additionally, inaccurate targeting by the user and optical limitations further increase the measurement uncertainty. Experienced surveyors increase the accuracy and reliability of such measurements by interpolating additional points, measured in the local neighborhood of the target. While such corrections are usually applied offline, instant estimation of the interest point (IP) can avoid expensive repetition of measurements at a later time in case of outliers. An extensive discussion of the problem is provided by Juretzko [8].

In this work, we analyze the benefits of online corrections of reflectorless measuring targets with at least one quasi-planar surface visible to the RTS (see Fig. 2). In particular, we compare three different correction methods, applied directly in the field. To keep the measurement effort low, we do not apply offline post-processing or high density 3D point cloud scans. As a side effect, the user constraints on the visual targeting precision are lowered, which allows even non-experts to perform reliable and robust measurements. We compare the different methods with a real-time simulation environment for RTS, and confirm the results by physical measurements. We further introduce an RTS algorithm design and device simulation setup, with Unity3D for real-time simulation, and a common interface for the simulator and the real device. This allows efficient algorithm development, the analysis of various RTS effects, and full control of the measurement setup, which would be hard to achieve with a physical environment.

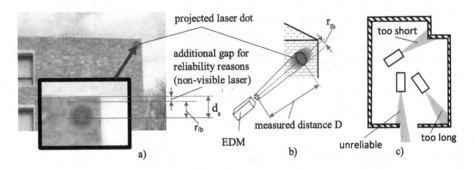

Fig. 2. Reliable measurements require that the laser fully hits a planar surface. Non-planar surfaces and multi-path-reflections increase the measurement uncertainties, as described in Klug *et al.* [7]. (a) Natural target, where the projected laser dot is indicated in green; in outdoor scenarios, the laser is barely visible. The *safety distance* d_s between the edges of the target and the laser hit reduces the risk of unreliable measurements, but increases the measurement uncertainty; d_s is mainly influenced by user experience, camera properties (e.g. image resolution, focal length or image blur), and by the scene setup (e.g. back light conditions, target surface properties). (b) The radius r_{lb} approximates the elliptical projection of the laser beam through a circle. (c) Effects of non-planar targets on EDM measurements [8]. (Color figure online)

2   Related Work

In the following, we shortly review related work about using robotic total stations for measuring.

Traditional surveying methods are described in Uren and Price [1], Coaker [4] and Zeiske [9]. More recently, image-based measurement methods are embedded in many modern total stations, including steering the RTS to selected pixels, selecting and visualizing 3D targets in the image or visualizing metadata. As an example, the device of Topcon [10] supports an image-based measurement feature for not directly measurable targets like corners and edges, but without providing any mathematical details or evaluation of the methods.

Since image-based features have been introduced, they were studied in different areas. Siu *et al.* [11] describe a close range photogrammetric solution for 3D reconstruction and target tracking by combining several total stations and cameras. Fathi *et al.* [12] generate 3D wire diagrams of a roof using video streams from a calibrated stereo camera set. Their algorithm combines feature point matching, line detection and a priori knowledge of roof structures to a structure from motion pipeline. Even if the results of these approaches are quite impressive, none of them can be applied for measuring corner and edge structures from a single position. Fathi *et al.* further notes accuracy problems of the reconstructed models. Ehrhart *et al.* [13] investigate image processing methods for deformation monitoring. In their work they detect movements of complete regions by comparing image patches, acquired with the camera of an RTS, but without explicitly performing any structural analysis of building corners or edges. Jadidi *et al.* [14] use image based modeling to reconstruct 3D point clouds and register as-built data to as-planned data.

Closely related to our approach is the work by Juretzko [8], who provides conceptional descriptions for not directly measurable target, using intersections of 3D rays, lines and planes. However, no comparative study between the methods, no detailed mathematical description and no suitable user interface is provided. Furthermore, the author mentions only minimal measured point sets for each method without any model fitting approach.

Klug *et al.* [7] implemented the proposed methods, but provided only a small number of physical experiments. In this work, we extend the work of the authors by analyzing effects of sensor and measurement uncertainties on the methods with a novel prototyping and real-time simulation setup for RTS. In particular, we run Monte-Carlo (MC) experiments in the RTS simulator to test different targets with different surfaces, the influence of the EDM sensor uncertainty and different incident angles of the EDM ray. The proposed simulation setup allows extracting ground truth data and varying various aspects of the measurement setup, which would be hard to achieve with physical installations. Klug *et al.* use a predecessor of the framework, which features driver abstraction, but no real-time simulation for testing various system effects. Also the authors did not include the description of the framework. Compared to the previous work, we provide more insights into the issues arising from sensor uncertainties and outside of laboratory conditions in a practical working environment.

To the best of our knowledge, we are the first to analyze the discussed methods with respect to varying EDM sensor uncertainty and surface properties. We provide a detailed mathematical formalism and a side-to-side comparison of the user flows to simplify the required training of RTS applicants. We also provide a comparative study of the methods, investigate the measurement concept in detail with a real-time RTS simulator, in a laboratory setup, and in an outdoor scenario.

In addition, we are the first to apply the novel real-time prototyping environment for RTS for interactive algorithm design and for extended MC simulations. The concept of the proposed prototyping and simulation environment is not limited to the proposed setup, but can be applied to different applications with similar requirements.

3   Concept

We compare four different measurement methods for measuring corner targets, all executed with an RTS in reflectorless measurement mode. In particular, we define the following methods: (a) measure a point close to the IP (*nearby method*), (b) estimate the IP with a single *support point method*, (c) estimate the IP with a *support line method*, and (d) estimate the IP with a *support plane method*.

In addition, we measure the IP directly (*direct method*). To allow the direct measurements of the IP, we modify the measurement target with modeling clay. In particular, we create a temporary planar area around the IP with modeling clay, which is removed for all other measurement methods. This allows for extracting reference data without a special laboratory setup. The *direct method* is used as reference, the *nearby method* is the standard method without any corrections. The support methods integrate in-the-field corrections for corner and edge measurements.

Figure 3 shows the nearby measurement method as well as the support point, support line and support plane method. Conceptual explanations of the methods are provided in the following sections, while the interested reader is referred to Klug *et al.* [7] for the mathematical details.

3.1   Test Hardware and Geometric Model Specification

Without loss of generality, we use the simplified geometric RTS model as shown in Fig. 1 to explain our proposed methods. The RTS for our experiments had been fully calibrated by the manufacturer. The driver provides access to sensors and actors of the device and transforms sensor data between the different coordinate systems; sensor data corrections are applied internally. As common for commercially available systems, details of the internal data processing are confidential and kept secret by manufacturers, and all drivers are closed source. The *instrument frame*, shown in Fig. 1, defines a common coordinate frame for points of a single *measurement set*. The registration of different measurement sets and the measurement targets in a common coordinate system relies on the measurement of control points. However, the point measurement methods themselves are the subject of the current analysis. Alternative registration methods use a fixed installation of reflective targets. In this work, we do not register the measured point sets in a common frame to avoid the physical installation. We apply an indirect analysis of the measurement error, which does not require a common coordinate frame for the measurement sets. Therefore, the results are not influenced by the registration uncertainty of the RTS, which increases the repeatability and reproducibility of the proposed experiments. The analysis of

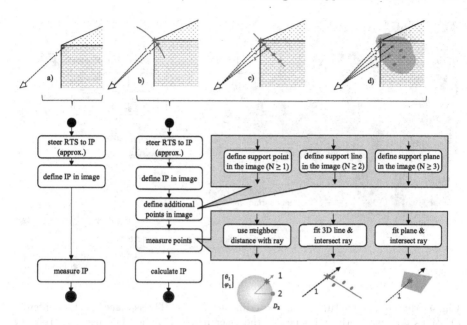

Fig. 3. Four different measurement methods of a corner with a single visible adjacent area as proposed in [7]: (a) direct and nearby method, (b) support point method, (c) support line method, and (d) support plane method. The view rays are enumerated according the measurement order used for our experiments.

different registration methods is beyond the scope of this work, but can be found in [1] (Fig. 4).

On the other hand, the simulation setup inherently provides ground truth and a common coordinate frame for all measurements, devices and targets. This allows for easier comparison of the different methods.

3.2 Standard Methods: Measuring the IP Directly or a Point Nearby

In reflectorless mode, the EDM laser should fully hit the planar measurement target. Non-planar surfaces increase the measurement uncertainty, partly reflected laser beams lower the measurement reliability. Figure 1 shows the simple geometric model for a single point measurement, Fig. 2 shows problematic measurement targets and the systematic error introduced by the aforementioned constraint. For an image-guided RTS, the simple work-flow for measuring an IP includes:

1. steering the laser to the IP using an interactive RTS video stream,
2. selecting the IP in the image, and
3. measuring distance and converting the sensor data to an Euclidean point.

For the *direct method*, the user measures the IP directly, the current angle and distance measurements are used for conversion to a 3D point. If no planar

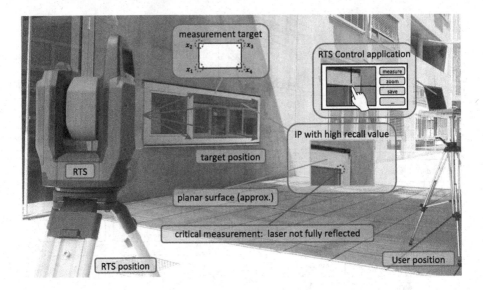

Fig. 4. Measurement setup for our experiments [7]. The RTS is placed on two different positions for testing the influence of the laser incident angle. The user controls the RTS remotely using a vision based prototyping software on the mobile PC. The laser is barley visible from close distance, but not from the user position or in the live camera stream.

surface is visible at the target, the distance uncertainty increases. If a fully reflected laser dot can not be guaranteed, the *nearby method* provides an intuitive approximation. The user does not aim for the IP directly, but for a measurable point close to it. Again, an increase of the measurement uncertainty occurs; but, in contrast to a direct IP measurement with partly-reflected laser beam, it is user-controlled. Repeated measurements with slowly decreasing safety gap between the laser and the edge of the target allows an experienced user to decrease the measurement uncertainty.

3.3   Support Point Method

To get the 3D coordinates of a building corner, the image pixel of the corner and a support point near the corner is defined, where the distance of the support point can be measured safely. Afterwards, the corner itself can simply be defined in the 2D image. The 3D coordinate of the target of interest is approximated by using the back-projected pixel of the first point and the measured distance of the support point. The approximation error becomes reasonable small for certain applications when following conditions hold: reasonable distance between the measurement device and the target, a perpendicular arrangement of the view ray and the measured surface, a small distance between the corner and the measured 3D point.

An offline version of this method is commonly used by surveying engineers [4,8,15]. With the support point method, the minimal measurement count for a 3D point is $N_{min} = 1$. Figure 3 shows the support point concept.

Measurement Flow. The simple measurement flow is defined by following steps:

1. Use the pan/tilt control interface, until the target-of-interest is visible in the image
2. Define target-of-interest in the image
3. Define support point with a single distance measurement
4. Calculate the 3D position of the target-of-interest by using the angle of the image point and the distance of the support point measurement.

3.4   Support Line Method

Several 3D points on the visible wall are measured by the user to estimate an 3D line which intersects the corner of interest. The corner itself can then simply be defined in the 2D image. The related 3D target is calculated by finding the intersection point of the back projected view ray with the previous estimated 3D doing with an least square approximation.

With support lines, the minimal measurement count for 3D points is $N_{min} = 2$. When using more than two points, a robust estimation like RANSAC based least square 3D line fitting can be applied [16]. Figure 3 shows the support line concept.

Measurement Flow. The simple measurement flow is defined by following steps:

1. Use the pan/tilt control interface, until the target-of-interest is visible in the image
2. Define target-of-interest in the image
3. Define support line with $N \geq 2$ measurements
4. Calculate the 3D position of the target-of-interest by intersecting the back-projected view ray with the support line.

3.5   Support Plane Method

To get the 3D coordinates of a building corner, the user measures several 3D points on the visible wall to estimate an planar approximation of this wall. The corner of interest can simply be defined in the 2D image. The related 3D target is calculated by intersecting the back-projected view ray with the previous estimated plane. The measurement concept is shown in Fig. 3. The target-of-interest can be moved freely on the plane.

Measurement Flow. The simple measurement flow is defined by following steps:

1. Use the pan/tilt control interface, until the target-of-interest is visible in the image
2. Define target-of-interest in the image
3. Define support plane with $N \geq 3$ measurements
4. Calculate the 3D position of the target-of-interest by intersecting the back-projected view ray with the support plane.

4   Experiments

In this section, we describe the experiments undertaken. First, we shortly outline
the experimental setup. Then we describe the results of MC simulations to analyze various aspects of the proposed measurement methods, such as influences
of the target surfaces and the incident angles. Finally we experimentally evaluate our methods in physical environments. Table 1 shows the test taxonomy for
both, MC simulations and physical setups. Note that a more detailed discussion
of the results is postponed to Sect. 5 to incorporate both the simulation and the
physical measurement results likewise and to draw relationships.

4.1   RTS Simulator and Interactive Testing

For proper testing the methods described above, we developed a novel RTS
prototyping environment. An abstraction layer on top of the RTS driver allows
for seamless exchange of an RTS simulator and the physical device; automatically generated multi-language bindings based on the gRPC library allows for
a flexible and modular prototyping environment. Figure 5 shows the software
architecture of the RTS prototyping and simulation environment. As a major
benefit of this approach, we can treat a real physical RTS like any simulated
virtual one. Furthermore, multi-language bindings allows for transfer, control
and streaming between different heterogeneous data sources and sinks, such as,
for example a mathematical analysis engine and a game engine[1].

For simulation experiments, the prototyping framework is set up to carry out
the MC simulation with a real-time RTS simulator implemented in Unity3D. The
test sets for the MC simulations are generated in MATLAB, control values and
simulation parameters are uploaded to Unity3D; the measurements are simulated
in Unity3D, results are streamed back and are evaluated in MATLAB.

For physical experiments and interactive tests, we designed a graphical user
interface which allows seamlessly interfacing the RTS simulator or the physical
RTS device. Figure 6 shows the test GUI for the different methods; The GUI
provides an intuitive work flow implementation for our experiments. This enables
even novice and non-expert users to use the proposed measuring methods within
a few minutes. For each test, the user selects a particular measurement method.
After selection of the method, the operator is automatically guided through the
process to fulfill the measuring task, with a final result given at the end.

For better repeatability, we explicitly avoid using a special laboratory for
surveying and measurement, but define a simple evaluation concept for comparison of the proposed methods. The setup can be applied in indoor and outdoor
environments[2].

---

[1] Unity3D and MATLAB can be used with gRPC by compiling the abstraction layer
to shared C++ libraries.

[2] The analysis does not follow the ISO 17123 standard [17], since we conduct only a
comparative studies of the proposed methods with non-direct measurable targets.

Table 1. Test taxonomy. (x) evaluated; (x*) evaluated, where the parameter approximately fits the specification; (-) not evaluated or not applicable.

Test configurations		Test environment			
Property	Value	MC simulation	Laboratory	Indoor	Outdoor
Surface type	Planar	x	x*	x*	x*
	Uneven	x	-	-	-
	Fillet	x	-	-	-
Incident angle α	0.5π	x	x	x	x
	0.25π	x	x	x	x
Measurement method	Direct	x	x	x	x
	Nearby	x	x	x	x
	Support point	x	x	x	x
	Support line	x	x	x	x
	Support plane	x	x	x	x
Noise	n1 (no noise)	x	-	-	-
	n2 (EDM noise)	x	-	-	-
	Physical	-	x	x	x
Evaluation method	Direct: $x_{i,IP,ref} - x_{i,IP,est}$	x	-	-	-
	Indirect: $x_{i,IP,est} - x_{i+1,IP,est}$	-	x	x	x

4.2 MC Simulation

Our simulator implements the simple RTS model as shown in Fig. 1. The model is converted to the scene graph shown on the right of Fig. 5. Additional tree nodes are introduced for placing the RTS and the measurement target freely in the scene. The EDM and the camera are modeled using ray casting and GPU based rendering, both provided by Unity3D. The camera image is rendered to a texture buffer and streamed through the simulator API for further processing. The scene graph and ray casting results can be accessed externally via the simulator API. The abstraction layer provides an unique API for both, the simulator and the RTS driver. In Fig. 7, the simulator and the MC simulation workflow is depicted.

Measurement Targets Variants. The basic target is a planar triangle mesh, placed at ten meter distance from the RTS. Different target variants are generated using following steps: 1. subdivide the surface of the basic target into small triangles, 2. translate the mesh vertices, and 3. remove faces and vertices outside of the region of interest (ROI) for performance reasons.

We simulate three different target variants with following surface properties: 1. planar surface, 2. uneven surface, and 3. round edges (fillet). The planar surface variant is simply the basic target. The uneven surface variant is generated using random translations of the mesh vertices along the vertex normals. Similar, the fillet of the target with round edges is generated by translating the vertices near the border as a function of the distance to the border. Figure 8 shows the generation of the mesh variants.

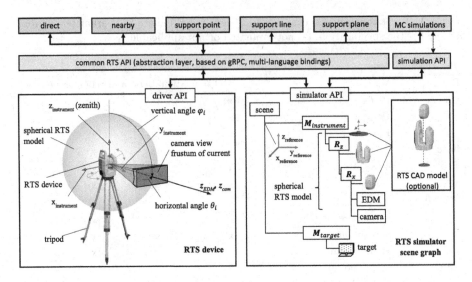

Fig. 5. RTS prototyping framework. The abstraction layer provides a common API for the RTS driver and for the simulator, with gRPC as communication library. The simulator implements the simplified geometric RTS model as scene graph in Unity3D, provides the RTS API and additional access to the scene graph.

RTS Sensor Uncertainty Simulation. We follow the JCGM 100:2008 Guide to the Expression of Uncertainty (GUM) [18] for modeling the sensor uncertainty. In particular, GUM standardizes the analysis and report of measurement uncertainties of measured physical quantities to allow repeatable experiments. The uncertainty of RTS sensors with normal distributed random noise can be specified in following general form:

$$p(|y - x| \leq ku_c(y)) = CI_k \tag{1}$$

where x is the measured quantity, $u_c(y)$ is the combined standard uncertainty of the measurement result y; k is the coverage factor, and CI_k is the confidence interval[3]. Let $u_a(y)$ be an additive and $u_p(y)$ be a proportional component of the combined sensor uncertainty, both provided by the device manufacturers. Then, $u_c(y)$ is given by [18]

$$u_c(y) \approx \sqrt{u_a(y) + (xu_p(y))^2} \tag{2}$$

Unity3D provides generators for uniform distributed random values. We use the Box-Muller transform [19] to simulate normal distributed noise for sensor readings:

---

[3] Analogue to GUM, we use the same symbol is as the physical quantity and as the random variable for economy of notation [18].

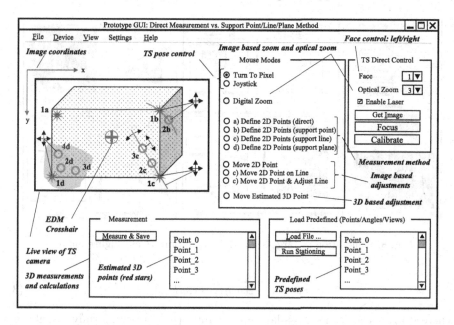

Fig. 6. Test GUI used in our system [7]. The interface guides the user through the measurement tasks. (Color figure online)

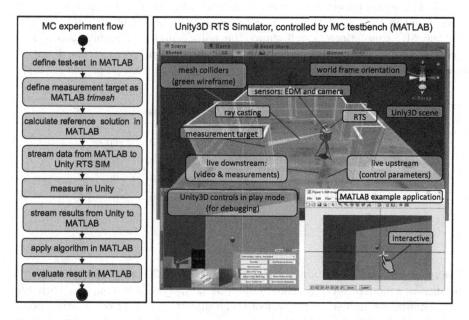

Fig. 7. MC simulation flow (left). Unity3D RTS simulator (right). (Color figure online)

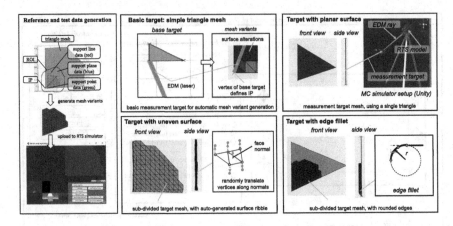

Fig. 8. Generation of targets for MC simulation. (Color figure online)

$$y = x + \sqrt{-2ln(g)} \cos\left(2\pi h u_c(y)\right) \tag{3}$$

where $u_c(y)$ is the desired standard uncertainty, $\{g, h\}$ are uniformly distributed random values, and x is the simulated sensor reading without noise. The EDM uncertainty has significant influence on the measurements and should be analyzed. The angle uncertainty of actors is negligibly small and therefore is not considered in the calculations. Table 2 provides the sensor uncertainty settings for the MC simulations, Fig. 9 shows the noise simulation architecture. More general error descriptions can include signal refraction, cyclic errors, pointing errors and camera calibration effects, but are beyond the scope of this work [1].

Table 2. MC sensor noise settings.

Description		EDM sensor		Angle sensor	
Label	Description	$u_a(d)$	$u_p(d)$	$u_a(\alpha)$	$u_p(\alpha)$
n1	Without noise	0	0	0	0
n2	With noise	$0.75e{-}3$m	$10e{-}6$m	0	0

Complex Collider Definition for Ray Casting. Unity3D allows to use triangle meshes as colliders for physical simulations [20]. The close coupling with the GPU limits the numeric precision of scene operations to 32 bit floating point arithmetic[4]. In general, a higher precision is not required for the proposed MC simulations. However, the non-convex measurement targets require non-convex

---

[4] Higher precision arithmetic require explicit implementation of the scene graph and related operations.

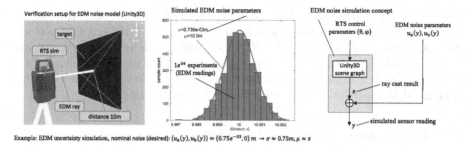

Fig. 9. Uncertainty simulation for RTS sensors.

colliders, which cause ray casting problems due to numeric round-off effects. Figure 10 shows a ray casting experiment where the ray simply passes through a surface when targeting a mesh vertex or edge directly. This is critical for our experiments, thus explicit colliders must be generated. We simply increase each triangle of the target surface by $0.5e-4m$. In particular, we perform the following steps: 1. First, we remove the links between connected triangles by duplicating shared vertices. 2. Then, we translate the vertices of a triangle along the medians, the line between a vertex and the centroid, to enlarge the surface. While this method decreases the simulation accuracy, it also increases the reliability of the ray casting. The generated colliders consist of overlapping triangles, and they counteract intersection issues caused by round-off errors.

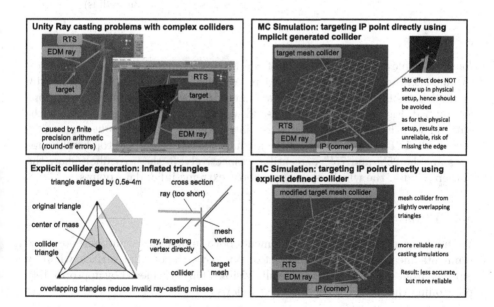

Fig. 10. Explicit collider generation for Unity3D to avoid ray casting issues of complex colliders.

Additional MC Parameters. The main parameters for the MC experiments are defined in Table 1, sensor noise parameters are given in Table 2. Additional settings are required for defining the MC experiments, such as measurement count for each method, distance between the IP point and the measured point for the nearby method, and properties for surface variant generation. Table 3 lists the additional MC simulation properties which we used for this work.

Table 3. Additional properties for the MC experiments used in this work.

Property	Value
Bounding box for basic target	2m
ROI radius	0.5m (region for picking additional points)
Subdivision iterations	Fillet target: 50; other targets: 25
Fillet surface jitter	10e−3m
Fillet radius	30e−3m
Test count per MC experiment	100
Distance between RTS and target	10m
Inflate vertex offset for colliders	0.5e−4m
RANSAC line/plane fitting	No
Minimum safety distance between ray and target edges for non-direct methods	2.5e−3m (circular approximation of the projected EDM ray at the intersection point, assuming 5e−3m radius)

Results. Table 4 shows the results of the MC experiments for all 60 simulation variants. The direct method is used to estimate reference values, the nearby method is assumed to be the standard method when no additional corrections are applied. Figure 11 shows the box-and-whisker plots for the simulations without and with EDM sensor noise. The plots visualize following *robust summary statistics*[5]: 1. The central mark is the median, 2. the bottom and top box boundaries are the 25th and 75th percentiles, respectively; 3. the + symbols show the outliers, and 4. the whiskers show the most extreme inlier data points.

4.3   Physical Measurements

We further performed several experiments both in laboratory and outdoor environments, measuring the distance between two corners of a flat surface, whereby only the front face of the surface is fully visible. This is achieved by appropriately positioning the RTS and the target as follows:

---

[5] MATLAB standard settings for box plots, function *boxplot, statistics toolbox.*

Table 4. MC simulation results. The direct method is usually not applicable for physical corner targets without target modifications.

	MC settings		EDM noise: $u_a(d) = 0m$, $u_p(d) = 0m$			EDM noise: $u_a(d) = 0.75e-3m$, $u_p(d) = 10e-6m$		
α	mesh variant	meas. method	$E(\mathbf{x}_{ip,ref} - \mathbf{x}_{ip,est})$ [m]	$\bar{d}$ [m]	$\sigma(d)$ [m]	$E(\mathbf{x}_{ip,ref} - \mathbf{x}_{ip,est})$ [m]	$\bar{d}$ [m]	$\sigma(d)$ [m]
		direct	$1.961e-06$	$1.961e-06$	$4.257e-21$	$6.076e-04$	$6.076e-04$	$4.114e-04$
		nearby	$2.500e-03$	$2.500e-03$	$4.359e-18$	$2.595e-03$	$2.595e-03$	$\mathbf{1.154e-04}$
	planar	support point	$2.500e-03$	$7.052e-05$	$9.535e-20$	$2.593e-03$	$5.652e-04$	$4.201e-04$
		support line	$2.525e-01$	$\mathbf{1.336e-06}$	$6.385e-22$	$2.525e-01$	$\mathbf{5.137e-04}$	$3.732e-04$
		support plane	$3.079e-01$	$1.527e-06$	$1.915e-21$	$3.071e-01$	$1.277e-03$	$9.642e-04$
		direct	$7.668e-07$	$\mathbf{7.668e-07}$	$\mathbf{1.064e-22}$	$6.260e-04$	$\mathbf{6.260e-04}$	$4.689e-04$
		nearby	$2.512e-03$	$2.512e-03$	$5.666e-18$	$2.597e-03$	$2.597e-03$	$\mathbf{1.419e-04}$
0.5π	uneven	support point	$2.545e-03$	$4.770e-04$	$9.807e-19$	$2.629e-03$	$6.852e-04$	$4.687e-04$
		support line	$3.268e-01$	$5.816e-03$	$9.589e-18$	$2.249e-01$	$5.971e-03$	$5.282e-04$
		support plane	$3.280e-01$	$5.011e-03$	$5.230e-18$	$3.713e-01$	$8.460e-03$	$1.158e-03$
		direct	$5.338e-08$	$\mathbf{5.338e-08}$	$\mathbf{1.197e-22}$	$6.112e-04$	$\mathbf{6.112e-04}$	$4.774e-04$
		nearby	$2.495e-03$	$2.495e-03$	$3.051e-18$	$2.608e-03$	$2.608e-03$	$\mathbf{1.895e-04}$
	fillet	support point	$2.495e-03$	$7.243e-05$	$5.448e-20$	$2.605e-03$	$6.148e-04$	$4.616e-04$
		support line	$2.637e-01$	$1.599e-02$	$1.395e-17$	$2.815e-01$	$1.320e-02$	$5.923e-04$
		support plane	$3.044e-01$	$3.003e-02$	$6.974e-17$	$3.446e-01$	$1.055e-02$	$1.020e-03$
		direct	$1.527e-07$	$1.527e-07$	$\mathbf{0}$	$5.453e-04$	$5.453e-04$	$4.290e-04$
		nearby	$2.500e-03$	$2.500e-03$	$1.743e-18$	$2.580e-03$	$2.580e-03$	$\mathbf{3.385e-04}$
	planar	support point	$2.500e-03$	$1.250e-03$	$\mathbf{0}$	$2.613e-03$	$1.337e-03$	$7.076e-04$
		support line	$2.618e-01$	$2.770e-07$	$\mathbf{0}$	$2.247e-01$	$\mathbf{5.306e-04}$	$4.124e-04$
		support plane	$3.325e-01$	$\mathbf{6.443e-09}$	$4.988e-24$	$2.993e-01$	$7.783e-04$	$5.983e-04$
		direct	$1.937e-07$	$\mathbf{1.937e-07}$	$\mathbf{1.862e-22}$	$6.223e-04$	$\mathbf{6.223e-04}$	$\mathbf{4.588e-04}$
		nearby	$2.491e-03$	$2.491e-03$	$5.230e-18$	$2.728e-03$	$2.728e-03$	$4.731e-04$
0.25π	uneven	support point	$2.813e-03$	$1.799e-03$	$2.179e-18$	$2.773e-03$	$1.640e-03$	$7.980e-04$
		support line	$1.584e-01$	$1.273e-03$	$1.308e-18$	$2.696e-01$	$2.950e-03$	$5.019e-04$
		support plane	$3.243e-01$	$4.674e-04$	$4.359e-19$	$4.219e-01$	$2.874e-02$	$1.933e-03$
		direct	$1.527e-07$	$\mathbf{1.527e-07}$	$\mathbf{0}$	$6.047e-04$	$6.047e-04$	$4.769e-04$
		nearby	$2.575e-03$	$2.575e-03$	$6.974e-18$	$2.650e-03$	$2.650e-03$	$\mathbf{4.088e-04}$
	fillet	support point	$2.575e-03$	$1.326e-03$	$\mathbf{0}$	$2.669e-03$	$1.361e-03$	$7.446e-04$
		support line	$1.777e-01$	$1.565e-02$	$\mathbf{0}$	$2.410e-01$	$4.244e-02$	$8.440e-04$
		support plane	$3.217e-01$	$2.919e-02$	$\mathbf{0}$	$3.055e-01$	$1.936e-02$	$9.770e-04$

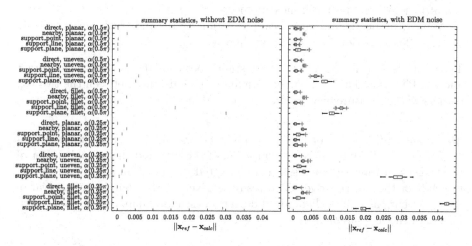

Fig. 11. Box-and-whisker plot of the MC simulation results. (Left) without EDM noise. (Right) with applied EDM noise.

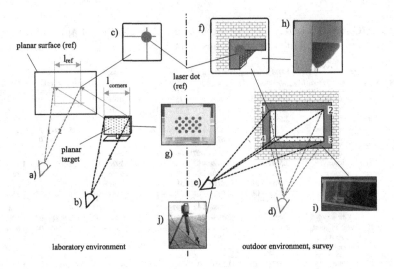

Fig. 12. Measurement setups for testing under laboratory conditions and for outdoor scenarios [7]: (a) measurement of the reference distance between the two top corners of the portable target, (b) portable target used to measure the distance between two corners in laboratory conditions, (c) detailed view of the projected laser dot during the reference measurement, (d) reference measurement of a window in indoor and outdoor conditions using perpendicular viewing angle, (e) the same windows measured with a viewing angle of 0.25π, (f) and (h) the modeling clay for reference measurements, (i), (g) and (j) the outdoor window, the portable laboratory target and the RTS.

- Approx. same height of target center and camera center
- Approx. perpendicular laser beam direction for laboratory experiments and outdoors for ground truth measurements
- Approx. perpendicular laser beam direction for ground truth measurements and 0.25π direction for outdoor evaluation.

The setup is shown in Fig. 12. The distance between the measurement target and the RTS is about 5 m in all experiments. The distance between the two top corners of the measurement indoor target is about 0.6 m.

Measurement Strategy. For Euclidean distance evaluation, a single set measurement consists of the measured 3D position of the first and the second corner of the target[6]. All measurements where converted to Euclidean coordinates using the API of the device driver. The result is given in the confidence interval of $\pm 2\hat{\sigma}_d$, with $\hat{\sigma}_d$ as unbiased standard deviation assuming unbiased normal distribution of the measurements:

---

[6] Note that we use a half-set for our evaluations, since we do not use the second telescope face (face right).

The Euclidean distance of measurement i between two points $p_{i,0}$ and $p_{i,1}$ is calculated by

$$d_i = ||\mathbf{p}_{i,1} - \mathbf{p}_{i,0}|| = || \begin{bmatrix} x_{i,1} \\ y_{i,1} \\ z_{i,1} \end{bmatrix} - \begin{bmatrix} x_{i,0} \\ y_{i,0} \\ z_{i,0} \end{bmatrix} || \tag{4}$$

and the average distance $\bar{d}$ and the unbiased standard deviation $\hat{\sigma}$ is given by

$$\bar{d} = \frac{\sum_{i=0}^{N-1} d_i}{N} \qquad \hat{\sigma} = \sqrt{\frac{\sum_{i=0}^{N-1} (d_i - \bar{d})^2}{N-1}} \tag{5}$$

For outlier removal, at least $N = 3$ sets must be measured. Outliers are removed using median absolute deviation (MAD) with $\pm 3\hat{\sigma}$ interval on distances [21]. The statistic evaluation is repeated on the reduced data set.

We calculate the distance error between two points d using

$$\Delta d = |\bar{d}_{ref} - \bar{d}| \pm 2 \cdot \sqrt{\hat{\sigma_{ref}}^2 + \hat{\sigma_1}^2} \tag{6}$$

with $\bar{d}_{ref} \pm 2\hat{\sigma}_{dref}$ as reference distance and $\bar{d} \pm 2\hat{\sigma}$ as measured distances between two corners.

For measuring the ground truth, we employed two different approaches. For the laboratory target, we aligned it with a planar surface and measured the distance using the RTS. Note that this method is suitable for portable targets and outer corners only. For ground truth estimation of immovable targets like windows, we filled the corners with modeling clay to create a quasi-planar surface around the corners, which could be measured by the RTS. This method is suitable for fixed and portable targets and is well suited for inner corners[7].

Laboratory Measurements. First, we conducted two experiments with the portable target. We measured the ground truth distance between the two top corners as shown in Fig. 12(a) and (b). Then we used the four different methods to perform the measurement again.

In a second experiment, we measured the same distance again with the RTS pointing at the target at an angle of approximately 0.25π.

Outdoor Measurements. We conducted four outdoor experiments, where we measured the extents of a window from a perpendicular and a 0.25π point of view. We measured the ground truth distance shown in Fig. 12(d), (f) and (h). Then, we applied the four measurement methods again as discussed in the previous paragraph above.

---

[7] Note that we performed the ground truth measurements immediately before the experiments, to ensure that errors due to changes in environmental conditions are negligible.

Results. The results for the laboratory measurements are given in groups 1,2,5 and 6 of Table 5. Overall, the support line and support plane based methods achieve considerably better results than the standard method and the support point method, or perform at least on par. The results for an angle of approximately 0.25π indicate that the support line and support plane based methods achieve considerably better results than the standard method and the support point method for non-orthogonal measurement setups.

The results of the physical experiments, in which the indirect evaluation method as discussed in Sect. 4.3 was applied, are given in groups 3 and 4 in Table 5. The Box-and-Whisker plots for some repeated distance measurements are presented in Fig. 13. Again, the support line and the support plane methods are overall more suitable and give better results, or perform at least on par.

Table 5. Expanded physical distance measurement results from [7]. For the indirect evaluation method, the error of the average distance between two measured target points is shown.

α	Record	Meth.	$\bar{d}$ [m]	$\hat{\sigma}_d$ [m]	N	$\overline{d_{ref}}$ [m]	$\Delta\bar{d}$ [m]
0.5π	Indoor	Direct	881.992e−3	362.719e−6	10.000	881.992e−3	0
		Nearby	893.240e−3	820.525e−6	8.000	881.992e−3	11.248e−3
		Support point	886.912e−3	1.921e−3	10.000	881.992e−3	4.920e−3
		Support line	887.088e−3	830.455e−6	10.000	881.992e−3	5.096e−3
		Support plane	885.561e−3	957.555e−6	9.000	881.992e−3	**3.569e−3**
	Lab.	Direct	600.191e−3	82.942e−6	4.000	600.191e−3	0
		Nearby	586.664e−3	273.151e−6	4.000	600.191e−3	13.527e−3
		Support point	599.712e−3	39.655e−6	3.000	600.191e−3	478.897e−6
		Support line	599.803e−3	866.189e−6	5.000	600.191e−3	**387.538e−6**
		Support plane	604.457e−3	3.636e−3	5.000	600.191e−3	4.266e−3
	Outdoor	Direct	883.245e−3	25.067e−6	4.000	883.245e−3	0
		Nearby	888.800e−3	14.479e−6	3.000	883.245e−3	5.555e−3
		Support point	882.519e−3	807.959e−6	4.000	883.245e−3	726.362e−6
		Support line	881.964e−3	813.967e−6	5.000	883.245e−3	1.282e−3
		Support plane	882.181e−3	249.838e−6	4.000	883.245e−3	**1.065e−3**
	Outdoor (long)	Direct	2.192	107.789e−6	10.000	2.192	0
		Nearby	2.196	1.182e−3	10.000	2.192	4.463e−3
		Support point	2.193	1.248e−3	10.000	2.192	1.761e−3
		Support line	2.189	819.832e−6	10.000	2.192	2.303e−3
		Support plane	2.190	1.212e−3	10.000	2.192	**1.587e−3**
0.25π	Lab.	Direct	600.191e−3	82.942e−6	4.000	600.191e−3	0
		Nearby	582.446e−3	1.192e−3	5.000	600.191e−3	17.745e−3
		Support point	584.189e−3	240.581e−6	4.000	600.191e−3	16.002e−3
		Support line	598.194e−3	229.861e−6	3.000	600.191e−3	1.997e−3
		Support plane	598.545e−3	654.487e−6	5.000	600.191e−3	**1.646e−3**
	Indoor	Direct	881.702e−3	221.990e−6	5.000	881.702e−3	0
		Nearby	897.636e−3	3.285e−3	5.000	881.702e−3	15.934e−3
		Support point	894.017e−3	2.142e−3	5.000	881.702e−3	12.314e−3
		Support line	882.071e−3	607.033e−6	5.000	881.702e−3	**369.144e−6**
		Support plane	882.079e−3	1.165e−3	5.000	881.702e−3	377.119e−6

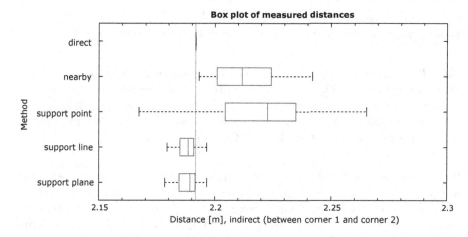

Fig. 13. Accuracy results [7] for distance measurements between two window corners. The reference distance (horizontal line) was estimated from repeated, perpendicular measurements, using the direct method and modeling clay as temporary planar surface.

5   Discussion

In the following, we briefly discuss the results for the individual experiments in more detail and draw relationships between the results of the simulation and the physical measurement results with respect to different aspects.

Planar Target Surface. The MC simulation results shown in Table 4 and Fig. 11 indicate the benefits of the proposed indirect measuring methods. For the perpendicular setup, the accuracies of the point, line and plane support methods are comparable with the reference result. We use the direct measurement method with the proposed temporary target modification. For the MC simulation, the proposed collider extension fulfills the same functionality and allows for direct measurement of edges and corners. All support methods significantly outperform the nearby method, for which we assumed a laser radius of $2.5e-3$ m near the target. In case of an incident angle of 0.25π, the support point method shows a significant systematic error, the support line and plane methods do not suffer from the same error and outperform the other methods. The results from the physical measurements shown in Table 5 and in Fig. 13 supports our findings.

Uneven Target Surface. The limitations of the proposed methods are clearly visible when measuring uneven and fillet targets. In this work, we use overdetermined line and plane fitting, but without outlier-robust estimation. We do not limit the support measurements to the proximity of the IP, but allow the measurements within an ROI with 0.5 m radius. If we assume no EDM measurement uncertainty, the accuracy of the support methods and the nearby method are

372   C. Klug et al.

in the same range. However, the support line and support plane method show stronger dependencies of the surface properties than the other methods.

Fillet Target Surfaces. Similar to uneven target surfaces, the support line and plane method are significantly influenced by the surface properties, while the other methods are less affected. Special care must be taken when choosing the best suitable method for a particular measurement. Different ROI radii would provide further insight, but are beyond the scope of this work.

Nearby and Support Point Method. By definition, both, the nearby and the support point method use a measurement close to the IP. The support point method is designed to reduce the systematic error by applying the angles of the IP while assuming reasonable surface properties. The support point method outperforms the nearby method in all experiments, as shown in Fig. 11. This method does not increase the distance measurement count, hence has no significant influence on the measurement duration. Given the fairly simple algorithm and user interface, we think the integration into new and existing RTS is reasonable.

Prototyping and Simulation Environment. The proposed prototyping and simulation environment lowered the implementation effort significantly. Varying physical properties of a measurement setup was easy. The laboratory measurements and our own findings during the physical measurements support this simulation setup for similar hardware configurations. They encourage further work on integrating more realistic sensor models and additional physical properties into the simulator.

Ray Casting in Simulation. While we used ray casting with a single ray to model the EDM in Unity3D in this work, a more realistic simulation would integrate multiple rays which are distributed within the laser beam. As a side effect, ray casting problems with complex mesh colliders due to round-off errors could be detected and corrected automatically, without the need of the workaround proposed previously.

Targeting Uncertainty. The proposed user interfaces support optical an digital zoom for all measurement methods. By zooming in, the targeting uncertainty can be reduced, but it is limited by physical properties of the camera and the measurement setup. An interesting aspect to investigate in the future is the influence of an operators physical condition on the results, such as *e.g.* concentration, distraction, exhaustion or eye strain. In particular, these properties can be modeled as targeting uncertainty, and can be simulated by angle sensor uncertainty.

6 Conclusion

In this work, we have evaluated different methods for indirect measurements using an RTS, based on previous work from Klug et al. [7]. The initial findings in [7] are confirmed by the simulation and extended physical experiments conducted: support based methods consistently outperform the standard method, where one reason for the huge gain in accuracy is due to the definition of the reference method, requiring the projected laser beam to be fully on the visible surface. This is also the main cause for the big systematic error of the reference measurement method.

We identified three major important avenues for future investigation: (i) outlier detection through the use of RANSAC schemes, (ii) the use of multiple ray casting operations in simulation, and (iii) the investigation of operator condition effects on measurement errors. The former two are targeted more towards improvements of our methods in terms of mathematics and engineering. However, the latter clearly falls into the HCI domain and is very relevant for designing and implementing user interfaces.

Acknowledgements. This work was enabled by the Competence Center VRVis. VRVis is funded by BMVIT, BMWFW, Styria, SFG and Vienna Business Agency under the scope of COMET - Competence Centers for Excellent Technologies (854174) which is managed by FFG.

References

1. Uren, J., Price, B.: Surveying for Engineers. Palgrave Macmillan, Basingstoke (2010)
2. Schulz, T.: Calibration of a terrestrial laser scanner for engineering geodesy. Ph.D. thesis. ETH Zurich, Switzerland (2007)
3. Nichols, J.M., Beavers, J.E.: Development and calibration of an earthquake fatality function. Earthq. Spectra **19**, 605–633 (2003)
4. Coaker, L.H.: Reflectorless total station measurements and their accuracy, precision and reliability. B.S. thesis. University of Southern Queensland (2009)
5. Reda, A., Bedada, B.: Accuracy analysis and calibration of total station based on the reflectorless distance measurement. Master's thesis. Royal Institute of Technology (KTH), Sweden (2012)
6. Martin, D., Gatta, G.: Calibration of total stations instruments at the ESRF. In: Proceedings of XXIII FIG Congress, pp. 1–14 (2006)
7. Klug, C., Schmalstieg, D., Arth, C.: Measuring human-made corner structures with a robotic total station using support points, lines and planes, pp. 17–27. INSTICC, SciTePress (2017)
8. Juretzko, M.: Reflektorlose Video-Tachymetrie - Ein Integrales Verfahren zur Erfassung Geometrischer und Visueller Informationen. Ph.D. thesis. Ruhr University Bochum, Faculty of Civil Engineering (2004)
9. Zeiske, K.: Surveying made easy (2004). https://www.aps.anl.gov/files/APS-Uploads/DET/Detector-Pool/Beamline-Components/Lecia_Optical_Level/Surveying_en.pdf. Accessed 22 May 2018
10. Corporation, T.: Imaging station is series, instruction manual (2011)

11. Siu, M.F., Lu, M., AbouRizk, S.: Combining photogrammetry and robotic total stations to obtain dimensional measurements of temporary facilities in construction field. Vis. Eng. **1**, 4 (2013)
12. Fathi, H., Brilakis, I.: A videogrammetric as-built data collection method for digital fabrication of sheet metal roof panels. Adv. Eng. Inf. **27**, 466–476 (2013)
13. Ehrhart, M., Lienhart, W.: Image-based dynamic deformation monitoring of civil engineering structures from long ranges. In: Image Processing: Machine Vision Applications VIII, vol. 9405, pp. 94050J–94050J-14 (2015)
14. Jadidi, H., Ravanshadnia, M., Hosseinalipour, M., Rahmani, F.: A step-by-step construction site photography procedure to enhance the efficiency of as-built data visualization: a case study. Vis. Eng. **3**, 1–12 (2015)
15. Scherer, M.: Intelligent scanning with robot-tacheometer and image processing: a low cost alternative to 3D laser scanning? In: FIG Working Week (2004)
16. Fischler, M.A., Bolles, R.C.: Random sample consensus: a paradigm for model fitting with applications to image analysis and automated cartography. Commun. ACM **24**, 381–395 (1981)
17. Iso 17123–3: Optics and optical instruments - field procedures for testing geodetic and surveying instruments. Standard, International Organization for Standardization, Geneva, CH (2001)
18. JCGM 100:2008 - Evaluation of measurement data - Guide to the expression of uncertainty in measurement. Standard, Int. Organ. Stand. Geneva ISBN (2008)
19. Box, G.E.P., Muller, M.E.: A note on the generation of random normal deviates. Ann. Math. Stat. **29**, 610–611 (1958)
20. Unity Technologies: Unity3D: Game engine. https://unity3d.com. Accessed 28 July 2017
21. Leys, C., Ley, C., Klein, O., Bernard, P., Licata, L.: Detecting outliers: do not use standard deviation around the mean, use absolute deviation around the median. J. Exp. Soc. Psychol. **49**, 764–766 (2013)

Author Index

Printed in the United States
By Bookmasters